T0183942

Lecture Notes in Artificial Intelligence   9592

Subseries of Lecture Notes in Computer Science

More information about this series at http://www.springer.com/series/1244

Tapabrata Ray · Ruhul Sarker
Xiaodong Li (Eds.)

Artificial Life and Computational Intelligence

Second Australasian Conference, ACALCI 2016
Canberra, ACT, Australia, February 2–5, 2016
Proceedings

Editors
Tapabrata Ray
University of New South Wales
Canberra, ACT
Australia

Ruhul Sarker
University of New South Wales
Canberra, ACT
Australia

Xiaodong Li
RMIT University
Melbourne, VIC
Australia

ISSN 0302-9743   ISSN 1611-3349   (electronic)
Lecture Notes in Artificial Intelligence
ISBN 978-3-319-28269-5   ISBN 978-3-319-28270-1   (eBook)
DOI 10.1007/978-3-319-28270-1

Library of Congress Control Number: 2015958838

LNCS Sublibrary: SL7 – Artificial Intelligence

Printed on acid-free paper

This Springer imprint is published by SpringerNature
The registered company is Springer International Publishing AG Switzerland

Preface

This volume contains the papers presented at the Australasian Conference on Artificial Life and Computational Intelligence (ACALCI 2016) held during February 2–5, 2016, in Canberra.

The research areas of artificial life and computational intelligence have grown significantly over recent years. The breadth is reflected in the papers addressing diverse aspects in the domain, from theoretical developments to learning, optimization, and applications of such methods for real-world problems.

This volume presents 30 papers, many of them authored by leading researchers in the field. After a rigorous evaluation of all 41 submissions by the international Program Committee, 30 manuscripts were selected for single-track oral presentation at ACALCI 2016. All papers underwent a full peer-review with at least three reviewers per paper.

The ACALCI 2016 international Program Committee consisted of over 75 members from 15 countries. We would like to thank the members of the international Program Committee, ACALCI Steering Committee, local Organizing Committee, and other members of the organization team for their commendable efforts and contributions to the conference.

We would like to acknowledge the support from the University of New South Wales, Canberra, and the organizers of the Australian Computer Science Week (ACSW), who kindly allowed ACALCI 2016 to be co-located with ACSW 2016 at the Australian National University (ANU), Canberra.

The support and assistance from Springer and EasyChair are gratefully acknowledged.

November 2015

Tapabrata Ray
Ruhul Sarker
Xiaodong Li

Organization

Conference Chairs

Tapabrata Ray   The University of New South Wales, Australia
  (General Chair)
Ruhul Sarker (Co-chair)   The University of New South Wales, Australia
Xiaodong Li (Co-chair)   RMIT University, Australia

Proceedings Chair

Hemant Kumar Singh   The University of New South Wales, Australia

Local Organizing Committee

Kathryn Merrick   The University of New South Wales, Australia
Sameer Alam   The University of New South Wales, Australia
George Leu   The University of New South Wales, Australia
Daoyi Dong   The University of New South Wales, Australia

Publicity Chairs

Hemant Kumar Singh   The University of New South Wales, Australia
Jiangjun Tang   The University of New South Wales, Australia

Treasurer and Registration Chairs

Kamran Shafi   The University of New South Wales, Australia
Saber Elsayed   The University of New South Wales, Australia

Special Session Chairs

Girija Chetty   University of Canberra, Australia
Xiuping Jia   The University of New South Wales, Australia

Paper and Poster Award Committee Chair

Mengjie Zhang   Victoria University of Wellington, New Zealand

Tutorial and Workshop Chair

Philip Hingston   Edith Cowan University, Australia

Steering Committee

Hussein Abbass	The University of New South Wales, Australia
Stephan Chalup	The University of Newcastle, Australia
Philip Hingston	Edith Cowan University, Australia
Kevin Korb	Monash University, Australia
Xiaodong Li	RMIT University, Australia
Frank Neumann	The University of Adelaide, Australia
Marcus Randall	Bond University, Australia
Mengjie Zhang	Victoria University of Wellington, New Zealand

Program Committee

Hernán Aguirre	Shinshu University, Japan
Sameer Alam	The University of New South Wales, Australia
Ahmed Shamsul Arefin	The University of Newcastle, Australia
Md Asafuddoula	The University of New South Wales, Australia
Yukun Bao	Huazhong University of Science and Technology, China
Regina Berretta	The University of Newcastle, Australia
Kalyan Shankar Bhattacharjee	The University of New South Wales, Australia
Alan Blair	The University of New South Wales, Australia
Tom Cai	The University of Sydney, Australia
Shelvin Chand	The University of New South Wales, Australia
Gang Chen	Victoria University of Wellington, New Zealand
Stephen Chen	York University, Canada
Girija Chetty	University of Canberra, Australia
Winyu Chinthammit	University of Tasmania, Australia
Raymond Chiong	The University of Newcastle, Australia
Carlos Coello Coello	CINVESTAV-IPN, Mexico
Kusum Deep	Indian Institute of Technology Roorkee, India
Grant Dick	University of Otago, New Zealand
Daoyi Dong	The University of New South Wales, Australia
Saber Elsayed	The University of New South Wales, Australia
Junbin Gao	Charles Sturt University, Australia
Tom Gedeon	Australian National University, Australia
Garry Greenwood	Portland State University, USA
Christian Guttmann	Institute of Value Based Reimbursement System, Sweden
Philip Hingston	Edith Cowan University, Australia
David Howard	CSIRO, Australia
Amitay Isaacs	IBM OzLabs, Australia
Hisao Ishibuchi	Osaka Prefecture University, Japan
Xiuping Jia	The University of New South Wales, Australia
Kevin Korb	Monash University, Australia

Paul Kwan	University of New England, Australia
Ickjai Lee	James Cook University, Australia
George Leu	The University of New South Wales, Australia
Xiaodong Li	RMIT University, Australia
Hui Ma	Victoria University of Wellington, New Zealand
Michael Mayo	The University of Waikato, New Zealand
Yi Mei	RMIT University, Australia
Alexandre Mendes	The University of Newcastle, Australia
Kathryn Merrick	The University of New South Wales, Australia
Efrén Mezura-Montes	University of Veracruz, Mexico
Irene Moser	Swinburne University of Technology, Australia
Keith Nesbitt	The University of New South Wales, Australia
Frank Neumann	The University of Adelaide, Australia
Oliver Obst	CSIRO, Australia
Hideaki Ogawa	RMIT University, Australia
Yew-Soon Ong	Nanyang Technological University, Singapore
Sanjay Pant	Inria, France
Somnuk Phon-Amnuaisuk	Institut Teknologi Brunei, Brunei
Daniel Polani	University of Hertfordshire, UK
Kai Qin	RMIT University, Australia
Marcus Randall	Bond University, Australia
Inaki Rano	University of Ulster, UK
Tapabrata Ray	The University of New South Wales, Australia
Ovi Chris Rouly	George Mason University, USA
Ruhul Sarker	The University of New South Wales, Australia
Dhish Saxena	Indian Institute of Technology Roorkee, India
Friedhelm Schwenker	Ulm University, Germany
Bernhard Sendhoff	Honda Research Institute Europe, Germany
Kamran Shafi	The University of New South Wales, Australia
Dharmendra Sharma	University of Canberra, Australia
Chunhua Shen	The University of Adelaide, Australia
Koji Shimoyama	Tohoku University, Japan
Karthik Sindhya	University of Jyväskylä, Finland
Hemant Kumar Singh	The University of New South Wales, Australia
Ankur Sinha	Indian Institute of Management Ahmedabad, India
Andrew Skabar	La Trobe University, Australia
Andrea Soltoggio	Loughborough Universitiy, UK
Andy Song	RMIT University, Australia
Kang Tai	Nanyang Technological University, Singapore
Eiji Uchibe	Okinawa Institute of Science and Technology, Japan
Bing Wang	Chinese Academy of Sciences, China
Dianhui Wang	La Trobe University, Australia
Peter Whigham	University of Otago, New Zealand
Kevin Wong	Murdoch University, Australia
Bing Xue	Victoria University of Wellington, New Zealand

Jianhua Yang   University of Western Sydney
Fabio Zambetta   RMIT University, Australia
Mengjie Zhang   Victoria University of Wellington, New Zealand

Contents

Planning and Scheduling

Feature Selection

Applications and Games

Mathematical Modeling and Theory

Fractal Dimension - A Spatial and Visual Design Technique for the Creation of Lifelike Artificial Forms

Dale Patterson[✉] and Daniel Della-Bosca

Griffith University, Nathan, Australia
d.patterson@griffith.edu.au

Abstract. Creating artificial entities that are lifelike and comfortable for human users to interact with is a critical challenge in a number of fields from robotics to human-computer interface design. Fractal systems are a mathematical model that can be observed in many natural systems from microscopic cellular biology through to satellite imagery. The recursive, self-similar nature of fractal systems makes them well suited to the automated creation of natural 3D forms. This research looked at the fractal dimension of artificially created forms, in particular looking at whether differing levels of fractal dimension made a difference to how natural, appealing or lifelike an item was to the user. A randomized trial (n = 25) identified that differing levels of fractal dimension did generate differing levels of response from users. This finding identifies the potential to use fractal dimension as a design principal when creating the physical forms that represent artificial life.

Keywords: Fractal · Design principals · Artificial life-forms · Human computer interaction · Experimental testing

1 Introduction

Artificial life and computational intelligence have given us many wonderful creations. From the highly successful game playing artificial intelligence systems, through virtual computer game characters, to lifelike robots with whom users can interact in near human like communications [1–3]. Yet one of the key challenges for artificial life, and digital virtual entities, is how they are perceived by the human user and how comfortably those users interact with the digital entity. In this vein the human computer interface plays a critical role in how lifelike and engaging the virtual entity can be. Whether that interface involves physically facing a mechanical robotic system, or interacting on screen with a virtual non-player game character, the visual and physical form of those items plays a key role in how believable they are as natural or life-like entities [4, 5].

In the pursuit of more natural artificial life forms, several approaches have been pursued by existing research. One of those is to take biological systems and, through complex bio-chemistry create what are essentially biological computer systems, using biological cells and systems to produce computational systems [6, 7]. This approach

© Springer International Publishing Switzerland 2016
T. Ray et al. (Eds.): ACALCI 2016, LNAI 9592, pp. 3–12, 2016.
DOI: 10.1007/978-3-319-28270-1_1

definitely creates a "living" entity but although the current systems offer potential for the future, they are extremely simple and lack the computational power to undertake any complex artificial intelligence or other practical functions that would produce an artificial life-form capable of interacting with humans in an effective manner [6, 7].

The second approach to creating artificial life involves taking digital systems and through combinations of physical, mechanical, computational, human-computer interaction, and ideally artificially intelligent capabilities, producing life like digital entities that can interact with real humans in meaningful ways. At the heart of these digital systems are often complex devices, both physical/mechanical and software based, that produce the intelligent life-like system. Yet at the surface of these digital systems exists the human computer interface. In the case of robots the physical appearance in both three-dimensional form and also interactive movement creates the initial contact with the human user. In the case of software based tools the user interface (or on screen visual presence and movement) and its appearance is the first interactive element the human senses deal with. Studies of robot use by human participants, such as those by Wu et al. in 2012, highlight the fact that the design of the robots appearance plays an important role in its acceptance and use [5]. This is supported by other studies, including those by DiSalvo et al. and Fong et al. that indicate that most of the studies on robot-human interaction have not focused on physical design, instead focusing on verbal interactions and movement [5, 8, 9].

In the field of computer game design similar circumstances are found where the focus of research has been on the verbal/textual interactions with non-player characters and the artificial intelligence related to this verbal field. The physical 3D design of spaces and characters, particularly procedural creation of 3D models, has been actively pursued, yet the design of "artificial living" characters and spaces, such that they appear natural and life-like has been less actively pursued [10–13]. In essence the key challenge is to create artificial forms, in either the real 3D world (e.g. robots) or in virtual 3D (e.g. game item) that are natural in spatial form and assist the user in understanding the "living" nature of the object and thus breaking down that initial barrier, to then allow the user to take better advantage of the other "lifelike" features of the system.

2   Fractals, Life and Nature

Fractal systems are essentially mathematical methods that use simple geometric shapes or mathematical functions, either in 2D or 3D, and repeat those shapes many times with subtle variations to create images or objects. Generally implemented using recursive programming methods, this repetitive process, using simple elements repeatedly, generates engaging and often uncannily natural patterns, images and even objects (see Fig. 1 for an example of a fractal form created from a simple geometric shape recursively repeated at differing transformations). These objects are often described as being self-similar in nature, featuring detail at differing scales and transformations.

Self-similarity plays a key role in the life-like or natural nature of fractal shapes. The fact that features are repeated at differing scales, positions and orientations creates a sense of uneven roughness, something that is less common in digital systems, and that plays a key role in the natural appearance of the outcome [14, 15]. Benoit

Fig. 1. Fractal Shell [16]

Mandelbrot, a key pioneer of fractal research, summarized his career as the 'ardent pursuit of the concept of roughness.' [14]. It is this "roughness" that creates the link to natural surfaces, spaces and objects, where fractal forms are comparatively common. Examples of inherently fractal real world phenomenon include clouds, coastlines, rivers, trees, ferns, shells and many more. Aside from recognizing fractal patterns in nature, these inherently fractal forms have also been successfully built by digital programs that automatically generate fractal systems and objects (see Fig. 2 for examples) [17].

(a) A tail of a lizard   (b) Oliva porphyria   (c) A horn of a Big-Horn Sheep

Fig. 2. Fractals in nature (upper left) & digital equivalents (lower right) [17]

Mathematically speaking, a fractal system meets a specific set of conditions, but in aesthetic terms, 'An object is said to be self-similar if it looks "roughly" the same at any scale' [14, 15], and images are called fractal if they display self-similarity, that is, they can be broken into parts, each of which is (approximately) a reduced size copy of the whole.

Significant research exists into the natural appearance of fractal images and objects and their relationship to real world living entities. In fact many research studies, such as those by Weibel et al. and West et al., highlight the fractal nature of life itself [18, 19].

As West et al. describe in their work, Fractal Geometry: a design principal for living organisms, 'It is concluded that to consider fractal geometry as a biological design principle is heuristically most productive and provides insights into possibilities of efficient genetic programming of biological form' [19]. The very nature of cell division, branching circulatory systems, genetic replication and many other fundamental biological systems can be effectively described through fractal systems where other mathematical models are ineffective.

Morphogenesis is a term used to describe development of structural features and patterns in living organisms. The study of morphogenesis when linked with fractal mathematics has led to a number of fractal techniques, used to create and describe natural forms, that have proven highly successful. In particular when looking at the creation of natural, and lifelike forms, Lindenmayer systems (L-systems), initially designed to describe simple algal growth, have been widely adapted and used to create realistic plant life and other branching systems (such as the pulmonary circulatory systems described by West et al.) [21, 22] (Fig. 3).

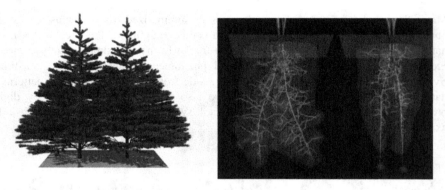

Fig. 3. Měch & Prusinkiewicz example L-Systems – Trees & Roots [23]

Other growth related systems, based on fractals, shape grammars and evolutionary models have had similar success in creating lifelike visual forms [12, 17]. These examples in conjunction with the widespread use of fractals to add natural roughness to clouds, fog, water and surfaces, amongst others, clearly demonstrate the potential of fractal systems to add a natural element to digitally created objects and images [16].

Yet this raises the question of whether simply being fractal in nature makes an item more natural, or whether there are specific types and levels of fractal content that more powerfully provide a sense of nature, and life, to the user.

2.1   Fractal Dimension

The concept of a fractal item, either a 2D pattern or 3D object, being self-similar does not directly indicate its complexity or structural nature. Such self-similar items can be either complex or simple. There exists a range of possible levels of fractal dimension (or complexity) within this fractal mathematical space. From a designers point of view this creates the possibility to consider the fractal dimension as a changeable variable to alter the visual and aesthetic nature of the fractal item being created. In terms of the quantification of fractal dimension, the numbers used refer to floating point value within a range of 1.0 unit representing fractal dimension. Mathematically it is the geometric space between the numbers 1 and 2 for the two dimensional plane, and between 2 and 3 for the 3 dimensional object. This space between integers or the fractional space is referred to as the parameter of fractal dimension or D value. The rule of self-similarity is that a pattern that fills the plane in very simplistic terms (a low order of roughness and irregularity) has a D value close to 1, and a pattern that fills the plane with detailed and intricate structure will have a D value close to 2. For objects with volume (real and virtual 3D structures), the D value lies between the 2 and 3 [24].

With this fractal dimension in mind, for designers of artificial life to effectively create the most life-like fractal items those designers need to understand the broader human preferences with regard to fractal dimension. There have been a number of research studies, including studies by Aks & Sprott as well as those by Spehar et al., that have measured the preferences of participants when viewing images containing varying levels of fractal dimension [25, 26]. By taking images from nature, art and digitally generated imagery, all with known fractal dimensional values, and presenting them to participants, the studies identified an average preference for a fractal dimension level in the range of 1.3 to 1.5 [25, 26]. As a result the findings of the studies found that most participants preferred images that were not too complex (below 1.5) but also not too simple (above 1.3).

For the designer of an artificial life form these dimension levels are valuable, providing insight into the level of visual fractal complexity (dimension) that users will find more natural. However for the designer of the physical form of a robot the visuals are not the only factor. From a sensory perspective the robot will be both a visual and tactile (and potentially audio as well) interactive entity. As outlined in the work of Prendinger et al. and Wu et al., the physical and tactile nature of such a device plays a crucial role in how well it is accepted [4, 5].

With increasing demands for both more natural robotic systems and also for the automated creation of digital 3D content (in User Interfaces, Games, AR and VR applications) there is a need to gain a greater understanding of fractal dimension [16, 26–29]. Understanding applied fractal dimension across the range of human senses, with the objective of enabling designers of artificial life, to enhance their creations through more targeted lifelike design [28].

3   Testing the Nature of Tactile and Visual Fractal Dimension

To test the nature of human interactions, in both visual and tactile sensory form, with items of differing levels of fractal dimension, an experimental trial was carried out. The goal of the trial was to measure the user response to physical surfaces and images with a range of varied levels of fractal dimension. The trial involved 50 participants who ranged in age from 18 to 52 years. The items used to represent differing fractal dimensions in the visual realm were simple grey scale images (see Fig. 4).

Colour was removed to simplify the task and remove the colour as a possible variable, thus allowing the only changing variable to be the fractal dimension itself. To maintain consistency throughout the trials the touch trial involved user interacting with

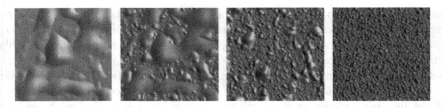

Fig. 4. Example Fractal images used in experimental trial.

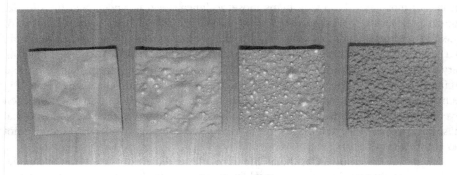

Fig. 5. Example Fractal 3D Printed Objects used in experimental trial.

the same set of fractal dimensional items only that these objects were 3D printed into physical objects as shown in Fig. 5.

The study involved each participant being presented with a range of surface options. These surface options included a range of digitally created fractal surfaces and objects, each with differing levels of fractal dimension and complexity. To avoid any bias or influence from experiencing one before the other, the trial group was split into two sub groups of 25 participants. Each sub group then completed one trial, either tactile (interacting with the physical 3D printed fractal forms) or visual (interacting with the image based fractal forms).

The trial items were designed and intended to be very simple in nature with surfaces that were generated for their aesthetic neutrality (lack of association to natural or synthetic commonly recognised form). Each surface was presented in consistent simple neutral color and the base shape/function used to create the fractal pattern was consistent through both the tactile and visual groups. The only variable that was different through the trials was the amount of fractal dimension in the surface patterns.

For the participants of both trial groups, they were initially asked a series of questions to establish basic information on age, sex and previous experience or possible biasing factors. For those participants who were in the visual trial group they were then shown the fractal items on screen (as arranged in Fig. 4). The participants were then observed interacting with the visual fractal surfaces before being questioned regarding their preferences. As the surfaces featured 3D relief elements in the tactile and bump maps in the visual, the D values presented here are in the 2 to 3 range for both groups to enable simpler comparative reporting of results. At the conclusion of the questions regarding the visual surface preferences the participants were asked several broad questions regarding their experience and overall feeling about the study before concluding.

For the tactile group, following the initial questions they were asked to place their hands on the 3D printed fractal objects, placed underneath a covered black sheet. This blinding process insured that the participants response was not effected by the visual appearance of the items and was purely based on the tactile experience (see Fig. 6).

They were then observed interacting with the tactile fractal surfaces before being questioned regarding their preferences and then their overall experience before concluding the trial.

Fig. 6. Example Tactile experimental trial (Note without black cover here to show hand interaction with 3D printed objects)

4 Results

Results from the study are reported using fractal dimension (D) and the resulting absolute effect sizes in conjunction with 95 % confidence intervals (CI). The results from participants in the visual trial group showed 18 of the 25 (72 %) participants indicated surfaces with a visual fractal dimension of D = 2.38 (±0.106 (CI)) was their preference. This result closely matches the findings from other studies including those by Aks & Sprott as well as those by Spehar et al., who found that the range of 2.3–2.5 was preferred [25, 26]. Of note was the fact that preference rates dropped off quickly the further away from the 2.3–2.5 range the dimensional value was (with values in the high 2.8–3.0 range being the furthest away and also the lowest in user preference (1 of 28 (3.5 %)).

The other interesting finding from the visual trial related to the time taken to make a judgement. For the visual trial, participants averaged more than 10 s (10.6 (±3.61(CI))) to make up their mind regarding their preference.

Results from the tactile trial group showed a similar pattern of favouring one level of fractal dimension, but notably the dimension that was favoured was lower D values (D = 2.25 (±0.142 (CI)), in the 2.1 to 2.4 range. Of significant interest from the tactile trials was the user observation study. In this study one of the most notable findings was that users in the tactile trial had significantly stronger emotional reactions to the surfaces than their counterparts in the visual group. The tactile groups response times were significantly faster at 3 s compared to 10.6 for the visual group. The response magnitude was also significantly higher, particularly with negative responses being strongly expressed. This was in contrast to the visual group for whom the responses were more measured and only given after careful comparison and categorization.

5 Analysis and Discussion

The visual fractal preferred dimensional results from this study closely match the results found for fractal dimension in images by other studies [25, 26]. With the average values in the 1.3–1.5 2D range and 2.3–2.5 3D range indicating that users found items that were neither too complex (>1.5 or 2.5) nor too simple (<1.3 or 2.3) ideal and most natural.

The tactile fractal dimensional results were notably different, and at a lower level of fractal dimension, to those of the visual trials. Users in the tactile trial also responded significantly more quickly and with stronger emotion. This finding that the ideal "natural" fractal dimension is different for touch and visual senses is a critical outcome from this research. The relative difference indicates that touch or tactile surfaces need to be measurably simpler, in terms of fractal dimension to be most natural and life-like. It also indicates that physical tactile or touchable surfaces are capable of generating stronger and faster responses. These findings carry significant impact for the design of surfaces for artificial life forms such as robots, touch screen interfaces as well as for the surfacing characteristics of other virtual or on-screen artificial life. In the robot example it may be that using a surface that has some surface complexity, but not a lot (2.1–2.3 fractal dimension) may be able to make a difference and remove some of that initial negative response that is commonly associated with robotic systems. In simple terms perhaps flat plastic (which has a fractal dimension of 2.0) could be replaced with a slightly more complex surface to make it more acceptable for users. This surface complexity could be applied in both 3D form and also in 2D textures and patterns for use in physical robotics as well as 3D user interfaces, games and VR systems [29–31].

6 Conclusions

The experimental study identified that differing fractal dimension plays a significant role in determining how natural an item feels to the user. The finding that there was a preferred fractal dimension, but that the dimension level was different for the two differing senses, applied in both the visual experiments and also the touch experiments. Interestingly for both visuals and surfaces the desirability, and natural feel, of the item reduced as the dimension moved away from the ideal dimensional value (both more complex dimension and less complex dimension were less desirable).

It is also important to note that there was not a single "ideal fractal dimension". The experimental findings showed that in both visual and tactile sensory systems the desired "natural" dimension was different and there is a need to design with these sensory differences in mind.

The results from the study indicate that fractal dimension can be applied as a design principal to automatically create items that are more (closer to desired natural fractal dimension) or less (further from desired natural fractal dimension) natural in form. The ability to use a mathematical technique of this kind allows for automated content creation tools, such as those involved in creation of artificial life forms to use fractal dimension as a guiding principal for making those forms more lifelike and natural. Understanding that the human response was different in differing senses, with touch using a lower fractal dimension for desired natural form than visuals allows for application of fractal dimension in differing sensory domains. For example when designing the physical "touchable" surface of an artificial life-form like a robot the lower fractal dimension could be applied to make the robots surface (or full physical shape/form) more natural and lifelike to the human tactile senses. Equally when designing the visual form of an on screen artificial life-form (for example a virtual game characters appearance) the higher visual fractal dimension could be applied to make that character more natural, and as a result more lifelike to the viewer.

References

1. Cohen, P., Feigenbaum, E. (eds.): The Handbook of Artificial Intelligence, vol. 3. Butterworth-Heinemann, Oxford (2014)
2. Yannakakis, G.: Game AI revisited. In: Proceedings of the 9th conference on Computing Frontiers, pp. 285–292. ACM (2012)
3. Haring, K, Matsumoto, Y., Watanabe, K.: How do people perceive and trust a lifelike robot. In: Ao, S., Douglas, C., Grundfest, W., Burgstone, J (eds.) Proceedings of the World Congress on Engineering and Computer Science, vol. 1 (2013)
4. Prendinger, H., Ishizuka, M. (eds.): Life-Like Characters: Tools, Affective Functions, and Applications. Springer Science & Business Media, Berlin (2013)
5. Wu, Y., Fassert, C., Rigaud, A.: Designing robots for the elderly: appearance issue and beyond. Arch. Gerontol. Geriatr. 54(1), 121–126 (2012)
6. Amos, M., Rasmussen, S., McCaskill, J., Dittrich, P.: Editorial. Artificial life 21(2), 193–194 (2015)
7. Cussat-Blanc, S., Pollack, J.: Cracking the egg: Virtual embryogenesis of real robots. Artif. Life 20(3), 361–383 (2014)
8. DiSalvo, C., Gemperle, F., Forlizzi, J., Kiesler, S.: All robots are not created equal: the design and perception of humanoid robot heads. In: Proceedings of the 4th Conference on Designing Interactive Systems: Processes, Practices, Methods, and Techniques, pp. 321–326. ACM (2002)
9. Fong, T., Nourbakhsh, I., Dautenhahn, K.: A survey of socially interactive robots. Robot. Auton. Syst. 42(3), 143–166 (2003)
10. Xu, K., Zhang, H., Cohen-Or, D., Chen, B.: Fit and diverse: set evolution for inspiring 3D shape galleries. ACM Trans. Graph. (TOG) 31(4), 57 (2012)
11. Cook, M., Colton, M., Gow, J.: Automating game design in three dimensions. In: Proceedings of the AISB Symposium on AI and Games, pp. 20–24 (2014)

12. Merrick, K.E., Isaacs, A., Barlow, M., Gu, N.: A shape grammar approach to computational creativity and procedural content generation in massively multiplayer online role playing games. In: Anacleto, J.C., Clua, E.W.G., Correa da Silva, F.S., Fels, S.,Yang, H.S. (eds.) Entertainment Computing, vol. 4(2), pp. 115–130 (2013)

13. Hendrikx, M., Meijer, S., Van Der Velden, J., Iosup, A.: Procedural content generation for games: A survey. ACM Trans. Multimedia Comput. Commun. Appl. (TOMM) 9(1), 1–22 (2013)

14. Mandelbrot, B.B.: The Fractal Geometry of Nature. Macmillan, New York (1983)

15. Mandelbrot, B.B.: Fractals: Form, Change and Dimension. WH Freemann and Company, San Francisco (1977)

16. Della-Bosca, D., Patterson, D., Costain, S.: Fractal complexity in built and game environments. In: Pisan, Y., Sgouros, N.M., Marsh, T. (eds.) ICEC 2014. LNCS, vol. 8770, pp. 167–172. Springer, Heidelberg (2014)

17. Harary, G., Tal, A.: The natural 3D spiral. Comput. Graph. Forum 30(2), 237–246 (2011). Blackwell Publishing Ltd

18. Weibel, E.R.: Fractal geometry: a design principle for living organisms. Am. J. Physiol. Lung Cell. Mol. Physiol. 261(6), 361–369 (1991)

19. West, G.B., Brown, J.H., Enquist, B.J.: The fourth dimension of life: fractal geometry and allometric scaling of organisms. Science 284(5420), 1677–1679 (1999)

20. Hamon, L., Richard, R., Richard, P., Boumaza, R., Ferrier, J.: RTIL-system: a real-time interactive L-system for 3D interactions with virtual plants. Virtual Reality 16(2), 151–160 (2012)

21. Pestana, P.: Lindenmayer systems and the harmony of fractals. Chaotic Model. Simul. 1(1), 91–99 (2012)

22. Prusinkiewicz, P., Lindenmayer, A.: The Algorithmic Beauty of Plants. Springer Science & Business Media, Berlin (2012)

23. Měch, R., Prusinkiewicz, P.: Visual models of plants interacting with their environment. In: Proceedings of the 23rd Annual Conference on Computer Graphics and Interactive Techniques, pp. 397–410. ACM (1996)

24. Sarkar, N., Chaudhuri, B.B.: An efficient differential box-counting approach to compute fractal dimension of image. IEEE Trans. Syst. Man Cybern. 24(1), 115–120 (1994)

25. Spehar, B., Clifford, C., Newell, B., Taylor, R.: Universal aesthetic of fractals. Comput. Graph. 27(5), 813–820 (2003)

26. Aks, D., Sprott, J.: Quantifying aesthetic preference for chaotic patterns. Empirical Stud. Arts 14(1), 1–16 (1996)

27. Patterson, D.: 3D Space: special project in advanced computer environments, Ph.D., Bond University (2003)

28. Della-Bosca, D., Patterson, D.: The imperatives of the application of fractal principles applied to compositional strategies for the static and moving image. In: ACUADS 2014 (2015)

29. Umedachi, T., Idei, R., Ito, K., Ishiguro, A.: A fluid-filled soft robot that exhibits spontaneous switching among versatile spatiotemporal oscillatory patterns inspired by the true slime mold. Artif. Life 19(1), 67–78 (2013)

30. Patterson, D.: 3D SPACE: using depth and movement for selection tasks. In: Proceedings of the Twelfth International Conference on 3D Web Technology, pp. 147–155. ACM (2007)

31. Patterson, D.: Using interactive 3D game play to make complex medical knowledge more accessible. Procedia Comput. Sci. 29, 354–363 (2014)

Using Closed Sets to Model Cognitive Behavior

John L. Pfaltz[(✉)]

Department of Computer Science, University of Virginia, Charlottesville, USA
jlp@virginia.edu

Abstract. We introduce closed sets, which we will call knowledge units, to represent tight collections of experience, facts, or skills, *etc.* Associated with each knowledge unit is the notion of its generators consisting of those attributes which characterize it.

Using these closure concepts, we then provide a rigorous mathematical model of learning in terms of continuous transformations. We illustrate the behavior of transformations by means of closure lattices, and provide necessary and sufficient criteria for simple transformations to be continuous. By using a rigorous definition, one can derive necessary alternative properties of cognition which may be more easily observed in experimental situations.

1 Introduction

We are concerned with modeling intelligence and learning, but not *artificial* intelligence or *machine* learning. Rather we want to model these phenomena as they might occur in a human mind. It is generally accepted that mental cognition occurs in the brain, which is itself comprised of a network of neurons, axons, and synapses. Neuroscientists have a rather clear understanding of the physical layout of the brain, including which portions are responsible for individual mental functions [6]. But, how mental processes actually occur is still elusive. Nevertheless, it is clear that the response to external stimuli occurs in a reactive network. Thus if we want to model cognitive behavior we must, at some level, come to grips with network behavior.

In Sect. 2, we will introduce the idea of an experiential operator, ρ, which expresses a relationship between the elements of a network. The elements can be raw visual stimuli, at a lower level, or concepts and ideas, at a higher level.

In Sect. 3 we introduce the concept of *closure*, which identifies closely related elements. Closure is central to our mathematics. Then, for want of a better term we call closed sets, *knowledge units*. Properties of these knowledge units are developed in Sect. 4.

It is not until Sect. 5 that we actually encounter network transformations that correspond to learning situations, and define the concept of *continuity*. We will examine several continuous network transformations and provide necessary and sufficient conditions for a simple transformation to be continuous. This section is the meat of the paper.

© Springer International Publishing Switzerland 2016
T. Ray et al. (Eds.): ACALCI 2016, LNAI 9592, pp. 13–26, 2016.
DOI: 10.1007/978-3-319-28270-1_2

2   The Experiential Operator

Let U denote a finite universe of awarenesses, sensations, *etc.* that an individual might experience, $U = \{\ldots, w, x, y, z\}$.[1] We denote sets by $\{\ldots\}$ and by upper case letters. Thus $Y = \{x, z\}$ is a set of two possible experiences in U. Y is said to be a subset of (or contained in) U, denoted $Y \subseteq U$.

Experiences are related to one another. If z is related to x, say for example that z can be experienced having once experienced x, we denote the relationship by $x \; \rho \; z$. Relationships may, or may not, be symmetric; we need not have $z \; \rho \; x$. Based on known neural morphology [6], most neural cells have many inputs and relatively few outputs, so we can assume many relationships will be asymmetric. Relationships come in a great many varieties. Experiential events can be simultaneous or sequenced in time; can be adjacent or distant in space; can be synonyms or antonyms in a lexical space; or can be friendly or threatening in an emotional space. But for this paper we assume only one generic relationship. By ρ we mean that some relationship exists. Throughout this paper we are going to let the term "experience" be generic. We might have related visual stimuli comprising a visual object, or related skills comprising a skill set, or related facts comprising an area of knowledge. All will be regarded as experiential.

Relationships are frequently visualized by means of graphs, or networks, such as Fig. 1. Here an edge between q and s denotes $q \; \rho \; s$. If no arrow head is present, it is assumed that the relation is symmetric.

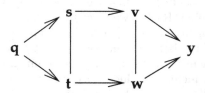

Fig. 1. A very small network depicting the relationships, ρ, between 6 experiential elements.

While network graphs can provide a valuable intuition, we actually prefer to regard relationships as operators that map subsets of U onto other subsets in U. Thus we will denote $q \; \rho \; s$ by the expression $\{q\}.\rho = \{s\}$, that is, ρ operating on q yields s, or because we tacitly assume q is related to itself, and because $q \; \rho \; t$, $\{q\}.\rho = \{q, s, t\}$. In Fig. 1, $\{s\}.\rho = \{s, t, v\}$ and $\{t\}.\rho = \{s, t, w\}$. Using this kind of suffix notation is a bit unusual, but it has value. One reason for preferring an operator notation is that in order to experience y it may be necessary to first experience both v and w, that is, $y \in \{v, w\}.\rho$, but $y \notin \{v\}.\rho$. For example, for a neuron y to respond, it may need signals from both v and w. So properly,

---

[1] This finiteness constraint can be relaxed somewhat, but there is relatively little yield for the resulting complexity.

ρ is a function on sets, not individual elements of U. A second reason is that in later sections we will compose the functional operators, and suffix notation lets us read the composition in a natural left to right manner.

To formalize this, we let 2^U denote all possible combinations of "experiences" in the universe U. Mathematically, it is called the **power set** of U. The relationship operator, ρ, maps subsets $Y \subseteq U$ into other subsets, $Z = Y.\rho \subseteq U$. By convention we assume that every experience is related to itself, so that, for all Y, $Y \subseteq Y.\rho$. Consequently, ρ is an **expansive** operator. This is precisely what we want; ρ denotes the possibility of expanding one's realm of experiences. For example, having the experiences x and y, it may be possible to also experience z, or $\{x, y\}.\rho = \{x, y, z\}$.

We will also assume that a greater collection of experience will permit a greater awareness of possible new experience. That is, $X \subseteq Y$ implies $X.\rho \subseteq Y.\rho$. Then ρ is said to be a **monotone** operator.

3   Closure Operators and Knowledge Units

Certain collections of experiences, of facts, of abilities, appear to be more robust than others. They go by many names in the literature. A cluster of perceived visual stimuli may be called an *external entity*, or *object*. If the granularity of the base experiential elements, U, is coarser, say that of *skills* or *facts*, we might call a cluster of abilities an *area of expertise*, such as *horseshoeing*; or a cluster of facts might be regarded as a *discipline*, such as *medieval history* or *high school algebra*. With so many possible terms and interpretations, we choose to use a more neutral term. We will call such clusters *knowledge units* without trying to specify precisely what such a unit is. In this section we will postulate that this organizing process can be approximately modeled by a mathematical *closure* operator.

An operator φ is said to be a **closure operator** if for all $X, Y \subseteq U$,

$$Y \subseteq Y.\varphi \qquad \varphi \text{ is expansive,}$$
$$X \subseteq Y \text{ implies } X.\varphi \subseteq Y.\varphi \qquad \varphi \text{ is monotone, and}$$
$$Y.\varphi.\varphi = Y.\varphi \qquad \varphi \text{ is idempotent.}$$

There is an extensive literature on closure and closure operators of which [2, 5, 9, 12, 14] are only representative.

Since ρ is both expansive and monotone, it is almost a closure operator itself. But, ρ need not be idempotent. In Fig. 1, we have $\{q\}.\rho = \{qst\} \subset \{qstuv\} = \{q\}.\rho.\rho$. However, we can define a closure operator φ_ρ with respect to ρ. Let,

$$Y.\varphi_\rho = \bigcup_{z \in Y.\rho} \{\{z\}.\rho \subseteq Y.\rho\}. \tag{1}$$

Readily, if $z \in Y$ then $z.\rho \subseteq Y.\rho$, so $Y \subseteq Y.\varphi$. We call φ_ρ the **experiential closure** because it is determined by the experiential operator ρ. Note that any relationship, ρ, of any type can give rise to a closure operator, φ_ρ.

Proposition 1. φ_ρ *is a closure operator.*

Proof. Readily, $Y \subseteq Y.\varphi_\rho$ by definition. Let $X \subseteq Y$ and let $z \in X.\varphi_\rho$. By (1) $z.\rho \subseteq X.\rho \subseteq Y.\rho$ hence $z \in Y.\varphi_\rho$. Now let $z \in Y.\varphi_\rho.\varphi_\rho$. Then $z.\rho \subseteq Y.\varphi_\rho.\rho = \bigcup_{z \in Y.\varphi_\rho} \{z.\rho \subseteq Y.\rho\}$, hence $z \in Y.\varphi_\rho$.   □

In the network of Fig. 1, observe that $\{y\}$ is closed, but $\{v\}$ is not, because $\{y\}.\rho = \{y\} \subseteq \{vwy\} = \{v\}.\rho$, so $\{v\}.\varphi_\rho = \{vwy\}$. Neither is $\{w\}$ closed, because $\{w\}.\varphi_\rho = \{vwy\} = \{v\}.\varphi_\rho$. So, singleton elements need not be closed.

A set Y is said to be **closed** if $Y = Y.\varphi$. Because φ is expansive, U itself must be closed. The empty set, $\emptyset$, is most often closed, but need not be. (Here, $\emptyset$ denotes an "empty set" that contains no elements.)

Normally, we omit the subscript ρ from the closure symbol φ because most results are valid for all closure operators. Only if some property of the relational closure is required will we use the symbol φ_ρ.

By a **knowledge unit**, K_i, we mean a set closed with respect to φ_ρ in U. That is, the elements of K_i are a tightly bound collection of related experiences that will be regarded as a unit of *knowledge awareness*. In Fig. 1, because $\{st\}$ is closed, it is a knowledge set, K_1. The set $\{qst\}$ is also closed, and thus also a knowledge unit, K_2. Here, $K_1 = \{st\} \subset \{qst\} = K_2$. We can think of increasing knowledge awareness with increasing experience or capability.

3.1   An Example of Experiential Closure

The formal definition of experiential closure, φ_ρ, as well as the more general definition with respect to expansive, monotonicity, and idempotency, conveys little intuitive sense of its being. Here we will examine an example which could occur in human cognition.

Consider the retina of the eye, where the close packing of cells (frequently called "pixels", and here shown as hexagonal, even though the retina is never quite so regular) endows each receptive cell with 6 neighbors. Figure 2 illustrates a simulated portion of the retinal structure with a mottled pattern of 43 excited cells (black dots) which we will denote by Y. We seek an experiential closure of Y based on an adjacency relation, ρ. The pixels, or neural cells, containing an $\times$ in Fig. 3(a) denote the extent of $Y.\rho$. If all the neighbors of an $\times$-cell are also $\times$-cells, then it is in $Y.\varphi_\rho$ which is shown as Fig. 3(b). Surely, a process that can extract more "solid" objects in a natural kind of mottled camouflage will convey survival benefit, and might be "built-in".

It was shown in [16] that this spatial closure operator can be implemented in parallel by "expanding" each stimulated element in Y then expanding its complement thus contracting Y.

Since it is assumed that virtually all processing of information passing back from the retina to the visual cortex occurs in parallel; that spatial retinal relationships are preserved in some of this visual pathway; and that this pathway consists of alternating odd/even cell layers [18], it is plausible to regard this example as an actual, but vastly oversimplified, cognitive process.

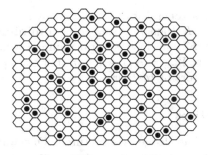

Fig. 2. A mottled pattern on a simulated retina.

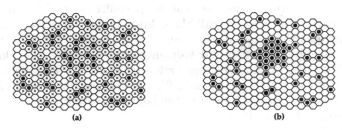

Fig. 3. Closure within the mottled pattern of Fig. 2

This example of a closure operator has been set within the context of visual cognition. It does not necessarily imply that this black and white "cartoon" example mimics an actual visual process. Real visual cognition is far more complex, for example, we see in multiple frequencies (color). But, it does establish that closure concepts are compatible with known aspects of visual physiology, and illustrates how a closure operator can extract "identifiable" objects from a pattern.

A well-known property of closure systems is that if X and Y are closed then their intersection $X \cap Y$ must be closed; or equivalently, $X.\varphi \cap Y.\varphi = (X \cap Y).\varphi$. Readily, we encounter many different kinds of experiential relationships in the real world, say $\rho_1, \rho_2, \ldots, \rho_n$. We can show by counter example that $X.\varphi_{\rho_1 \& \rho_2} \neq X.\varphi_{\rho_1} \cap X.\varphi_{\rho_2}$. But, for all X, $X.\varphi_{\rho_1} \cap X.\varphi_{\rho_2} = X.\varphi_{\rho_1 \cdot \rho_2}$. That is, the intersection of closed sets corresponds to closure based on concatenated, rather than concurrent, relationships, which seems to be what occurs in the visual pathway.

4   Generators and Knowledge Lattices

If K is a closed knowledge unit there exists at least one set $Y \subseteq K$ such that $Y.\varphi = K$. (It may be K itself.) Y is said to be a **generator** of K. A reasonable interpretation of generating sets is that these are a set of features of K that serve to characterize K.

Readily, the set Y is a generator of $Y.\varphi$, as is any set Z, $Y \subset Z \subseteq Y.\varphi$. If for all $X \subset Y$, $X.\varphi \subset Y.\varphi = K$ then Y is said to be a **minimal generator** of K.[2] In general, a closed set K may have several minimal generating sets, denoted $K.\Gamma = \{Y_1, \ldots Y_m\}$ where $Y_i.\varphi = K$, $1 \leq i \leq m$. For example, in Fig. 1, $\{qv, qw\}$ are both minimal generators of $\{qstvwy\}$.

4.1   Knowledge Lattices

It is assumed that our knowledge is structured. One way of doing this is to partially order the knowledge units by containment to form a lattice. Because U itself must be closed (φ is expansive) and because $X \cap Y$ must be closed, any collection of discrete closed sets can be partially ordered by containment to form a complete lattice. We call them **knowledge lattices**, denoted $\mathcal{L}_\varphi$. Figure 4 illustrates the knowledge lattice, $\mathcal{L}_\varphi$, associated with the experiential operator, ρ, of Fig. 1. Doignon and Falmange called such lattices "knowledge spaces" [4]. This idea of *knowledge spaces* has generated a considerable amount of psychological literature.[3] Ganter and Wille [5] regard a lattice of closed sets as a "concept lattice". In both theories the lattice structure is central; for us, it will be important, but ancillary.

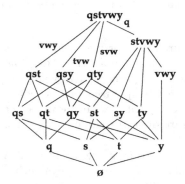

Fig. 4. Closed set lattice, $\mathcal{L}_\varphi$, of Fig. 1. Four set differences have been labeled.

A closed set K_m in $\mathcal{L}_\varphi$ is said to **cover** K_i if $K_i \subset K_m$ and there exists no set K_j such that $K_i \subset K_j \subset K_m$. That is, K_m is the next set above K_i in the lattice.[4] We can think of the **difference**, $K_m - K_i$, as being the skill/experience set differentiating an individual with knowledge unit K_i from one with K_m.

---

[2] If for all closed sets K, there is a *unique* minimal generating set, the closure operator is said to be *antimatroid*. While antimatroid knowledge systems, such as [4,5], are mathematically most interesting, they seem, in practice, to be most rare.

[3] Over 400 references can be found at the web site <cord.hockemeyer@uni-graz.at>.

[4] Because U is discrete, there always is a "next" set above K_i in $\mathcal{L}$, unless $K_i = U$, the maximal element.

In Fig. 4, $\{gstvwy\} - \{qst\} = \{vwy\}$ and $\{qstvwy\} - \{stvwy\} = \{q\}$. Explicitly showing the set differences as we have done in 4 instances in Fig. 4 can be an aid to understanding Proposition 2 which follows.

Proposition 2. *If a closed set K covers the closed sets $K_1, \ldots, K_m$ in $\mathcal{L}_\rho$, then X is a generator of K if and only if $X \cap (K - K_i) \neq \emptyset$ for all $1 \leq i \leq m$.*

Proof. A rigorous proof can be found in [8], here we present a more intuitive argument.

A knowledge unit is the smallest closed set containing some set, X, of experiences. Suppose X is a generator of K. Now, if X does not embrace at least one element from $K - K_i$ then $X.\varphi = K_i$, not K.

Conversely, $\mathcal{L}_\rho$ contains a number of knowledge units, K_i, and if X includes at least one experience that differentiates each one from K, then X must characterize K; it must be a generator. □

That is, the generators of a knowledge unit are precisely those features which differentiate it from other knowledge units in the lattice. By Proposition 2, if one knows the generators of a closed knowledge unit, one knows the closed sets it covers, and conversely given the lattice of closed sets one can determine all the generators. It is worthwhile convincing oneself of this unusual result by actual trial. In Fig. 4, $\{qstvwy\}$ covers $\{qst\}$, $\{qsy\}$, $\{qty\}$, and $\{stvwy\}$ with respective differences being $\{vwy\}$, $\{tvw\}$, $\{svw\}$, and $\{q\}$. Using Fig. 1, convince yourself that both of the sets $\{qv\}$ and $\{qw\}$, each of which intersect all four set differences are actually generators of $\{qstvwy\}$.

Suppose U consists of visual stimuli. If X generates K, a closed set of related stimuli, constituting a visual object, then X consists of those visual attributes that characterize the object; and differentiate it from other similar objects, K_i. On the other hand, if K represents an ability level in high-school algebra, as in [4], then X represents those skills necessary to advance from lesser sets of algebraic abilities, K_i to K. Finally, if K represents knowledge of the Napoleonic wars, then questions embodying the facts found in a generator, X, would comprise an excellent test of the student's knowledge. The concept of generators resonates with many educational themes depending on the network granularity.

Experiential networks are real. The neural networks of the mind are real; our social networks are real; the related collections of facts we call knowledge are real. Our rendition of these real networks by ρ may be an over simplification; but it is an abstract depiction of real phenomena. In contrast, these *knowledge lattices* are **not** real. They have no existential counterpart that we know of. They are purely a mathematical construct designed to help us understand the organization and structure of real networks; and in the next section, to help us understand how their structure can change under dynamic transformation. This is an important distinction. While in this section, and the next, we may seem to be fixated on these *knowledge lattices*. We are really most concerned about the underlying network of experiential relationships.

Do the concepts of *closure* and *generators* correspond to real phenomena? Even though we have no compelling proof, we believe they do. It seems clear that our minds are capable of identifying and labeling, in some fashion, related collections of experiential input. Several cognitive psychologists have emphasized this fact. Objects that are linguistic nouns appear to invariably behave as closed concepts, with adjectives often fulfilling the role of generating features. Replacing a cluster of primitive experiential elements with a single label can optimize neuron use because it facilitates the internal representation at a coarser granularity. It seems necessary for "abstract" thought.

Similarly, it seems apparent that the mind, on many levels, apprehends objects and abstractions of the real world by abbreviated collections of salient features. This, too, represents an economical use of neurons — which must be important to all organisms. Whether *generators* exactly model this phenomenon is unclear; but surely they represent an abstraction of this capability.

Our imposition of a formal lattice structure as a mathematical device to comprehend the organization of experiential networks may be a major contribution of this paper. In the following sections we will see where this leads us.

5   Transformation as Learning

The notion of *transformation* is a familiar one in educational psychology; for example, the process of *internalization* has been described by the Russian psychologist, Lev Vygotsky, as a "series of transformations" [3]. In this section we will develop the idea of transformation as a mathematical function. Most of us are familiar with polynomial functions, which describe numerical change — the speed of a falling object is a quadratic function of it's time of flight. But now, we let a transformation be a function that describes a change of *structure*. It requires a different mathematical mind set. It is one reason we use suffix notation.

By a **transformation**, $U \xrightarrow{f} U'$, we mean a function f which for every set $Y \subseteq U$, assigns a set $Y.f = Y' \subseteq U'$. (We use Y' to denote the image of Y in U'). Of most interest will be the effect, $K.f$ of transforming closed knowledge units, and how the transformation will affect their relationship with other knowledge units, $K_i.f$. The importance of using a power set as the domain and codomain of a transformation is that elements can be functionally inserted or removed from the system. For example, consider the transformation f depicted by Fig. 5 which adds a completely new element, r, to the network of Fig. 1. That is, $\emptyset.f = \{r\}$, so $\{y\}.f = \{ry\}$, and all closed sets containing q now contain $\{qr\}$.

In the mathematics of the real line, the behavior of functions is typically visualized by the familiar graph plotting the value $y = f(x)$ for all x along the x-axis. When the function is defined on sets of discrete elements a different approach must be taken. We prefer to illustrate its behavior by what happens to the closed set/knowledge lattice. Although f must be defined for all sets, $Y \subseteq U$, we use only these closed sets to visualize the process. In Fig. 5 the lower transformation $\mathcal{L}_\varphi \xrightarrow{f*} \mathcal{L}'_{\varphi'}$ illustrates its behavior with respect to the knowledge lattice. This transformation, f, is a classic example of a smooth, well-behaved lattice morphism.

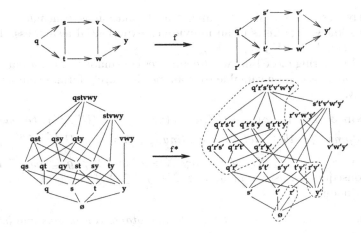

Fig. 5. A transformation $U \xrightarrow{f} U'$ that adds a completely new element r' to the network of Fig. 1.

A transformation $U \xrightarrow{f} U'$ is said to be **monotone** if for all sets X, Y in U, $X \subseteq Y$ implies $X.f \subseteq Y.f$. Monotonicity is essential throughout the following mathematical approach.[5] Observe that the transformation f of Fig. 5 is monotone, in that $K_i \subseteq K_m$ in $\mathcal{L}_\varphi$ implies $K_i.f \subseteq K_m.f$ in $\mathcal{L}'_{\varphi'}$.

5.1 Continuous Transformations

In high school we are told that a "continuous" function, $f(x)$, is one whose graph can be drawn without lifting one's pencil from the paper. The more precise definition encountered in real analysis is quite analogous to the definition that follows.[6] A discrete transformation, $U \xrightarrow{f} U'$, is said to be **continuous** if for all $Y \subseteq U$,

$$Y.\varphi.f \subseteq Y.f.\varphi' \qquad (2)$$

This is the traditional definition of continuity for functions on discrete spaces [9–11,20,21]. Yet this short equation conveys little intuitive sense of its import. The transformation f of Fig. 5 is continuous; it is "smooth". Continuity takes on additional importance when viewed as a function on knowledge lattices.

---

[5] In artificial intelligence (A.I.), learning is said to be "monotonic" if no new piece of information can invalidate any existing "knowledge" as represented by a set of rules. That concept of knowledge involves a notion of logical contradiction, not just the simple inclusion or deletion of experiential input. There is an abundance of literature about A.I. architectures which support both monotonic and non-monotonic reasoning [13,17]. Our use of the term is rather different.

[6] A real function $y = f(x)$ is said to be continuous if for any open set O_y containing y, there exists an open set O_x containing x such that $f(O_x) \subseteq O_y = O_{f(x)}$, or using suffix notation $x.O.f \subseteq y.f.O'$.

It effectively asserts that if a learning transformation is continuous, it only expands the knowledge units of an individuals experiential awareness. That is, if $K = Y.\varphi$ then $K.f \subseteq Y.f.\varphi_{\rho'} = K'$.

Before considering more fully what comprises continuous transformations in a cognitive context it can be valuable to examine the purely formal characteristics of continuity.

Proposition 3. Let $(U, \varphi) \xrightarrow{f} (U', \varphi')$, $(U', \varphi') \xrightarrow{g} (U'', \varphi'')$ be monotone transformations. If both f and g are continuous, then so is $U \xrightarrow{f \cdot g} U''$.

Proof. We have $X.\varphi.f \subseteq X.f.\varphi'$ for any $X \in U$ and $Y.\varphi'.g \subseteq Y.g.\varphi''$ for any $Y \in U'$. Consequently, as g is monotone, $X.\varphi.f.g \subseteq X.f.\varphi'.g \subseteq X.f.g.\varphi''$. Thus $f \cdot g$ is continuous. □

Proposition 4. Let $(U, \varphi) \xrightarrow{f} (U', \varphi')$ be monotone, continuous and let $Y.f = Y'$ be closed. Then $Y.\varphi.f = Y'$.

Proof. Let $Y.f$ be closed in U'. Because f is continuous $Y.\varphi.f \subseteq Y.f.\varphi' = Y.f$, since $Y.f$ is closed. By monotonicity, $Y.f \subseteq Y.\varphi.f$, so $Y.\varphi.f = Y.f$. □

Proposition 5. Let $(U, \varphi) \xrightarrow{f} (U', \varphi')$ be monotone. Then f is continuous if and only if $X.\varphi = Y.\varphi$ implies $X.f.\varphi' = Y.f.\varphi'$.

Proof. Let f be continuous, and let $X.\varphi = Y.\varphi$. By monotonicity and continuity, $X.f \subseteq X.\varphi.f = Y.\varphi.f \subseteq Y.f.\varphi'$. Similarly, $Y.f \subseteq X.f.\varphi'$. Since $Y.f.\varphi'$ is the smallest closed set containing $X.f$ and $X.f.\varphi'$ is the smallest closed set containing $Y.f$, $X.f.\varphi' = Y.f.\varphi'$.

Conversely, assume f is not continuous. So there exists Y with $Y.\varphi.f \nsubseteq Y.f.\varphi'$ There exists $X \in Y.\varphi^{-1}$. $X.f \subseteq X.\varphi.f = Y.\varphi.f \nsubseteq Y.f.\varphi'$, so $X.f.\varphi' \neq Y.f.\varphi'$, contradicting the condition. □

Corollary 1. If $(U, \varphi) \xrightarrow{f} (U', \varphi')$ is a monotone, continuous transformation and X generates K $(X.\varphi = K)$ then $X.f$ generates $K.f.\varphi'$.

Note that even though f is monotone and continuous, and K is closed with respect to φ, $K.f$ need not be closed with respect to φ'. However, by Corollary 1, $K.f$ must be a generating set of $K.f.\varphi'$.

Continuous transformations are very well-behaved with other demonstrable properties, *c.f.* [11]. It is our conjecture that continuous transformations of a human's experiential network (as exemplified by ρ) corresponds to our "natural" reaction to new experience and stimuli. It is an, almost automatic, response to novel experiences.

5.2   Small Incremental Change

The key to continuous learning is not just exposure to new experience, but how that new experience is integrated with other related experience. It has been suggested that new experience, new stimuli, is integrated into our memory, or knowledge structure, as we sleep. Apparently this occurs through the creation of new axons and synaptic connections [1]. Some researchers believe that the elimination of connections may be as equally important as creating new ones [19].

It was shown in [14], that if a discontinuity exists, it will manifest itself at a single experiential event.

Proposition 6. *If there exists Y such that $Y.\varphi.f \not\subseteq Y.f.\varphi'$ then there exists a singleton set $\{y\} \subseteq Y.\rho$ such that $\{y\}.\varphi.f \not\subseteq \{y\}.f.\varphi'$.*

This makes testing for continuity viable.

The following two propositions characterize continuous transformations that add, or delete, edges/relationships within a network. In both Propositions 7 and 8, we assume that $U' = U$, and that f is the identity function on $\mathcal{L}_\varphi$, and that $y' = \{y\}.f$ denotes the same node, but within the new structure of $\mathcal{L}'_{\varphi'}$. In the statement of these propositions we use the term $x.\eta$. By $Y.\eta$, which we call the **neighborhood** of Y, we mean the set $Y.\eta = Y.\rho - Y$, that is, the immediate neighbors of Y with respect to ρ.[7]

In Proposition 7 we show that new links can be continuously created between two experiential events x and z if there already exists a reasonably close relationship. Granovetter [7], and many other sociologists have observed this phenomenon.

Proposition 7. *Let $U \xrightarrow{f} U'$ be the identity transformation. If f adds an edge (x', z') to create a network ρ', it will be continuous at x if and only if for all $y \in x.\eta$, if $x \in y.\varphi$ then $z \in y.\rho$.*

Proof. Assume that $\exists y \in x.\eta, x \in y.\varphi$ but $z \notin y.\eta$. Since $x \in y.\varphi$, $x.\eta \subseteq y.\rho$. But, because $z \notin y.\eta$, $x'.\eta' \not\subseteq y'.\rho'$ and $y.\varphi.f \not\subseteq y.f.\varphi'$.

Conversely, assume f is discontinuous. First, we observe that $x.\varphi.f \subseteq x.f.\varphi'$, since the addition of an edge (x', z') cannot reduce the closure $x'.\varphi'$. So, f must be discontinuous at $y \in x.\eta$; that is, $\exists w \in y.\varphi$ such that $w' \notin y'.\varphi'$, because $w'.\eta \not\subseteq y'.\rho'$. Readily $w' = x'$ (or z'). After adding the edge (x', z'), $x'.\eta' \not\subseteq y'.\rho'$ only if $z' \notin y'.\eta$, that is $z \notin y.\eta$.   □

We say f is "discontinuous at x" even though the actual *discontinuity* may occur at $y \in \{x\}.\eta \subseteq \{x\}.\rho$ as noted in Proposition 6. This slight abuse of terminology allows us to focus on the structure surrounding the node x before (x', z') is created.

Observe that the creation of the link (t', v') in Fig. 6 is continuous because for $\{s, w\} \subseteq t.\rho$, we have $t \notin s.\varphi$ and $t \notin w.\varphi$, so Proposition 7 is satisfied vacuously.

Next we show that a link between two experiential events x and z can be continuously deleted if they are not too closely connected.

Proposition 8. *Let $U \xrightarrow{f} U'$ be the identity transformation. If f deletes an edge (x, z) from ρ', it will be discontinuous at x if and only if either*
  (a) $z \in x.\varphi$ and $z.\varphi \neq x.\varphi$ or
  (b) there exists $y \in x.\varphi$, with $z \in y.\eta$.

---

[7] Note that the η operator is normally neither expansive nor monotone.

Proof. Suppose (a), $z \in x.\varphi$. Since (x, z) is being deleted $z' \notin x'.\eta'$. Consequently, $\{x\}.\varphi.f \not\subseteq \{x'\}.f.\varphi'$. The last conjunct $x.\varphi \neq z.\varphi$ of condition (a) covers the special case described in [15].

Suppose (b) that $\exists y \in x.\varphi$ and $z \in y.\eta$. $\{y'\} \subseteq x.\varphi.f$, but $z' \notin x'.\eta'$ implies that $y'.\eta' \not\subseteq x'.\eta'$, hence $y' \notin x'.\varphi' = x.f.\varphi'$. Now, $\{x\}.\varphi.f \not\subseteq \{x\}.f.\varphi'$, and f is discontinuous.

Conversely, suppose f is not continuous at x. Then by Proposition 6, either (1) $\{x\}.\varphi.f \not\subseteq \{x\}.f.\varphi'$ or (2) for some $y \in \{x\}.\eta$, $\{y\}.\varphi.f \not\subseteq \{y\}.f.\varphi'$.

Assume the former, then $\exists$ some $w \in \{x\}.\varphi$ such that $w' = w.f \notin \{x\}.f.\varphi'$. Since (x, z) is the only edge being deleted, w must be z.

Now assume the latter. If $y \in \{x\}.\varphi$ then $y.\eta \subseteq x.\rho$. If $z \notin y.\eta$ then $\{y\}.\varphi.f \subseteq \{y\}.f.\varphi'$; but f is assumed to be discontinuous, so $z \in y.\eta$. $\square$

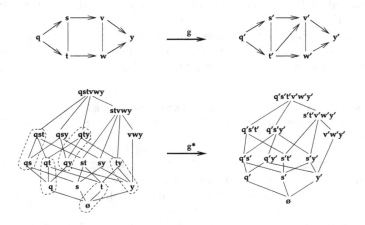

Fig. 6. A transformation g that adds a new connection (t', v') to the network of Fig. 1.

In Fig. 6, consider the inverse function, g^{-1} which removes the edge (t', v'). By Proposition 8, it is not continuous because $s' \in t'.\varphi'$ and $v' \in s'.\eta'$ satisfying condition (b) for discontinuity. We can verify the discontinuity, because $t'\varphi' = \{s't'\}$ in $\mathcal{L}'$, so $t'.\varphi'.g^{-1} = \{st\} \not\subseteq \{t\} = \{t'\}.g^{-1}.\varphi$.

If f and g are both continuous single edge additions or deletions, then by Proposition 3, their composition $f \cdot g$ is as well. It would be mathematically satisfying, if conversely every continuous restructuring of ρ could be decomposed into primitive single edge transformations; but in [14], it is shown that this need not be true.

6   Summary

Our goal has been to explore whether properties of closure operators and closed set systems can be relevant to modeling cognitive processes. We have presented ρ

as an *experiential* operator. We have considered closed sets as units of *knowledge* that can be characterized by their generators and partially ordered to form a *knowledge lattice* We have couched *learning* in terms of transformations.

Proposition 8 provides necessary and sufficient conditions for a specific kind of transformation which removes a link in a relationship to be continuous. It seems to be a widely held contention that *learning* involves the acquisition of more experiences and more data. In early childhood when our neural capabilities are growing this would seem so. But, even at an early age, children appear to be condensing raw stimuli into abstract identifiable concepts. In the process of *learning*, deletion seems to be as valuable as addition. In many forms of autism, it is the inability to delete and control an overload of raw sensory images that is problematic.

We believe we have demonstrated that an approach to network comprehension based on closed sets and continuous transformation can be a potentially valuable tool for modeling cognitive behavior. It will certainly take further refinement, including consideration of multiple experiential relationships, and considerable experimental testing to validate that claim.

References

1. Bernier, A., Beauchamp, M., Bourette-Turcot, A.-A., Carlson, S.M., Carrier, J.: Sleep and cognition in preschool years: specific links to executive functioning. Child Dev. **84**(5), 1542–1553 (2013)
2. Caspard, N., Monjardet, B.: The lattices of closure systems, closure operators and implicational systems on a finite set: a survey. Discrete Appl. Math. **127**(2), 241–269 (2003)
3. Cole, M., John-Steiner, V., Scribner, S., Souberman, E.: Mind in Society. Harvard University Press, Cambridge (1978)
4. Doignon, J.-P., Falmagne, J.-C.: Knowledge Spaces. Springer, Berlin (1999)
5. Ganter, B., Wille, R.: Formal Concept Analysis - Mathematical Foundations. Springer, Heidelberg (1999)
6. Gazzaniga, M.S., Ivry, R.B., Mangun, G.R., Steven, M.S.: Cognitive Neuroscience, The Biology of the Mind. W.W. Norton, New York (2009)
7. Granovetter, M.S.: The strength of weak ties. Am. J. Sociol. **78**(6), 1360–1380 (1973)
8. Jamison, R.E., Pfaltz, J.L.: Closure spaces that are not uniquely generated. Discrete Appl. Math. **147**, 69–79 (2005). also in Ordinal and Symbolic Data Analysis, OSDA 2000. Brussels, Belgium, July 2000
9. Ore, O.: Mappings of closure relations. Ann. Math. **47**(1), 56–72 (1946)
10. Ore, O.: Theory of Graphs. Colloquium Publications, vol. XXXVIII. American Mathematical Society, Providence (1962)
11. Pfaltz, J., Šlapal, J.: Transformations of discrete closure systems. Acta Math. Hungar. **138**(4), 386–405 (2013)
12. Pfaltz, J.L.: Closure lattices. Discrete Math. **154**, 217–236 (1996)
13. Pfaltz, J.L.: Establishing logical rules from empirical data. Int. J. Artif. Intell. Tools **17**(5), 985–1001 (2008)
14. Pfaltz, J.L.: Mathematical continuity in dynamic social networks. Soc. Netw. Anal. Min. (SNAM) **3**(4), 863–872 (2013)

15. Pfaltz, J.L.: Mathematical evolution in discrete networks. Math. Appl. **2**(2), 153–167 (2013)
16. Rosenfeld, A., Pfaltz, J.L.: Sequential operations in digital picture processing. J. ACM **13**(4), 471–494 (1966)
17. Russell, S., Norvig, P.: Artificial Intelligence: A Modern Approach. Prentice Hall, Englewood Cliffs (2003)
18. Sarti, A., Citti, G., Petitot, J.: Functional geometry of the horizontal connectivity in the primary visual cortex. J. Physiol. (Paris) **103**(1–2), 37–45 (2009)
19. Tononi, G., Cirelli, C.: Perchance to Prune. Sci. Am. **309**(2), 34–39 (2013)
20. Šlapal, J.: Complete-lattice morphisms compatible with closure operators. Thai J. Math. **8**(2), 255–262 (2010)
21. Šlapal, J.: On categories of ordered sets with a closure operator. Publicationes Mathematicae Debrecen **78**(1), 61–69 (2011)

Learning and Optimization

Solving Dynamic Optimisation Problems
with Known Changeable Boundaries

AbdelMonaem F.M. AbdAllah[✉], Daryl L. Essam,
and Ruhul A. Sarker

School of Engineering and Information Technology,
University of New South Wales, (UNSW@ADFA), Canberra 2600, Australia
abdelmonaem.abdallah@student.adfa.edu.au,
{d.essam,r.sarker}@adfa.edu.au

Abstract. Dynamic optimisation problems (DOPs) have become a challenging research topic over the last two decades. In DOPs, at least one part of the problem changes as time passes. These changes may take place in the objective function(s) and/or constraint(s). In this paper, we propose a new type of DOP in which the boundaries of variables change as time passes. This is called a single objective unconstrained dynamic optimisation problem with known changeable boundaries (DOPKCBs). To solve DOPKCBs, we propose three repair strategies. These algorithms have been compared with other repairing techniques from the literature that have been previously used in static problems. In this paper, the results of the conducted experiments and the statistical analysis generally demonstrated that one of the proposed strategies, which uses the overall elite individual (OEI) as a repair strategy, obtained much better results than the other strategies.

Keywords: Changeable boundaries · Dynamic optimisation · Genetic algorithm · Overall elite individual · Repair strategy

1 Introduction

Optimisation is one of the important research areas that directly relates to our everyday decision making, such as in transportation and management. There are different categories of optimisation problems. These problems can be either discrete or continuous [1, 2], single objective or multi-objective [3, 4], unconstrained or constrained [2], and they may either be stationary (static) [5], or dynamic, where they have at least one part that changes over time [6].

Several real-world problems change over time, e.g., transportation, production and economic systems, hence the ability to optimise dynamic problems is important. These problems are called Dynamic Optimisation Problems (DOPs). In DOPs, at least one part of the problem changes as time passes. Therefore, addressing and solving DOPs is challenging, since they need an optimisation algorithm to not only locate optimal solutions, but also must track the changes in optimal solutions over time [7, 8].

In the literature, most of the conducted research in DOPs dealt with changes in the objective function and/or constraints [7, 8]. However, changes in the boundaries of

© Springer International Publishing Switzerland 2016
T. Ray et al. (Eds.): ACALCI 2016, LNAI 9592, pp. 29–40, 2016.
DOI: 10.1007/978-3-319-28270-1_3

variables as time passes have not yet been considered. Furthermore, because of the dynamicity of DOPs, solutions might not be normally distributed, so we need to consider non-parametric tests, e.g., Friedman tests [8].

Motivated by the literature, in this paper we propose single objective unconstrained dynamic optimisation problems with known changeable boundaries (DOPKCB). DOPCD is a DOP in which the boundaries of variables change as time passes. In this paper, we will consider GA-based approaches for solving DOPKCBs. In solving DOPKCBs, when we move from one time slot/window to the next, some solutions may become infeasible by violating the boundary condition of one or more variables. In this case, it is appropriate to apply repairing mechanisms before we continue the optimisation process using GA. Such a repair process may also be needed when the optimisation process takes place, as we are interested in feasible solutions as well as optimal values. A good number of repair techniques have been applied to static optimisation problems. For example, repair mechanisms are used for static optimisation problems with particle swarm (PS) [9, 10] and Evolutionary Algorithms (EAs) [11] whereby the variables that exceed boundaries are brought back inside the search space while solving optimisation problems. These repair mechanisms include stochastic procedures such as random [9] and the stochastic strategy with respect to the new boundaries [10]. They may be deterministic, such as periodic, set on the nearest boundary [9] and deterministic "Midpoint" [10]. In this paper, we have investigated the performance of these approaches with GA in solving DOPKCBs. We have also proposed three new repair methods: stochastic strategy with respect to old boundaries, scaling and overall elite individual. The experiments were conducted by solving a set of test problems that were developed in this paper. They are based on well-known problems from the literature. Note that in this paper, the words "dimensions" and "variables" can be used interchangeably.

The rest of this paper is organised as follows. In Sect. 2, DOPs are briefly investigated. In Sect. 3, DOPKCB is described and a framework is provided for generating its test problems. This section also describes the repair strategies investigated in this paper, as well as our three proposed strategies. Section 4 includes the experimental results, and a comparison of all the repair techniques for solving DOPKCBs. Finally, conclusions and directions for future work are presented in Sect. 5.

2   Dynamic Optimisation Problems

In dynamic optimisation problems (DOPs), at least one part of each problem changes as time passes. DOPs are usually solved using population based approaches, such as Genetic Algorithms (GAs) [12] and Evolutionary Algorithms (EAs) [13]. Researchers have considered many different issues and mechanisms while solving DOPs. In this section, we briefly investigate three such issues, namely change detection, optimisation and test problem generators.

2.1 Change Detection

The simplest approach to solve DOPs is to ignore changes in the problem; however, this could be an impractical strategy for many problems [6]. In DOPs, the goal of the solution technique is to track the changes in a problem, and locate the optimal solution [7]. Additionally, the correlation between the problem-after-change and the problem-before-change must be considered. In this paper, we assume that the system can detect the variables that violate the boundary condition, by directly comparing the value of the variables with their current boundaries.

2.2 Optimisation Approaches

In this section we briefly introduce some of the most typical approaches that have been proposed to solve DOPs. The first approach is introducing diversity when changes occur, in which diversity is introduced into the population when any change is detected [14, 15]. The second approach is maintaining diversity during the search process, in which solution techniques maintain the diversity in the population during the search process [16, 17]. The third approach is a memory approach. This can be useful in reusing previously found solution(s), if the changes in a problem are periodical or recurrent. To solve these problems, using memory could save computational time [7, 18]. This category might be particularly effective in solving DOPs with periodically changing environments [12]. We refer the reader to the surveys [7, 8] for more details and more critical reviews of DOP solution approaches.

The memory approach might be the closest to one of the proposed approaches in this paper, which is overall elite individual (OEI). In this approach, we use the previously found best solution to reset any violated variables.

2.3 Test Problem Generators

In the literature, there are various benchmark problems to test the performance of algorithms for solving DOPs. Some test problems in the continuous search space are mentioned below:

- Moving Peaks Benchmark (MPB): this was proposed by Branke [19], and has been widely used in the literature [20].
- Dynamic Composition Benchmark Generator (GDBG): the dynamic composition functions [21] are actually generated from the static functions that were devised by Liang et al. [22].
- Dynamic test problems of CEC 2009 Competition: the GDBG was used to construct these test problems [23]. These dynamic test problems consist of Sphere, Rastrigin, Weierstrass, Griewank and Ackley's functions.

3 Dynamic Optimisation Problems with Known Changeable Boundaries (DOPKCB)

A dynamic optimisation problem with changeable boundaries (DOPKCB) is a DOP in which the boundaries of the variables change as time passes. In real-life situations, such problems may arise due to the fact that the range or limit of decision variables may change over time, because of both internal and external factors. For example:

- in a production process: when we produce multiple products based on the range of the available resources, this range may be change over time;
- in stock exchange: when we want to optimise a group of illiquid stocks, and their range of availability may change as time passes.

3.1 DOPKCB Benchmark Problems

To construct a framework for designing DOPKCB, benchmark function(s) containing multiple dimensions are used. In this paper, Sphere, Rastrigin, Weierstrass, Griewank and Ackley are used. Generally, this paper only considers minimisation problems.

Here, we have considered three main parameters to construct a problem. The first parameter is ProbOfChange that determines the probability of a problem change as time passes. The second parameter is MaxDim that represents the maximum number of dimensions that a problem contains. Finally, PercOfChangedDim is the percentage of dimensions in the time slot that have their boundaries change. DOPKCBs are generated as follows:

- For each generation, generate a random value (g_random $\in [0, 1]$)

  - If (g_random < ProbOfChange)

    Change the boundaries of some variables of the problem
  - Else

    Do not change

To determine which dimensions are ineffective, while all others are effective, a problem mask is randomly generated. If we have a problem with ten dimensions (MaxDim = 10), where three are changed (PercOfChangedDim = 30 %). Then three unique indices $\in [1, 10]$ are randomly generated, and those dimensions are chosen to change their boundaries as follows: generate a random value, r, $\in \{1, 2, 3\}$ for each variable of those variables that are change its boundaries:

- If (r == 1): change the lower boundary of the variable
- Else if (r == 2): change the upper boundary of the variable
- Else: change both the lower and upper boundaries of the variable

The change in the lower and upper boundaries is made by choosing random and different values from a predefined set of values. Hence the efficiency of an algorithm for solving DOPKCB depends on how to repair the infeasible and out-of-boundary value(s). Therefore, their efficiency depends on the used repair method.

3.2 DOPKCB Repair Techniques

The DOPKCB repair technique basically repairs the variables of an individual (solution) that are outside the current given boundaries. In other words, the solutions are moved from an infeasible region, to the feasible region, by changing the values of the violated variables. Repair techniques can be classified into two main categories. The first category is stochastic techniques that randomly determine a value of the infeasible variable in a specific range inside its current boundaries. The second category is deterministic techniques that deterministically determine a value of each infeasible variable in a specific location inside its current boundary. In this section, we discuss the previously used repair techniques, as well as our proposed techniques.

Firstly, we discuss stochastic approaches as follows:

Random. Random strategy is one of the simplest stochastic methods. This strategy randomly generates a valid value for the infeasible variable inside the new boundaries [9, 11]. This strategy does not use any information, either from previous boundaries, or the infeasible value.

Stochastic Strategy with Respect to New Boundaries. The stochastic strategy with respect to new boundaries method is a stochastic repair method [10]. This strategy places a new valid value of the infeasible variable randomly in the nearest half of the new boundaries. It works as follows:

$$X_{new} = \begin{cases} U_{new} - (0.50 * \text{rand}()) * (U_{new} + L_{new}) & \text{if } X_{infeasible} > U_{new} \\ L_{new} - (0.50 * \text{rand}()) * (U_{new} + L_{new}) & \text{if } X_{infeasible} < L_{new} \end{cases} \quad (1)$$

where L_{new} and U_{new} are the new lower and upper boundary of the variable respectively, and rand() is a random value $\in [0, 1]$.

Now, we will introduce our proposed stochastic repair approach.

Stochastic Strategy with respect to Old Boundaries. A stochastic Strategy with respect to Old Boundaries method is our first proposed repair technique in this paper. This method uses information of the position of the infeasible value with respect to the old boundaries. This strategy places the new valid value of the variable in the same half of the new search space, but with respect to the old boundaries. It works as follows:

$$X_{new} = \begin{cases} U_{new} - (0.50 * \text{rand}()) * (U_{new} + L_{new}) & \text{if } X_{infeasible} > U_{old} \\ L_{new} - (0.50 * \text{rand}()) * (U_{new} + L_{new}) & \text{if } X_{infeasible} < L_{old} \end{cases} \quad (2)$$

where L_{new} and U_{new} are the new lower and upper boundary of the variable respectively, rand() is a random value $\in [0, 1]$, and L_{old} and U_{old} are the old lower and upper boundary of the variable respectively. This strategy supposes that it would be better for the optimisation algorithm to continue its investigation in the same half of the search space as its previous infeasible value was located.

Now we discuss the deterministic approaches as follows:

Periodic. A periodic repair method is a deterministic strategy that assumes that the search space of the variable has a periodic shape [9, 11]. This strategy brings the infeasible value into the current search space from an end which is opposite to where it is located out of the current feasible boundaries [11] as follows:

$$X_{new} = \begin{cases} U_{new} - (L_{new} - X_{\text{infeasible}}) \% S_{new} \text{ if } X_{\text{infeasible}} < L_{new} \\ L_{new} + (X_{\text{infeasible}} - U_{new}) \% S_{new} \text{ if } X_{\text{infeasible}} > U_{new} \end{cases} \quad (3)$$

where L_{new} and U_{new} are the new lower and upper boundary of the variable respectively, '%' is the modulus operator, and $S_{new} = |U_{new} - L_{new}|$, that is the boundary width of the variable.

Set on the Nearest Boundary. Set on the nearest boundary repair method is a deterministic strategy that resets the infeasible value of the variable, on the boundary which it exceeded, based on the position of the infeasible location [9, 11]. It works as follows:

$$X_{new} = \begin{cases} L_{new}, \text{ if } X_{\text{infeasible}} < L_{new} \\ U_{new}, \text{ if } X_{\text{infeasible}} > U_{new} \end{cases} \quad (4)$$

where L_{new} and U_{new} are the new lower and upper boundary of the variable respectively. This would work well when optimum values of the current problem are located on the boundaries.

Midpoint. The midpoint method is a deterministic strategy that resets the infeasible value of the variable to the middle position between the infeasible value and the most distant current lower or upper boundaries [10]. It works as follows:

$$X_{new} = \begin{cases} 0.50 * (X_{infeasible} + L_{new}) & \text{if } X_{infeasible} > U_{new} \\ 0.50 * (X_{infeasible} + U_{new}) & \text{if } X_{infeasible} < L_{new} \end{cases} \quad (5)$$

where L_{new} and U_{new} are the new lower and upper boundary of the variable respectively. Note that the equation of midpoint method is repeated until it finds a feasible value in the current boundaries.

Now, we will introduce our novel proposed deterministic repair approaches.

Scaling. The scaling method is our second proposed repair techniques. It is a deterministic method that uses information of the previous boundaries and the infeasible value. This strategy places the old infeasible value in the same scaled value in a new search space. It works as follows:

$$X_{new} = U_{new} - (U_{old} - X_{infeasible}) * \frac{S_{old}}{S_{new}} \tag{6}$$

where L_{new} and U_{new} are the new lower and upper boundary of the variable respectively, U_{old} is the old upper boundary of the variable, and S_{old} and S_{new} are the width of the old and the new boundary of the variable respectively. This strategy supposes that it would be better for the optimisation algorithm to continue its investigation in the same scaled value as its previous infeasible value.

Overall Elite Individual. Overall Elite Individual method (OEI) is our last proposed repair technique. It is a deterministic repair method that uses information from the search space during the optimisation process to guide the repair process. We propose this approach, as all the previous repair techniques do not take into consideration any information from the best found area during the optimisation process. This strategy keeps track of the best found solution during the search process. Then it uses this solution to repair the violated variables as follows:

$$X_{new} = \begin{cases} X_{bestIndividual} \text{ if } X_{bestIndividual} \in [U_{new}, L_{new}] \\ L_{new} \text{ if } X_{bestIndividual} < L_{new} \\ U_{new} \text{ if } X_{bestIndividual} > U_{new} \end{cases} \tag{7}$$

where $X_{bestIndividual}$ is the value of the best found individual for the infeasible variable X, and L_{new} and U_{new} are the current lower and upper boundaries of the variable respectively. This assumes that when the boundaries change it would be better to reset the location of the violated values near to the best found search space, guided by the previously best found solution. Note that the overall elite individual is updated if and only if the current elite individual is better than it.

4 Experimental Results, Analyses and Discussion

To test the performance of our proposed and previously used repair methods, all the repair methods were paired with genetic algorithms (GAs) to solve DOPKCBs. Therefore, eight variants of real-coded GAs were implemented for experimentation on a set of unconstrained separable benchmark functions, namely Sphere, Rastrigin, Weierstrass, Griewank and Ackley [23]. The eight GAs variants are represented as follows:

- GA with random repair (RaGA).
- GA with stochastic strategy with respect to new boundaries repair (SNBGA).
- GA with stochastic strategy with respect old boundaries repair (SOBGA).
- GA with periodic repair (PerGA).
- GA with set on the nearest boundary repair (SONBGA).
- GA with midpoint repair (MpGA).
- GA with scaling repair (ScGA).
- GA with Overall Elite Individual repair (OEIGA).

Note that the change in the lower and/or upper boundaries of the variable occurred by randomly choosing a value from a predefined set. The sets of lower and upper boundaries are $\in \{-20, -15, -5, 5, 10, 15\}$ and $\{-10, -5, 5, 10, 20, 25\}$ respectively. Consequently, the boundaries change by choosing from those predefined values. Note that in this paper, all the algorithms were coded in Microsoft C++, on a 3.4 GHz/16 GB Intel Core i7 machine, Windows 7 operating system.

For a fair evaluation, every algorithm ran for one million fitness evaluations. To compare these algorithms, a group of points was determined for calculations over the fitness evaluations. In this paper, 20 calculation points were determined, so the value for every $\frac{1000000}{20} = 50000$ fitness evaluations solutions were recorded. A variation of the Best-of-Generation measure was used, where the best-of-generation values were averaged over all generations at each calculation point [24]. It is calculated as follows:

$$\bar{F}_{BOG} = \frac{1}{G} \sum_{i=1}^{i=G} \left(\frac{1}{N} \sum_{j=1}^{j=N} F_{BOG_{ij}} \right) \tag{8}$$

where $\bar{F}_{BOG}$ is the mean best-of-generation fitness, G is the number of generations, N is the total number of runs and $F_{BOG_{ij}}$ is the best-of-generation fitness of generation i of run j of an algorithm on a problem [25].

Table 1 shows the used parameters of the implemented GAs and settings of DOPKCBs. Note that every run of an instance of a problem has initially the search space of all variables, i.e. $[-5, 5]$ [23]. Also, for a fair comparison, all GAs had the same initial population at the beginning of each run.

Table 1. Parameters of experiments

Parameter	Value
Population size	100
Max. number of fitness evaluations /run	1000000
Probabilities of problem change (ProbOfChange)	0.01, 0.50
Selection procedure	Tournament
Tournament size	2
Selection pressure	0.90
Elitism percentage	2
Crossover	Single-point
Crossover rate	0.90
Mutation	Uniform
Mutation rate	0.15
Number of dimensions (MaxDim)	20
Changed dimensions (PercOfChangedDim)/ change	Randomly $\in\{[0\ \%, 25\ \%], [75\ \%, 100\ \%]\}$

In order to compare the algorithms accurately, we performed statistical significance tests. Therefore, the non-parametric Friedman test, that is similar to the parametric repeated measure ANOVA, was used [8, 26]. As mentioned before, when each algorithm solved a problem, it had overall 20 $\overline{F}_{BOG}$ s. We performed the Friedman test with a confidence level of 95 % ($\alpha = 0.05$) on all the values with regard to particular variations of the parameters of DOPKCBs, with the null hypothesis that there is no significant differences among the performances of the compared algorithms. The computational value of the p-value was less than 0.05. Consequently, there are significant differences among the performances of the compared algorithms, therefore, we reject the null hypothesis.

Tables 2, 3, 4, and 5 show Friedman ranks of the comparisons among the algorithms with different settings of DOPKCBs. In these tables, lower values indicate better results and the best results are marked in bold.

Table 2. ProbOfChange = 0.01, PercOfChangedDim = [0 %, 25 %]

Function	RaGA	SNBGA	SOBGA	PerGA	SONBGA	MpGA	ScGA	OEIGA
Ackley	4.5	3.1	5	7.4	1.95	6.35	6.65	**1.05**
Griewank	3.85	3	5.05	4.5	7.1	**2.45**	3.9	6.15
Rastrigin	4.3	3.1	5.2	7.6	1.85	6.15	6.65	**1.15**
Sphere	4.35	3.05	4.95	7.8	1.72	6.05	6.8	**1.28**
Weierstrass	5.15	5.65	6.45	3	1.65	7.35	5.4	**1.35**
Average	4.43	3.58	5.33	6.06	2.854	5.67	5.88	**2.196**

Table 3. ProbOfChange = 0.50, PercOfChangedDim = [0 %, 25 %]

Function	RaGA	SNBGA	SOBGA	PerGA	SONBGA	MpGA	ScGA	OEIGA
Ackley	4	3	5.25	5.8	2	6.95	8	**1**
Griewank	4	3	5.8	8	2	5.2	7	**1**
Rastrigin	4	3	5.75	8	2	5.25	7	**1**
Sphere	4	3	5.8	8	2	5.2	7	**1**
Weierstrass	5.35	4	5.65	3	1.8	8	7	**1.2**
Average	4.27	3.2	5.65	6.56	1.96	6.12	7.2	**1.04**

Table 4. ProbOfChange = 0.01, PercOfChangedDim = [75 %, 100 %]

Function	RaGA	SNBGA	SOBGA	PerGA	SONBGA	MpGA	ScGA	OEIGA
Ackley	4.1	3	5.15	6.9	2	6.25	7.6	**1**
Griewank	3.85	3.15	4.7	7.4	3.2	4.4	6.9	**2.4**
Rastrigin	4.05	3	5.6	7.65	1.95	5.45	7.25	**1.05**
Sphere	4.05	3	5.65	7.8	1.95	5.3	7.2	**1.05**
Weierstrass	6.85	5.35	7.25	3	**1.5**	6.45	4.1	**1.5**
Average	4.58	3.5	5.67	6.55	2.12	5.57	6.61	**1.4**

Table 5. ProbOfChange = 0.50, PercOfChangedDim = [75 %, 100 %]

Function	RaGA	SNBGA	SOBGA	PerGA	SONBGA	MpGA	ScGA	OEIGA
Ackley	5.55	4	7	3	2	5.45	8	1
Griewank	4.95	3	6	7.5	2	4.05	7.5	1
Rastrigin	5	3	6	7.15	2	4	7.85	1
Sphere	4.95	3	6	7.5	2	4.05	7.5	1
Weierstrass	6	4	5	3	1.95	7.95	7.05	**1.05**
Average	5.29	3.4	6	5.63	1.99	5.1	7.58	**1.01**

The following observations can be drawn from the previous tables:

- For the previous techniques, SONBGA performed better when the optimal solutions were located near to the boundaries, especially Weierstrass function where the optimal solutions are located exactly on the changed boundaries. Also, SNBGA is the best stochastic strategy. This is because it would be better for the optimisation algorithm to continue its investigation near to its previous infeasible value.
- The proposed SOBGA and ScGA did not present any competitive results. Regarding SOBGA, searching in the same half of the current search space as the previous infeasible value that had been located was not effective, because it placed the new feasible value in un-guided areas, unlike SNBGA. Whereas, ScGA was not effective because boundaries were moving, but were not scaled. However, ScGA strategy could perform better if the new boundaries were scaled.
- Our last proposed method, OEIGA, which used overall elite individual as a repair strategy was the best strategy, especially when the ProbOfChange increased. This is because it lets the GA explore more search space when the boundaries moved more and explored more search spaces. Consequently, OEIGA found better elite individual(s) to effectively guide the optimisation process. However, OEIGA performance degraded in Table 2 when the ProbOfChange = 0.01 for the Griewank function. This is because OEIGA could not explore the search space enough to find a better overall elite individual that could be used effectively to repair violated values.
- In general, OEIGA outperformed all the other GAs. This is because the OEI repair method guided GAs towards good search areas when boundaries were moved.

5   Conclusions and Future Work

Motivated by the literature [7, 8], in this paper we propose a new type of dynamic optimisation problem: single objective unconstrained DOPs with known changeable boundaries (DOPKCBs). This is a class of DOPs in which the boundaries of the dimensions change as time passes.

Moreover, we have proposed three repair procedures to solve DOPKCBs. Based on the experimental results and statistical tests, one of the proposed approaches, the one that uses the overall elite individual as a repair strategy (OEI), outperformed the other repair strategies. This procedure guided the algorithm to repair to near the previously best found solution, therefore it guided GAs towards good search areas when boundaries were moved.

There are several possible directions for future work. The first direction is solving problems with more dimensions, e.g. forty and eighty dimensions. This direction also includes solving non-separable functions. The second direction is to use hybrid repair procedures, e.g. pairing two or more repair strategies, especially a deterministic with a stochastic strategy.

References

1. Gendreau, M., Potvin, J.-Y., Bräysy, O., Hasle, G., Løkketangen, A.: Metaheuristics for the vehicle routing problem and extensions: a categorized bibliography. In: Golden, B., Raghavan, S., Wasil, E. (eds.) The Vehicle Routing Problem: Latest Advances and New Challenges. Springer, New York (2008)
2. Nocedal, J., Wright, S.J.: Numerical Optimization, 2nd edn. Springer, New York (2006)
3. Miettinen, K., Ruiz, F., Wierzbicki, A.P.: Introduction to multiobjective optimization: interactive approaches. In: Branke, J., Deb, K., Miettinen, K., Słowiński, R. (eds.) Multiobjective Optimization. LNCS, vol. 5252, pp. 27–57. Springer, Heidelberg (2008)
4. Bandyopadhyay, S., Saha, S.: some single - and multiobjective optimization techniques. In: Unsupervised Classification, pp. 17–58. Springer, Heidelberg (2013)
5. Dadkhah, K.: Static optimization. In: Foundations of Mathematical and Computational Economics, pp. 323–346. Springer, Berlin (2011)
6. Branke, J.: Evolutionary Optimization in Dynamic Environments. Kluwer, Dordrecht (2001)
7. Nguyen, T.T., Yangb, S., Branke, J.: Evolutionary dynamic optimization: a survey of the state of the art. Swarm Evol. Comput. 6, 1–24 (2012)
8. Cruz, C., González, J.R., Pelta, D.A.: Optimization in dynamic environments: a survey on problems, methods and measures. Soft. Comput. 15, 1427–1448 (2011)
9. Wen-Jun, Z., Xiao-Feng, X., De-Chun, B.: Handling boundary constraints for numerical optimization by particle swarm flying in periodic search space. In: Congress on Evolutionary Computation, CEC 2004, vol. 2302, pp. 2307–2311 (2004)
10. Shi, C., Yuhui, S., Quande, Q.: Experimental study on boundary constraint handling in particle swarm optimization: from population diversity perspective. In: Yuhui, S. (ed.) Recent Algorithms and Applications in Swarm Intelligence Research, pp. 96–124. IGI Global, Hershey (2013)
11. Padhye, N., Deb, K., Mittal, P.: An Efficient and Exclusively-Feasible Constrained Handling Strategy for Evolutionary Algorithms. Technical Report (2013)
12. Yang, S.: Genetic algorithms with memory- and elitism-based immigrants in dynamic environments. Evol. Comput. 16, 385–416 (2008)
13. Branke, J., Schmeck, H.: Designing evolutionary algorithms for dynamic optimization problems. In: Advances in Evolutionary Computing: Theory and Applications, pp. 239–262. Springer, Heidelberg (2003)
14. Cobb, H.G.: An investigation into the use of hypermutation as an adaptive operator in genetic algorithms having continuous, time-dependent nonstationary environments. Naval Research Laboratory (1990)
15. Goh, C.-K., Chen Tan, K.: A competitive-cooperative coevolutionary paradigm for dynamic multiobjective optimization. IEEE Trans. Evol. Comput. 13, 103–127 (2009)

16. Grefenstette, J.J.: Genetic algorithms for changing environments. In: Maenner, R., Manderick, B. (eds.) Parallel Problem Solving from Nature, vol. 2, pp. 137–144. North Holland, Amsterdam (1992)

17. Yang, S., Yao, X.: Experimental study on population-based incremental learning algorithms for dynamic optimization problems. Soft. Comput. **9**, 815–834 (2005)

18. Nguyen, T.T., Yang, S., Branke, J., Yao, X.: Evolutionary dynamic optimization: methodologies. In: Yang, S., Yao, X. (eds.) Evolutionary Computation for DOPs. SCI, vol. 490, pp. 39–63. Springer, Heidelberg (2013)

19. Branke, J.: Memory enhanced evolutionary algorithms for changing optimization problems. In: Proceedings of the 1999 Congress on Evolutionary Computation, CEC 1999, vol. 1883, p. 1882 (1999)

20. Moser, I., Chiong, R.: Dynamic function optimization: the moving peaks benchmark. In: Alba, E., Nakib, A., Siarry, P. (eds.) Metaheuristics for Dynamic Optimization. SCI, vol. 433, pp. 37–62. Springer, Heidelberg (2013)

21. Li, C., Yang, S.: A generalized approach to construct benchmark problems for dynamic optimization. In: Li, X., et al. (eds.) SEAL 2008. LNCS, vol. 5361, pp. 391–400. Springer, Heidelberg (2008)

22. Liang, J.J., Suganthan, P.N., Deb, K.: Novel composition test functions for numerical global optimization. In: Proceedings 2005 IEEE, Swarm Intelligence Symposium, SIS 2005, pp. 68–75. (2005)

23. Li, C., Yang, S., Nguyen, T.T., Yu, E.L., Yao, X., Jin, Y., Beyer, H.-G., Suganthan, P.N.: Benchmark Generator for CEC 2009 Competition on Dynamic Optimization (2008)

24. Morrison, R.W.: Performance measurement in dynamic environments. In: GECCO Workshop on Evolutionary Algorithms for Dynamic Optimization Problems, pp. 5–8 (2003)

25. Yang, S., Nguyen, T.T., Li, C.: Evolutionary dynamic optimization: test and evaluation environments. In: Yang, S., Yao, X. (eds.) Evolutionary Computation for DOPs. SCI, vol. 490, pp. 3–37. Springer, Heidelberg (2013)

26. García, S., Molina, D., Lozano, M., Herrera, F.: A study on the use of non-parametric tests for analyzing the evolutionary algorithms' behaviour: a case study on the CEC'2005 Special Session on Real Parameter Optimization. J. Heuristics **15**, 617–644 (2009)

Compaction for Code Fragment Based Learning Classifier Systems

Isidro M. Alvarez[✉], Will N. Browne, and Mengjie Zhang

School of Engineering and Computer Science,
Victoria University of Wellington, Wellington, New Zealand
{isidro.alvarez,will.browne,mengjie.zhang}@ecs.vuw.ac.nz
http://www.victoria.ac.nz/ecs

Abstract. Learning Classifier Systems (LCSs) originated from artificial cognitive systems research, but migrated such that LCS became powerful classification techniques in single domains. Modern LCSs can extract building blocks of knowledge utilizing Code Fragments in order to scale to more difficult problems in the same or a related domain. Code Fragments (CF) are GP-like sub-trees where past learning can be reused in future CF sub-trees. However, the rich alphabet produced by the code fragments requires additional computational resources as the knowledge and functional rulesets grow. Eventually this leads to impractically long chains of CFs. The novel work here introduces methods to produce Distilled Rules to remedy this problem by compacting learned functions. The system has been tested on Boolean problems, up to the 70 bit multiplexer and 3x11 bit hidden multiplexer, which are known to be difficult problems for conventional algorithms to solve due to large and complex search spaces. The new methods have been shown to create a new layer of rules that reduce the tree length, making it easier for the system to scale to more difficult problems in the same or a related domain.

Keywords: LCS · Learning · Classifier · Code Fragments · Compaction

1 Introduction

Learning Classifier Systems (LCSs) fall under the umbrella of a set of techniques known as Evolutionary Computation (EC) [4], which are inspired by Darwinian principles. LCSs were originally cognitive systems. A cognitive system is one that is inspired by the principles of stimulus-response in cognitive psychology. This type of system was first introduced by Holland and it was designed to evolve a set of rules that would convert a given input into useful output for a multitude of problem domains [7]. However, they became powerful classifiers in single domains. To progress as cognitive systems, they need the capability of scaling to similar and related domains. Although EC techniques are applicable to many problems and have enabled advances in the field of machine learning, they have an inherent weakness. Each time a problem is solved, conventional EC techniques tend to throw away any learned knowledge and must start anew

© Springer International Publishing Switzerland 2016
T. Ray et al. (Eds.): ACALCI 2016, LNAI 9592, pp. 41–53, 2016.
DOI: 10.1007/978-3-319-28270-1_4

when tasked with a new challenge. This is a problem because by removing any learned information, the technique loses the potentially useful information that previously learned blocks of knowledge represent.

Recently, reusing learned knowledge has been shown to increase scalability and can provide shortcuts that decrease the search space of the problem at hand [14,15]. The past work showed that the reuse of knowledge through the adoption of code fragments (CFs), GP-like sub-trees, into the most common LCS framework, XCS, can provide dividends in scaling. CFs are initially limited to a depth of two. This depth was chosen, based on empirical evidence, to limit bloating, a common occurrence in Genetic Programming (GP). Analysis suggests that there is an implicit pressure for parsimony within CFs [14]. However, at each new problem, including at each new scale, a CF can contain previously learned CFs. Thus the depth of the sub-tree can increase by a factor of two at each successive problem.

CFs are a practical extension to XCS and have enabled the solution to previously intractable problems. Initially this was only to scale to more complex problems in the same domain [15], as CFs were only used in the leaf nodes of the sub-trees. In addition to this, the functions used by the system were hard coded, e.g. OR, NOT, MULTIPLICATION. This creates bias in the choice of hard coded functions and does not contain building blocks related to functions (only the terminal leaf nodes). Subsequently, it has been demonstrated that it is possible to reuse learned rulesets as functions.

These learned rulesets map inputs to outputs, therefore they act as learned functions. The following illustration may serve to clarify this point:

$$'If < Conditions > Then < Actions >' \qquad (1)$$

$$'If < Input > Then < Output >' \qquad (2)$$

$$Function(Arguments < Input > Return < Output >) \qquad (3)$$

Equation 1 is the standard way that a classifier would process its conditions to achieve an action, which is analogous to 2. Equation 3 is the analogy with a function where a complete rule-set acts as a single function. These functions will take a number of arguments as their input and will return an output [2].

It was determined that reusing learned functionality at the root and leaf nodes of CF sub-trees can increase scalability by reducing the search space, as relevant CFs are attached to the learned functions reducing the search for the appropriate input to functions. Furthermore, it was shown that by progressively accumulating learned functionality in the form of 'rule-sets', it is possible to further reduce the search space [1,2].

Compaction (Reduction) techniques, have the goal of reducing the number of classifiers based on given criteria [20]. The most common method for achieving this is a form of Subsumption as implemented in [18]. It extended an XCS that had been implemented with CFs, giving it the functionality to subsume unnecessary classifiers. Subsumption occurs in XCS in the action set, after the discovery step, and consists of identifying classifiers that are both accurate and sufficiently experienced. Less general classifiers are deleted (subsumed) and the subsumer has its numerosity counter increased. This has the benefit of reducing the computing cost while producing simpler and more condensed final populations [3].

An alternative compaction method is a post-processing step that condenses the population of classifiers and is additional to the different mechanisms that exert parsimony pressure on the population, such as subsumption and niche mutation [19]. Wilson's technique consists of three main steps [5,20]. First, a subset of classifiers that achieve 100 % performance is identified. Then any classifiers that do not advance performance are eliminated from this subset. Last, the classifiers are ordered by the number of inputs matched, until all the inputs are matched. This process was designed to happen after the normal processing of XCS and in this respect is similar to the proposed work. With one major difference, whereas Wilson's technique produces a compact set of optimal classifiers, the proposed work aims to translate the final set of optimal CF classifiers produced by XCS into a more compact alphabet to facilitate a faster evaluation of learned knowledge.

CRA2 is a similar compaction method to [20], but is executed during the normal training processing of XCS [5]. Classifiers are marked as 'useful' if they have the highest payoff prediction, numerosity product. At the end of the run all the classifiers not marked 'useful' are removed. In some respects this is equivalent to restarting XCS with a constantly revised and potentially improved initial classifier set [5]. Although this algorithm does tend to produce a correct result, it is dependent on having at least one dominant classifier in each matchset. Also, according to Dixon, this algorithm only works correctly if all the classifiers have zero errors with payoffs equal to the environmental reward value.

Compaction methods are needed with CF rules as they contain long chains of rules that are slow to process. At the end of each run, a method is needed to produce a new layer of rules that can be processed efficiently. There still needs to be a tight linking between the CFs and the final, efficient, rule-set functions, termed Distilled Rules (DR). The link is required as the CFs are reused by the system and they include feature construction while the DRs are utilized instead of the evaluation of the long chains of CFs.

The aim of this work is to improve the efficiency, without reducing the effectiveness of the CF approach. The research objective is: **Create** a method(s) to reduce the length of CF chains as the problem scales and functionality is transferred to related domains.

The benefits of the new work, known as XCSCF3, will be tested by running experiments against XCS and XCS with standard CFs (XCSCFC in this case). XCS is an acceptable benchmark as it is widely used and has been studied profusely. The methods will be illustrated using the basic Boolean operators, while being tested on the multiplexer problems and finally the hidden multiplexer.

2   Background

Learning Classifier Systems were first proposed by John H. Holland almost 40 years ago [7]. The original description of the LCS was of a cognitive system. The implication was that this type of system could learn about its environment, about its state, and could also execute actions on its environment.

The first cognitive system or (CS-1) was proposed by Holland and Rietman and featured a Genetic Algorithm (GA) component that made it possible to learn. The Learning System One (LS-1) of Smith exhibited an advantage over CS-1 in that it could learn from two different problem domains [8,16].

LCSs can select features using generality in the don't care operator. Originally, they utilized a ternary alphabet composed of: { 0, 1, # }; the '#' hashmark stands for a don't care (or an OR operator). Since the original inception of LCSs, they have been expanded to include richer alphabets in their representation, such as S-Expressions [11]. These new alphabets have equivalent don't care identifiers. XCS is the standard LCS used for research, but it cannot solve certain problems. In order to achieve better results, Code Fragments have been added to XCS (see [3] for further details on XCS).

Code Fragments (CFs) were introduced to XCS in the form of GP-like subtrees. They have a maximum depth of two, as this number was deemed important to limit bloating. CFs have enhanced XCS in terms of increased scalability and a much richer alphabet. CFs have been instrumental in arriving at a solution for the 135 Bit Multiplexer, a problem that until then, had been considered intractable for standard XCS [15].

LCSs can reuse learned knowledge to scale to problems beyond the capabilities of non-scaling techniques. One such technique is XCSCFC. This approach uses CFs to represent each of the condition bits such that it allows feature construction in the condition of rules. Another advantage of LCSs is that they can select and construct features to find reusable patterns in the antecedents of feature space to map conditions to actions. Although XCSCFC exhibits better scalability than XCS, eventually, a computational limit in scalability will be reached [13]. The reason for this is because multiple code fragments can be used at the terminals, each one potentially containing CFs from previous lower scale problems. As the problem increases in size, it is possible to create trees having a depth of twice the number of scaled problems.

Another type of CF system is XCSCFA, where the condition part retains its original ternary alphabet representation but the action part of the classifier is replaced by a code fragment. The terminals in the code fragment sub-tree can be replaced with either the corresponding bits from the environment message or with bits from the classifier condition [15]. This method produced optimal populations in discrete domain problems as well as in continuous domain problems [15]. This however lacked scaling to very large problems, even if they had repeated patterns in the data.

A slightly different approach to increase scalability was sought in $XCSCF^2$ [1]. Since LCSs can reuse sets of condition:action rules as functions as in the input:output of the function corresponds to the condition:action of rules,

XCSCF^2 [1] captures building blocks of knowledge together with associated functionality. By linking the rulesets to the learned function the system was able to reduce the search space. This provided certain benefits in scaling in the simpler boolean problems such as the 11 and 20 bit multiplexers. The drawback of the CF approach is that chains of CFs (and rules in CFs) are created, which slows the performance [2].

Sensor Tagging [17], was introduced based on the notion of messy coding as described in [6,10], in order to quicken the learning in XCS-based systems. The classifiers utilize a hash table to keep track of the binary values paired with a particular condition bit. The approach was successful in solving up to the 135 bit multiplexer. However, it is heavily memory intensive, therefore it reduces the scalability, which is required to solve any of the more complex multiplexer problems. The main difference between the two approaches is that while CFs can be referred to as an alphabet, because they can represent the condition, when paired with a system that is scalable, they become a method by which to learn new building blocks of knowledge. They identify the relationships between different features that are useful in solving more complex problems in the same or a related domain. Although Sensor Tagging [17], subsumption for XCS with CFs [18] and the precursor compaction techniques are useful approaches, the proposed work here considers the task of compaction from a slightly different direction. The compaction takes place at the end of the run and produces the set of DRs from classifiers with a rich alphabet to a simple alphabet to increase efficiency in future reuse of knowledge.

3   The Method

Although CFs produce maximally general and correct rules, as well as being readily interpretable by the human eye, they represent a solution through many logical layers that require computing resources. The aim is that by compacting CF rules into a new layer using a ternary alphabet, it will be possible to lessen the computing needs for solving a particular problem. Moreover, the new rules are anticipated to be simpler to interpret than long chains of CFs. Furthermore, this will enable learning without the need for hard coded functions.

3.1   Proposed System

The objective is to reduce the CF chain length, i.e., depth. There are existing methods for creating compacted ternary rulesets, but this work aims to use CFs to generate the final compact rules by directly translating each CF rule to multiple compact ternary rules. The compact rules will also be associated with the uncompacted CFs, which can be reused in future problems as they encode the knowledge of relationships between the features.

The boot-strap function of NAND needs to be created from a standard XCS system. The rules-set produced is then fed into the proposed system to serve as a seed function. From this initial function, other Boolean operators are learned, such as NOT, OR, AND, and so forth [2].

The proposed system will follow the normal XCS steps, i.e., create a matchset, choose a valid action, create an action set, execute said action and update the action set based on what reward the environment returns. In conjunction with the aforementioned steps, the system will construct features composed of code fragments, following the method of XCSCFC [15]. It will create new CFs for each of the condition bits but will retain the binary alphabet, {0, 1}, for the action part of the classifiers.

Once the final population of each problem has been determined, the system will begin to translate each CF rule into a set of rules based on the ternary alphabet i.e., {0, 1, #}. These new rules are called Distilled Rules (DRs). As the rules are being translated, (please see Algorithm 1), care will be taken to omit duplicate rules or rules that can be subsumed by existing rules. The compaction method will loop through the growing set of DRs to optimize the final population. The first step in learning the DRs is to determine which of the final classifiers have enough experience and are always correct and accurate. Since XCS produces a complete map solution, i.e., both completely correct and completely incorrect rules that the system categorizes as accurate (consistently incorrect), one must ensure to only process the classifiers that are always correct, as these will provide the correct DRs. Next, a series of states is presented to the classifiers and the CFs are evaluated to determine if they evaluate to a 1. Any don't care CFs are ignored and this reduces the number of potential states that must be processed. If all the CFs return a 1 then the ternary rule becomes a potential *candidate* for further processing and is inserted into the temporary list of rules. If the new candidate is a duplicate then the numerosity of the existing DR is increased by one and the candidate is ignored. Likewise if the new candidate can be subsumed or can be a subsumer, meaning that the subsumer rule is accurate and more general than the classifier to be subsumed, the numerosity of the appropriate rule is updated and the subsumed rule is deleted. The final list of DRs is the translation of the original CFs into a ternary alphabet.

Usage of Distilled Rules. The distilled rules produced by the system at the end of each run will be reused by the system when solving any of the following, more complex tasks. Since the proposed system does not avail itself of hard coded functions, the DRs will serve as the functions that will be used instead. Each time a CF forming part of a classifier condition has to be compared with the message string, e.g. when forming a matchset, the CF sub-tree will be traversed and the appropriate functions at the root nodes will receive their inputs from the terminals at the leaf nodes. These inputs would be compared with the list of DRs linked to the aforementioned function. Where all inputs match a particular rule, the linked action becomes the output and potential input for any higher levels in the chain of CFs.

Algorithm 1. Rules Compaction Method

```
1: for all valid classifiers do        ▷ Classifiers with enough experience and always correct
2:       for all  condition bits do
3:             if currentBit not don't care then
4:                   TempList[currentBit] ← 0        ▷ Array element will be permuted
5:             else if currentBit is don't care then
6:                   TempList[currentBit] ← NOOPERATION
7:                        ▷ Array element set to constant - will not be permuted
8:             end if
9:       end for
10:      while unprocessed bits do        ▷ While there are unprocessed condition bits
11:            TempList[currentBit] ← NextPermutation
12:            Evaluate current classifier using TempList
13:            if All Code Fragments = 1 then
14:                  Add TempList to currentRule
15:                        ▷ Current State is a valid candidate DR
16:            end if
17:      end while
18: end for
19: N ← 0        ▷ DRs Counter
20: while numSubsumed > 0 AND N < MAX_LOOPS do
21:            ▷ Continue until the number of DRs subsumed is 0
22:            ▷ or the maximum number of loops is reached
23:      if currentRule is duplicate then
24:            ignore currentRule
25:      else if currentRule is subsumable then
26:            subsume currentRule
27:      else if currentRule is subsumer then
28:            subsume existingRule
29:      end if
30:      update currentRule numerosity
31:      N ← N + 1
32: end while
```

---

4   Results

The Boolean operators, multiplexer and hidden multiplexer problems are notable in their complexity and difficulty, and therefore provide a good testing scheme for the proposed LCS [4].

4.1   Multiplexer Problem

The multiplexer problem is highly non-linear and exhibits epistasis; the address bits are fundamental in determining the importance of the corresponding data bits [12]. The number of address bits is a function of the length of the message string and grows along with the length of the input string as the problem scales. The search space of the problem is also adequate to show the benefits of the proposed work. For example, for the 70-bit multiplexer the search space consists of 2^{70} combinations [9]. One of the underlying reasons for choosing this problem domain for the proposed work is because it can be solved by continually building functionality from the basic Boolean Operators such as NAND, which leads to OR, NOR, and so forth. The reason for providing the system with a learned 'NAND rules' seed file is because with the NAND function any of the other Boolean operators can be derived.

4.2 Hidden Multiplexer Problem

The hidden multiplexer is considered a hierarchical problem, as it is designed in a two-level hierarchy. The lower level is evaluated by one set of Boolean operators and the output of the lower-level is then fed to the higher level. In the proposed system the lower level is a parity problem while the higher level is a multiplexer problem [4].

This problem is an interesting challenge for the proposed work because it combines the complexity of two different types of problems, resulting in a challenging search space. The reason is that the hierarchical dependency of the problems require effective building block processing; the classifiers must identify the parity blocks and then recombine them effectively [4].

4.3 Experimental Setup

The experiments were run 30 times with each having an independent random seed. The stopping criteria was when the agent completed the allotted number of training instances, which were chosen based on preliminary empirical tests on the convergence of systems. The proposed system was compared with XCSCFC and with XCS. The settings for the single step experiments were as follows: Payoff 1,000; the learning rate $\beta = 0.2$; the Probability of applying crossover to an offspring $\chi = 0.8$; the probability of using a don't care symbol when covering $P_{don'tCare} = 0.33$; the experience required for a classifier to be a subsumer $\Theta_{sub} = 20$; the initial fitness value when generating a new classifier $F_I = 0.01$; the fraction of classifiers participating in a tournament from an action set 0.4.

4.4 Boolean Problems

The number of rules produced by the proposed system increased with the complexity of the problem, as was anticipated. For instance, after having learned the OR operator the system had learned three distilled rules, see Fig. 1 which shows a listing of the final Code Fragments along with their Id. After having learned the 6 bit multiplexer, there were 12 DRs associated with the resulting solution, see Table 1. It is apparent that the learning algorithm did not subsume some of the DRs such as rules 3 and 5 and then again rules 7 and 12, (this was probably due to not having used an enumeration method due to time constraints). The emphasis of the compaction algorithm is to produce a ternary alphabet to diminish the number of comparisons made by the system, but it is not expected to produce an optimal compaction of rules because it would be time consuming. In essence, there is a tradeoff between shorter CF trees for a less optimal DRs set. The method processes just enough potential rules to derive an optimized set, this in turn will help in reducing the CF chains to be evaluated by using the DRs instead. With a problem like the 6 bit multiplexer this would not present much of a difficulty but a much more difficult problem, such as the 70 bit multiplexer, could produce an exorbitant number of duplicate rules, slowing the technique.

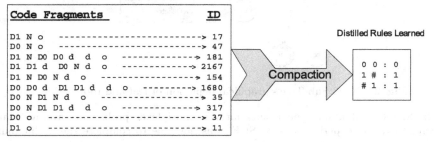

Fig. 1. OR - Final CFs and their corresponding DRs - D0 and D1 are features from the environment while N and d represent learned functions - o is a stop symbol and identifies the end of the CF.

Table 1. 6-Mux - Distilled rules

1	1	#	#	#	0	:	0
0	0	0	#	#	#	:	0
1	0	0	#	0	0	:	0
1	0	1	#	0	1	:	0
1	0	#	#	0	#	:	0
0	1	#	1	#	#	:	1
1	1	#	#	#	1	:	1
0	1	#	0	#	#	:	0
1	0	#	#	1	#	:	1
0	0	1	#	#	#	:	1
1	1	0	#	1	1	:	1
1	1	1	#	0	1	:	1

Table 2. 6-Mux - Code fragments

CF ID	CF Terms
CF_27	D1 D1 m D0 d o
CF_31	D0 D1 d o
CF_43	D0 D0 D1 c m o
CF_47	D1 D1 d D0 N c o
CF_86	D1 D0 M N o

Table 2 shows one example rule of the CF terms pertaining to the 6 Bit Multiplexer. CF_43 makes use of the AND Boolean operator (c) and it has D0 and D1 as its inputs. Likewise (m) is the tag given by the system to the OR operator and its inputs are state bit 0 and the output of the AND operator. The output from the OR node is the final result for the sub-tree. Please see Fig. 2 for a graphical description.

Table 3 shows the average time in seconds that was spent evaluating the CFs. XCS was evaluated at the matchset step and took the least amount of time. XCSCFC performed better than the other two CF systems, followed by the proposed system, XCSCF3. $XCSCF^2$ was not able to complete the 20 bit Multiplexer due to its acute memory requirements, however during the 6 and 11 bit Multiplexers it is apparent that $XCSCF^2$ requires much longer time spans to process its CFs. The timing experiments were repeated 30 times on a Windows

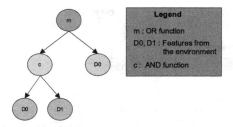

Fig. 2. CF 43 Sub-Tree - graphical depiction of leaf and root nodes.

Table 3. CF evaluation time results for the multiplexer problems - average time (Seconds) over 30 experiments - XCSCF^2 was not able to complete the 20 bit multiplexer due to memory requirements

System	6 Bit	11 Bit	20 Bit
XCS	0.29 ± 0.04	1.41	7.94
XCSCFC	1.62 ± 0.23	13.49	73.89
XCSCF^2	91.23 ± 11.99	449.29	NA
XCSCF3	23.23 ± 2.14	54.93	172.38

machine with an i5-3470 CPU and 8.0 GB of RAM. The code profiler was used to measure the elapsed times in the particular functions.[1] This table is important because it provides evidence supporting the theory that by compacting the CF rulesets it is possible to garner dividends in execution time, making it possible to solve the more difficult problems.

5   Discussion

5.1   Importance of the Distilled Rules

Although it may seem as if the proposed system is only producing rules akin to what XCS normally learns, it is important to keep in mind the following:

i. The Distilled Rules are a direct result of the final rules composed of Code Fragments. These same rules are the building blocks that the system would have identified as an optimal solution to the problem at hand.
ii. The CFs remain linked to the DRs produced, therefore they can be reused in future problems.
iii. The system is not using hard-coded functions but learned functions accrued throughout its learning history, which can help avoid human bias in function choice.

---

[1] CodeBlocks - code profiler.

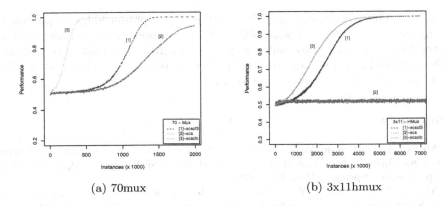

(a) 70mux   (b) 3x11hmux

Fig. 3. Mux and Hidden Mux

In spite of its potential, the new compaction algorithm still lacks the ability to produce more complex DRs in a scalable fashion. Meaning that once the system begins to tackle the 70 bit multiplexer and beyond, the execution times increase to an impractical level. Either a parallel or off-line training can be used. DRs could also not be used for large scale problems that are unlikely to form the base of chains of rules in any case.

The results show a positive impact in the number of instances needed to fully converge for some of the problems. As can be observed, during the 70-Mux problem, the proposed system needs more training instances than XCSCFC to solve the problem and less than XCS, see Fig. 3a. Initially, XCS was not able to solve the 70-Mux problem with comparable settings and therefore it was given a P# setting of 1.0 and Population of 20k individuals, which relies on mutation, rather than covering, to discover useful features. During the 3 bit Parity, 11 bit Hidden Multiplexer, the proposed system utilizes more training instances than XCSCFC to converge and XCS was incapable of learning the problem, see Fig. 3b.

The proposed system has performed better than anticipated with respect to XCS in terms of instances needed to fully learn the problem. However, it has not performed as well as XCSCFC during the Multiplexer experiments described in this work. It is to be determined if the increased complexity of the CF sub-trees in the proposed system has any bearing in this disparity.

6   Conclusions

The proposed system has been shown to reuse information learned from the tasks given to it. It accomplished this with both, simple problems i.e. Boolean operators, and with complex problems such as the 70 bit multiplexer. It can also produce an additional layer of rules based on a simple alphabet. These new rules are key in reducing the time requirements for the system when it evaluates the

CFs it uses. This was demonstrated by the time results produced by the proposed system, XCSCF3 compared with XCSCF^2. The proposed system averaged a shorter time requirement to evaluate its CFs. There is room for improvement as the proposed system demonstrated larger time requirements than XCSCFC, which does not reuse rulesets as functions.

References

1. Alvarez, I.M., Browne, W.N., Zhang, M.: Reusing learned functionality to address complex boolean functions. In: Dick, G., et al. (eds.) SEAL 2014. LNCS, vol. 8886, pp. 383–394. Springer, Heidelberg (2014)
2. Alvarez, I.M., Browne, W.N., Zhang, M.: Reusing learned functionality in XCS: code fragments with constructed functionality and constructed features. In: Genetic and Evolutionary Computation Conference GECCO '14 Companion, pp. 969–976. ACM (2014)
3. Butz, M.V., Wilson, S.W.: An algorithmic description of XCS. Soft Comput. **6**, 144–153 (2002)
4. Butz, M.V.: Rule-Based Evolutionary Online Learning Systems: A Principal Approach to LCS Analysis and Design. Springer, Berlin (2006)
5. Dixon, W.: An Investigation of the XCS Classifier System in Data Mining. The University of Reading, Reading (2004)
6. Goldberg, D.E., Korb, B., Deb, K.: Messy genetic algorithms: motivation, analysis, and first results. Complex Syst. **3**, 493–530 (1989)
7. Holland, J.H.: Adaptation. In: Rosen, R., Snell, F.M. (eds.) Progress in Theoretical Biology, vol. 4, pp. 263–293. Academic Press, New York (1976)
8. Holland, J.H.: Adaptation in Natural and Artificial Systems: An Introductory Analysis with Applications to Biology, Control, and Artificial Intelligence. The University of Michigan Press, Ann Arbor (1975)
9. Koza, J.R.: A hierarchical approach to learning the boolean multiplexer function. In: Foundations of Genetic Algorithms, pp. 171–192. Morgan Kaufmann (1991)
10. Lanzi, P.L.: Extending the representation of classifier conditions Part I : from binary to messy coding. In: Proceedings of the Genetic and Evolutionary Computation Conference (GECCO-1999), vol. 1, pp. 337–344, July 1999
11. Lanzi, P.L., Perrucci, A.: Extending the representation of classifier conditions Part II : from messy coding to S-Expressions. In: Proceedings of the Genetic and Evolutionary Computation Conference (GECCO-1999), vol. 1, pp. 345–352, July 1999
12. Iqbal, M., Browne, W.N., Zhang, M.: Comparison of Two Methods for Computing Action Values in XCS with Code-Fragment Actions. In: GECCO'13 Companion, pp. 1235–1242 (2013)
13. Iqbal, M., Browne, W.N., Zhang, M.: Extending learning classifier system with cyclic graphs for scalability on complex, large-scale boolean problems. In: Proceedings of the Genetic and Evolutionary Computation Conference, pp. 1045–1052 (2013)
14. Iqbal, M., Browne, W.N., Zhang, M.: Learning overlapping natured and niche imbalance boolean problems using XCS classifier systems. In: Proceedings of the IEEE Congress on Evolutionary Computation, pp. 1818–1825 (2013)
15. Iqbal, M., Browne, W.N., Zhang, M.: Reusing building blocks of extracted knowledge to solve complex, large-scale boolean problems. IEEE Trans. Evol. Comput. **17**(3), 503–518 (2013)

16. Schaffer, J.D.: Learning multiclass pattern discrimination. In: Proceedings of the 1st International Conference on Genetic Algorithms and their Applications (ICGA85), pp. 74–79. Lawrence Erlbaum Associates (1985)
17. Liang-Yu, C., Po-Ming, L., Tzu-Chien, H.: A sensor tagging approach of knowledge in learning classifier systems. In: Proceedings of the IEEE Congress on Evolutionary Computation, pp. 2953–2960 (2015)
18. Hsuan-Ta, L., Po-Ming, L., Tzu-Chien, H.: The subsumption mechanism for XCS using code fragmented conditions. In: Proceedings Companion of the Genetic and Evolutionary Computation Conference, pp. 1275–1282 (2013)
19. Wilson, S.W.: Classifier fitness based on accuracy. Evol. Comput. **3**(2), 149–175 (1995)
20. Wilson, S.W.: Compact rulesets from XCSI. In: Lanzi, P.L., Stolzmann, W., Wilson, S.W. (eds.) Advances in Learning Classifier Systems 2002. LNCS, vol. 2321, pp. 196–208. Springer, Berlin (2002)

The Boon of Gene-*Culture* Interaction
for Effective Evolutionary Multitasking

Bingshui Da[1], Abhishek Gupta[1], Yew Soon Ong[2]([⊠]), and Liang Feng[3]

[1] Computational Intelligence Lab, School of Computer Engineering,
Nanyang Technological University, Singapore, Singapore
[2] Rolls-Royce@NTU Corporate Lab C/o, School of Computer Engineering,
Nanyang Technological University, Singapore, Singapore
ASYSONG@ntu.edu.sg
[3] College of Computer Science, Chongqing University, Chongqing, China

Abstract. Multifactorial optimization (MFO) is a recently proposed paradigm for *evolutionary multitasking* that is inspired by the possibility of harnessing underlying synergies between outwardly unrelated optimization problems through the process of *implicit genetic transfer*. In contrast to traditional single-objective and multi-objective optimization, which consider only a single problem in one optimization run, MFO aims at solving multiple optimization problems simultaneously. Through comprehensive empirical study, MFO has demonstrated notable performance on a variety of complex optimization problems. In this paper, we take a step towards better understanding the means by which MFO leads to the observed performance improvement. In particular, since (a) genetic and (b) cultural transmission across generations form the crux of the proposed *evolutionary multitasking engine*, we focus on how their interaction (i.e., gene-culture interaction) affects the overall efficacy of this novel paradigm.

1 Introduction

Evolutionary algorithms (EAs) are generic population-based metaheuristics for optimization that employ mechanisms inspired by biological evolution, namely, Darwinian principles of *Natural Selection* or *Survival of the Fittest* [1]. Through computational analogues of sexual reproduction and mutation, EAs are capable of exploring and exploiting promising regions of the search space, with the survival pressure encouraging evolution of the entire population towards fitter regions of the objective function landscape [2]. In the literature, EAs have demonstrated powerful search capability and have been successfully applied on a wide variety of real-world problems [3].

Over the past few decades, EAs have attracted much research attention, with several variants proposed for single-objective optimization [4], multi-objective optimization [5], and many-objective optimization [6]. It is worth noting that the majority of these works focus on efficiently dealing with only a single problem at a time. Seldom has an attempt been made to multitask, i.e., to solve

© Springer International Publishing Switzerland 2016
T. Ray et al. (Eds.): ACALCI 2016, LNAI 9592, pp. 54–65, 2016.
DOI: 10.1007/978-3-319-28270-1_5

multiple optimization problems (or multiple *tasks*) simultaneously using a single population of evolving individuals. It is only very recently that A. Gupta *et al.* have proposed a new paradigm, labeled *multifactorial optimization* (MFO) [7], that attempts to harness the intrinsic potential for *evolutionary multitasking* possessed by population-based search strategies (here the 'multifactorial' is used to imply that every task contributes a different *factor* influencing the evolution of the population). For example, consider a scenario where two popular benchmarks from continuous optimization, such as the Rastrigin function and the Ackley function, are to be solved simultaneously. In such cases, evolutionary multitasking provides the scope for *autonomously* exploiting underlying synergies (or what we term as the *latent genetic complementarities* [7]) between otherwise independent tasks, through the process of *implicit genetic transfer*.

To realize the MFO paradigm, a novel algorithm, namely, the *multifactorial evolutionary algorithm* (MFEA), has also been proposed in [7]. The MFEA is inspired by bio-cultural models of *multifactorial inheritance* [8], which contend that the complex developmental traits among offspring are influenced by *gene-culture interactions*. The computational equivalent of multifactorial inheritance, for the purpose of efficient evolutionary multitasking, is established by considering each optimization task to create a *distinct environment* in which offspring can be reared. In other words, from the standpoint of the MFEA, multitasking leads to the coexistence of multiple blocks of cultural bias (or *memes* [9]), one corresponding to each task. The subsequent evolution of encoded individuals in the composite landscape is simulated through an interplay of genetic and cultural transmission, where cultural aspects are manifested by two major components of the MFEA acting in concert, namely, (a) *non-random* or *assortative mating*: which states that individuals prefer to mate with those sharing a similar cultural background, and (b) *vertical cultural transmission*: which states that the phenotype of an offspring is strongly influenced by that of its parents. While the basic structure of the proposed algorithm is similar to a classical EA, it is augmented by the aforementioned features that are borrowed from the models of multifactorial inheritance. Using the proposed algorithm, the MFO paradigm has been thoroughly studied in [7] via several computational experiments. These included multitasking across continuous optimization tasks, or combinatorial optimization tasks, or even a mixture of combinatorial and continuous tasks (*cross-domain multitasking*). In the majority of cases, MFEA demonstrated noteworthy performance by accelerating convergence for complex optimization tasks.

Bearing in mind the need for future algorithmic developments in the field of MFO, we find it essential, at this juncture, to investigate and fully acknowledge the key contribution of gene-culture interaction while designing effective *evolutionary multitasking engines*. To this end, in this paper, we present a variant of the MFEA, labeled as *polygenic evolutionary algorithm* (PGEA), which curtails the cultural aspects of the evolutionary process as are manifested in the models of multifactorial inheritance. On comparing the performance of the MFEA and the PGEA on the same set of benchmark instances, it becomes possible to decipher the benefits to the multitasking procedure provided by gene-culture interaction.

The remainder of the paper is organized as follows. Section 2 covers the preliminaries. It introduces the basic concepts of MFO, describes the MFEA, and presents an overview of cultural transmission in multifactorial inheritance. In Sect. 3, we describe the PGEA and discuss our strategy for investigating and verifying the efficacy of the cultural aspects of the MFEA. In Sect. 4, computational experiments are carried out on a variety of benchmark functions from continuous optimization. These serve the purpose of highlighting the key contribution of gene-culture interaction towards effective evolutionary multitasking. Finally, Sect. 5 concludes the paper by summarizing the presented work.

2 Preliminaries

In this Section, we present an overview of the basic concepts in evolutionary multitasking, as have been proposed in [7].

2.1 Multifactorial Optimization (MFO)

Consider a scenario where K distinct optimization tasks are presented simultaneously to a single evolutionary solver. Let the jth task be denoted as T_j, and the dimensionality of its search space X_j be D_j. Without loss of generality, all tasks are assumed to be minimization problems, with the objective function of task T_j being given by $f_j : X_j \to \mathbb{R}$. In such a setting, MFO is defined as an *evolutionary multitasking paradigm* that builds on the implicit parallelism of population-based search with the aim of concurrently finding $\{x_1, x_2, \cdots, x_K\} = \operatorname{argmin}\{f_1(x), f_2(x), \cdots, f_K(x)\}$. Here, x_j denotes a feasible solution in X_j. Note that each f_j is treated as an additional factor influencing the whole evolutionary process. For this reason, the composite problem is referred to as a K-factorial problem.

The fundamentals of designing an EA are based on the Darwinian principle of natural selection. Hence, in order to develop a suitable algorithm for MFO, it is necessary to first conceive a valid measurement to evaluate the fitness of individuals in a multitasking environment. To this end, the following set of properties are defined for every individual p_i, where $i \in 1, 2, ..., |P|$, in a population P:

- *Factorial Rank*: The *factorial rank* r_{ij} of p_i on task T_j is simply the index of p_i in the list of population members sorted in ascending order with respect to f_j.
- *Scalar Fitness*: The list of *factorial ranks* $\{r_{i1}, r_{i2}, \cdots, r_{iK}\}$ of an individual p_i is reduced to a *scalar fitness* φ_i based on its best rank over all tasks; *i.e.* $\varphi_i = 1/\min\{r_{i1}, r_{i2}, \cdots, r_{iK}\}$.
- *Skill Factor*: The *skill factor* τ_i of p_i is the one task, amongst all other tasks in MFO, on which the individual is the most effective, *i.e.* $\tau_i = \operatorname{argmin}_j\{r_{ij}\}$, where $j \in \{1, 2, \cdots, K\}$.

Based on the definition of scalar fitness, the comparison between individuals can be achieved in a straightforward manner. For instance, an individual p_a is considered to dominate individual p_b in *multifactorial sense* simply if $\varphi_a > \varphi_b$.

Also, it is clear that the aforementioned fitness assignment and comparison procedure guarantees that if an individual p^* maps to the global optimal of any task, then, $\varphi_* \geq \varphi_i$ for all $i \in \{1, 2, \cdots, |P|\}$. Therefore, the evolutionary environment built under the above definitions is indeed compatible with the ensuing definition of *multifactorial optimality*.

– *Multifactorial Optimality*: An individual p^* is considered *optimum* in multi-factorial sense iff $\exists j \in \{1, 2, \cdots, K\}$ such that $f_j^* \leq f_j(x_j)$, for all feasible $x_j \in X_j$.

2.2   An Overview of the Multifactorial Evolutionary Algorithm

The MFEA is inspired by the bio-cultural models of multifactorial inheritance. The algorithm is in fact classified under the broad umbrella of *memetic computation* [9,10] as it considers the transmission of biological as well as cultural building blocks (genes and memes) [11,12] from parents to their offspring. In particular, cultural effects are incorporated via two aspects of multifactorial inheritance acting in concert, namely (a) assortative mating and (b) vertical cultural transmission.

The basic structure of the MFEA is presented in Algorithm 1. Details of its various distinctive features are discussed next.

Algorithm 1. Multifactorial evolutionary algorithm.

1: Generate an initial population of solutions and store it in *current-pop*.
2: Evaluate every solution with respect to every optimization task in the multitasking environment.
3: Compute the skill factor of each individual.
4: **while** (stopping conditions are not satisfied) **do**
5:     Apply genetic operators on *current-pop* to generate an *offspring-pop* (see Algorithm 2).
6:     Evaluate the individuals in *offspring-pop* for certain optimization tasks only (see Algorithm 3).
7:     Concatenate *offspring-pop* and *current-pop* to form an *intermediate-pop*.
8:     Re-compute the scalar fitness and skill factor of all individuals.
9:     Select the fittest individuals from *intermediate-pop* to survive into the next generation and form the new *current-pop*.
10: **end while**

2.3   Chromosome Description and Decoding Procedure

Assuming there to be K optimization tasks, we define a *unified search space* Y with dimensionality ($D_{multitask}$) equal to $\max_j\{D_j\}$. Thus, during population initialization, every individual is assigned a vector of $D_{multitask}$ random-keys [13,14] which lie in the fixed range $[0, 1]$. This vector constitutes the chromosome of that individual. While addressing task T_j, only the first D_j random-keys of the chromosome are considered.

There is a strong theoretical motivation behind using the aforementioned encoding scheme. In particular, it is considered to be an effective means of accessing the power of population-based search. As the *schemata* (or genetic building blocks) [15] corresponding to different optimization tasks are contained within a unified pool of genetic material, they get processed by the EA in parallel. Most importantly, this encourages the discovery and implicit transfer of useful genetic material from one task to another in an efficient manner. Moreover, as a single individual in the population may inherit genetic building blocks corresponding to multiple optimization task, the analogy with multifactorial inheritance becomes more meaningful.

Given a chromosome $y \in Y$, a decoding scheme must first be employed to transform y into a meaningful task-specific solution representation. In the case of continuous optimization, this can be achieved by linearly mapping each random-key from the unified space to the original search space of the optimization task. For instance, consider a task T_j in which the ith variable (x_i) is bounded in the range $[L_i, U_i]$. If the ith random-key of a chromosome y takes value $y_i \in [0, 1]$, then the decoding procedure is given by $x_i = L_i + (U_i - L_i) \cdot y_i$

2.4   Cultural Aspects of the MFEA

In the MFEA, we interpret the skill factor (τ) of an individual as a computational representation of its cultural background. Accordingly, while simulating genetic operations (via crossover and mutation), the phenomenon of assortative mating (which states that individuals prefer to mate with those sharing a similar cultural background) is enforced by prescribing a set of conditions that must be satisfied for two randomly selected parent candidates to undergo crossover. A summary is provided in Algorithm 2. The occurrence of assortative mating in the natural world is used in the models of multifactorial inheritance to explain pedigreed traits that extend over several generations [8]. In the case of the MFEA, we introduce a tunable parameter called the *random mating probability* (*rmp*) which follows the principle of assortative mating and is used to balance exploration and exploitation during evolution of individuals in the search space.

Algorithm 2. Assortative mating

1: **for** $i = 1 : |P|/2$ **do**
2:    Randomly select two parents P_1 and P_2 from *current-pop*.
3:    Generate a random number *rand* between 0 and 1.
4:    **if** $(\tau_1 == \tau_2)$ or $(rand < rmp)$ **then**
5:       Parents P_1 and P_2 crossover to give two offspring individuals C_1 and C_2.
6:    **else**
7:       P_1 is mutated slightly to give an offspring C_1.
8:       P_2 is mutated slightly to give an offspring C_2.
9:    **end if**
10:    Append C_1 and C_2 to *offspring-pop*.
11: **end for**

Setting $rmp \approx 0$ implies that only culturally alike individuals are allowed to crossover, while setting $rmp \approx 1$ permits completely random cross-cultural mating. In the former case, the predominantly intra-cultural mating and the small genetic variations produced by mutation (see Algorithm 2) facilitate the scanning of confined regions of the search space. As a result however, there is always the tendency for solutions to get trapped in local optima. On the other hand, when rmp is sufficiently greater than 0, the increased cross-cultural mating leads to the creation of offspring with diverse genetic properties, thereby facilitating the escape from local optima. In addition, it is contended that exclusive mating between individuals belonging to the same cultural background could lead to the loss of good and diverse genetic material available from other cultural backgrounds. In Algorithm 1, notice that the MFEA is bootstrapped by evaluating every individual in the initial population with respect to every task in the multitasking environment. However, it is evident that carrying out exhaustive evaluations in all subsequent generations is likely to be computationally too expensive. For that reason, it is considered practical for an offspring to only be evaluated for a particular task on which it is most likely to be effective. The algorithmic realization of the aforementioned notion is achieved via a *selective imitation* strategy [7] as a form of vertical cultural transmission (see Algorithm 3). Accordingly, an offspring in the MFEA is only evaluated with respect to the task at which at least one of its parents is highly skilled. In other words, the offspring *randomly imitates* the skill factor (or cultural background) of any one of its parents. Furthermore, *every offspring undergoes local improvements* with respect to the skill factor that it chooses to imitate (details of the local search algorithm shall be provided in Sect. 4). Notice that since the genetic composition of an offspring is a combination of the genetic material of its parents, it is reasonable to expect its skill factor to liken that of its parents.

Algorithm 3. Vertical cultural transmission

1: Consider an offspring C which either has 2 parents P_1 and P_2, or a single parent P_1 (or P_2) (see Algorithm 2).
2: **if** (C has 2 parents) **then**
3:     Generate a random number $rand$ between 0 and 1.
4:     **if** ($rand < 0.5$) **then**
5:         C imitates P_1 → Evaluate and locally improve C with respect to task τ_1 (skill factor P_1).
6:     **else**
7:         C imitates P_2 → Evaluate and locally improve C with respect to task τ_2 (skill factor P_2).
8:     **end if**
9: **else**
10:     C is evaluated and locally improved with respect to task τ_1 (or τ_2).
11: **end if**
12: Objective function values of C with respect to all unevaluated tasks are artificially set to ∞.

A crucial outcome emerges from the combined effect of assortative mating and vertical cultural transmission. On occasions when parents with different skill factors happen to crossover, a multicultural environment is created for offspring to be reared in. In such situations, it is possible for an offspring that is genetically closer to one parent to imitate or be culturally influenced by the other. It is this feature of the MFEA that leads to implicit genetic transfer across tasks. Refined genetic material created within individuals of a particular skill factor, if also useful for a different task, can be effectively transferred via the proposed mechanism.

3   The Polygenic Evolutionary Algorithm

As described above, assortative mating and vertical cultural transmission represent the core forms of cultural interaction in the MFEA. In order to understand their importance towards effective evolutionary multitasking, we herein propose an alternate *polygenic evolutionary algorithm* (PGEA) which curtails the cultural aspects of the evolutionary process as prevalent in the MFEA. Thus, in comparison to the PGEA, the credit of any improvement in performance achieved by the MFEA can be entirely assigned to gene-culture interactions.

In the PGEA, the first step to removing cultural bias is taken by ignoring the phenomenon of assortative mating. Thus, any two members of the PGEA population, regardless of whether they possess the same skill factor or not, are allowed to mate freely. In other words, the value of rmp is essentially fixed at 1, implying that uninhibited cross-cultural mating is allowed to occur; which is accompanied by probabilistic mutation of the generated offspring. Secondly, the effect of vertical cultural transmission is minimized by permitting the generated offspring to randomly select any task for evaluation regardless of the skill factor(s) of their parents (i.e., the strategy of selective imitation is also ignored). For a complete overview of the incorporated modifications, see Algorithm 4. The ramifications of these modifications towards the overall performance of the multitasking engine shall be investigated in the next section.

4   Empirical Study

The main aim behind the computational experiments is to better understand the effects of gene-culture interactions towards the overall efficacy of evolutionary multitasking. The simplest way of acquiring a qualitative understanding of the effects is to compare the performance of the MFEA (which incorporates a variety of cultural biases through assortative mating and vertical cultural transmission) and the PGEA (which removes all cultural bias). The aforementioned approach is therefore adopted herein.

Algorithm 4. Genetic mechanisms of the polygenic evolutionary algorithm

---

1: Consider two parents P_1 and P_2 randomly selected from *current-pop*.

2: P_1 and P_2 crossover to give two offspring solutions C_1 and C_2.

3: Offspring C_1 and C_2 may be slightly mutated with a predefined probability.

4: Each offspring is evaluated for any one randomly selected task (individual learning will be applied here). The objective values of the offspring with respect to all unevaluated tasks are artificially set to ∞.

4.1 Experimental Setup and Algorithmic Specifications

In this section, we carry out several computational experiments on popular benchmark problems in continuous optimization. We consider a unimodal function: (a) sphere (search region $[100, 100]$), and four complex multimodal functions [16]: (b) shifted and rotated Rastrigin (search region $[-5, 5]$) (search region denotes the box constraint on every dimension), (c) shifted and rotated Ackley (search region $[-32, 32]$), (d) shifted and rotated Griewank (search region $[-600, 600]$) and (e) rotated Weierstrass (search region $[-0.5, 0.5]$). The dimensionality of each of the benchmark functions is fixed at 30, and the rotation matrix corresponding to each function is randomly generated. During computational experiments, we combine any two of the benchmark functions together to form a single 2-factorial problem. Moreover, the instances are setup such that the global optima of the two constitutive tasks in a single MFO problem are largely separated (demonstrated in Fig. 1a). This ensures that there is no *apparent* source of synergy (or genetic complementarity) between the tasks.

In Table 1, we list the descriptions of four pairs of 2-factorial problems that have been considered in this paper. The second column of the table states the combined functions. For example, $(Task_1, Task_2) \equiv (Sphere, Rastrigin)$ implies that the sphere function and the Rastrigin function have been combined into a single MFO run. The third column of Table 1 represents the location of the global optimum of $Task_1$, while the fourth column represents the location of the global optimum of $Task_2$. With regard to the MFEA and the PGEA, we set the population size to 100 individuals which are evolved over 500 generations. The *rmp* (which only occurs in the MFEA) is configured to 0.3 in all experiments so as to allow sufficient cross-cultural mating. With regard to the variation operators [17], we employ the Simulated Binary Crossover (SBX) with no variable swap [18] and Gaussian mutation operators throughout. Particularly, in the PGEA, the probability of mutation was kept fixed at 10%. Further, in order to facilitate the discovery of high quality solutions, we include a BFGS quasi-Newton individual learning step into each task evaluation call (note that learning proceeds in the spirit of Lamarckism [3, 19]). We realize that hybridizing EAs with individual learning (via local search) is traditionally perceived as a form of cultural evolution or as a *first generation memetic algorithm* [19, 20]. However, judging from the standpoint of multifactorial inheritance, in the present work, local search is not viewed as a separate source of cultural influence that acts over and above assortative mating and vertical cultural transmission.

Table 1. Description of MFO test instances. ($Task_1$, $Task_2$) implies that $Task_1$ and $Task_2$ are combined in a single MFO run.

No.	MFO problems	Global optimum of $Task_1$	Global optimum of $Task_2$
1	(Sphere, Rastrigin)	$x_i = 50, \forall i$	$x_i = 0, \forall i$
2	(Ackley, Weierstrass)	$x_i = 20, \forall i$	$x_i = 0, \forall i$
3	(Griewank, Weierstrass)	$x_i = 300, \forall i$	$x_i = 0, \forall i$
4	(Sphere, Ackley)	$x_i = 50, \forall i$	$x_i = 0, \forall i$

4.2   Discussions

Figure 1a depicts a 1-D illustration of the separated sphere and Rastrigin functions. The convergence trends of the multimodal Rastrigin function in this scenario (given a 30-D search space), as obtained by the MFEA and the PGEA, is provided in Fig. 1b. In addition, the figure also contains a third curve, labeled as SOEA, which represents a traditional single-objective optimization-based approach to solving the Rastrigin function (note that the SOEA employs identical variation operators and local search process as the MFEA and the PGEA, with a mutation probability of 10 %). For fairness of comparison, the SOEA is also enhanced with the same Lamarckian local search algorithm as the MFEA and the PGEA. It is clear from the convergence trends that the performance of the MFEA and the PGEA far exceed that of the SOEA on this instance. The observation underpins our broader claim that provisions for enhanced population diversity and implicit genetic transfer, as facilitated by the evolutionary multitasking paradigm, are potentially invaluable tools for accelerating the convergence process of complex optimization tasks.

On further inspecting Fig. 1b, it is observed that the performance achieved by the MFEA is even superior to that of the PGEA. This result provides strong evidence of the fact that gene-cultural interactions play an important role in improving convergence characteristics. As has been discussed in Sect. 2.4, the cultural aspects of the MFEA (manifested by assortative mating and vertical cultural transmission, acting in concert) lead to a favorable balance between exploration (via population diversification and genetic transfer during *controlled* cross-cultural mating) and exploitation (via assortative mating) of the search space. In contrast, in the PGEA, the removal of cultural bias disrupts the aforementioned balance. The uninhibited cross-cultural mating leads to excessive mixing of genes, eventually causing the loss of pedigreed high quality genetic material [7]. Moreover, by ignoring vertical cultural transmission, the systematic search of fitter regions of the objective function landscape is impeded. Therefore, it comes as little surprise that the performance of the resultant multitasking engine (i.e., the PGEA) is inferior to that of the MFEA. The convergence trends depicted in Figs. 2, 3 and 4 (corresponding to problem numbers 2–4 in Table 1) have similar qualitative characteristics as those presented in Fig. 1. This empirical observation goes a long way towards further reinforcing our inferences as drawn previously. In Fig. 2, the convergence trends of Ackley function (in Fig. 2a) and the

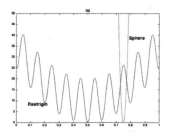
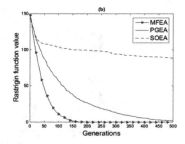

Fig. 1. (a) 1-D illustration of separated Rastrigin and sphere functions in the unified search space, and (b) convergence trends of Rastrigin function in (*Sphere, Rastrigin*).

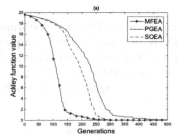
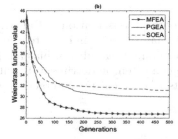

Fig. 2. The convergence trends of (a) Ackley function and (b) Weierstrass function in (*Ackley, Weierstrass*).

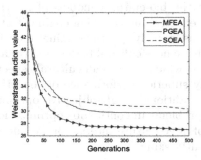

Fig. 3. The convergence trends of Weierstrass function in (*Weierstrass, Griewank*).

Weierstrass function (in Fig. 2b) are presented, when solved in conjunction as (*Ackley, Weierstrass*). Note that both functions in this 2-factorial problem are complex and multimodal. Nevertheless, the convergence rate achieved by the MFEA is found to be accelerated in both cases, in comparison to the PGEA as well as the SOEA. Thus, it is contended that the provision for implicit genetic transfer, appropriately supervised by gene-culture interactions as prescribed by the models of multifactorial inheritance, allows the population to successfully exploit the landscape of multiple complex functions simultaneously, thereby efficiently bypassing obstacles to converge faster.

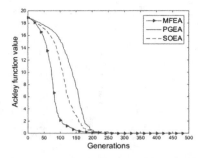

Fig. 4. The convergence trends of Ackley function in (*Sphere, Ackley*).

An important observation we also make here is that the performance of the PGEA may be even inferior to the SOEA in some of the examples. This shows that eliminating cultural bias altogether from an evolutionary multitasking engine can often be detrimental to its overall performance. In other words, the benefits of gene-culture interaction are strongly highlighted in these examples.

5   Conclusion

The main aim of this paper was to show the importance of gene-culture interaction, as manifested in the bio-cultural models of multifactorial inheritance, towards the design of an effective multitasking engine. To this end, we have presented a pair of algorithms, namely, (a) the original multifactorial evolutionary algorithm (MFEA) which includes cultural biases, and (b) a new polygenic evolutionary algorithm (PGEA) which curtails all cultural aspects of the evolutionary process. The consistently superior performance of the MFEA, as compared to the PGEA (and also a traditional single-objective optimization approach), on a variety of benchmark problems in continuous optimization, has demonstrated that the incorporation of gene-culture interaction is indeed a pivotal aspect of effective evolutionary multitasking.

Acknowledgement. This work was conducted within the Rolls-Royce@NTU Corporate Lab with support from the National Research Foundation (NRF) Singapore under the Corp Lab@University Scheme.

References

1. Koza, J.R.: Genetic Programming: On the Programming of Computers by Means of Natural Selection, vol. 1. MIT Press, Cambridge (1992)
2. Konak, A., Coit, D.W., Smith, A.E.: Multi-objective optimization using genetic algorithms: a tutorial. Reliab. Eng. Syst. Saf. **91**(9), 992–1007 (2006)

3. Ong, Y.S., Keane, A.J.: Meta-Lamarckian learning in memetic algorithms. IEEE Trans. Evol. Comput. **8**(2), 99–110 (2004)
4. Bäck, T., Hammel, U., Schwefel, H.P.: Evolutionary computation: comments on the history and current state. IEEE Trans. Evol. Comput. **1**(1), 3–17 (1997)
5. Fonseca, C.M., Fleming, P.J.: An overview of evolutionary algorithms in multiobjective optimization. Evol. Comput. **3**(1), 1–16 (1995)
6. Ishibuchi, H., Tsukamoto, N., Nojima, Y.: Evolutionary many-objective optimization: a short review. In: IEEE Congress on Evolutionary Computation, pp. 2419–2426. Citeseer (2008)
7. Gupta, A., Ong, Y.S., Feng, L.: Multifactorial evolution. IEEE Trans. Evol. Comput. **PP**(99), 1–1 (2015)
8. Rice, J., Cloninger, C.R., Reich, T.: Multifactorial inheritance with cultural transmission and assortative mating. I. Description and basic properties of the unitary models. Am. J. Hum. Genet. **30**(6), 618 (1978)
9. Chen, X., Ong, Y.S., Lim, M.H., Tan, K.C.: A multi-facet survey on memetic computation. IEEE Trans. Evol. Comput. **15**(5), 591–607 (2011)
10. Ong, Y.S., Lim, M.H., Chen, X.: Research frontier-memetic computation past, present & future. IEEE Comput. Intell. Mag. **5**(2), 24 (2010)
11. Iqbal, M., Browne, W.N., Zhang, M.: Reusing building blocks of extracted knowledge to solve complex, large-scale Boolean problems. IEEE Trans. Evol. Comput. **18**(4), 465–480 (2014)
12. Mills, R., Jansen, T., Watson, R.A.: Transforming evolutionary search into higher-level evolutionary search by capturing problem structure. IEEE Trans. Evol. Comput. **18**(5), 628–642 (2014)
13. Bean, J.C.: Genetic algorithms and random keys for sequencing and optimization. ORSA J. Comput. **6**(2), 154–160 (1994)
14. Gonçalves, J.F., Resende, M.G.C.: Biased random-key genetic algorithms for combinatorial optimization. J. Heuristics **17**(5), 487–525 (2011)
15. Wright, A.H., Vose, M.D., Rowe, J.E.: Implicit parallelism. In: Cantú-Paz, E., et al. (eds.) GECCO 2003. LNCS, vol. 2724, pp. 1505–1517. Springer, Heidelberg (2003)
16. Ong, Y.S., Zhou, Z., Lim, D.: Curse and blessing of uncertainty in evolutionary algorithm using approximation. In: 2006 IEEE Congress on Evolutionary Computation, CEC 2006, pp. 2928–2935. IEEE (2006)
17. Fogel, D.B.: What is evolutionary computation? IEEE Spec. **37**(2), 26–28 (2000)
18. Deb, K., Agrawal, R.B.: Simulated binary crossover for continuous search space. Complex Syst. **9**(3), 1–15 (1994)
19. Meuth, R., Lim, M.H., Ong, Y.S., Wunsch II, D.C.: A proposition on memes and meta-memes in computing for higher-order learning. Memetic Comput. **1**, 85–100 (2009)
20. António, C.C.: A memetic algorithm based on multiple learning procedures for global optimal design of composite structures. Memetic Comput. **6**(2), 113–131 (2014)

A Study on Performance Metrics to Identify Solutions of Interest from a Trade-Off Set

Kalyan Shankar Bhattacharjee[✉], Hemant Kumar Singh,
and Tapabrata Ray

School of Engineering and Information Technology, University of New South Wales,
Canberra, Australia
k.bhattacharjee@student.adfa.edu.au, {h.singh,t.ray}@adfa.edu.au

Abstract. Optimization algorithms typically deliver a set of trade-off solutions for problems involving multi/many-objectives in conflict.The number of such solutions could be in hundreds, thousands or even more. A decision maker typically identifies a handful of preferred trade-off solutions (*solutions of interest* (SOI)) from the above set based on secondary indicators e.g. expected marginal utility, convex bulge, hypervolume contribution, bend angle, reflex angle etc. In this paper, we first highlight that members of SOI could be significantly different depending on the choice of the secondary indicator. This leads to an important question *"what metrics should a decision maker use to choose a solution over another ?"* and more importantly *"how to identify a handful of solutions ?"* from a potentially large set of solutions. In this paper we introduce an approach based on **local curvature** to select such solutions of interest. The performance of the approach is illustrated using a bi-objective test problem, and two many-objective engineering optimization problems.

Keywords: Solutions of interest · Decision making · Performance metrics

1 Introduction

Real life optimization problems often require optimizing two or more conflicting objectives simultaneously. The optimum is thus a set of trade-off solutions, which in the objective space represents the Pareto Optimal Front (POF). By definition, all solutions on the POF are equally preferable in absence of any preference information. Typically, the choice of a solution from the above POF for implementation is left to the decision maker (DM). It is well known in decision making literature that the ability of a DM to select a solution diminishes significantly with increasing number of solutions and/or objectives. This decision making problem becomes even more acute when one attempts to select solutions arising out of many objective optimization problems.

To support decision makers in such scenarios, it is theorized that certain *interesting* solutions on the Pareto front may be preferred over others. To this end, the concept of *knee* solutions of a POF has been suggested in the literature [3, 5, 7, 13].

© Springer International Publishing Switzerland 2016
T. Ray et al. (Eds.): ACALCI 2016, LNAI 9592, pp. 66–77, 2016.
DOI: 10.1007/978-3-319-28270-1_6

Conceptually, a solution is referred to as a *knee* if in order to gain a small benefit in one objective, a large compromise is necessary in at (at least) one other objective. This notion of *knee*, however has been interpreted differently by various researchers and we broadly refer them as *solutions of interest* since many do not confirm to the above definition of *knee*. In this paper, we first review the existing metrics used to search for the knee solutions. Subsequently, we construct a bi-objective test problem to illustrate the behavior of each of these metrics in terms of ranking these solutions. Thereafter we discuss certain drawbacks of these techniques, and propose an alternative scheme to overcome them.

Rest of the paper is organized as follows. A study using existing knee measures is given in Sect. 2. An alternative proposal for identification of SOI is described in Sect. 3. Numerical experiments are presented in Sect. 4, and finally the conclusions of the study are given in Sect. 5.

2 Different Metrics to Identify SOI

For a multi/many objective problem, the optimum consists of a set of solutions not dominated by any other in the objective space. This best trade-off set is termed as POF, which contains several solutions, out of which one (or at most a few) solutions of interest have to be chosen for implementation. A brief description of different indicators to aid in decision making are given below. In order to search for solutions that rank high in terms of these indicators, they are often incorporated in an evolutionary search as a secondary metric (apart from non-dominance).

- Expected marginal utility: Branke et al. [3] proposed an alternative method to focus on knees during the course of optimization. It calculates the utility of a solution corresponding to a function $\lambda f_1 + (1 - \lambda)f_2$, with a number of uniform values of λ. A solution in the POF with the largest marginal utility is identified as the *knee* solution. This measure will ignore points in a local convex bulge region as *knee* candidates. However, it can identify multiple global *knees* if they exist.

- Maximum convex bulge/distance from hyperplane: Das [5] noted that often in practice, the solutions are chosen from the middle section of the POF, thereby avoiding the extreme sections of the Pareto front. This central section is referred as *maximum bulge*, wherein solutions that are away from the hyperplane are identified as *solutions of interest*. This concept was subsequently used in a number of works for ranking during the course of optimization [2, 8, 10]. More recently, Zhang et al. [13] illustrated that such solutions have a large hypervolume contribution and thus promoting them during the course of search could inherently offer a solution set with a larger hypervolume.

- Reflex/bend angle: These two methods essentially measure a *kink* (abrupt change in slope) in a two-objective POF. In the reflex angle approach introduced by Branke et al. [3], it is quantified as the external angle formed by the two lines joining the point in consideration with its neighboring points.

The solution in the POF having the largest reflex angle is considered as a *knee*. This was used as a secondary ranking measure in NSGA-II [6] to find solutions concentrated around the knee. Noting that the reflex angle is a local phenomenon, a slightly modified quantification based on bend angle was proposed by Deb and Gupta [7]. The method can be used to identify *knee* solutions between two given solutions in the POF.

- Trade-off approach: For two-objective case, this particular approach was proposed by Deb and Gupta [7]. The approach relies on a user-prescribed trade-off information provided as a pair of values $(\alpha > 1, \beta > 1)$. In order to qualify as a *knee*, a unit gain in f_1 should incur at least α sacrifice in f_2, and similarly a unit gain in f_2 should incur at least β sacrifice in f_1, where all objective values are considered in a normalized space.

- eps-Dominance: In the context of multi/many-objective optimization, a solution a is said to ϵ-dominate a solution b [14] if and only if $f_i(a) + \epsilon \geq f_i(b)\ \forall i = 1, \ldots, m$ where m is the number of objectives and $f_i(x)$ is the ith objective value corresponding to a solution x. Thus, for every point in the Pareto front, the ϵ value can be computed. A higher eps-dominance value for a solution indicates that the solution is having higher trade-offs and one would have to add a larger quantity to each objective of that solution to make it dominated with respect to other solutions in the Pareto set. Therefore, a point in the Pareto front corresponding to a solution having higher eps-dominance value is preferred to a decision maker.

2.1   Illustration on a Bi-objective Example

To illustrate the differences, consider the bi-objective optimization problem presented in Eq. 1.

$$\text{Min. } f_1 = x_1, f_2 = (y - 3.5) \times g/20.5$$

$$\text{where } y = \begin{cases} 24 - \sqrt{20 - (14x_1 - 5)^2}, & \text{if} \quad 0 \leq x_1 \leq 5/14, \\ 18 + \sqrt{(1 - (14x_1 - 5)^2)} & \text{if} \quad 5/14 \leq x_1 \leq 6/14 \\ 18 - \sqrt{(1 - (14x_1 - 7)^2)} & \text{if} \quad 6/14 \leq x_1 \leq 7/14 \\ 59 - 84x_1 & \text{if} \quad 7/14 \leq x_1 \leq 8/14 \\ -3.5x_1 + 13 & \text{if} \quad 8/14 \leq x_1 \leq 10/14 \\ 50.5 - 56x_1 & \text{if} \quad 10/14 \leq x_1 \leq 11/14 \\ 17.5 - 14x_1 & \text{otherwise} \end{cases} \tag{1}$$

$$g = 1 + \sum_{2}^{n} (x_i - 0.5)^2, \quad 0 \leq x_i \leq 1, \quad i = 1, 2, \ldots, n$$

The POF of the function sampled using 14001 points is presented in Fig. 1(a). All the points on the POF correspond to $g = 1$. Specific points on the POF are listed below:

- A: Left extremity of the POF (minimum f_2)
- B: Solution with the maximum hypervolume contribution. An important thing to note is that the solution with the maximum hypervolume contribution may not always lie near the *knee* region, as it is highly dependent on the neighbouring solutions on POF. In this case B is almost coincident with A.
- C: Solution at the maximum bulge in convex region

Table 1. Solutions of interest on the POF

Solution	f_1	f_2	Rank based on					
			EMU	Conv. bulge	Ref. angle	Bend angle	Hypervolume	eps-Dominance
A	0	1	2	8072	9	9	14000	1680
B	7.1429e-05	0.99512	4	7624	6	6	1	1681
C	0.062214	0.86245	194	1	1874	1874	3219	2256
D	0.40764	0.74182	5710	13617	13707	13707	7053	7055
E	0.4495	0.67282	6296	12181	410	410	4048	4049
F	0.5	0.65854	7003	14001	14001	14001	13997	13998
G	0.57143	0.36585	8003	1626	1	1	1096	741
H	0.71429	0.34146	10003	10681	14000	14000	12300	10986
I	0.78571	0.14634	3	1039	2	2	2209	1384
J	1	0	1	8073	3	3	14001	4410

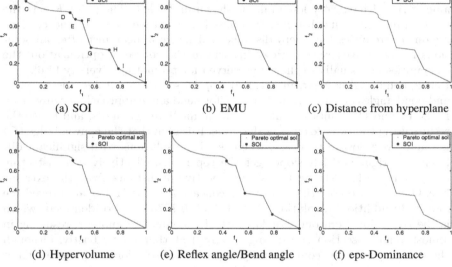

(a) SOI   (b) EMU   (c) Distance from hyperplane

(d) Hypervolume   (e) Reflex angle/Bend angle   (f) eps-Dominance

Fig. 1. Top 10 solutions (out of 14001 uniformly sampled points on the POF) using different decision making metrics.

- D: Solution at the maximum concave bulge from extreme line
- E: Solution at "local" convex bulge closest to extreme line
- F: Solution at intersection between quadratic and linear portions of POF
- G: A strong knee (convex) formed by intersection of two linear portions of POF.
- H: A strong knee (concave) formed by intersection of two linear portions of POF.
- I: A strong knee (convex) formed by intersection of two linear portions of POF. It is possible to draw a line from I to a different part of the curve (say C), such that G lies to the left of the line. Thus optimization of a linear aggregated function such as $\lambda f_1 + (1 - \lambda)f_2$ will not identify G. I is thus a "global strong

knee" in this sense. However, its distance from the extreme line is less than that of point C.

- J: Right extremity of the POF (minimum f_1)

We now compute the metrics (convex bulge, bend/reflex angle, EMU and hypervolume contribution) for all these solutions and list solutions A to I in Table 1.

The top 10 SOI derived using the above metrics are represented in Fig. 1, followed by the discussion.

- EMU: As seen in Fig. 1(b) EMU identifies the "global strong knee" (I) as well as two extremities of the Pareto front (A, J). These three solutions are followed by a range of solutions close to the extreme point A.
- Convex bulge: Based on convex bulge, point C and some others in its neighborhood are identified as top 10 solutions as seen in Fig. 1(c). All other solutions among $A - J$ have very low rank, as shown in Table 1. The point F gets the lowest rank, since its distance is counted as negative being in the concave region. Extremities have zero distance and hence appear just after all solutions in the convex region. However, within the course of optimization, the extremities are usually explicitly preserved for promoting diversity [2,6].
- Reflex/bend angles: Next, in Fig. 1(e), top 10 solutions obtained using reflex and bend angles are shown. In this case, for bend angle approach, for any given $\mathbf{f}$, the $\mathbf{f^L}$ and $\mathbf{f^R}$ points are taken as the immediate neighbors, and hence the results using the two are exactly the same. It is seen that the convex bulge (C) is ranked very low in this case, whereas all the solutions with significant difference in right and left slopes get the top ranks, effectively demonstrating the preference for "strong knees", irrespective of distance from the extreme line. One can also note that the strong concave knees F and H are ranked the lowest. In addition, a solution ($K \equiv 0.4286, 0.7073$) is also identified, which is the transition from one circular part of the curve to another, resulting in almost vertical section (reflex angle ≈ 180) at that point. Lastly, although these two approaches could identify a number of solutions of interest, it not easy to extend the concept to ≥ 3 objectives.
- Hypervolume contribution: Fig. 1(d) shows the top 10 solutions obtained using hypervolume contribution. Unlike the studies in [13], it can be seen that the hypervolume contribution can be highly dependent on the neighboring points on the Pareto front. If knee solution is in a region surrounded with a number closely accumulated solutions, its overall contribution may be small and it could be ranked low. In this particular case, the points lying on the vertical sections (B and K) of the POF are ranked the highest, as for the same increase in f_1 they have the highest increase in f_2, thereby increasing their hypervolume contribution. Also to be noted is that the extreme solutions once again get lowest ranks as the lie on the same level as the Nadir solution, resulting in a zero hypervolume contribution.
- eps-Dominance: Fig. 1(f) shows the top 10 solutions obtained based on the ϵ-dominance value for each point in the Pareto front. This metric is also

dependent on neighboring points in the objective space. The point G gets the highest rank and point F gets the lowest rank among all the points $(A - J)$ in the Pareto front. If a decision maker were supposed to choose based on eps-dominance as a metric, point G would be the most desired location among points $A - J$ and point F would be the least desired location.

2.2 Limitations of Existing Methods

It is clear from the above example that the metrics have quite different values and the choice of one over another could lead to completely different set of solutions being selected. The main limitations of the existing methods could be interpreted as follows. The angle-based approaches (reflex or bend angle) have the limitation of being applicable in two-objectives only in the current form. Although the extension to higher number of objectives is possible conceptually, the calculations will be significantly more involved due to spatial arrangements of the points in the higher dimensions. The trade-off based approach also faces the same limitation, since several trade-off parameters need to be defined in higher dimensions as the number of objective combinations increase. The hypervolume measure although can be calculated in higher dimensions, is computationally expensive. Moreover, the hypervolume contribution is also largely dependent on the neighboring non-dominated solutions. The maximum bulge is relatively faster to compute, even for higher dimensions, but may not capture any trade-off information between the points corresponding to the solutions. Expected marginal utility as defined in [3] takes into account the trade-off information, and can be extended to problems with higher number of objectives. Given these properties, it seems most suitable to identify SOI on the Pareto-front. However, on closer look, two of its properties may reduce its effectiveness as a good SOI measure:

- Dependence on neighboring points: The expected marginal utility effectively measures the loss in performance if the best solution along a preferred direction is replaced by the second best solution along that particular direction. This

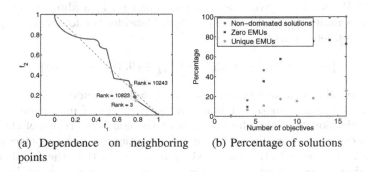

(a) Dependence on neighboring points

(b) Percentage of solutions

Fig. 2. Rank based on EMU: Dependence on neighboring points

means that if two points are very close to each other (or a copy), or have same utility in a particular direction i.e. located symmetric about the solution having best utility along any preferred direction, they are likely to get a very low rank in the absence of one. Consider, for example the following case of the problem above, when the solutions are *not* uniformly distributed. It can be seen that due to a high density of points around the knee, the solutions get lower rank than the one away.

- Secondly, it is observed that for many-objective problems, only a small percentage of the population gets assigned a non-zero value of EMU. This is not an issue when identifying a few knee solution(s) from a given set, but it reduces the effectiveness of the EMU as a secondary ranking measure for evolutionary search. This is because if large number of solutions have the same (zero) value, those solutions effectively remain unranked. As a result, a small number of solutions (with non-zero EMU) are left to drive the population, which results in a very slow migration of the population towards the POF. To demonstrate this, consider populations of randomly generated solutions for different number of objectives, and the corresponding proportion of zero EMU solutions in the non-dominated population. In Fig. 2(b), it is clear that as number of objectives increases the number of non-zero EMU solutions decreases and very few solutions with unique EMU values are left.

It can be clearly observed that none of the method could focus on all possible regions of interest or regions having higher trade-offs. To overcome this limitation, we introduce a new metric, which is based on local curvature discussed in [12]. We show in the next section how this metric can be used to identify potential solutions of interest with high trade-offs.

3   Proposed Metric

Pareto front geometry estimation is important in the context of multi/many-objective optimization problem in terms of decision making. Wang [12] described about choosing adaptive L_p scalarising function which shows significant search improvement over standard MOEA/D. In terms of decision making, the geometry of the Pareto front gives the decision maker an idea about the regions of interest for a multi/many-objective problem. Consider the following property of a family of reference curves:

$$\{y_1{}^\alpha + y_2{}^\alpha + \cdots + y_m{}^\alpha = 1 \; ; y_j \in (0,1], \alpha \in (0,\infty)\} \tag{2}$$

It can be inferred from Fig. 3(a) that for $\alpha > 1$, the curve is non-convex; for $\alpha = 1$ it is linear and for $\alpha < 1$ it is convex. In terms of maximum trade offs for a minimization problem, the solutions at the convex portions of the Pareto front are most important. This is because if a solution lies in the convex portion, improvement in one objective causes significant loss in the other(s). Therefore, convex region appeals more to a decision maker to find solutions of interest. In the context of a multi/many-objective problem the geometry of the Pareto front can be obtained by solving Eq. 3 for α which results in the smallest $h(\alpha, Q)$:

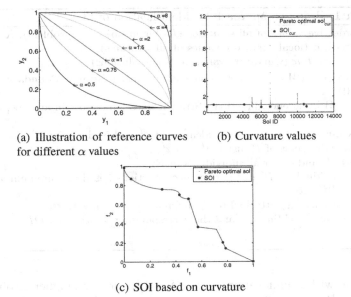

(a) Illustration of reference curves for different α values

(b) Curvature values

(c) SOI based on curvature

Fig. 3. Curvature and top 7 solutions (out of 14001 uniformly sampled points on the POF) using different decision making metrics

$$h(\alpha, Q) = \sum_{\forall x^k \in Q} \left(\sum_{i=1,\dots,m} \left(f_i(x^k) \right)^\alpha - 1 \right)^2, \ \alpha \in P \tag{3}$$

The value of α is determined locally for each point in the Pareto front taking certain number of nearest neighbors along each objective direction for each point in the objective space. For a convex Pareto front, all the regions having an α less than 1 can be considered as potential knee solutions. For a non-convex Pareto front, solutions having minimum curvature get preference over others. This phenomenon can be well explained using the test example from the previous section. Figure 3 shows the curvature values of the solutions with respect to the solution ids. It can be seen that the solutions having larger trade-off correspond to lower values of α.

Based on our algorithm using 8 neighbors in each objective direction (total $8 \times 2 = 16$ neighbors), local curvature values for most of the region were less than 1 which would indicate the convex nature of the Pareto front in most of the regions (Fig. 3(b)). However some portion of the Pareto front is non-convex in nature (Fig. 3(c)) which results in high value (> 1) of curvature in those regions. The pseudocode of our approach is given in Algorithm 1, followed by an outline of the key steps.

- **Generate:** A structured set of $|W|$ reference points is generated spanning a hyperplane with unit intercepts in each objective axis using normal boundary intersection method (NBI) [4]. The approach generates $|W|$ points on the

Algorithm 1. Proposed approach for identification of SOI

Input: f (objective values of all solutions (P) for m objective problem), K (number of SOI required), α (local curvature values of all solutions)
Output: SOI, $Metric$ (Curvature values of Knee solutions)
 1: **Generate** $|W|$ ($|W| \leq K$) reference points using Normal Boundary Intersection (NBI)
 2: **Construct** $|W|$ reference directions; Straight lines joining origin and $|W|$ reference points
 3: For individuals in P compute the ideal point z^I and Nadir point z^N
 4: **Scale** the individuals of P^i using z^I and z^N
 5: **Compute** d_1 and d_2 for all individuals in P^i
 6: **Assign** individuals of P^i to the reference directions based on minimum d_2
 7: **for** $j = 1 : |W|$ **do**
 8:    Find solutions P_{W_i} attached to W_i reference direction with α_{W_i}
 9:    **Set** $Metric_j = \underset{\alpha_{W_i}}{\text{Min}}\ \alpha_{W_i}$ and the corresponding solution is SOI_j
10: **end for**

---

hyperplane with a uniform spacing of $\delta = 1/s$ for any number of objectives m with s unique sampling locations along each objective axis. The reference directions are formed by constructing a straight line from the origin to each of these reference points.

- **Scale:** The process of scaling converts the objective values between 0 and 1. In the event any coordinate of the ideal point matches with the corresponding coordinate of the Nadir point, the scaled value of the corresponding objective is set to 0.

- **Compute:** Two measures d_1 and d_2 are computed for all solutions as done in [1]. The first measure d_1 is the Euclidean distance between origin and the foot of the normal drawn from the solution to the reference direction, while the second measure d_2 is the length of the normal.

- **Assign:** For each solution, d_2 with each reference direction is calculated and solutions are attached to the reference directions based on minimum d_2. Therefore some reference direction will have a cloud of solutions attached to it and some reference directions might not have solutions at all.

- **Set:** For the reference directions having at least one solution attached to it, this process identifies Solutions of interest (SOI) along those. Among the cloud of solutions attached to a reference direction, the solution with the minimum α is identified and considered to be the SOI along that particular reference direction. Hence, the metric corresponding to the SOI is the minimum α value within that cloud attached to the reference direction.

4   Numerical Experiments

Following the bi-objective illustration in previous section, we now discuss two practical many-objective problems. Both of these problems show interesting differences among the regions of interest obtained using our method and others.

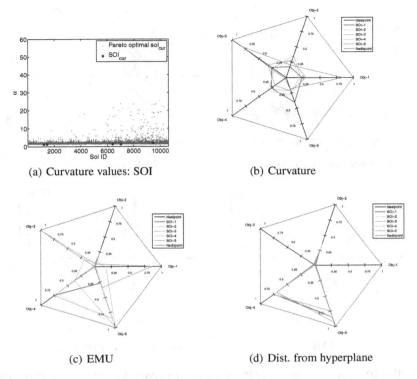

(a) Curvature values: SOI

(b) Curvature

(c) EMU

(d) Dist. from hyperplane

Fig. 4. Top 10 solutions (out of 10626 uniformly distributed points on the POF) using different metrics

4.1 Water Resource Problem

First, we consider the five-objective Water Resource problem [9]. Decomposition based evolutionary algorithm (DBEA) [1] was used with a population size of 10626, run for 100 generation. All 10626 individuals in the final generation are non-dominated. It is interesting to note that all the local curvature values obtained were more than 1 (Fig. 4(a)), which indicates the non-convex nature of the overall Pareto front. For non-convex Pareto fronts, the theoretical concept of knee does not apply. Therefore, in this case, the solutions having lower values of local curvature (Fig. 4(a)) can be considered important to decision maker because those are the only solutions having relatively higher trade-off values compared to the rest of the points. Similarly top 10 solutions in terms of lower curvature values, higher EMU values and higher distance from the hyperplane values are presented in Fig. 4. It can be also observed that solutions with higher trade-off are likely to be closer to the Ideal point of the Pareto front. Our method in Fig. 4(b) shows that the SOIs are closer to the Ideal point of the scaled plot compared to all other methods.

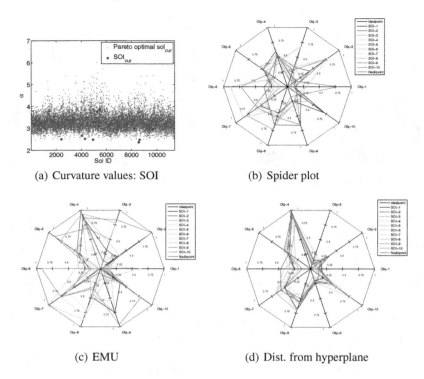

(a) Curvature values: SOI   (b) Spider plot

(c) EMU   (d) Dist. from hyperplane

Fig. 5. Top 10 solutions (out of 11440 uniformly distributed points on the POF) using different decision making metrics

4.2   General Aviation Aircraft Problem

Next, we consider a 10-objective General aviation aircraft problem introduced in [11]. For this problem, DBEA [1] was run for 100 generation with a population size of 11440. All solutions in the final generation were non-dominated. Figure 5 represents the top 10 solutions out of 11440 non-dominated solutions based on different metrics. For this problem, once again it is observed that all curvature values more than 1 (Fig. 5(a)), indicating a non-convex Pareto front. SOI's delivered by different metrics are shown in Fig. 5. It can be seen that the proposed method was able to deliver the SOIs closer to the ideal point (having higher trade-offs) of the Pareto front for the problem.

5   Conclusions

Multi-objective optimization algorithms typically deliver a set of trade-off solutions known as POF. Choosing one or a few solutions for final implementation from the POF is not trivial as it may contain huge number of solutions in high dimensions. In absence of any additional preferences, certain metrics need to be used to identify solutions of interest (SOI). This paper reviews existing measures in this regard and illustrates the different solutions that will be obtained using them. It also highlights some of their shortcomings, followed by a proposal based on local curvature. Lastly, numerical experiments are presented on many-objective problems do illustrate the potential benefits of the proposed approach.

References

1. Asafuddoula, M., Ray, T., Sarker, R.: A decomposition-based evolutionary algorithm for many objective optimization. IEEE Trans. Evol. Comput. **19**(3), 445–460 (2015)
2. Bechikh, S., Said, L.B., Ghédira, K.: Searching for knee regions of the pareto front using mobile reference points. Soft Comput. **15**(9), 1807–1823 (2011)
3. Branke, J., Deb, K., Dierolf, H., Osswald, M.: Finding knees in multi-objective optimization. In: Yao, X., Burke, E.K., Lozano, J.A., Smith, J., Merelo-Guervós, J.J., Bullinaria, J.A., Rowe, J.E., Tiňo, P., Kabán, A., Schwefel, H.-P. (eds.) PPSN 2004. LNCS, vol. 3242, pp. 722–731. Springer, Heidelberg (2004)
4. Das, I., Dennis, J.E.: Normal-bounday intersection: a new method for generating pareto optimal points in multicriteria optimization problems. SIAM J. Optim. **8**(3), 631–657 (1998)
5. Das, I.: On characterizing the knee of the pareto curve based on normal-boundary intersection. Struct. Optim. **18**(2–3), 107–115 (1999)
6. Deb, K., Pratap, A., Agarwal, S., Meyarivan, T.: A fast and elitist multiobjective genetic algorithm: NSGA-II. IEEE Trans. Evol. Comput. **6**(2), 182–197 (2002)
7. Deb, K., Gupta, S.: Understanding knee points in bicriteria problems and their implications as preferred solution principles. Eng. Optim. **43**(11), 1175–1204 (2011)
8. Rachmawati, L., Srinivasan, D.: Multiobjective evolutionary algorithm with controllable focus on the knees of the pareto front. IEEE Trans. Evol. Comput. **13**(4), 810–824 (2009)
9. Ray, T., Tai, K., Seow, K.C.: An evolutionary algorithm for multiobjective optimization. Eng. Optim. **33**(3), 399–424 (2001)
10. Schütze, O., Laumanns, M., Coello, C.A.C.: Approximating the knee of an MOP with stochastic search algorithms. In: Rudolph, G., Jansen, T., Lucas, S., Poloni, C., Beume, N. (eds.) PPSN 2008. LNCS, vol. 5199, pp. 795–804. Springer, Heidelberg (2008)
11. Simpson, T.W., Chen, W., Allen, J.K., Mistree, F.: Conceptual design of a family of products through the use of the robust concept exploration method. AIAA/USAF/NASA/ISSMO Symp. Multi. Anal. Optim. **2**, 1535–1545 (1996)
12. Wang, R., Zhang, Q., Zhang, T.: Pareto adaptive scalarising functions for decomposition based algorithms. In: Gaspar-Cunha, A., Henggeler Antunes, C., Coello, C.C. (eds.) EMO 2015. LNCS, vol. 9018, pp. 248–262. Springer, Heidelberg (2015)
13. Zhang, X., Tian, Y., Jin, Y.: A knee point driven evolutionary algorithm for many-objective optimization. IEEE Trans. Evol. Comput. **PP**(99), 1 (2014)
14. Zitzler, E., Laumanns, M., Bleuler, S.: A tutorial on evolutionary multiobjective optimization. In: Gandibleux, X., Sevaux, M., Sörensen, K., T'kindt, V. (eds.) Metaheuristics for Multiobjective Optimisation. Lecture Notes in Economics and Mathematical Systems, vol. 535, pp. 3–37. Springer, Heidelberg (2004)

Dynamic Configuration of Differential Evolution Control Parameters and Operators

Saber Mohammed Elsayed$^{(\boxtimes)}$ and Ruhul Sarker

School of Engineering and Information Technology,
University of New South Wales at Canberra, Canberra, Australia
{s.elsayed,r.sarker}@adfa.edu.au

Abstract. Differential evolution has shown success in solving different optimization problems. However, its performance depends on the control parameters and search operators. Different from existing approaches, in this paper, a new framework which dynamically configures the appropriate choices of operators and parameters is introduced, in which the success of a search operator is linked to the proper combination of control parameters (scaling factor and crossover rate). Also, an adaptation of the population size is adopted. The performance of the proposed algorithm is assessed using a well-known set of constrained problems with the experimental results demonstrating that it is superior to state-of-the-art algorithms.

1 Introduction

Over decades, evolutionary algorithms (EAs) have been used to solve optimization problems. Such problems may have different mathematical properties. Among EAs, genetic algorithms (GA) [1], differential evolution (DE) [2] and evolution strategy (ES) [3] are very popular. Like any other EAs, the choice of DE's search operators and control parameters (scaling factor (F), crossover rate (Cr) and population size (PS)) plays a pivotal role in its success [4]. A trial-and-error approach is a possible way to define them. However, such an approach is known tedious. As a matter of fact, one combination of control parameters and/or search operators may work well for a set of problems, but may not perform the same for another. As a consequence, different research studies have been introduced for adapting DE's control parameters and/or search operators. Some of them are discussed below.

Elsayed et al. [5] proposed a general framework that divided the population into four sub-populations, each of which used one combination of search operators. During the evolutionary process, the sub-population sizes were adaptively varied based on the success of each operator, which was calculated based on changes in the fitness values, constraint violations and feasibility ratios. The algorithm performed well on a set of constrained problems. Elsayed et al. [6] also proposed two novel DE variants, each of which utilized the strengths of multiple mutation and crossover operators, to solve 60 constrained problems, with their results superior performance to those from state-of-the-art algorithms.

© Springer International Publishing Switzerland 2016
T. Ray et al. (Eds.): ACALCI 2016, LNAI 9592, pp. 78–88, 2016.
DOI: 10.1007/978-3-319-28270-1_7

Zamuda and Brest [7] introduced an algorithm that employed two DE muta-tion strategies and a population was adaptively reduced during the evolutionary process. The algorithm was tested on 22 real-world applications and showed bet-ter performance than two other algorithms. The authors then extended the algo-rithm by embedding a self-adaptation mechanism for parameter control [8], in which the population was divided into sub-populations to apply more DE strate-gies and a population diversity mechanism introduced. The mutation strategies used depended on the population size, which was reduced as the number of function evaluations increased. In [9], with a probability (q), one, out of 12, set of control parameters was selected and during the evolutionary process, q was updated based on the success rate in the previous steps. Sarker et al. [10] proposed a DE algorithm that used a mechanism to dynamically select the best performing combinations of Cr and F for a problem during the course of a single run. The results demonstrated that the proposed algorithm was superior to other state-of-the-art algorithms. Mallipeddi et al. [11] proposed using a mix of four constraint handling techniques (CHTs) based on a DE algorithm (ECHT-DE) to solve constrained problems, in which four populations were initialized and each on which used a different CHT. Additionally, a mix of mutation strategies and a pool of F and Cr values were employed.

To deal with DE's control parameters, Liu and Lampinen [12] proposed a self-adaptive mechanism to determine the right values of F and Cr using the fuzzy logic concept. Brest et al. [13] introduced a self-adaptation method for F and Cr, in which each individual in the population assigned with a different combination of F and Cr values. Zhang et al. [14] proposed an adaptive DE (JADE). In it, at each generation, Cr_z, $\forall z = 1, 2, ..., PS$, was independently generated $\left(N(\overline{Cr}, Cr_\sigma = 0.1)\right)$. $\overline{Cr}$ was initially set to a value of 0.5 and then dynamically updated. Similarly, F_z was generated according to a Cauchy dis-tribution with a location parameter $(\overline{F})$, its initial value was 0.5, and a scaling parameter of 0. At the end of each generation, $\overline{F}$ was updated.

From the literature, it was found that the current approaches did not assume that one operator might work well due to the assigned combination of Cr and F or vice versa and might perform badly, if it used another combination of control parameters. Motivated by this fact, in this paper, a new framework, which bears in mind the above-mentioned issue is introduced. In it, three sets (F_{set}, Cr_{set} and SO_{set}) are considered, which represent the scaling factor, crossover rate and search operators, respectively. Then, each individual in the population is assigned a random combination of (F, Cr and SO). The success rate of each combination is accumulated over generations. Then, the number of combinations is linearly reduced along with PS. The performance of the proposed algorithm is tested on a well-known set of constrained problems [15]. The algorithm shows consistently better performance in comparison with state-of-the-art algorithms.

The rest of this paper is organized as follows. A brief overview of DE is dis-cussed in Sect. 2. The proposed algorithm is then described in Sect. 3. The exper-imental results and conclusions are then discussed in Sects. 4 and 5, respectively.

2   Differential Evolution

DE is a population-based algorithm that uses three operators (mutation, crossover and selection) to guide the individuals to find the (near) optimal solutions [16], such that

- **Mutation:** In its simplest form (DE/rand/1 [2]), a mutant vector is generated by multiplying the difference between two random vectors by F and the result is added to a third random vector as

$$\overrightarrow{v}_z = \overrightarrow{x}_{r_1} + F.(\overrightarrow{x}_{r_2} - \overrightarrow{x}_{r_3}) \tag{1}$$

where r_1, r_2, r_3 are different random integer numbers $\in [1, PS]$ and none of them is similar to z. The type of mutation operator has a great effect on the performance of DE. There are many variants of this operator, such as DE/best/1 [2], DE/rand-to-best/1 [17] and DE/current-to-best [14].

- **Crossover:** There are two well-known crossover schemes, exponential and binomial. In the former, a trial vector $\overrightarrow{u}$ is generated as follows:

$$u_{z,j} = \begin{cases} v_{z,j} \ \forall j = \langle l \rangle_D, \langle l+1 \rangle_D, ..., \langle l+L-1 \rangle_D \\ x_{z,j} \qquad\qquad \forall j \in [1, D] \end{cases} \tag{2}$$

where l is randomly selected from a range $[1, D]$, $j = 1, 2..., D$, $\langle l \rangle_D$ denotes a modulo function with a modulus of D and $L \in [1, D]$.

On the other hand, the binomial crossover is conducted on every $j \in [1, D]$ with a predefined crossover probability, that is

$$u_{z,j} = \begin{cases} v_{z,j} & if(rand \leq cr | j = j_{rand}) \\ x_{z,j} & \text{otherwise} \end{cases} \tag{3}$$

$j_{rand} \in 1, 2, ..., D$ is a randomly selected index, which ensures $\overrightarrow{u_z}$ gets at least one component from $\overrightarrow{v_z}$.

- **Selection:** The selection process is simple, in which a tournament between $\overrightarrow{u}_z$ and $\overrightarrow{x}_z$, $\forall z = 1, ..., PS$, takes place and the winner survives to the next generation.

3   Dynamic Configuration of DE's Control Parameters and Operators

Here, the proposed dynamic configuration of DE parameters and operators algorithm (DCDE) is described.

3.1   DCDE

It has been proven that the performance of a DE operator and a set of parameters may work well on a specific problem and may perform badly on another [5]. This motivated researchers to introduce DE variants that incorporated an

---

Algorithm 1. General framework of DCDE

1: $PS \leftarrow PS_{max}$; define PS_{min}; $F_{set} \leftarrow F_1, F_2, ..., F_{nf}$; $Cr_{set} \leftarrow Cr_1, Cr_2, ..., Cr_{ncr}$; $SO_{set} \leftarrow SO_1, SO_2, ..., SO_{nso}$; $cfe \leftarrow 0$;

2: Generate an initial random population. The variables of each individual $(\overrightarrow{x_z})$ must be within its boundaries;

3: Calculate the fitness value and constraint violation of $(\overrightarrow{x_z})$;

4: $cfe \leftarrow 2 \times PS$ as evaluating the constraints is counted;

5: Sort the whole population.

6: **while** $cfe < cfe_{max}$ **do**

7:    Each individual is assigned a random combination of parameter segments F, Cr and SO;

8:    Convert discrete segments of F and Cr to continuous values.

9:    **for** $z = 1 : PS$ **do**

10:      Generate a new individual $(\overrightarrow{u_z})$ using its assigned combination;

11:      Calculate the constraints violation $\Theta(\overrightarrow{u_z})$;

12:      **if** $\Theta(\overrightarrow{u_z}) > 0$ // the individual is infeasible **then**

13:        $cfe \leftarrow cfe + 1$;

14:        Fitness value $(fit(\overrightarrow{u_z})) \leftarrow fit(\overrightarrow{x_z})$;

15:      **else if** $\Theta(\overrightarrow{u_z}) = 0$ // the individual is feasible **then**

16:        Calculate the fitness value $(fit(\overrightarrow{u_z}))$;

17:        $cfe \leftarrow cfe + 2$;

18:      **end if**

19:      **if** $\overrightarrow{u_z}$ is better than $\overrightarrow{x_z}$ **then**

20:        $\overrightarrow{u_z}$ is survived to the next generation; $com_{y,suc} \leftarrow com_{y,suc} + 1$; $SO_{p,suc} \leftarrow SO_{p,suc} + 1$;

21:      **end if**

22:      Update and sort the new population.

23:    **end for**

24:    Calculate the rank of each combination based on Eq. 4.

25:    Reduce PS and number of combinations if required.

26:    Go to step 9;

27: **end while**

---

ensemble of DE operators and parameters. However, such studies used to calculate the success of search operators separately from control parameters; and then used some adaptive mechanisms to place emphasis on the best-performing operators. However, after selecting the best operators, they may not perform well as expected. One reason for this is the change in the control parameters. Therefore, in this section, a new framework is proposed which keeps track of the best combinations of operators and control parameters. The proposed algorithm is presented in Algorithm 1.

To begin with, three sets are defined as: F_{set}, Cr_{set} and SO_{set}, where F_{set} and Cr_{set} contain nf and ncr discrete values, respectively, and each discrete value represents a range of continuous values. For example, if $F = 8$, and $Cr = 9$, it means that $0.8 \leq F < 0.9$ and $0.9 \leq Cr < 1$, while $SO_{set} = \{SO_1, SO_2, ..., SO_{nso}\}$ is a set of different DE variants. This means that the total number of combinations (NoC) is equal to $(nf \times ncr \times nso)$.

First, PS random individuals are generated within the variables bounds, i.e., $x_{i,j} = \underline{x_j} + rand(\bar{x}_j - \underline{x_j})$, where $\underline{x_j}$ and $\bar{x}_j$ are the lower and upper bounds of the j^{th}variable, respectively. Each individual in the population $(\overrightarrow{x_z})$ is assigned a combination that has three values (F_z, Cr_z and SO_z). To make it clear, each combination is assigned to at least one individual. In case of NoC is less than PS, the rest $PS - NoC$ individuals are assigned with random combinations. Then, for each $\overrightarrow{x_z}$, a new offspring $(\overrightarrow{u_z})$ is generated by using its assigned combination of operators and parameters. If $\overrightarrow{u_z}$ is better than $\overrightarrow{x_z}$, it survives to the next generation and the success of the corresponding combination ($com_{y,suc}$) is increased by 1, where $y = 1, 2, ..., NoC$. It is worth mentioning that to reduce the number of fitness evaluations, if $\overrightarrow{u_z}$ is infeasible, its objective value is not calculated. Instead, it takes the fitness value of its parent. Hence, the number of fitness evaluations (cfe) is only increased by 1. On the other hand, if $\overrightarrow{u_z}$ individual is feasible, its fitness value is calculated and hence cfe is increased by 2. At the end of each generation, the ranking of any combination (R_y) is calculated using Eq. (4), where N_y is the number of individuals updated by a combination y. Note that the initial value of R_y was set at a value of 0.

$$R_y = \frac{com_{y,suc}}{N_y} \tag{4}$$

At the same time, a linear reduction of PS takes place, i.e., PS is set to a large value at the start of the evolutionary process and then linearly reduced (by removing one or more individual from the worst 5 % solutions), such that

$$PS_{iter} = \text{round}\left(\left(\left(\frac{PS_{min} - PS_{max}}{FFE_{max}}\right) \times cfe\right) + PS_{max}\right), \tag{5}$$

where, PS_{max} and PS_{min} are the maximum and minimum values of PS, respectively, and FFE_{max} the maximum number of fitness evaluations. The main motivation behind adapting PS is to maintain diversity during the early stages of the evolutionary process, while placing emphasis on the intensification process at later stages [18].

At the same time, all combinations are sorted based on their ranks and the worst $(PS_{iter-1} - PS_{iter})$ combinations are then removed. The process continues until a stopping criterion is met.

3.2 Selection Process

The selection process between any offspring and its parent is based on the superiority of feasible solutions technique [19], as it does not require user-defined parameters. In it, three conditions exist: (1) between two feasible candidates, the fittest one (according to the fitness value) is selected; (2) a feasible point is always better than an infeasible one; and (3) between two infeasible solutions, the one with a smaller sum of constraint violations (Θ) is chosen, where Θ of an individual ($\overrightarrow{x_z}$) is calculated such that:

$$\Theta_z = \sum_{k=1}^{K} max(0, g_k(\overrightarrow{x_z}) - \delta_k) + \sum_{e=1}^{E} max(0, |h_e(\overrightarrow{x_z})| - \epsilon_e) \tag{6}$$

where $g_k(\overrightarrow{x_z})$ is the kth inequality constraints, $h_e(\overrightarrow{x_z})$ the eth equality constraint. As some inequality constraints may be difficult, a new parameter δ is considered in Eq. (6) which is set to a large value at the beginning of optimization process and then reduced to be zero. This also applies to the equality constraints, whereby ϵ_e is initialized with a large value and then reduced to 0.0001 [15]. Setting the initial value of ϵ is a problem dependent, as discussed in [20].

4   Experimental Results

In this section, the computational results of DCDE are presented and analyzed on the CEC2010 constrained problems set [15]. All algorithms were run 25 times for each test problem, where the stopping criterion was to run for up to $200,000$ and $600,000$ FEs for the 10D and 30D problems, respectively.

To begin with, in regards to the possible parameter values used in this study,

- $SO_{set} = \{DE_1, DE_2\}$, in which
  1. DE_1: DE/φ-best/1/bin [10]

  $$u_{z,j} = \begin{cases} x_{\phi,j} + F_z.(x_{r_1,j} - x_{r_2,j}) & if(rand \leq cr_z | j = j_{rand}) \\ x_{z,j} & otherwise \end{cases} \tag{7}$$

  2. DE_2: $DE/current$-to-$\phi best$ with archive/1/bin [14]

  $$u_{z,j} = \begin{cases} x_{z,j} + F_z.(x_{\phi,j} - x_{z,j} + x_{r_1,j} - \widetilde{x}_{r_3,j}) & if(rand \leq cr_z | j = j_{rand}) \\ x_{z,j} & otherwise \end{cases} \tag{8}$$

  where $\varphi = 0.5$ as suggested in [10], $\phi = 0.1$ [14], $r_1 \neq r_2 \neq r_3 \neq z$ are random integer numbers, $\widetilde{x}_{r_2,j}$ randomly chosen from $PS \cup AR$, i.e., the union of PS and archive AR. Initially, the archive was empty, then the unsuccessful parent vectors were added to the it and once its size $(arch_{size})$ exceeds a threshold, randomly selected elements were deleted to make space for the newly inserted ones [14]. The reason for using DE_1 was to obtain a balance between diversity and intensification, as described in [10], while DE_2 had a high convergence rate.
- $F_{set} = \{F_3 \in [0.3 - 0.4[, F_4 \in [0.4 - 0.5[, F_5 \in [0.5 - 0.6[, F_6 \in [0.6 - 0.7[, F_7 \in [0.7 - 0.8[, F_8 \in [0.8 - 0.9[, F_9 \in [0.9, 1[\}$.
- $Cr_{set} = \{Cr_2 \in [0.2 - 0.3[, Cr_3 \in [0.3 - 0.4[, Cr_4 \in [0.4 - 0.5[, Cr_5 \in [0.5 - 0.6[, Cr_6 \in [0.6 - 0.7[, Cr_7 \in [0.7 - 0.8[, Cr_8 \in [0.8 - 0.9[, Cr_9 \in [0.9, 1[\}$, hence $NoC_{total} = 7 \times 8 \times 2 = 112$ combinations.
- $PS_{max} = 125$ and $PS_{min} = 30$.
- $arch_{size}$ was set to a value of $1.4PS$ and $2.6PS$ for the 10D and 30D problems, respectively. The reason for its value when solving the 30D problems was to maintain diversity.

The results obtained are presented in Table 1. For the 10D problems, it was found that the algorithm was able to obtain the optimal solution for every problem. Its performance was robust (the average results achieved were the optimal) for all test problems, except C02, C07 and C11. For the 30D test problems, the algorithms was able to obtain very good results, in comparison with those in the literature. Although its performance was robust for most of the test problems, it faced difficulties to achieve similar performance for some multi-modal problems, i.e., C13.

Also, Fig. 1 presents the best 10 combinations of Cr, F and SO, for all problems with 10D, recorded the end of the evolutionary process, of a single run. From this figure, it can be concluded that one set of control parameters can be suitable for one search operator, but it may not suit another search operator. To add to this, no single combination of operators and parameters is the best for all test problems.

4.1   Comparison with the State-of-the-Art Algorithms

The DCDE's results were also compared to those of (1) dynamic selection of DE parameters (DE-DPS) [10], (2) adaptive ranking mutation operator based DE (ECHT-ARMOR-DE) [21], which used an ensemble of CHTs, parameters and operators; and (3) εDEag [22] (the winner of the CEC2010 competition). The detailed results are shown in Table 1.

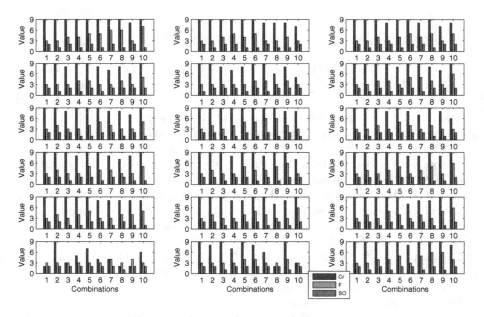

Fig. 1. Best 10 combinations of Cr, F and SO for all problems with 10D recorded at the end of the evolutionary process

Table 1. Function values achieved by DCDE, εdeag, ECHT-ARMOR-DE and DE-DPS for the CEC2010 constrained problems. "*" and "-" refer to infeasible solutions

Prob.	Algorithm	10D			30D		
		Best	Mean	Std.	Best	Mean	Std.
C01	DCDE	-7.473104E-01	-7.473104E-01	8.535312E-14	-8.218844E-01	-8.207086E-01	1.790135E-03
	DE-DPS	-7.473104E-01	-7.473104E-01	2.26623E-16	-8.21884E-01	-8.212036E-01	1.79648E-03
	εDEag	-7.473104E-01	-7.470402E-01	1.323339E-03	-8.218255E-01	-8.208687E-01	7.103893E-04
	ECHT-ARMOR-DE	-7.4730E-01	-7.4700E-0	1.4E-03	-8.1806E-01	-7.8992E-01	2.51E-02
C02	DCDE	-2.2777E+00	-2.2754E+00	9.54058E-03	-2.280919E+00	-2.197439E+00	1.062499E-01
	DE-DPS	-2.2777E+00	-2.2775E+00	2.54035E-04	-2.280671E+00	-2.244631E+00	5.20548E-02
	εDEag	-2.2777E+00	-2.2695E+00	2.38978E-02	-2.169248E+00	-2.151424E+00	1.197582E-02
	ECHT-ARMOR-DE	-2.2777E+00	-2.2770E+00	3.3E-03	-2.2607E+00	-2.1706E+00	7.36E-02
C03	DCDE	0.000000E+00	0.000000E+00	0.000000E+00	0.000000E+00	2.609221E-24	1.974308E-24
	DE-DPS	0.000000E+00	0.000000E+00	0.000000E+00	1.6200E-19	1.8479E-13	4.17994E-13
	εDEag	0.000000E+00	0.000000E+00	0.000000E+00	2.867347E+01	2.883785E+01	8.047159E-01
	ECHT-ARMOR-DE	0.000000E+00	0.000000E+00	0.000000E+00	2.5801E-24	2.6380E+01	7.94E+00
C04	DCDE	-1.000000E-05	-1.000000E-05	0.00000E+00	-3.333333E-06	-3.333333E-06	2.267611E-15
	DE-DPS	-1.000000E-05	-1.000000E-05	9.09633E-15	-3.3318E-06	-3.3123E-06	2.03926E-08
	εDEag	-9.992345E-06	-9.918452E-06	1.5467300E-07	4.698111E-03	8.162973E-03	3.067785E-03
	ECHT-ARMOR-DE	-1.00000E-05	-1.0000E-05	0.00000E+00	-3.3326E-06	8.3713E-02	2.89E-01
C05	DCDE	-4.836106E+02	-4.836106E+02	3.480934E-13	-4.836106E+02	-4.836106E+02	2.568459E-13
	DE-DPS	-4.836106E+02	-4.836106E+02	1.25826E-10	-4.836106E+02	-4.836106E+02	4.42074E-06
	εDEag	-4.836106E+02	-4.8361E+02	3.89035E-13	-4.531307E+02	-4.495460E+02	2.899105E+00
	ECHT-ARMOR-DE	-4.8361E+02	-4.8361E+02	0.0E+00	-4.8122E+02	-4.3355E+02	1.46E+02
C06	DCDE	-5.786624E+02	-5.786624E+02	1.292068E-13	-5.306379E+02	-5.306379E+02	3.370340E-12
	DE-DPS	-5.786624E+02	-5.78662E+02	8.05379E-04	-5.306379E+02	-5.306329E+02	5.89364E-03
	εDEag	-5.786581E+02	-5.786528E+02	3.6271690E-03	-5.285750E+02	-5.279068E+02	4.748378E-01
	ECHT-ARMOR-DE	-5.7866E+02	-5.7866E+02	4.0E-13	-5.2465E+02	-4.8931E+02	1.32E+02
C07	DCDE	0.000000E+00	0.000000E+00	0.0000000E+00	0.000000E+00	4.035279E-26	6.703154E-26
	DE-DPS	0.000000E+00	0.000000E+00	0.0000000E+00	5.48786E-20	1.03359E-13	2.20540E-13
	εDEag	0.000000E+00	0.000000E+00	0.0000000E+00	1.147112E-15	2.603632E-15	1.233430E-15
	ECHT-ARMOR-DE	0.000000E+00	0.000000E+00	0.000000E+00	0.000000E+00	1.0789E-25	2.20E-25
C08	DCDE	0.000000E+00	7.585162E+00	5.041295E+00	0.000000E+00	1.176962E-25	2.939178E-25
	DE-DPS	0.00000E+00	3.950387E+00	5.01904E+00	4.575719E-13	3.447568E-09	8.86366E-09
	εDEag	0.00000E+00	6.727528E+00	5.560648E+00	2.518693E-14	7.831464E-14	4.855177E-14
	ECHT-ARMOR-DE	0.00000E+00	7.5262E+00	5.0E+00	0.000000E+00	2.0101E+01	4.70E+01
C09	DCDE	0.00000E+00	0.000000E+00	0.0000000E+00	2.079289E-27	1.152400E-25	1.323484E-25
	DE-DPS	0.000000E+00	0.000000E+00	0.0000000E+00	3.81580E-23	5.29059E-14	1.27939E-13
	εDEag	0.00000E+00	0.000000E+00	0.0000000E+00	2.770665E-16	1.072140E+01	2.821923E+01
	ECHT-ARMOR-DE	0.000000E+00	1.7633E-01	8.8E-01	0.000000E+00	4.6110E+00	2.31E+01
C10	DCDE	0.00000E+00	0.000000E+00	0.0000000E+00	0.000000E+00	9.839902E-26	1.027787E-25
	DE-DPS	0.000000E+00	0.000000E+00	0.0000000E+00	1.63778E-21	2.23928E-13	6.24058E-13
	εDEag	0.000000E+00	0.000000E+00	0.0000000E+00	3.252002E+01	3.326175E+01	4.545577E-01
	ECHT-ARMOR-DE	0.000000E+00	0.000000E+00	0.000000E+00	6.029E-13	6.5536E+01	1.07E+02
C11	DCDE	-1.522713E-03	-1.522713E-03	1.760165E-14	-3.923439E-04	-3.923438E-04	9.750780E-11
	DE-DPS	-1.52271E-03	-1.52271E-03	3.14275E-12	-3.92344E-04	-3.923423E-04	8.77688E-10
	εDEag	-1.52271E-03	-1.52271E-03	6.3410350E-11	-3.268462E-04	-2.863882E-04	2.707605E-05
	ECHT-ARMOR-DE	-1.5227E-03	-	4.4E-02	-3.9234E-04	-	5.28E-03
C12	DCDE	-5.700899E+02	-2.597412E+02	1.430207E+02	-1.992635E-01	-1.992635E-01	4.099412E-09
	DE-DPS	-1.9925E-01	-1.9925E-01	4.19599E-01	-1.992635E-01	-1.9926E-01	2.60287E-08
	εDEag	-5.700899E+02	-3.367349E+02	1.7821660E+02	-1.991453E-01	3.562330E+02	2.889253E+02
	ECHT-ARMOR-DE	-1.9925E-01	-1.9925E-01	1.6E-13	-1.9926E-01	-1.6076E-01	1.93E-01
C13	DCDE	-6.84294E+01	-6.84294E+01	5.674449E-06	-6.8429E+01	-6.1863E+01	2.53349E+00
	DE-DPS	-6.84294E+01	-6.84294E+01	0.0000000E+00	-6.8429E+01	-6.63314E+01	2.08493E+00
	εDEag	-6.84294E+01	-6.842936E+01	1.0259600E-06	-6.64247E+01	-6.53531E+01	5.73301E+01
	ECHT-ARMOR-DE	-6.8429E+01	-6.7169E+01	2.1E+00	-6.7416E+01	-6.4646E+01	1.97E+00
C14	DCDE	0.000000E+00	0.000000E+00	0.0000000E+00	0.000000E+00	3.537636E-26	6.760738E-26
	DE-DPS	0.000000E+00	0.000000E+00	0.000000E+00	8.925796E-21	5.137406E-14	1.31791E-13
	εDEag	0.000000E+00	0.000000E+00	0.000000E+00	5.015863E-14	3.089407E-13	5.608409E-13
	ECHT-ARMOR-DE	0.000000E+00	0.000000E+00	0.000000E+00	1.5809E-27	6.6135E+02	2.47E+03
C15	DCDE	0.000000E+00	0.000000E+00	0.0000000E+00	0.000000E+00	3.216546E-26	2.776381E-26
	DE-DPS	0.000000E+00	5.438912E-26	2.19329E-25	6.336258E-20	1.957805E-13	5.22687E-13
	εDEag	0.000000E+00	1.798980E-01	8.8131560E-01	2.160345E+01	2.160376E+01	1.104834E-04
	ECHT-ARMOR-DE	0.0000E+00	2.8246E+00	1.6E+00	1.1716E-04	3.1316E+08	1.20E+09
C16	DCDE	0.000000E+00	0.000000E+00	0.0000000E+00	0.000000E+00	0.000000E+00	0.000000E+00
	DE-DPS	0.000000E+00	0.000000E+00	0.0000000E+00	0.000000E+00	0.000000E+00	0.0000000E+00
	εDEag	0.000000E+00	3.702054E-01	3.7104790E-01	0.000000E+00	2.168404E-21	1.062297E-20
	ECHT-ARMOR-DE	0.000000E+00	2.8478E-02	5.0E-02	0.000000E+00	0.000000E+00	0.000000E+00
C17	DCDE	0.000000E+00	2.988057E-30	1.327924E-29	2.060608E-17	1.133124E-06	3.979964E-06
	DE-DPS	0.000000E+00	1.061273E-24	3.88726E-24	3.236013E-12	8.766191E-03	1.55966E-01
	εDEag	1.463180E-17	1.249561E-01	1.9371970E-01	2.165719E-01	6.326487E+00	4.986691E+00
	ECHT-ARMOR-DE	0.00000E+00	3.6978E-33	3.1E-33	3.3564E-16	4.0336E-01	3.51E-01
C18	DCDE	0.000000E+00	5.272224E-24	1.649100E-23	3.322699E-21	1.291713E-13	6.203728E-13
	DE-DPS	0.000000E+00	3.209082E-23	7.12457E-23	6.747743E-13	9.459914E-08	1.91224E-07
	εDEag	3.731440E-20	9.678765E-19	1.8112340E-18	1.226054E+00	8.754569E+01	1.664753E+02
	ECHT-ARMOR-DE	0.000000E+00	0.000000E+00	0.000000E+00	0.000000E+00	0.000000E+00	0.000000E+00

In comparison with the above mentioned algorithms, DCDE and DE-DPS were able to reach a 100 % feasibility rate (FR), but εDEag attained a 12 % FR for C12 and the FR of ECHT-ARMOR-DE was less than 100 % (no exact FR was reported in the corresponding paper).

Considering the quality of the solutions obtained, a summary is reported in Table 2. The results for the 10D problems clearly showed the ability of DCDE to obtain better results for more test problems than the other algorithms. DCDE had superior performance in solving the 30D problems.

Statistically, based on the Wilcoxon signed rank test, the algorithm was found superior to all the other algorithms, especially for the 30D problems. Also, the Friedman test was undertaken to rank all algorithms based on the average fitness values achieved. The results are shown in Table 3. Generally, DCDE was ranked 1st followed by DE-DPS, ECHT-ARMOR-DE and εDEag, respectively.

Table 2. A Comparison Summary of DCDE against DE-DPS, ECHT-ARMOR-DE and εDEag

Algorithms	Results	10D			30D		
		Better	Similar	Worse	Better	Similar	Worse
DCDE vs. DE-DPS	Best	1	17	0	11	7	0
	Mean	6	10	2	13	2	3
DCDE vs. ECHT-ARMOR-DE	Best	4	14	0	12	4	2
	Mean	7	7	4	15	1	2
DCDE vs. εDEag	Best	1	17	0	17	1	0
	Mean	9	7	2	16	0	2

Table 3. Ranks of DCDE, DE-DPS, ECHT-ARMOR-DE and εDEag based on the Friedman Test

Rank	Algorithms			
	DCDE	DE-DPS	ECHT-ARMOR-DE	εDEag
10D	2.11	2.25	2.75	2.89
30D	1.47	2.03	3.22	3.28

5 Conclusions and Future Work

To cover a research gap found in the literature, that was the current DE algorithms measure the success or failure of a DE operator without considering the set of parameters that was assigned to it during the optimization process. Therefore, in this paper, a new framework, was introduced. In it, three sets (F_{set}, Cr_{set} and SO_{set}) were initiated. Then, each individual in the population was assigned a random combination of F, Cr and SO. The success rate of each combination was accumulated over generations. Then, the number of combinations was linearly reduced along with the population size.

The performance of the proposed algorithm was tested on a well-known set of constrained problems. From the results obtained, the proposed algorithm showed consistently better performance in comparison with three state-of-the-art algorithms, in terms of its ability to obtain a 100 % feasibility rate and better quality solutions. Statistical tests were also undertaken which showed the superiority of the proposed methodology.

For future work, we intend to analyze the algorithm's components and solve real-world problems.

Acknowledgment. This work was supported by an Australian Research Council Discovery Project (Grant# DP150102583) awarded to A/Prof. Ruhul Sarker.

References

1. Davis, L., et al.: Handbook of Genetic Algorithms, vol. 115. Van Nostrand Reinhold, New York (1991)
2. Storn, R., Price, K.: Differential evolution-a simple and efficient heuristic for global optimization over continuous spaces. J. Global Optim. **11**(4), 341–359 (1997)
3. Hansen, N., Müller, S., Koumoutsakos, P.: Reducing the time complexity of the derandomized evolution strategy with covariance matrix adaptation (cma-es). Evol. Comput. **11**(1), 1–18 (2003)
4. Feng, L., Yang, Y.-F., Wang, Y.-X.: A new approach to adapting control parameters in differential evolution algorithm. In: Li, X., et al. (eds.) SEAL 2008. LNCS, vol. 5361, pp. 21–30. Springer, Heidelberg (2008)
5. Elsayed, S.M., Sarker, R.A., Essam, D.L.: Multi-operator based evolutionary algorithms for solving constrained optimization problems. Comput. Oper. Res. **38**(12), 1877–1896 (2011)
6. Elsayed, S.M., Sarker, R.A., Essam, D.L.: Self-adaptive differential evolution incorporating a heuristic mixing of operators. Comput. Optim. Appl. **54**(3), 771–790 (2013)
7. Zamuda, A., Brest, J.: Population reduction differential evolution with multiple mutation strategies in real world industry challenges. In: Rutkowski, L., Korytkowski, M., Scherer, R., Tadeusiewicz, R., Zadeh, L.A., Zurada, J.M. (eds.) EC 2012 and SIDE 2012. LNCS, vol. 7269, pp. 154–161. Springer, Heidelberg (2012)
8. Brest, J., Boskovic, B., Zamuda, A., Fister, I., Mezura-Montes, E.: Real parameter single objective optimization using self-adaptive differential evolution algorithm with more strategies. In: IEEE Congress on Evolutionary Computation (CEC), pp. 377–383. IEEE (2013)
9. Tvrdík, J., Polakova, R.: Competitive differential evolution for constrained problems. In: IEEE Congress on Evolutionary Computation (CEC), pp. 1–8. IEEE (2010)
10. Sarker, R., Elsayed, S., Ray, T.: Differential evolution with dynamic parameters selection for optimization problems. IEEE Trans. Evol. Comput. **18**(5), 689–707 (2014)
11. Mallipeddi, R., Suganthan, P.N.: Ensemble of constraint handling techniques. IEEE Trans. Evol. Comput. **14**(4), 561–579 (2010)
12. Liu, J., Lampinen, J.: A fuzzy adaptive differential evolution algorithm. Soft Comput. **9**(6), 448–462 (2005)

13. Brest, J., Greiner, S., Boskovic, B., Mernik, M., Zumer, V.: Self-adapting control parameters in differential evolution: a comparative study on numerical benchmark problems. IEEE Trans. Evol. Comput. **10**(6), 646–657 (2006)
14. Zhang, J., Sanderson, A.C.: Jade: adaptive differential evolution with optional external archive. IEEE Trans. Evol. Comput. **13**(5), 945–958 (2009)
15. Mallipeddi, R., Suganthan, P.N.: Problem definitions and evaluation criteria for the cec 2010 competition on constrained real-parameter optimization. Technical report, Nanyang Technological University, Singapore (2010)
16. Storn, R., Price, K.: Differential evolution-a simple and efficient adaptive scheme for global optimization over continuous spaces, vol. 3. ICSI, Berkeley (1995)
17. Qin, A.K., Huang, V.L., Suganthan, P.N.: Differential evolution algorithm with strategy adaptation for global numerical optimization. IEEE Trans. Evol. Comput. **13**(2), 398–417 (2009)
18. Tanabe, R., Fukunaga, A.: Improving the search performance of shade using linear population size reduction. In: IEEE Congress on Evolutionary Computation (CEC), pp. 1658–1665, July 2014
19. Deb, K.: An efficient constraint handling method for genetic algorithms. Comput. Methods Appl. Mech. Eng. **186**(2), 311–338 (2000)
20. Mezura Montes, E., Coello Coello, C.A.: Adding a diversity mechanism to a simple evolution strategy to solve constrained optimization problems. In: IEEE Congress on Evolutionary Computation, vol. 1, pp. 6–13. IEEE (2003)
21. Gong, W., Cai, Z., Liang, D.: Adaptive ranking mutation operator based differential evolution for constrained optimization. IEEE Trans. Cybern. **45**(4), 716–727 (2015)
22. Takahama, T., Sakai, S.: Constrained optimization by the ε constrained differential evolution with an archive and gradient-based mutation. In: IEEE Congress on Evolutionary Computation (CEC), pp. 1–9. IEEE (2010)

Exploring the Feasible Space Using Constraint Consensus in Solving Constrained Optimization Problems

Noha M. Hamza$^{(\boxtimes)}$, Daryl L. Essam, and Ruhul A. Sarker

School of Engineering and Information Technology,
University of New South Wales at Canberra, Canberra, Australia
noha.hamza@student.adfa.edu.au

Abstract. Over the last few years, constraint consensus methods have been used for the movement of infeasible solutions towards feasible space, when solving constrained optimization problem. In this paper, a novel approach is proposed that is based on the concept of constraint consensus to improve feasible individuals, rather than infeasible ones, in which a feasible individual is considered as an infeasible one, if its fitness value is worse than a dynamic reference point. The obtained new solutions are then passed to differential evolution to be evolved. The proposed algorithm has been tested on the CEC2010 benchmark constrained problems. The results demonstrate better performance of the proposed algorithm, in terms of quality of solutions and computational time, in comparison with a standard differential evolution algorithm, as well as a set of state-of-the-art algorithms.

Keywords: Constrained optimization · Constraint consensus · Differential evolution

1 Introduction

There exist a considerable number of real-world decision processes that require the solution of constrained optimization problems (COPs). These COPs may contain linear and non-linear functions with equality and in-equality constraints. Some of these functions may not satisfy certain properties, such as differentiability, continuity and convexity [1, 2], that are required by conventional optimization methods [3]. Thus the existence of any non-standard functions in COPs makes them challenging to solve [4].

Evolutionary algorithms (EAs), such as genetic algorithm (GA) [5] and differential evolution (DE) [6], are population based algorithms that mimic some sort of selection, crossover and mutation to find an optimal solution. EAs do not require the satisfaction of specific mathematical properties [2], are robust to dynamic changes and have broader applicability in practice [7]. Although EAs have a successful history of solving COPs, there is no guarantee that they will reach an optimal solution [8], and they are often slow in reaching the feasible region in many cases.

Recently, the constraint consensus (CC) methods have been incorporated with EAs to help infeasible solutions to move toward feasible space. Such techniques are based

© Springer International Publishing Switzerland 2016
T. Ray et al. (Eds.): ACALCI 2016, LNAI 9592, pp. 89–100, 2016.
DOI: 10.1007/978-3-319-28270-1_8

on projection algorithms, which employ some form of a projection for each violated constraint, most commonly a projection in the gradient or anti gradient direction [9]. The performance of such algorithms has shown the benefit of incorporating CC with EAs. In a few recent research studies, an additional operation has been applied to selected infeasible individuals in each generation to help to move them closer to feasible space [10–13]. Such an operation used a modified version of the traditional CC method. In fact, CC assists infeasible solution vectors to quickly move towards feasible region, by making a consensus among the currently violated constraints. It determines the direction and step size that are required to move towards feasibility in each step [14]. However, the CC methods deal only with constraints, but not with the fitness function. The approach introduced by [10–13] is a two-step sequential approach, where the CC methods assist in reducing the constraint violations of a few infeasible individuals in each generation and then the usual evolutionary search operators are applied to the population. In those research studies, the CC methods were applied to the infeasible individuals for making possible improvements in feasibility, where a projection mechanism was used for each violated constraint. Note that the constraint violation of any feasible individual is zero.

In this paper, our interest is to deal with feasible individuals, rather than infeasible ones. To develop the new approach based on feasible individuals, we define a new term "fitness deviation", which means the deviation of the fitness value of a feasible individual, from the fitness value of a reference point. Also, the CC method works with DE, with an objective of minimizing this deviation. In the proposed algorithm, the population is divided into two groups; feasible and infeasible, if any exist. Some of the feasible individuals are then evolved using the CC method. Then the generated new points replace the old ones, and the entire population is updated. After that, the DE mutation is applied to the whole population. The process continues until a stopping criterion is met.

The performance of the proposed algorithm was tested by solving a set of constrained benchmark problems with 30 dimensions [15]. The results show that the proposed algorithm is able to obtain better solutions than standard DE with lower computational time and it also shows superiority to state-of-the-art algorithms.

This paper is organized as follows. After the introduction, Sect. 2 describes the DE algorithm. Section 3 discusses an overview of the constraint consensus method. Section 4 demonstrates the design of the proposed algorithm, while the experimental results and analysis are presented in Sect. 5. Finally, the conclusions are given in Sect. 6.

2 Differential Evolution

Differential Evolution (DE) is a population based stochastic direct search method, in which for each parent (target vector), $\vec{x}_{i,t}$, in the population, a new mutated vector (mutant vector), $\vec{v}_{i,t}$, is generated using a mutation strategy [6]. A final vector, $\vec{u}_{i,t}$, is then created by combining the mutant vector with the target vector while using a pre-specified crossover rate. A comparison is then made between each parent and its offspring, and the better one is copied to the next generation.

DE has been successfully applied in solving different optimization problems, including non-linear and non-differentiable ones. However DE prematurely converges when solving problems with multiple local optima, because it loses diversity [16].

2.1 Mutation Strategy

For DE, a considerable number of mutation operators have been introduced. These mutation operators often possess different search capabilities in various stages of the evolution process [17]. The variants are classified using the notation DE/base/num/cross; "base" indicates the method of selecting a parent that will form the base vector, "num" indicates the number of difference vectors that are used to perturb the parent and "cross" indicates the crossover operator. For example, in the simplest mutation, "DE/rand/1/bin", a mutant vector is generated by multiplying the amplification factor (F) by the difference of two random vectors, and the result is added to a third random vector [18], as follows:

$$\vec{v}_{i,t} = \vec{x}_{r_1,t} + F \times \left(\vec{x}_{r_2,t} - \vec{x}_{r_3,t} \right) \tag{1}$$

where r_1, r_2, r_3 are random numbers $(1, 2, \ldots, NP)$, $r_1 \neq r_2 \neq r_3 \neq z$, $\vec{x}$ is a decision vector, which represents the individuals at the current population, NP is the population size, the scaling factor F is a positive control parameter for scaling the difference vector, $F \in [0, 1]$, and t is the current generation.

2.2 Crossover

Two crossover operators, known as exponential and binomial crossover, are widely used in DE [16].

The binomial crossover is performed as follows:

$$u_{i,j,t} = \begin{cases} v_{i,j,t}, & if\,(rand \leq Cr\ or\ j = j_{rand}) \\ x_{i,j,t}, & \text{otherwise.} \end{cases} \tag{2}$$

where $rand \in [0, 1]$, $j_{rand} \in [1, 2, \ldots, D]$ is a randomly chosen index, which ensures $\vec{u}_{i,t}$ gets at least one component from $\vec{v}_{i,t}$, and the crossover rate, $Cr \in [0, 1]$, is a user defined parameter, which control the contribution of the mutant vector while producing the trial one.

3 Constraint Consensus (CC) Method

The projection algorithms employ some form of a projection for each violated constraint, most commonly a projection in the gradient or anti gradient direction to solve feasibility problems with a set of convex constraints. However, the Constraint Consensus (CC) method [19] uses different types of projection algorithms that provide approximate solutions to feasibility problems, which can include nonlinear and non-convex constraints. The main idea is to assist a currently infeasible point to quickly move towards a feasible region, by making a consensus among the currently violated constraints to define the direction and distance that are required to achieve feasibility. The movements are updated repeatedly until a stopping condition is met [14].

In the process, CC starts from an initial infeasible solution and then constructs a feasibility vector for each violated constraint of some existing solution. The feasibility vector approximates the move from the current infeasible point, to the closest feasible solution, for each violated constraint. The calculation of the feasibility vectors in CC is exact for linear constraints; however a linear approximation can be generated (known as linear feasibility vectors) for nonlinear constraints. The linear feasibility vector moves the infeasible solution in a parallel direction to the gradient of the violated constraint and the step size of the movement is calculated by using a first order Taylor series expansion of the constraint function around the current solution [12, 14, 20], such that:

$$\left(\vec{x}_{k+1,c} - \vec{x}_k \right) = \frac{-vio_c}{\left\| \nabla g_c(\vec{x}_k)^T \right\|^2} \nabla g_c(\vec{x}_k)^T \tag{3}$$

where

- $\nabla g_c(\vec{x}_k)$ is the gradient of the cth violated constraint, $c \in C = (1, 2, \ldots, m)$, $\nabla g_c(\vec{x}_k)^T$ is the transposition of its gradient, and $\left\| \nabla g_c(x_k)^T \right\|$ is its length.
- vio_c: is the constraint violation $|g_c(\vec{x}_k) - b_c|$, $vio_c = 0$ for satisfied constraints.
- k is the number of CC generations, $k = 0, 1, \ldots, \mu$, where μ is the maximum number of CC generations.
- $\vec{x}_k$ is the current infeasible point at k^{th} generation "current iteration", and $\vec{x}_{k+1,c}$ is the estimated feasible point for each c violated constraint at $k + 1^{th}$ generation.

To deal with non-differentiable and discontinuous functions, an approximate gradient $(\nabla g_c(\vec{x}_k))$ is calculated numerically in our algorithm. $\nabla g_c(\vec{x}_k)$ is equal to $(\frac{g_c(\vec{x}+\Delta) - g_c(\vec{x})}{\Delta})$, where Δ represents a small change in $\vec{x}$ (here it is equal to 0.0001).

The feasibility vectors for all violated constraints are joined into a consensus vector which is then used to update the current point. The CC steps are repeated until a predefined stopping condition is satisfied [9, 14], such that (1) the length of every feasibility vector is less than a predefined feasibility distance threshold (α) (e.g. 10^{-6}), (2) the length of the consensus vector is less than a movement tolerance (β) which is caused when the consensus vector becomes too short, or (3) more than μ generations have been completed.

4 Exploring Feasible Space Using Constraint Consensus

In this section, the proposed algorithm (EFS-CC-DE) is introduced, and then the constraint handling technique is discussed.

4.1   Proposed Algorithm

As mentioned earlier, the CC method helps infeasible points to quickly move towards the feasible region by making a consensus among the currently violated constraints. However, can we use a similar concept for feasible individuals (those with their sum the constraints violations being zero) for improving their fitness values?

The proposed approach has two stages. In the first, CC is applied for a selected number of feasible solutions, if any exist. Then, those individuals, along with any remaining individuals, are evolved by DE. To clarify, the proposed approach starts with setting a reference point (z^*) in each generation, which represents the best solution found so far, either feasible or infeasible. The CC method is then used to help feasible solutions to move towards the reference point. In other words, any feasible solution, which is evaluated as greater than z^*, in the case of a minimization problem, may be handled by the concept of CC method to minimize its objective function deviation ($f_i - z^*$), where f_i is the objective function of individual i.

The main steps of the proposed algorithm are shown in Algorithm 1. Firstly, EFS-CC-DE randomly generates a set of NP individuals. Each $x_{i,j}$ is generated within a boundary based on the following equation:

$$x_{i,j} = L_j + rand \times (Upper_j - Lower_j) \tag{4}$$

where $Lower_j$ and $Upper_j$ are the lower and upper bounds for decision variable $x_{i,j}$, while $rand$ is a random number within $[0, 1]$. The fitness function value $f(x_{i,j})$ of each individual $x_{i,j}$ is then evaluated, and the individual which has the best fitness function value, either feasible or infeasible, serves as a reference point (z^*) [21].

$$z^* = \min(f(x_{i,j}) | x \in \Omega) \tag{5}$$

If there are feasible individuals, then some of them are selected. For the selected individuals (P_{fes}); the objective violation of the ith individual (obj_{vio_i}) is calculated as follows:

$$obj_{vio_i} = |z^* - f(x_{i,j})|, \text{ where } 1 \le i \le P_{fes} \tag{6}$$

For each individual $obj_{vio_i} > 0$, the linear feasibility vector is calculated to approximate the move from the current feasible point (x_i) to z^*, say $\vec{x}_{fv,i}$, to z^*, such that

$$\vec{x}_{fv,i} - \vec{x}_i = \frac{-obj_{vio_i}}{||\nabla f(\vec{x}_i)||^2} \nabla f(\vec{x}_i)^T \tag{7}$$

where $\nabla f(\vec{x}_i)$ is the gradient of the objective function of $\vec{x}_i$, and $\vec{x}_{fv,i} - \vec{x}_i$ is the feasibility vector in the CC method.

Then the population is updated, in which the new (P_{fes}) individuals are merged with the remaining $NP-P_{fes}$ individuals. Then for each individual in NP, new offspring are generated according to:

Algorithm 1: EFS-CC-DE

STEP 1: In generation $t = 0$, generate an initial random population of size NP. The variables in each individual (i) are generated using equation 4. Update the Fitness Evaluations (FEs).

STEP 2: for each individual (i) in NP, generate its F_i, Cr_i and φ_i

STEP 3: Divide NP into two groups. The first group contains the feasible solutions, if found, and the second group contains the infeasible solutions, if found.

STEP 4: At each generation, if there are feasible solutions and FEs are less than 300,000, **then** to P_{fes} feasible individuals, calculate the feasibility vector, for each, using equation 7, and update FEs; **else;** go to **Step 6**.

STEP 5: The new P_{fes} individuals, obtained from **Step 4**, will replace the older ones, if they are better, and are then merged with the other individuals.

STEP 6: For each individual ($\vec{x}_i$) in NP, a new offspring ($\vec{u}_i$) is generated using (8), and FEs are updated.

STEP 7: Selection: if $\vec{u}_i$ is better than $\vec{x}_i$, based on the fitness value and/or constraints violation, accept it for the next generation. Sort the entire population based on the objective value and/or constraint violation.

STEP 8: Stop if the termination criterion is met; else set $t = t + 1$, and go to **Step 3**.

$$
u_{i,j} = \begin{cases} x_{i,j} + F_i \cdot \left(x_{r_{i1},j} - x_{r_{i2},j} \right) + F_i \cdot \left(x_{\varphi,j} - x_{i,j} \right) & if\,(rand \leq Cr_i\ or\ j = j_{rand}) \\ x_{i,j} & \text{otherwise} \end{cases} \quad (8)
$$

where φ is an integer number between $[1-0.1NP]$.

For each newly generated individual, if it is better than its parent, it survives for the next generation, and the entire population is sorted based on the fitness function and/or constraint violation.

4.2 Constraint Handling

In this paper, the superiority of feasible solution technique is used to select individuals [22], in which: (i) between two feasible solutions, the fittest one (according to fitness value) is better, i.e. $f(\vec{x}_1) < f(\vec{x}_2)$, (ii) a feasible solution is always better than an infeasible one, (iii) between two infeasible solutions, the one having the smaller sum of its constraint violation is preferred, i.e. $vio(\vec{x}_1) < vio(\vec{x}_2)$. Equality constraints are transformed into inequalities of the following form, where ε is a small tolerance, i.e. 0.0001, and E is the number of equality constraints:

$$
|h_e(\vec{x})| - \varepsilon \leq 0,\ for\ e = 1, \ldots, E \quad (9)
$$

5 Experimental Results

In this section, we present and analyze the experimental results of the proposed algorithm by solving set of benchmark problems introduced in the CEC2010 special session and competition on constrained optimization problems (30D) [15] (we assume 30D problems are much difficult than 10D ones). These problems possess different mathematical properties, such as the objective function and/or the constraints are either linear or non-linear, the constraints are of either equality or inequality type, the objective function is either unimodal or multi-modal, and the feasible space may be very tiny compared to the search space.

The algorithm has been coded using Matlab, and has been run on a PC with a 3.40 GHz Core (TM) i7 processor, 8G RAM and Windows 7. Based on the analysis presented in [23], the values of the parameters, are set such that NP is 100 individuals and $P_{fes} = 10$ % of the feasible solutions. F_i is a random number $\in [0.4 - 0.9]$. In regard to Cr_i, for each individual in the population at generation t, $Cr_{i,t}$ is randomly selected from $\{0.95, 0.75$ or $0.4\}$ [24], the total number of Fitness Evaluations (FEs) was set to 20000D, and the number of independent runs for each problem was set to 25. CC's parameters were chosen as follows: $\alpha = 10^{-6}$ and $\mu = 1.0$ CC generation, we use linear feasibility vectors as shown in (7).

5.1   Effect of Proposed Algorithm

The comparison summary of DE and the proposed algorithm, for the 30D test problems, is presented in Table 1. From this table, it is clear that the number of problems in which better average fitness values were obtained by the proposed algorithm, is higher than those obtained by DE. In regards to the best fitness values obtained, EFS-CC-DE is slightly better in terms of the number of best values obtained in comparison to DE by 8. Based on the average results, EFS-CC-DE is better than the DE by 14 test problems.

Table 1. Comparison among EFS-CC-DE and DE based on the 30D test problems

D	Comparison	Results	Better	Equal	Worse	Decision
30D	EFS-CC-DE - to - DE	Best	8	7	3	$\approx$
		Average	14	3	1	$+$

A non-parametric statistical significance test, namely the Wilcoxon Signed Rank Test [4, 25], has also been performed. The Wilcoxon test results, regarding the best and average fitness values are presented in Table 1. As a null hypothesis, it is assumed that there is no significant difference between the best and/or mean values of two samples, while the alternative hypothesis is that there is a significant difference in the best and/or average fitness values of the two samples, using a 5 % significance level. Based on the test results/rankings, we have assigned one of three signs (+, -, and $\approx$) for the comparison of any two algorithms (shown in the 'Decision' column), where the "+" sign means that the first algorithm is significantly better than the second, the "$-$" sign means that the first algorithm is significantly worse, and the "$\approx$" sign means there is no significant difference between the two algorithms. From Table 1, it is clear that EFS-CC-DE is significantly better than DE, based on the average results obtained for all test problems. However, there is no statistically significant difference among EFS-CC-DE and DE in regard to the best results obtained.

In addition to judging the quality of solutions, we have compared the average computational time and the number of fitness evaluations required to obtain the optimal solution with an error margin of 0.0001, i.e. the stopping criteria is $[f(\vec{x}) - f(\overrightarrow{x^*}) \le 0.0001]$, where $f\left(\overrightarrow{x^*}\right)$ was the best known solution. The comparisons are shown in Table 2. From this table, it is clear that EFS-CC-DE is the best, as it consumes 16.19 % less computational time than DE. The number of average fitness evaluations taken by EFS-CC-DE is less than those of DE. EFS-CC-DE saves 22.35 % in comparison to DE.

Table 2. Comparison among EFS-CC-DE and DE, based on the average computational time and FEs

D	Algorithm	Total average Time	Total average FEs
30D	EFS-CC-DE	**58.06**	**318063.58**
	DE	67.45	389135.27

To further illustrate this, an example convergence plot, is depicted in Fig. 1, which shows that EFS-CC-DE converges at a faster rate than DE. In the plot, the x-axis represents the fitness evaluations, while the y-axis represents the average fitness value.

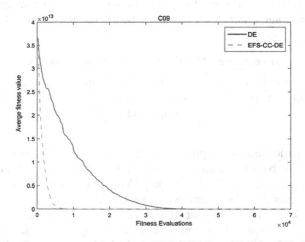

Fig. 1. Convergence plot for both EFS-CC-DE and DE for C09 (30D)

5.2   Comparison to State-of-the-Art Algorithms

Here the computational results of EFS-CC-DE are compared with a number of state-of-the-art algorithms εDEag [26], which won the CEC2010 constrained optimization competition, Adaptive Ranking Mutation Operator Based Differential Evolution for Constrained Optimization, ECHT-ARMOR-DE [27], and Co-evolutionary

Comprehensive Learning Particle Swarm Optimizer (Co-CLPSO) [28]. The detailed results are shown in Appendix A.

Considering the quality of the solutions obtained, a summary is reported in Table 3. From this table, EFS-CC-DE was clearly better than εDEag and Co-CLPSO for the majority of the test problems. EFS-CC-DE was found superior when compared with ECHT-ARMOR-DE for 10 and 14 test problems, based on the best and average results, respectively. Finally, based on the Wilcoxon test, EFS-CC-DE was significantly better than εDEag, Co-CLPSO and ECHT-ARMOR-DE.

Table 3. Comparison between of EFS-CC-DE, εDEag and ECHT-ARMOR-DE

D	Comparison	Results	Better	Equal	Worse	Decision
30D	EFS-CC-DE – to – εDEag	Best	17	1	0	+
		Average	13	0	5	+
	EFS-CC-DE – to – ECHT-ARMOR-DE	Best	10	6	2	+
		Average	14	1	3	+
	EFS-CC-DE – to – Co-CLIPSO	Best	16	2	0	+
		Average	17	0	1	+

6   Conclusions and Future Work

In this research, the concept of the CC method has been utilized to improve feasible individuals, rather than infeasible ones, to solve constrained optimization problems. This approach was inspired by the usefulness of the concept of the constraint consensus method that is used in the traditional optimization domain. However, it required the modification of the CC method for its appropriate use with feasible individuals. This approach was applied to only some of the feasible individuals in each generation, to minimize computational time while maintaining good diversity within the population.

The proposed algorithm (EFS-CC-DE) was tested on a well-known set of constrained problems and the results were compared with the same DE without applying the CC method. The results showed the effectiveness of using the CC method in terms of obtaining quality solutions at relatively lower computational time.

The results of the proposed algorithm were also compared with three state-of-the-art algorithms, and based on the quality of the solutions obtained, as well as a non-parametric statistical test, it showed that the proposed algorithm was superior to those algorithms.

For the future work, we intend to apply the proposed method for both feasible and infeasible individuals within a single framework.

Appendix A

See Appendix Table 4.

Table 4. Function values obtained by DE, EFS-CC-DE, εDEag, ECHT-ARMOR-DE and CO-CLIPSO for the CEC2010 (30D) test problems

Prob.	Algorithm	DE	EFS-CC-DE	εDEag	ECHT-ARMOR-DE	CO-CLIPSO
C01	Best	**−8.218843E-01**	−8.218825E-01	−8.218255E-01	−8.1806E-01	−8.0688E-01
	Average	−8.147209E-01	−7.980977E-01	**−8.208687E-01**	−7.8992E-01	−7.1598E-01
	St. d	7.387809E-03	2.901320E-02	**7.103893E-04**	2.51E-02	5.0252E-02
C02	Best	**−2.280973E + 00**	**−2.280973E + 00**	−2.169248E + 00	−2.2607E + 00	−2.2809
	Average	−2.273549E + 00	**−2.275677E + 00**	−2.151424E + 00	−2.1706E + 00	−2.2029
	St. d	4.195948E-03	**4.046198E-03**	1.197582E-02	7.36E-02	1.9267E-01
C03	Best	**0.000000E + 00**	**0.000000E + 00**	2.867347E + 01	2.5801E-24	–
	Average	4.436202E-21	**3.538459E-25**	2.883785E + 01	2.6380E + 01	–
	St. d	1.403361E-20	**4.619381E-25**	8.047159E-01	7.94E + 00	–
C04	Best	−3.332553E-06	**−3.332864E-06**	4.698111E-03	−3.3326E-06	−2.9300E-06
	Average	−3.309584E-06	**−3.329799E-06**	8.162973E-03	8.3713E-02	1.1269E-01
	St. d	2.629157E-08	**3.926758E-09**	3.067785E-03	2.89E-01	5.6335E-01
C05	Best	−4.836106E + 02	−4.836106E + 02	−4.531307E + 02	−4.8122E + 02	**−4.8360E + 02**
	Average	**−4.836106E + 02**	**−4.836106E + 02**	−4.495460E + 02	−4.3335E + 02	−3.1249E + 02
	St. d	3.147886E-08	2.533516E-06	2.899105E + 00	1.46E + 02	8.8332E + 01
C06	Best	−5.306378E + 02	**−5.306379E + 02**	−5.285750E + 02	−5.2465E + 02	−2.8601E + 02
	Average	−4.054263E + 02*	**−5.306348E + 02**	−5.279068E + 02	−4.8931E + 02	−2.4470E + 02
	St. d	2.580869E + 02	**7.556911E-03**	4.748378E-01	1.32E + 02	3.9481E + 01
C07	Best	**0.000000E + 00**	**0.000000E + 00**	1.147112E-15	**0.000000E + 00**	3.7861E-11
	Average	6.378598E-01	6.378598E-01	2.603632E-15	**1.0789E-25**	1.1163
	St. d	1.491658E + 00	1.491658E + 00	1.233430E-15	**2.20E-25**	1.8269
C08	Best	6.175302E-30	**0.000000E + 00**	2.518693E-14	**0.000000E + 00**	4.3114E-14
	Average	1.594650E-01	**4.133150E-27**	7.831464E-14	2.0101E + 01	4.7517E + 01
	St. d	7.973248E-01	**6.367448E-27**	4.855177E-14	4.70E + 01	1.1259E + 02
C09	Best	2.189841E-27	**0.000000E + 00**	2.770665E-16	**0.000000E + 00**	1.9695E + 02
	Average	2.102604E-01	**2.329347E-26**	1.072140E + 01	4.6110E + 00	1.4822E + 08
	St. d	7.425869E-01	**2.364385E-26**	2.821923E + 01	2.31E + 01	2.4509E + 08
C10	Best	3.215946E-25	**0.000000E + 00**	3.252002E + 01	6.0209E-13	3.1967E + 01
	Average	2.672508E-19	**2.051003E-26**	3.326175E + 01	6.5536E + 01	1.3951E + 09
	St. d	5.804783E-19	**1.793996E-26**	4.545577E-01	1.07E + 02	5.8438E + 09
C11	Best	−3.923439E-04	**−3.923439E-04**	−3.268462E-04	**−3.9234E-04**	–
	Average	1.132727E-03*	3.701916E-04	**−2.863882E-04**	–	–
	St. d	5.278412E-03	3.812677E-03	**2.707605E-05**	5.28E-03	–
C12	Best	**−1.992635E-01**	**−1.992635E-01**	−1.991453E-01	**−1.9926E-01**	−1.9926E-01
	Average	−1.992634E-01	**−1.992635E-01**	–	−1.6076E-01	−1.9911E-01
	St. d	4.325678E-09	**2.675864E-09**	2.889253E + 02	1.93E-01	1.1840E-04
C13	Best	**−6.770243E + 01**	−6.680096E + 01	−6.642473E + 01	−6.7416E + 01	−6.2752E + 01
	Average	−5.929649E + 01	−6.262695E + 01	−6.535310E + 01	**−6.4646E + 01**	−6.0774E + 01
	St. d	5.864591E + 00	3.312371E + 00	5.733005E-01	**1.97E + 00**	1.1176
C14	Best	2.111503E-22	**0.000000E + 00**	5.015863E-14	1.5809E-27	3.28834e-09
	Average	**1.594650E-01**	3.189299E-01	3.089407E-13	6.6135E + 02	0.0615242
	St. d	7.973248E-01	1.103846E + 00	**5.608409E-13**	2.47E + 03	0.307356
C15	Best	5.191573E-26	**0.000000E + 00**	2.160345E + 01	1.1716E-04	5.7499E-12

(Continued)

Table 4. (*Continued*)

Prob.	Algorithm	DE	EFS-CC-DE	εDEag	ECHT-ARMOR-DE	CO-CLIPSO
	Average	1.039801E-20	**4.603477E-28**	2.160376E + 01	3.1316E + 08	5.1059E + 01
	St. d	4.356723E-20	**1.178836E-27**	1.104834E-04	1.20E + 09	9.1759E + 01
C16	Best	**0.000000E + 00**	**0.000000E + 00**	**0.000000E + 00**	**0.000000E + 00**	**0.000000E + 00**
	Average	**0.000000E + 00**	**0.000000E + 00**	2.168404E-21	**0.000000E + 00**	5.2403E-16
	St. d	**0.000000E + 00**	**0.000000E + 00**	1.062297E-20	**0.000000E + 00**	4.6722E-16
C17	Best	**1.065707E-20**	5.968297E-19	2.165719E-01	3.3564E-16	1.5787E-01
	Average	1.018438E-03	**4.142044E-11**	6.326487E + 00	4.0336E-01	1.3919
	St. d	5.092191E-03	**1.020993E-10**	4.986691E + 00	3.51E-01	4.2621
C18	Best	3.121982E-17	3.089920E-19	1.226054E + 00	**0.000000E + 00**	6.0047E-02
	Average	1.312716E-08	3.646924E-12	8.754569E + 01	**0.000000E + 00**	1.0877E + 01
	St. d	6.560113E-08	1.223348E-11	1.664753E + 02	**0.000000E + 00**	3.7161E + 01

References

1. Barkat-Ullah, A.S.S.M.: An integrated evolutionary system for solving optimization problems. University of New South Wales At Australian Defence Force Academy (2009)
2. Sarker, R., Kamruzzaman, J., Newton, C.: Evolutionary optimization (EvOpt): a brief review and analysis. Int. J. Comput. Intell. Appl. **3**(4), 311–330 (2003)
3. Dantzig, G., Mukund, N.: Linear Programming 1: Introduction. Springer, New York (1997)
4. Elsayed, S.M., Sarker, R.A., Essam, D.L.: Multi-operator based evolutionary algorithms for solving constrained optimization Problems. Comput. Oper. Res. **38**(12), 1877–1896 (2011)
5. Goldberg, D.: Genetic Algorithms in Search, Optimization, and Machine Learning. Addison-Wesley, MA (1989)
6. Storn, R., Price, K.: Differential evolution - a simple and efficient adaptive scheme for global optimization over continuous spaces. Technical report, International Computer Science Institute (1995)
7. Fogel, L., Owens, J., Walsh, M.: Artificial Intelligence Through Simulated Evolution. Wiley, New York (1966)
8. Deb, K.: Multi-objective genetic algorithms: problem difficulties and construction of test problems. Evol. Comput. **7**(3), 205–230 (1999)
9. Chinneck, J.W.: The constraint consensus method for finding approximately feasible points in nonlinear programs. INFORMS J. Comput. **16**(3), 255–265 (2004)
10. Hamza, N., Sarker, R., Essam, D.: Differential evolution with multi-constraint consensus methods for constrained optimization. J. Glob. Optim. **57**(2), 583–611 (2013)
11. Hamza, N.M., Sarker, R.A., Essam, D.L.: Differential evolution with a mix of constraint consenus methods for solving a real-world optimization problem. In: 2012 IEEE Congress on Evolutionary Computation (CEC), pp. 1–7, 10-15 June 2012
12. Hamza, N.M., Elsayed, S.M., Essam, D.L., Sarker, R.A.: Differential evolution combined with constraint consensus for constrained optimization. In: IEEE Congress on Evolutionary Computation, pp. 865–872, 5-8 June 2011
13. Hamza, N.M., Sarker, R.A., Essam, D.L., Deb, K., Elsayed, S.M.: A constraint consensus memetic algorithm for solving constrained optimization problems. Eng. Optim. **46**(11), 1447–1464 (2013)
14. Ibrahim, W., Chinneck, J.W.: Improving solver success in reaching feasibility for sets of nonlinear constraints. Comput. Oper. Res. **35**(5), 1394–1411 (2008)

15. Mallipeddi, R., Suganthan, P.N.: Problem definitions and evaluation criteria for the CEC 2010 competition and special session on single objective constrained real-parameter optimization. Technical report, Nangyang Technological University, Singapore (2010)
16. Das, S., Suganthan, P.N.: Differential evolution: a survey of the state-of-the-art. IEEE Trans. Evol. Comput. **15**(1), 4–31 (2011)
17. Pan, Q.-K., Suganthan, P.N., Wang, L., Gao, L., Mallipeddi, R.: A differential evolution algorithm with self-adapting strategy and control parameters. Comput. Oper. Res. **38**(1), 394–408 (2011)
18. Storn, R.: On the usage of differential evolution for function optimization. In: Biennial Conference of the North American Fuzzy Information Processing Society (NAFIPS), pp. 519–523 (1996)
19. Censor, Y., Gordon, D., Gordon, R.: Component averaging: an efficient iterative parallel algorithm for large and sparse unstructured problems. Parallel Comput. **27**(6), 777–808 (2001)
20. Smith, L.: Improved placement of local solver launch points for large-scale global optimization. Carleton University (2011)
21. Yong, W., Zixing, C., Guo, G., Yuren, Z.: Multiobjective optimization and hybrid evolutionary algorithm to solve constrained optimization problems. IEEE Trans. Syst. Man Cybern. Part B Cybern. **37**(3), 560–575 (2007)
22. Deb, K.: An efficient constraint handling method for genetic algorithms. Comput. Meth. Appl. Mech. Eng. **186**, 311–338 (2000)
23. Hamza, N., Sarker, R., Essam, D.: Differential evolution with multi-constraint consensus methods for constrained optimization. J. Glob. Optim. **57**(2), 1–29 (2012)
24. Elsayed, S., Sarker, R.: Differential evolution with automatic population injection scheme. In: IEEE Symposium Series on Computational Intelligence, Singapore, accepted, 16–19 April 2013
25. Corder, G.W., Foreman, D.I.: Nonparametric Statistics for Non-Statisticians: A Step-by-Step Approach. John Wiley, Hoboken (2009)
26. Takahama, T., Sakai, S.: Constrained optimization by the ε constrained differential evolution with an archive and gradient-based mutation. In: IEEE Congress on Evolutionary Computation, pp. 1–9 (2010)
27. Gong, W., Cai, Z., Liang, D.: Adaptive ranking mutation operator based differential evolution for constrained optimization. IEEE Trans. Cybern. **45**(4), 716–727 (2014)
28. Liang, J.J., Shang, Z., Li, Z.: Coevolutionary comprehensive learning particle swarm optimizer. In: IEEE Congress on Evolutionary Computation, 18-23 July 2010, pp. 1–8 (2010)

A Nested Differential Evolution Based Algorithm for Solving Multi-objective Bilevel Optimization Problems

Md Monjurul Islam, Hemant Kumar Singh$^{(\boxtimes)}$, and Tapabrata Ray

School of Engineering and Information Technology, University of New South Wales,
Canberra, ACT 2600, Australia
md.islam5@student.adfa.edu.au, {h.singh,t.ray}@adfa.edu.au
http://www.unsw.adfa.edu.au, http://www.mdolab.net

Abstract. Bilevel optimization is a challenging class of problems, with applicability in several domains such as transportation, economics and engineering. In a bilevel problem, the aim is to identify the optimum solution(s) of an upper level ("leader") problem, subject to optimality of a corresponding lower level ("follower") problem. Most of the studies reported in the literature have focussed on single-objective bilevel problems, wherein both the levels contain only one objective. Several nested algorithms have been proposed in the literature to solve single objective problems, which have been subsequently enhanced through hybridization with local search in order to improve computational efficiency. The handful of algorithms used for multi-objective algorithms so far have used additional enhancements such as use of scalarization, sub-populations or hybridization. However, interestingly, unlike single-objective problems, the performance of a simple nested evolutionary algorithm has not been reported for multi-objective bilevel problems. In this paper, we attempt to address this gap by designing an algorithm which uses differential evolution at both levels. Numerical experiments show that on popular benchmarks, the proposed algorithm exhibits competitive performance with respect to existing state-of-the-art methods.

Keywords: Bilevel optimization · Multi objective · Evolutionary algorithms

1 Introduction

Bilevel optimization is a specific class of problems where optimization needs to be performed at two levels, upper ("leader") and lower ("follower"). The earliest appearance of bilevel optimization dates back to 1950s in the context of Stackelberg game theory [26]. In recent years, research in the field of bilevel optimization has gathered pace and it is increasingly being used to solve problems in several domains including engineering [12], logistics [27], transportation [17] and many more. Rapid increase in the size and complexity of the problems emerging

© Springer International Publishing Switzerland 2016
T. Ray et al. (Eds.): ACALCI 2016, LNAI 9592, pp. 101–112, 2016.
DOI: 10.1007/978-3-319-28270-1_9

from these domains has prompted active interest in design of efficient algorithms for bilevel optimization in the recent years. The increase in complexity could be attributed to having a larger number of system variables, multiple objectives, many constraints and highly non-linear and/or discontinuous functions. Additionally, the problems often need to be solved in real time, which necessitates that the solution be obtained in minimum computational time possible.

Bilevel problems can be further segregated into single-objective (both upper and lower levels contain one objective each) or multi-objective (upper/lower level contain more than one objective). Majority of the works reported to date deal with single objective bilevel optimization problems. A number of classical and population based methods have been developed to solve them. The classical methods include simplex method [6, 19], feasible interior point method with Karush-Kuhn-Tucker (KKT) conditions [10], branch and bound [1], descent methods [29] and penalty based approach [31]. Population based approaches include variants of genetic algorithms [9, 15, 16, 30], particle swarm optimization [14] and evolutionary algorithm [24]. As with single-level optimization problems, classical approaches tend to be vulnerable to getting stuck in local optima, whereas population based approaches take relatively longer time to converge. For bilevel problems, obtaining the optimum of the lower level problem is critical to generate valid solutions (an evaluation at upper level is *valid* only if the corresponding lower level variables used for the evaluation are optimum for lower level problem). Considering this as well as the aim to solve the problems within reasonable computational effort, *hybrid* techniques have also been proposed, where a local/classical search approach is used in conjunction with evolutionary approach (typically local for one of the level and global for other) [11, 13, 34]. Approximation of lower level optimum variable values has also been suggested [22, 23].

As for multi-objective bilevel problems, very few studies have been reported so far. In [7], an adaptive scalarization approach was used for problems with one variable at the upper level. For the case of interactive decision making between leader and follower, the problem was transformed into two separate multi-objective decision making problems in [20]. This work was further extended to include multiple interconnected decision makers at lower level in [21]. For linear bilevel multiobjective problems, mathematical programming was used in [18] for three different situations based on anticipation of upper level decision maker - optimistic anticipation, pessimistic anticipation and anticipation based on past behavior of lower level decision maker. In [32], a genetic algorithm is used to solve a transportation management and planning problems with two objectives at upper level and one at the lower level.

Among the evolutionary algorithms to solve generic multi-objective bilevel problems, some notable works include [2, 4]. Both of these algorithms divide the population at upper level into a number of sub-populations to solve lower level problems independently. While the former uses a non-dominated sorting algorithm as the base method, the latter uses a particle swarm optimizer. To reduce the computational complexity further, use of hybrid search has also been proposed. The work presented in [5] combines evolutionary algorithm with a local search, whereas that in [33] incorporates a crossover operator within a particle swarm optimization. A few different applications have been reported in these papers, including decision making in a company's scenario [5,33] and mining [25].

Interestingly, unlike single-objective bilevel domain, there seem to be no studies using a simple nested evolutionary algorithm for multi-objective bilevel problems. Most studies discussed above use certain specific enhancements, such as special population structure and/or hybridization. The intent of this paper is to investigate the performance of a simple nested evolutionary algorithm for multi-objective optimization, and how it compares to some of these existing techniques. Towards this goal, we propose a nested algorithm which uses differential evolution to solve the problem at both levels. We use three different problems from the literature to test the algorithm, of which two are mathematical benchmarks and third is based on a real-life application.

The rest of the paper is organized as follows. In Sect. 2, the basics of a bilevel optimization problem formulation are discussed. Section 3 provides overview of the proposed algorithm, followed by numerical experiments in Sect. 4. A summary of observations is given in Sect. 5.

2 Bilevel Multi Objective Optimization

A generic bilevel optimization problem is an extended version of a standard (single level) optimization problem, in which the optimization has to be performed at two levels, upper and lower. Each level has its variables, objectives and constraints. The subscript u will be henceforth used to denote attributes of the upper level problem, whereas subscript l will be used for those corresponding to the lower level problem. The critical link between the two levels is that for a given upper level vector $\mathbf{x}_u$, the evaluation of upper level function is valid *only if* the $\mathbf{x}_l$ for the corresponding lower level problem (with $\mathbf{x}_u$ held constant) is the optimum of the lower level problem. This relation gives rise to the nested nature of the bilevel problem. Formally, the mathematical representation of a generic bilevel problem is shown in Eq. 1.

$$
\begin{aligned}
\underset{\mathbf{x}_u}{\text{Minimize}} \quad & F_1(\mathbf{x}_u, \mathbf{x}_l), F_2(\mathbf{x}_u, \mathbf{x}_l), \ldots, F_{M_u}(\mathbf{x}_u, \mathbf{x}_l), \\
\text{S.t.} \quad & G_k(\mathbf{x}_u, \mathbf{x}_l) \leq 0, k = 1, \ldots, q_u, \\
& H_k(\mathbf{x}_u, \mathbf{x}_l) = 0, k = 1, \ldots, r_u, \\
\\
\underset{\mathbf{x}_l}{\text{Minimize}} \quad & f_1(\mathbf{x}_u, \mathbf{x}_l), f_2(\mathbf{x}_u, \mathbf{x}_l), \ldots, f_{M_l}(\mathbf{x}_u, \mathbf{x}_l), \\
\text{S.t.} \quad & g_k(\mathbf{x}_u, \mathbf{x}_l) \leq 0, k = 1, \ldots, q_l, \\
& h_k(\mathbf{x}_u, \mathbf{x}_l) = 0, k = 1, \ldots, r_l, \\
\text{where} \quad & \mathbf{x}_u \in \mathbb{X}_u, \quad \mathbf{x}_l \in \mathbb{X}_l
\end{aligned}
\tag{1}
$$

In Eq. 1, the upper objective (real-valued) functions are $F_i(\mathbf{x}_u, \mathbf{x}_l), i = 1, 2, \ldots, M_u$ and the lower level objective (real-valued) functions are $f_i(\mathbf{x}_u, \mathbf{x}_l), i = 1, 2, \ldots, M_l$. $\mathbf{x}_u$ is the vector of the n_u upper level variables in the domain $\mathbb{X}_u$, and $\mathbf{x}_l$ is the vector of the n_l lower level variables in the domain $\mathbb{X}_l$.

G represents the set of q_u inequality constraints and H is the set of r_u equality constraint for the upper level problem. Similarly, g and h have q_l and r_l inequality and equality constraints respectively for the lower level. The upper level objective function is optimized with respect to $\mathbf{x}_u$ where $\mathbf{x}_l$ acts as a fixed parameter. The lower level is optimized with respect to $\mathbf{x}_l$, considering $\mathbf{x}_u$ as a fixed parameter. For all the problems studied in this paper, both levels are bi-objective, i.e., $M_u=2$ and $M_l=2$.

3 Proposed Algorithm

As mentioned before, the proposed algorithm is a nested differential evolution based bilevel multi-objective algorithm, which is referred to here as DBMA. In synopsis, the algorithm is as follows. A population of size N_u is initialized randomly for upper level problem. For each upper level individual ($\mathbf{x}_u$), the lower level problem is optimized using a differential evolution based algorithm (discussed below), with population N_l. The search at lower level yields a Pareto-front for the given ($\mathbf{x}_u$). The upper level functions are then evaluated using each of the lower level solutions in the Pareto-front. Thereafter, new child solutions are generated using DE crossover and mutation and evaluated in the same way. All solutions thus obtained (parent+child) are collated at upper level, sorted and the top N_u solutions are then chosen for the next generation at the upper level. The process repeats until a prescribed number of generations to give the final solutions. The sorting used at both levels is non-dominated sorting and crowding distance [3], whereas the constraint handling is done based on ϵ level comparisons [28], as opposed to explicit *feasibility-first* schemes.

The DE operators used in the proposed algorithm are the same as in ϵ-constrained differential evolution (ϵDE) algorithm proposed in [28]. The initialization of the population is done using a uniform random distribution in the search space, by creating each design vector as:

$$x_{i,j} = x_{j,min} + \text{rand}([0,1]).(x_{j,max} - x_{j,min}) \tag{2}$$
$$i = 1, 2, \ldots N; \quad j = i = 1, 2, \ldots n \tag{3}$$

Here, N is the population size and n is the number of variables. $\mathbf{x}_{j,max}$ and $\mathbf{x}_{j,min}$ are the upper and lower bounds of jth variable respectively.

For evolution, mutation and crossover operators are used. For each population member $\mathbf{x}_i$, mutation is used to generate a trial vector by choosing three unique vectors $\mathbf{x}_{r1}, \mathbf{x}_{r2}, \mathbf{x}_{r3}$ from the population and generating a trial vector as:

$$\mathbf{x}_t = \mathbf{x}_{r1} + F.(\mathbf{x}_{r2} - \mathbf{x}_{r3}), \tag{4}$$

where F is a parameter known as the scaling factor. This trial vector then undergoes crossover with the parent vector $\mathbf{x}_i$. In this study, a binomial crossover with DE/1/rand/bin strategy is used for exploration, which is known to consistently perform well [8]. A child solution $\mathbf{x}_t$ is created using binomial crossover of parent vector $\mathbf{x}_i$ and trial vector $\mathbf{x}_t$, by using the following operation for each variable:

$$j_{rand} = \text{randint}(1, n)$$

$$x_{c,j} = \begin{cases} x_{t,j} \text{ if } \text{rand}[0,1] \leq CR \quad or \quad j = j_{rand}, \\ x_{i,j} \text{ otherwise} \end{cases} \quad (5)$$

Here CR is a user defined parameter known as crossover probability and n is the number of variables. This global search using the DE is run for a prescribed number of generations.

Algorithm 1. Differential Evolution based Bilevel Multi-objective Algorithm (DBMA)

Require: N_u: Population size for upper level DE
    Gen_{max_u}: Maximum number of upper level DE generations
    $\mathbf{F}_u = [F_{u_1}, F_{u_2}]$: Upper level Objective Functions
    $\mathbf{f}_l = [f_{l_1}, f_{l_2}]$: Lower Level Objective functions
1: Set $gen_u = 0$
2: Initialize N_u number of individuals for upper level.
3: For each upper level individual $\mathbf{x}_u$ perform the lower level optimization (Algorithm 2) to identify set of solutions $\mathbf{x}_l^*$ and corresponding upper and lower objective functions.
4: **while** $gen_u \leq Gen_{max_u}$ **do**
5:    **for** $i{=}1{:}N_u$ **do**
6:       Generate a child individual $\mathbf{x}_u^i$ using DE operators.
7:       Evaluate the upper level objective function by using new $\mathbf{x}_u^i$ and corresponding $\mathbf{x}_l^*$ (obtained through lower level optimization).
8:    **end for**
9:    Collate parent and child populations.
10:   Sort the (parent+child) population at upper level and select N_u best solutions for next generation.
11:   Update best solutions $\mathbf{F}_u$ and corresponding upper level individuals $\mathbf{x}_u$.
12:   $gen_u = gen_u{+}1$.
13: **end while**
14: Return upper level Pareto front $\mathbf{F}_u^*$, corresponding lower level Pareto fronts $\mathbf{f}_l^*$ and optimum variables $\mathbf{x}_u^*, \mathbf{x}_l^*$.

This concludes the overview of the proposed DBMA. In the next section, we present results on some of the existing multiobjective bilevel optimization problems using the algorithm.

4 Numerical Experiments

In this section, we discuss the numerical experiments using the proposed DBMA on three different problems. Out of these, two are benchmark problems, while the third is an application. The parameter settings for the first two (benchmark) problems are $N_u = 50$, $Gen_{max_u} = 5$, $N_l = 50$, $Gen_{max_l} = 25$. For the third problem (application), same population sizes are used with $Gen_{max_u} = 25$,

Algorithm 2. Lower level optimization

Require: Gen_{max_l}: Maximum number of lower level generations
   N_l: Population size for lower level DE
   $\mathbf{f}_l=[f_{l_1}, f_{l_2}]$: Lower Level Objective functions
   $\mathbf{x}_u$: Upper level variables (act as parameters for lower level)
1: Set $gen_l = 0$
2: Initialize N_l number of individuals for lower level problem.
3: **while** $gen_l \leq Gen_{max_l}$ **do**
4:    **for** $i=1:N_l$ **do**
5:       Generate a child individual $\mathbf{x}_l^i$ using DE operators.
6:       Evaluate the lower level objective function using $\mathbf{x}_l^i$ and $\mathbf{x}_u$
7:    **end for**
8:    Collate parent and child populations resulting in $2N_l$ individuals.
9:    Sort the (parent+child) population based on lower level objectives and select N_l
      best solutions for next generation.
10:    Update best $\mathbf{f}_l$ and corresponding $\mathbf{x}_l$.
11:    $gen_l = gen_l + 1$.
12: **end while**
13: Return best Pareto front $\mathbf{f}_l^*$ and corresponding $\mathbf{x}_l^*$.

$Gen_{max_l} = 30$. The scaling factor(F) of 0.7 and the crossover probability (CR) of 0.5 is used at both levels. For each problem, the statistics correspond to 21 independent runs. For comparison with other algorithms, hypervolume metric [35] is used, which calculates dominated volume (area in case of 2-objectives) with respect to a reference point. Nadir point is used as the reference point for calculating hypervolume in this study. For the first two problems, the true optima (and hence true nadir point) is known, whereas for the third problem the nadir point is computed based on the final non-dominated solutions obtained across all runs. Higher value of the metric indicates a better approximation.

4.1   Problem 1

The first problem [5] contains three decision variables, one at the upper level and two at the lower level. There is one constraint at each level. The mathematical formulation of the problem is given in Eq. 6.

$$\begin{aligned}
\text{Minimize} \quad & F_1(\mathbf{x}_u, \mathbf{x}_l) = x_{l_1} - x_u, \\
& F_2(\mathbf{x}_u, \mathbf{x}_l) = x_{l_2}, \\
& G_1(\mathbf{x}_u, \mathbf{x}_l) = 1 + x_{l_1} + x_{l_2} \geq 0; \\
\text{Minimize} \quad & f_1(\mathbf{x}_u, \mathbf{x}_l) = x_{l_1}, \\
& f_2(\mathbf{x}_u, \mathbf{x}_l) = x_{l_2}, \\
& g_1(\mathbf{x}_u, \mathbf{x}_l) = x_u^2 - x_{l_1}^2 - x_{l_2}^2, \\
& 0 \leq x_u \leq 1, -1 \leq x_{l_1}, x_{l_2} \leq 1
\end{aligned} \tag{6}$$

The Pareto front approximation for the median run of DBMA (based on hypervolume) is shown in Fig. 1. It is seen that the population converges close

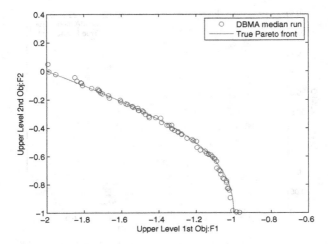

Fig. 1. Pareto front approximation (median) obtained for Problem 1

to the true optimum. The statistics on hypervolume and function evaluations are given in Tables 1 and 2 respectively (after description of all problems). It is seen that the median hypervolume value obtained using DBMA is 0.3076, which is higher than that obtained by BLEMO [4] and OMOPSO-BL [2] which achieve 0.3024 and 0.3068 respectively. It is to be noted, however, that due to the unavailability of their data, the results shown for their algorithms have been taken from [2]. This means that the reference point (nadir) used in their study for this calculation might be different from the one obtained using DBMA. The figures show, however, that all the algorithms have converged very close to the true front [2], which means that the error induced is likely to be minor as nadir points obtained using each algorithm are very close to each other. The mean function evaluations for the previous studies are not reported, but the population sizes and generations used by them are significantly higher than those used in DBMA.

4.2 Problem 2

The problem is an unconstrained problem at both upper and lower levels, taken from [4]. The mathematical formulation of the problem is given in Eq. 7.

$$\begin{aligned}
\text{Minimize} \quad & F_1(\mathbf{x}_u, \mathbf{x}_l) = (x_{l_1} - 1)^2 - \sum_{i=2}^{k} x_{l_i}^2 + x_u^2, \\
& F_2(\mathbf{x}_u, \mathbf{x}_l) = (x_{l_1} - 1)^2 - \sum_{i=2}^{k} x_{l_i}^2 + (x_u - 1)^2, \\
\text{Minimize} \quad & f_1(\mathbf{x}_u, \mathbf{x}_l) = x_{l_1}^2 - \sum_{i=2}^{k} x_{l_i}^2 \\
& f_2(\mathbf{x}_u, \mathbf{x}_l) = (x_{l_1} - x_u)^2 - \sum_{i=2}^{k} x_{l_i}^2, \\
& -1 \leq (x_u, x_{l_1}, x_{l_2}, ..., x_{l_k}) \leq 2,
\end{aligned} \tag{7}$$

Here, the upper level problem has one variable, whereas the lower level is scalable with k variables, which is set to one in this study. The statistics on

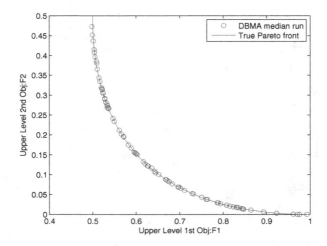

Fig. 2. Pareto front approximation (median) obtained for Problem 2(k=1)

hypervolume and function evaluations are given in Tables 1 and 2 respectively. The median hypervolume obtained by DBMA (0.2068) is slightly less than the by OMOPSO-BL (0.2074) but marginally better than BLEMO (0.2067) for $k = 1$ at the lower level. Similar to Problem 1, the reference (nadir) points for these calculations are very close to that of the true optimum. At the same time, the median function evaluations using DBMA are likely to be much lower than the other two approaches, given the lower population sizes and generations, although this could not be established due to unavailability of the function evaluations in [2]. The Pareto front approximation for the problem (median run) is shown in Fig. 2.

4.3   Problem 3

The last problem discussed here is a real-world application obtained from [5,33]. The problem represents a company scenario where the upper level represents the CEO whose main objectives are to maximize company profit and the product quality. On the other hand, the departmental head is represented as a lower level decision maker whose main objectives are to maximize organizational profit and worker satisfaction. The mathematical formulation of the problem is given in Eq. 8. The problem has two inequality constraints at upper level and three at lower level. The median Pareto front approximation obtained using DBMA is shown in Fig. 3, which looks very similar to that obtained using H-BLEMO [5]. A marginal difference in hypervolume is seen (0.4809 using DBMA vs 0.52 in [5]). However, once again, the exact reference point used in [5] is not available. The median function evaluations using H-BLEMO are $1,966,982$ [5], whereas that using DBMA are $1,876,309$.

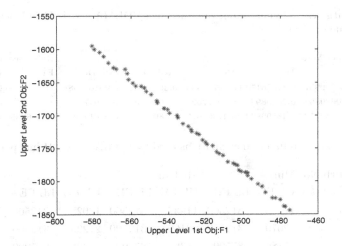

Fig. 3. Pareto front approximation (median) obtained for Problem 3

$$
\begin{aligned}
\text{Maximize} \quad & F_1(\mathbf{x}_u, \mathbf{x}_l) = (1,9)(x_{u_1}, x_{u_2})^T + (10,1,3)(x_{l_1}, x_{l_2}, x_{l_3})^T \\
& F_2(\mathbf{x}_u, \mathbf{x}_l) = (9,2)(x_{u_1}, x_{u_2})^T + (2,7,4)(x_{l_1}, x_{l_2}, x_{l_3})^T \\
& G_1(\mathbf{x}_u, \mathbf{x}_l) = (3,9)(x_{u_1}, x_{u_2})^T + (9,5,3)(x_{l_1}, x_{l_2}, x_{l_3})^T \le 1039 \\
& G_2(\mathbf{x}_u, \mathbf{x}_l) = (-4,-1)(x_{u_1}, x_{u_2})^T + (3,-3,2)(x_{l_1}, x_{l_2}, x_{l_3})^T \le 94
\end{aligned}
$$

$$
\begin{aligned}
\text{Maximize} \quad & f_1(\mathbf{x}_u, \mathbf{x}_l) = (4,6)(x_{u_1}, x_{u_2})^T + (7,4,8)(x_{l_1}, x_{l_2}, x_{l_3})^T \\
& f_2(\mathbf{x}_u, \mathbf{x}_l) = (6,4)(x_{u_1}, x_{u_2})^T + (8,7,4)(x_{l_1}, x_{l_2}, x_{l_3})^T \\
& g_1(\mathbf{x}_u, \mathbf{x}_l) = (3,-9)(x_{u_1}, x_{u_2})^T + (-9,-4,0)(x_{l_1}, x_{l_2}, x_{l_3})^T \le 61 \\
& g_2(\mathbf{x}_u, \mathbf{x}_l) = (5,9)(x_{u_1}, x_{u_2})^T + (10,-1,-2)(x_{l_1}, x_{l_2}, x_{l_3})^T \le 924 \\
& g_3(\mathbf{x}_u, \mathbf{x}_l) = (3,-3)(x_{u_1}, x_{u_2})^T + (0,1,5)(x_{l_1}, x_{l_2}, x_{l_3})^T \le 420 \\
& x_{u_1}, x_{u_2}, x_{l_1}, x_{l_2}, x_{l_3} \ge 0
\end{aligned}
\tag{8}
$$

Overall, it is seen that the performance of the proposed DBMA is competitive with the existing state of the art approaches for the problems studied. The algorithm is intuitive and simple to implement, and to the authors' knowledge provides a first study of extending a differential evolution based algorithm for bilevel multi-objective problems. The algorithm is also free of any additional parameters, other than those of a standard DE. The performance on two benchmark and one application problem indicate its potential to be used for solving generic bilevel multi-objective problems.

5   Summary

Bilevel optimization has gained significant attention in recent years, owing to their applicability in various domains such as such as transportation, economics and engineering. Most studies reported to date deal with single objective problems at both levels, but the interest in multi-objective versions has been steadily growing. In this paper, we reviewed some of the existing algorithms for solving

110   M.M. Islam et al.

Table 1. Statistics on hypervolume obtained using DBMA across 21 independent runs (* means True optima)

Prb No.	Hyper Volume					Reference point	
	Min	Max	Mean	Median	Std. Dev	F1	F2
1	0.30309957	0.31075173	0.30745333	0.30758072	0.001881988	-1*	0*
2	0.20639863	0.20698947	0.20677626	0.20683586	0.00017195	1*	0.5*
3	0.43609273	0.48509894	0.47866625	0.48087895	0.010154085	-473.6935	-1595.4000

Table 2. Statistics on function evaluations used by DBMA across 21 independent runs

Prb No	Min		Median		Max	
	UL FE	LL FE	UL FE	LL FE	UL FE	LL FE
1	11410	312500	11837	312500	12028	312500
2	22079	312500	22169	312500	22229	312500
3	1180	1875000	1309	1875000	1398	1875000

bilevel multi-objective problems. Thereafter, we proposed a simple nested differential evolution based algorithm to deal with generic bilevel multi-objective problems. Numerical experiments show that on often studied benchmarks, the proposed algorithm exhibits comparable performance with the state-of-the-art methods. The study also prompts a deeper look into other schemes such as hybridization, and in particular more studies on what kind of problems may they be more advantageous for compared to simple nested strategies.

Acknowledgment. The third author acknowledges support from *Australian Research Council Future Fellowship*.

References

1. Bard, J.F., Falk, J.E.: An explicit solution to the multi-level programming problem. Comput. Oper. Res. **9**(1), 77–100 (1982)
2. Carrasqueira, P., Alves, M.J., Antunes, C.H.: A bi-level Multiobjective PSO algorithm. In: Gaspar-Cunha, A., Henggeler Antunes, C., Coello, C.C. (eds.) EMO 2015. LNCS, vol. 9018, pp. 263–276. Springer, Heidelberg (2015)
3. Deb, K., Pratap, A., Agarwal, S., Meyarivan, T.: A fast and elitist multiobjective genetic algorithm:NSGA-II. IEEE Trans. Evol. Comput. **6**(2), 182–197 (2002)
4. Deb, K., Sinha, A.: Solving bilevel multi-objective optimization problems using evolutionary algorithms. In: Ehrgott, M., Fonseca, C.M., Gandibleux, X., Hao, J.-K., Sevaux, M. (eds.) EMO 2009. LNCS, vol. 5467, pp. 110–124. Springer, Heidelberg (2009)
5. Deb, K., Sinha, A.: An efficient and accurate solution methodology for bilevel multi-objective programming problems using a hybrid evolutionary-local-search algorithm. Evol. Comput. **18**(3), 403–449 (2010)
6. Dempe, S.: A simple algorithm for the-linear bilevel programming problem. Optimization **18**(3), 373–385 (1987)

7. Eichfelder, G.: Multiobjective bilevel optimization. Math. Program. **123**(2), 419–449 (2010)
8. Gong, W., Cai, Z., Ling, C.X., Li, C.: Enhanced differential evolution with adaptive strategies for numerical optimization. IEEE Trans. Syst. Man Cybern. Part B: Cybernetics **41**(2), 397–413 (2011)
9. Hejazi, S.R., Memariani, A., Jahanshahloo, G., Sepehri, M.M.: Linear bilevel programming solution by genetic algorithm. Comput. Operat. Res. **29**(13), 1913–1925 (2002)
10. Herskovits, J., Leontiev, A., Dias, G., Santos, G.: Contact shape optimization: a bilevel programming approach. Struct. Multi. Optim. **20**(3), 214–221 (2000)
11. Islam, M.M., Singh, H.K., Ray, T.: A memetic algorithm for the solution of single objective bilevel optimization problems. In: IEEE Congress on Evolutionary Computation (CEC) (2015) (In press)
12. Kirjner-Neto, C., Polak, E., Der Kiureghian, A.: An outer approximations approach to reliability-based optimal design of structures. J. Optim. Theor. Appl. **98**(1), 1–16 (1998)
13. Koh, A.: A metaheuristic framework for bi-level programming problems with multidisciplinary applications. In: Talbi, E.-G., Brotcorne, L. (eds.) Metaheuristics for bi-level Optimization. SCI, vol. 482, pp. 153–187. Springer, Heidelberg (2013)
14. Kuo, R., Huang, C.: Application of particle swarm optimization algorithm for solving bi-level linear programming problem. Comput. Mathtt. Appl. **58**(4), 678–685 (2009)
15. Legillon, F., Liefooghe, A., Talbi, E.: Cobra: a cooperative coevolutionary algorithm for bi-level optimization. In: IEEE Congress on Evolutionary Computation (CEC), pp. 1–8. IEEE (2012)
16. Mathieu, R., Pittard, L., Anandalingam, G.: Genetic algorithm based approach to bi-level linear programming. RAIRO Rech. Opérationnelle **28**(1), 1–21 (1994)
17. Migdalas, A.: Bilevel programming in traffic planning: models, methods and challenge. J. Glob. Optim. **7**(4), 381–405 (1995)
18. Nishizaki, I., Sakawa, M.: Stackelberg solutions to multiobjective two-level linear programming problems. J. Optim. Theor. Appl. **103**(1), 161–182 (1999)
19. Önal, H.: A modified simplex approach for solving bilevel linear programming problems. Eur. J. Oper. Res. **67**(1), 126–135 (1993)
20. Shi, X., Xia, H.: Interactive bilevel multi-objective decision making. J. Oper. Res. Soc. **48**(9), 943–949 (1997)
21. Shi, X., Xia, H.S.: Model and interactive algorithm of bi-level multi-objective decision-making with multiple interconnected decision makers. J. Multi-Criteria Decis. Anal. **10**(1), 27–34 (2001)
22. Sinha, A., Malo, P., Deb, K.: An improved bilevel evolutionary algorithm based on quadratic approximations. In: IEEE Congress on Evolutionary Computation (CEC), pp. 1870–1877, July 2014
23. Sinha, A., Malo, P., Deb, K.: Efficient evolutionary algorithm for single-objective bilevel optimization (2013). arXiv preprint arXiv:1303.3901
24. Sinha, A., Malo, P., Deb, K.: Test problem construction for single-objective bilevel optimization. Evol. Comput. **22**(3), 439–477 (2014)
25. Sinha, A., Malo, P., Frantsev, A., Deb, K.: Multi-objective stackelberg game between a regulating authority and a mining company: a case study in environmental economics. In: IEEE Congress on Evolutionary Computation (CEC), pp. 478–485. IEEE (2013)
26. von Stackelberg, H.: Theory of the Market Economy. Oxford University Press, New York (1952)

27. Sun, H., Gao, Z., Wu, J.: A bi-level programming model and solution algorithm for the location of logistics distribution centers. Appl. Math. Model. **32**(4), 610–616 (2008)
28. Takahama, T., Sakai, S.: Constrained optimization by the ϵ constrained differential evolution with gradient-based mutation and feasible elites. In: 2006 IEEE Congress on Evolutionary Computation. CEC 2006, pp. 1–8. IEEE (2006)
29. Vicente, L., Savard, G., Júdice, J.: Descent approaches for quadratic bilevel programming. J. Optim. Theory Appl. **81**(2), 379–399 (1994)
30. Wang, G.M., Wang, X.J., Wan, Z.P., Jia, S.H.: An adaptive genetic algorithm for solving bilevel linear programming problem. Appl. Math. Mech. **28**, 1605–1612 (2007)
31. White, D.J., Anandalingam, G.: A penalty function approach for solving bi-level linear programs. J. Glob. Optim. **3**(4), 397–419 (1993)
32. Yin, Y.: Multiobjective bilevel optimization for transportation planning and management problems. J. Adv. Transp. **36**(1), 93–105 (2002)
33. Zhang, T., Hu, T., Guo, X., Chen, Z., Zheng, Y.: Solving high dimensional bilevel multiobjective programming problem using a hybrid particle swarm optimization algorithm with crossover operator. Knowl.-Based Syst. **53**, 13–19 (2013)
34. Zhu, X., Yu, Q., Wang, X.: A hybrid differential evolution algorithm for solving nonlinear bilevel programming with linear constraints. In: Proceedings of 5th IEEE International Conference on Cognitive Informatics (ICCI06), pp. 126–131 (2006)
35. Zitzler, E., Thiele, L.: Multiobjective optimization using evolutionary algorithms - a comparative case study. In: Eiben, A.E., Bäck, T., Schoenauer, M., Schwefel, H.-P. (eds.) PPSN 1998. LNCS, vol. 1498, pp. 292–301. Springer, Heidelberg (1998)

Parkinson's Disease Data Classification Using Evolvable Wavelet Neural Networks

Maryam Mahsal Khan$^{(\boxtimes)}$, Stephan K. Chalup, and Alexandre Mendes

School of Electrical Engineering and Computer Science,
The University of Newcastle, Callaghan, Australia
maryammahsal.khan@uon.edu.au,
{stephan.chalup,alexandre.mendes}@newcastle.edu.au

Abstract. Parkinson's Disease is the second most common neurological condition in Australia. This paper develops and compares a new type of Wavelet Neural Network that is evolved via Cartesian Genetic Programming for classifying Parkinson's Disease data based on speech signals. The classifier is trained using 10-fold and leave-one-subject-out cross validation testing strategies. The results indicate that the proposed algorithm can find high quality solutions and the associated features without requiring a separate feature pruning pre-processing step. The technique aims to become part of a future support tool for specialists in the early diagnosis of the disease reducing misdiagnosis and cost of treatment.

Keywords: Parkinson's Disease · Neuroevolution · Wavelet neural network · Cartesian genetic programming · Artificial neural network

1 Introduction

Parkinson's Disease (PD) is a central nervous system disorder that is chronic, progressive and incurable. The main symptoms of PD are rigidity, bradykinesia, tremor and postural instability. In addition to those, other symptoms include impaired speech; difficulty in chewing and swallowing; and urinary and constipation problems. The treatment of the disease is very costly, with the average lifetime financial cost for a patient living with PD for 12 years being \$144,000. For comparison purposes, that is similar to the lifetime cost of treatment for a cancer patient (\$165,000) [1].

Decision support systems play an important role in the field of health care. Given the huge volume of information present in medical data repositories, data mining solutions are frequently employed to extract relevant information. The field of Artificial and Computational Intelligence (artificial neural networks, expert systems, fuzzy logic, evolutionary algorithms, genetic programming, etc.) can provide support tools to the medical experts thus reducing the time required to diagnose the disease. There are several studies in the scientific literature specifically on PD diagnosis. It has been estimated that about 90 % of individuals [2] with Parkinson's Disease have some kind of vocal disorder, known as *dysphonia*.

T. Ray et al. (Eds.): ACALCI 2016, LNAI 9592, pp. 113–124, 2016.
DOI: 10.1007/978-3-319-28270-1_10

That high incidence is the main reason why this research focuses on biomedical voice measurements, or speech signals.

In this study we aim to improve our understanding of how the Wavelet Neural Network functions thus making it effective for data classification tasks. The neuroevolutionary algorithm has already been applied on classifying digital mammograms as benign or malignant [3]. The current research complements the authors' previous research by providing an extended study on the PD dataset. As a result we have more comprehensive performance results, a better understanding of how the method can be utilised in critical applications and how robust it is when the application domain changes. For this particular case study, the long term aim is to obtain a non-invasive test that is highly sensitive to early signs of PD in speech signals. In the next section, we describe the features present in the PD dataset, and review some of the previous studies that have used this relatively challenging data. Then, a novel neuroevolutionary algorithm – a Wavelet Neural Network evolved via Cartesian Genetic Programming (CGPWNN) – is discussed and explained with examples. Section 3 presents the methodology, followed by an analysis of the results in Sect. 4. Section 5 concludes with the main findings and future research.

2 Background

2.1 Parkinson's Disease: Dataset and Features

The dataset used in this case study was obtained from an online machine learning database repository in the University of California at Irvine (UCI) [4–6] and has been studied previously [7–9]. The dataset is composed of 195 rows (samples), each with 22 different biomedical voice measurements. These voice measurements were taken from 31 individuals, where 23 had Parkinson's Disease (PD). Each patient had between 6 and 7 records in the dataset, totalling 195 samples as mentioned before. The main objective is to classify healthy from diseased subjects. The features and their descriptions are listed in Table 1.

2.2 Literature Survey

The PD dataset used in this research was originally published by Little et al. [10] in 2009. Their study was divided into three main sections: (1) Feature acquisition and calculation; (2) Feature pruning, where 10 non-correlated features were identified; and (3) Use of the pruned feature set and its different combinations (via exhaustive search) on a Support Vector Machine with a Gaussian radial kernel under bootstrap re-sampling. The maximum average classification accuracy attained was 91.4 % when using four features, namely HNR, $RDPE$, DFA and PPE.

Okan et al. [7] first pruned the dataset features by applying a mutual information measure, and ranked them based on the maximum relevance, minimum redundancy criterion 'mRMR'. They selected four key features, namely $Spread1$,

Table 1. Parkinson's dataset features and their descriptions [10]

Features	Description
MDVP: $F_0(Hz)$	Average vocal fundamental frequency
MDVP: $F_{hi}(Hz)$	Maximum vocal fundamental frequency
MDVP: $F_{lo}(Hz)$	Minimum vocal fundamental frequency
MDVP: Jitter (%)	Several measures of variation in fundamental frequency
MDVP: Jitter (Abs)	
MDVP: RAP	
MDVP: PPQ	
Jitter: DDP	
MDVP: Shimmer	Several measures of variation in amplitude
MDVP: Shimmer (dB)	
Shimmer: APQ3	
Shimmer: APQ5	
MDVP: APQ	
Shimmer: DDA	
RPDE	Two nonlinear dynamical complexity measures
D2	
DFA	Signal fractal scaling exponent
Spread1	Three nonlinear measures of fundamental frequency variation
Spread2	
PPE	
NHR	Two measures of ratio of noise to tonal components in the voice
HNR	
Status	Healthy / Diseased

$MDVP : F_0$, $Shimmer : APQ3$ and $D2$, which were then used in a classification model based on SVM. Using a leave-one-subject-out cross validation strategy they achieved an accuracy of 81.53 %. The same strategy, when applied to the original data of Little et al. [10], reduced the classification accuracy to 65.13 %, while using 10-fold cross-validation with their features increased the accuracy to 92.75 %.

Akin [8] also pruned the features first, via a linear SVM feature selection strategy where 10 features ($spread1$, $MDVP : F_0$, $D2$, $spread2$, $MDVP : F_{hi}$, $MDVP : APQ$, DFA, HNR, PPE and $RPDE$) were selected. These features were then used to train six rotation forest (RF) ensemble classifiers created using two ANN architectures *(MLP, RBF)*, two lazy learners *(KSTAR, IBk (WEKA[1]*

---

[1] http://www.cs.waikato.ac.nz/ml/weka/.

implementation of KNN)) and two decision trees *(LADTree, J48)*. A 10-fold cross-validation strategy was adopted. Among the six RF ensemble classifiers, the classification accuracy of IBk was the highest – 96.93 %.

Caglar et al. [9] used an Adaptive Neuro Fuzzy Classifier with Linguistic Hedges *(ANFC-LH)* to first select the strong features from the dataset. The technique identified four features of interest: $Spread1$, $MDVP : F_{hi}$, $RPDE$ and $D2$. Based on these features the dataset was split into equal parts: 50 % for training and 50 % for testing. As the dataset contained individuals with 6–7 records each, if the number of 'true checks' associated with an individual was high, then it was classified as healthy. Multilayer perceptrons (MLP), radial basis function neural networks (RBFNN) and ANFC-LH were used as classifiers for training. The author found ANFC-LH to yield the best result with 95.38 % training and 94.72 % testing accuracies.

Pei et al. [11] used a minimum distance classifier to assess genetic programming combined with expectation maximization algorithm. They used a 10-fold cross validation strategy for training and testing the classifiers using all features. The method resulted in a training accuracy of 95.06 % and a testing accuracy of 93.12 %.

Chen et al. [12] used a fuzzy k-nearest neighbour (FKNN) approach on a feature reduced dataset based on PCA. They trained the FKNN using the 10-fold cross validation strategy and obtained an accuracy of 96.07 %. While Polat [13] used a feature weighting method on the basis of fuzzy C-means clustering. Weighting the features based on the C-means approach improved the performance of classification and the method achieved 97.03 % accuracy using a KNN classifier with a 50-50 % training-testing partition.

Hariharan et al. [14] evaluated the dataset based on a three-step process. First, a Gaussian mixture model is used to weight the features, which are then ranked and reduced using different feature selection strategies (PCA, LDA) and feature subset selection methods (SFS and SBS). The reduced feature space is then classified using 10-fold cross validation with three different classifiers: LS-SVM, Probabilistic Neural Networks (PNN) and General Regression Neural Networks (GRNN). The authors found that LDA and SBS provided a feature space which was perfectly separable by the LS-SVM, PNN and GRNN classifiers. Their approach obtained an accuracy of 100 %.

Spadoto et al. [15] used three evolutionary mechanisms, namely Particle Swarm Optimization (PSO), Harmony Search (HS) and Gravitational Search Algorithm (GSA). The reduced dataset was then classified via an Optimum-Path Forest (OPF) classifier. They obtained an average of 84.01 % with an execution time of 0.16 s on a hold-out dataset.

Most of the techniques applied on the Parkinson's dataset surround feature selection or weighting prior to classification, as shown in Table 3. Choosing a pre-processing method comes with its advantages and disadvantages; disadvantages being complicating a classification process and thus increasing computational time. Our intent is to keep the process simple i.e. to implement an algorithm that does not require pre-processing of the features. The neuroevolution itself will select features that are significant and evolve to produce good quality solutions, i.e. feature selection and classification all in one. So far, there has been no technique that used neuroevolution to classify the dataset, and thus our technique would be the first of its kind to be tested. Even though neuroevolution has greater prospects in the reinforcement learning domain, e.g. for the design of efficient, intelligent controllers, our current research focus is to apply it on the supervised learning domain and check its applicability.

2.3 Wavelet Neural Network Evolved via CGP

Wavelet Neural Networks (WNN) represent a class of neural networks that use wavelets; i.e. they combine the theory of wavelets and neural networks. It has been found that WNN provide better function approximation ability than standard multilayer perceptrons (MLP) and radial basis function (RBF) neural networks [16]. Wavelet Neural networks have a feed-forward topology, with one hidden layer, whose activation functions are drawn from an orthonormal wavelet family. The common wavelet activation functions are Gaussian, Mexican hat, Morelet and Haar [16].

In this paper, a novel algorithm based on the concept of Cartesian Genetic Programming is used to evolve the wavelet neural network parameters. Cartesian Genetic Programming (CGP) is an evolutionary programming technique developed by Miller et al. [17] and has been particularly used for digital circuit optimization. The concept of CGP has also been used to train artificial neural networks; named Cartesian Genetic Programming Artificial Neural Network (CGPANN) and was proposed by Khan et al. [18]. The motivation behind using CGP for evolving parameters is that CGP doesn't bloat [19] i.e. it does not rapidly grow in size with time as the nodes and layers are fixed, the networks are dominated by redundant genes that have a neutral effect [20–22] on the performance. Also applications [18] using CGP representation are found to produce solutions that are robust and with good accuracy [23–26].

The main entity of WNN are the wavelons 'ψ'. Wavelons represent a wavelet function with predefined scaling 'α' and dilation 'β' values. Given an input x_{ij} and wavelet function ψ_j with scaling α and dilation β, the input is transformed into $\psi_j((x_{ij} - \beta)/\alpha)$, where $x_{ij} \in [1, \text{Total Inputs}]$, $\alpha \in [-1, 1]$ and $\beta \in [0, 1]$, $\psi_j \in [1, \text{Total wavelet functions}]$. Input, switch, scale and dilate genes occur in pairs, so if there are 2 or more inputs, then there should be 2 or more sets of input,

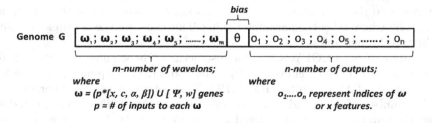

Fig. 1. Structure of a CGPWNN genome.

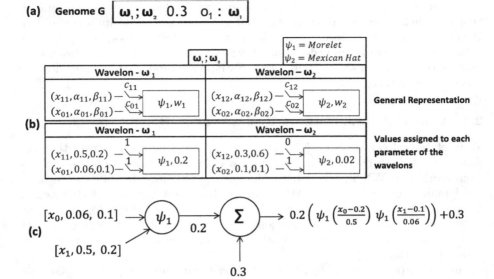

Fig. 2. (a) A 2×1 CGPWNN genome with 2 inputs and 1 output. (b) Generalized representation of a wavelon ψ structure with random values assigned. (c) Phenotype of the example genome in (a). Since it is a one output genome, it requires the use of a single wavelon.

switch, scale and dilate genes, respectively. Each of the inputs in the wavelons is connected via a c_{ij} gene known as the switch gene, where $c_{ij} \in \{0,1\}$. Each of the wavelons within a network has an associated weight represented by $w_{ij} \in [-1, 1]$. All these genes are combined together to form a wavelon structure 'ω'.

The CGP genotype consists of nodes and output genes, whereas the CGP-WNN genotype contains wavelons, output and bias 'θ' genes. There are two basic types of evolution strategies (μ, λ)-ES and $(\mu + \lambda)$-ES [27]. μ represents the number of individuals in the parent population and λ refers to the offspring produced in a generation. In (μ, λ)-ES the offspring replaces the parents as the fittest is selected from λ, while in $(\mu + \lambda)$-ES the fittest is selected from both parents and offspring for the next generation. Cartesian Genetic Programming uses the $(1 + \lambda)$-ES strategy, i.e. a single parent is mutated based on a mutation rate 'τ' to produce λ offsprings. The fittest of the genotypes becomes the parent and moves to the next generation. α, β and w_{ij} are perturbed within the range $[0.8v, 1.2v]$ where 'v' is the parameter value. This captures the continuous aspect of the wavelet networks.

Figure 1 shows a CGPWNN genome structure. The genome consists of three main sections: (1) m-Wavelons ω_m, (2) a bias θ and (3) n-outputs O_n. Figure 2(a) is an example of 2×1 architecture CGPWNN genotype, where 2×1 corresponds to the number of rows and columns, respectively. As WNNs have one hidden layer, the number of columns is fixed at 1, while there are 2 wavelons ω_m along the row. The number of inputs to the network is 2, i.e. x_0 and x_1, and the number of outputs is 1. The number of inputs to each wavelon structure is also fixed at 2. Figure 2(b) shows the random assignment of values to each gene of the wavelons ω_m. Figure 2(c) is the phenotypic representation of the genome in Fig. 2(a), along with its mathematical expression.

3   Experimental Setup

3.1   Training and Testing Sets

Two different training and testing sets were generated in order to investigate the performance of the algorithm.

- **Leave-one-subject-out strategy:** The dataset consists of 31 individuals, or subjects, where each individual can have 6 or 7 associated records. In the leave-one-subject-out cross-validation approach, it is not one record that is left out for testing, but one individual (i.e. all associated 6 or 7 records). The remaining 30 individuals (each with 6 or 7 records) are used for training. This approach is similar to [7] with the exception that no feature pruning was used as a pre-processing step.
- **10-fold cross-validation strategy:** The training set was composed of the records of 28 individuals while the testing set consisted of the records of 3 individuals.

Due to the fact that each individual has between 6 and 7 records in the dataset, if more than half of an individual's records are classified as PD, then the individual itself is classified as diseased (PD), otherwise not. This approach was adopted from [9]. The purpose of this approach is to avoid overfitting as records from the same patient are potentially very similar.

3.2   Performance Measures

The classifiers are evaluated based on the following performance metrics:

1. **Training accuracy** (Tr_{Acc}): fraction of correctly classified training samples.
2. **Testing accuracy** (Te_{Acc}): fraction of correctly classified testing samples, also known as the classification accuracy. The higher the percentage, the better is the classifier performance.

3.3   CGPWNN Parameters

Random structure of CGPWNN with a hidden layer size (HLS) of $[10, 15]$ were evolved with different parameter settings and a mutation rate of 0.01% and a $(1+25)$-ES as shown in Table 2. The wavelet functions used were Gaussian, Morelet, Mexican hat and Haar. Each network was evolved for 100,000 generations. The number of outputs O_p from the genotype was set at 5, 8, 10 and 15, and the number of inputs to each neuron I_E was set to 6, 11 and 22. The genotypes were evolved with the two strategies mentioned before, i.e. leave-one-subject-out and 10-fold cross-validation. Table 2 shows the results for CGPWNN, averaged for 50 independent evolutionary runs in each configuration. Results are divided into training accuracy 'Tr_{Acc}', testing accuracy 'Te_{Acc}', the percentage of active neurons in the search space 'A_{Neu}' and the percentage of features selected 'F_{sel}'.

Table 2. Performance of CGPWNN with leave-one-subject-out and 10-fold cross validation strategies. The best configurations are indicated in boldface.

Structure			Leave-one-subject-out				10-fold cross validation			
HLS	I_E	O_p	Tr_{Acc} (%)	$Te_{Acc}(\sigma)$ (%)	A_{Neu} (%)	F_{sel} (%)	Tr_{Acc} (%)	$Te_{Acc}(\sigma)$ (%)	A_{Neu} (%)	F_{sel} (%)
10	6	5	99.39	82.84(21.33)	30.93	26.27	99.32	88.73(15.26)	30.80	26.33
	11		98.48	82.00(18.84)	21.02	27.87	98.51	89.27(12.84)	21.44	28.35
	22		96.17	83.10(14.51)	7.72	30.33	95.94	89.53(11.01)	8.04	30.58
	6	10	99.98	83.03(19.68)	30.36	48.42	99.99	92.60(11.98)	30.64	47.68
	11		99.67	83.94(16.69)	26.97	56.03	99.61	92.73(11.04)	26.54	55.71
	22		96.87	82.90(15.14)	15.65	63.12	96.61	91.60(11.00)	15.74	63.93
15	6	8	99.94	**85.29**(17.86)	37.85	43.12	99.91	91.93(12.65)	38.38	43.63
	11		99.60	82.39(18.88)	32.11	52.10	99.51	90.13(13.28)	31.83	51.85
	22		96.85	82.00(15.65)	19.50	59.55	96.54	90.00(11.95)	19.85	60.40
	6	15	100.00	84.39(20.50)	35.90	65.78	99.99	91.80(14.10)	36.55	65.78
	11		99.91	84.65(18.14)	31.29	74.75	99.91	**92.93**(11.77)	32.33	75.46
	22		97.34	83.74(14.97)	24.95	87.72	96.97	91.27(11.49)	24.85	87.68

4   Results and Discussion

Table 2 shows the performance of CGPWNN on the PD dataset classification. The method obtained a maximum classification accuracy of 85.29 % with the leave-one-subject-out strategy and 92.93 % with the 10-fold cross-validation. The results show that increasing the number of inputs to each wavelon ω_i causes a reduction in training accuracy; and no clear trend was observed for the testing accuracy. On the other hand, increasing the number of outputs O_p causes an increase in training accuracy; and again no trend was observed for the testing accuracy. In the former case, the reduction in the training accuracy is associated with a property of wavelet neural networks, i.e. WNN performs better in applications with small input dimensions [16]. In the latter case, the output gene has a predominant role in improving the accuracy. Output is represented by either a wavelon(s), an input multiplied by a weight value, or the sum of both. Therefore, increasing the number of links that the output layer can have with the previous layers (input/hidden) improves the accuracy.

The percentage of active neurons/wavelons indicates the complexity of the problem investigated. In Table 2, the active percentage of neurons/wavelons is similar for each structure in both training and testing datasets. This indicates that any training/testing split of a dataset would not affect the active percentage of neurons/wavelons in the cartesian space. The percentage of active neurons was dependent on the number of inputs to each wavelon; where structures with less inputs I_E had higher percentages of active neurons and lower percentages of features selected. This indicates that the neuroevolutionary algorithm was able to find solutions with less features that are transformed by the wavelons in the structure. We can also observe a clear ascending trend in the percentage of features selected when the number of inputs to a wavelon I_E and the number of outputs O_p are increased.

Figure 3 shows the histogram of the number of wavelet activation functions utilized by the best solutions for all the evolved structures. Both training strategies resulted in similar selections. Gaussian activation functions were utilized more often, and Haar the least. Future research should examine the behaviour of the genotypes when using a single type of activation function.

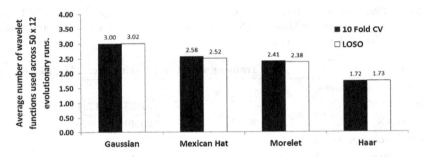

Fig. 3. Histogram of the average active wavelons for all the genotypes in the 12 configurations for both leave-one-individual-out & 10-fold cross-validation strategies.

Figure 4 shows the frequency of selection of the 22 features in the CGPWNN genotypes with both training strategies. The histogram represents the average number of features used in all the genotypes within each configuration; thus providing an average over 50×12 evolutionary runs; where 50 is the number of genotypes and 12 is the number of configurations. We can clearly see that out of 22 features, 4 of them were predominantly used in both the training strategies. They were PPE, $Spread1$, $Spread2$ and $D2$. The selected features are found to be a subset of features in most of the feature selection algorithms used by researchers in literature [8, 10]. This indicates that the feature selection process is an independent process and the presence of any features in the feature set doesn't affect the performance of the classifier.

Table 3 shows the comparison of the neuroevolutionary algorithm with other techniques using 10-fold cross validation and leave-one-subject-out strategy as training sets. We can clearly see that CGPWNN performed competitively even though no feature pre-processing step was adopted. This indicates its potential to classify vocal features for PD diagnosis.

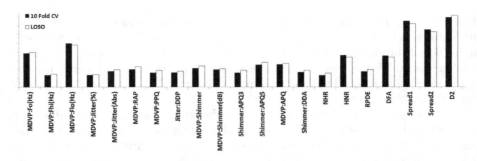

Fig. 4. Histogram of the average selected features for all the genotypes in the 12 configurations evolved for both leave-one-individual-out & 10-fold cross validation strategies.

Table 3. Comparison of techniques using leave-one-subject-out and 10-fold cross-validation strategies in Parkinson's Disease classification. Notice no pre-processing is required in the CGPWNN method.

Algorithm	Training acc. (%)	Testing acc. (%)	Reference
Leave-one-subject-out			
mRMR+SVM	–	81.53 ± 2.17	[7]
CGPWNN	99.94	85.29	
10-fold cross validation			
Preselection filter+exhaustive search+SVM	–	91.4 ± 4.4	[10]
mRMR+SVM	–	92.75 ± 1.21	[7]
SVM+MLP-ensemble	–	90.8	[8]
SVM+RBF-ensemble	–	88.71	[8]
SVM+LADTree-ensemble	–	92.82	[8]
SVM+J48-ensemble	–	92.3	[8]
SVM+KSTAR-ensemble	–	96.41	[8]
SVM+IBk-ensemble	–	96.93	[8]
GP-EM	95.06	93.12	[11]
PCA+FKNN	–	96.07	[12]
GMM+LDA+LS-SVM or PNN or GRNN	–	100	[14]
CGPWNN	99.90	92.93	

5   Conclusion

In this research, a novel neuroevolutionary algorithm - WNN evolved via CGP (CGPWNN) was tested to verify its effectiveness towards an accurate classification system for PD diagnosis. The dataset was composed of features based on biomedical voice measurements of both PD patients and healthy individuals.

It was found that CGPWNNs are successful in locating high-quality solutions; and are not dependent on a *'feature selection process'* as a pre-processing step before training occurs. CGPWNN obtained an accuracy of 92.93 % with a 10-fold cross-validation strategy, performing competitively with other techniques present in the literature.

CGPWNN selected four dominant features more frequently than the others, which illustrates their importance in the classification process. The four features identified were *Spread*1, *Spread*2, *D*2 and *PPE*, which are found to be subsets of features selected in other feature selective algorithms reported in literature.

Acknowledgments. We acknowledge Max Little, from the University of Oxford, UK, who created the database in collaboration with the National Center for Voice and Speech, Denver, Colorado, USA, who recorded the speech signals.

References

1. Parkinson's Australia, Living with Parkinson's disease; Deloitte Access Economics Pty Ltd, update - October 2011. http://www.parkinsonsnsw.org.au/. Accessed August 2014
2. Das, R.: A comparison of multiple classification methods for diagnosis of Parkinson disease. Expert Syst. Appl. **37**(2), 1568–1572 (2010)
3. Khan, M.M., Chalup, S.K., Mendes, A.: Evolving wavelet neural networks for breast cancer classification. In: 12th Australasian Data Mining Conference, Brisbane, Australia, 27th-28th November 2014
4. Lichman, M.: UCI machine learning repositry. http://archive.ics.uci.edu/ml
5. UCI machine learning repositry - Parkinsons data set. http://archive.ics.uci.edu/ml/datasets/Parkinsons.html. Accessed May 2014
6. Little, M.A., McSharry, P.E., Roberts, S.J., Costello, D.A.E., Moroz, I.M.: Exploiting nonlinear recurrence and fractal scaling properties for voice disorder detection. BioMed. Eng. Online **6**(1), 23 (2007)
7. Sakar, C.O., Kursun, O.: Telediagnosis of Parkinson's disease using measurements of dysphonia. J. Med. Syst. **34**(4), 591–599 (2010)
8. Ozcift, A.: Svm feature selection based rotation forest ensemble classifiers to improve computer-aided diagnosis of Parkinson disease. J. Med. Syst. **36**(4), 2141–2147 (2012)
9. Caglar, M.F., Cetisli, B., Toprak, I.B.: Automatic recognition of Parkinson's disease from sustained phonation tests using ann and adaptive neuro-fuzzy classifier. J. Eng. Sci. Des. **2**, 59–64 (2010)
10. Little, M.A., McSharry, P.E., Hunter, E.J., Spielman, J.L., Ramig, L.O.: Suitability of dysphonia measurements for telemonitoring of Parkinson's disease. IEEE Trans. Biomed. Eng. **56**(4), 1015–1022 (2009)
11. Guo, P.-F., Bhattacharya, P., Kharma, N.: Advances in detecting Parkinson's disease. In: Zhang, D., Sonka, M. (eds.) ICMB 2010. LNCS, vol. 6165, pp. 306–314. Springer, Heidelberg (2010)
12. Chen, H.-L., Huang, C.-C., Xin-Gang, Y., Xin, X., Sun, X., Wang, G., Wang, S.-J.: An efficient diagnosis system for detection of parkinson's disease using fuzzy k-nearest neighbor approach. Expert Syst. Appl. **40**(1), 263–271 (2013)

13. Polat, K.: Classification of parkinson's disease using feature weighting method on the basis of fuzzy c-means clustering. Int. J. Syst. Sci. **43**(4), 597–609 (2012)
14. Hariharan, M., Polat, K., Sindhu, R.: A new hybrid intelligent system for accurate detection of parkinson's disease. Comput. Meth. Program. Biomed. **113**(3), 904–913 (2014)
15. Spadoto, A.A., Guido, R.C., Carnevali, F.L., Pagnin, A.F., Falcao, A.X., Papa, J.P.: Improving parkinson's disease identification through evolutionary-based feature selection. In: 2011 Annual International Conference of the IEEE Engineering in Medicine and Biology Society, EMBC, pp. 7857–7860, August 2011
16. Alexandridis, A.K., Zapranis, A.D.: Wavelet neural networks: a practical guide. Neural Netw. **42**, 1–27 (2013)
17. Miller, J.F., Thomson, P.: Cartesian genetic programming. In: Poli, R., Banzhaf, W., Langdon, W.B., Miller, J., Nordin, P., Fogarty, T.C. (eds.) EuroGP 2000. LNCS, vol. 1802, pp. 121–132. Springer, Heidelberg (2000)
18. Khan, M.M., Khan, G.M., Ahmad, A.M., Miller, J.F.: Fast learning neural networks using cartesian genetic programming. Neurocomputing **121**, 274–289 (2013)
19. Miller, J.: What bloat? cartesian genetic programming on boolean problems. In: Genetic and Evolutionary computation Conference Late Breaking Papers, pp. 295–302. Morgan Kaufmann (2001)
20. Vassilev, V.K., Miller, J.F.: The advantages of landscape neutrality in digital circuit evolution. In: Miller, J.F., Thompson, A., Thompson, P., Fogarty, T.C. (eds.) ICES 2000. LNCS, vol. 1801, pp. 252–263. Springer, Heidelberg (2000)
21. Yu, T., Miller, J.F.: Neutrality and the evolvability of boolean function landscape. In: Miller, J., Tomassini, M., Lanzi, P.L., Ryan, C., Tetamanzi, A.G.B., Langdon, W.B. (eds.) EuroGP 2001. LNCS, vol. 2038, pp. 204–217. Springer, Heidelberg (2001)
22. Yu, T., Miller, J.F.: Finding needles in haystacks is not hard with neutrality. In: Foster, J.A., Lutton, E., Miller, J., Ryan, C., Tettamanzi, A.G.B. (eds.) EuroGP 2002. LNCS, vol. 2278, pp. 13–25. Springer, Heidelberg (2002)
23. Khan, M.M., Khan, G.M., Miller, J.F.: Efficient representation of recurrent neural networks for markovian/non-markovian non-linear control problems. In: International Conference on System Design and Applications (ISDA), pp. 615–620 (2010)
24. Walker, A., Miller, J.F.: Solving real-valued optimisation problems using cartesian genetic programming. In: Proceedings of the Genetic and Evolutionary Computation Conference GECCO, pp. 1724–1730. ACM Press (2007)
25. Walker, J.A., Miller, J.F.: Predicting prime numbers using cartesian genetic programming. In: Ebner, M., O'Neill, M., Ekárt, A., Vanneschi, L., Esparcia-Alcázar, A.I. (eds.) EuroGP 2007. LNCS, vol. 4445, pp. 205–216. Springer, Heidelberg (2007)
26. Walker, J.A., Miller, J.F.: Changing the genospace: solving GA problems with cartesian genetic programming. In: Ebner, M., O'Neill, M., Ekárt, A., Vanneschi, L., Esparcia-Alcázar, A.I. (eds.) EuroGP 2007. LNCS, vol. 4445, pp. 261–270. Springer, Heidelberg (2007)
27. Beyer, H.G., Schwefel, H.P.: Evolution strategies: a comprehensive introduction. Natural Comput. **1**(1), 3–52 (2002)

GO-PEAS: A Scalable Yet Accurate Grid-Based Outlier Detection Method Using Novel Pruning Searching Techniques

Hongzhou Li[1], Ji Zhang[2(✉)], Yonglong Luo[3], Fulong Chen[3], and Liang Chang[1]

[1] Guangxi Key Laboratory of Trusted Software, Guilin University of Electronic Technology, Guilin, China
homzh@163.com, changl@guet.edu.cn
[2] University of Southern Queensland, Toowoomba, Australia
ji.zhang@usq.edu.au
[3] Anhui Normal University, Wuhu, China
ylluo@ustc.edu.cn, long005@mail.ahnu.edu.cn

Abstract. In this paper, we propose a scalable yet accurate grid-based outlier detection method called GO-PEAS (stands for Grid-based Outlier detection with Pruning Searching techniques). Innovative techniques are incorporated into GO-PEAS to greatly improve its speed performance, making it more scalable for large data sources. These techniques offer efficient pruning of unnecessary data space to substantially enhance the detection speed performance of GO-PEAS. Furthermore, the detection accuracy of GO-PEAS is guaranteed to be consistent with its baseline version that does not use the enhancement techniques. Experimental evaluation results have demonstrated the improved scalability and good effectiveness of GO-PEAS.

1 Introduction

Outlier detection is an important data analytic/mining problem that aims to find objects and/or patterns that are considerably dissimilar, exceptional and inconsistent with respect to the majority data in an input database. Outlier detection has become one of the key enabling technologies for a wide range of applications in industry, business, security and engineering, etc., where outliers represent abnormal patterns that are critical for domain-specific decision-making and actions.

Due to its inherent importance in various areas, considerable research efforts in outlier detection have been taken in the field and a number of outlier detection techniques have been proposed that leverage different detection mechanisms and algorithms. The majority of them deal with the traditional relational datasets which can be generally classified into the distribution-based methods [2], the distance-based methods [4,10], the density-based methods [8,11,13,16–18] and the clustering-based methods [6,9], which feature different levels of performance in terms of detection accuracy and efficiency. The research on outlier detection has also been carried out for other types of datasets such as temporal data

© Springer International Publishing Switzerland 2016
T. Ray et al. (Eds.): ACALCI 2016, LNAI 9592, pp. 125–133, 2016.
DOI: 10.1007/978-3-319-28270-1_11

[7] and semistructured data (e.g., XML) [5] and in the distributed computing environment [12, 14, 15, 19].

Detecting outliers from increasingly large datasets is a very computationally expensive process. To improve the efficiency performance of outlier detection when dealing with large datasets, a grid structure can be created through a space partitioning that discretizes each continuous attribute to a few intervals. Using the grid structure can considerably reduce the computational overhead as the major operation of detection is now performed on the grid cells, a typically much smaller set compared to the total number of data instances in the dataset. This makes them much more scalable to datasets with a large number of instances. In addition, the grid structure greatly facilitates the calculation of data synopsis to capture data distribution and characteristics for the purpose of outlier detection.

Despite being generally more efficient than other categories of outlier detection methods, the existing grid-based outlier detection methods still suffer from some major limitations. First, using data synopsis of grid cells alone through a single round of data scan will compromise the detection effectiveness and may not be able to meet the requirement for high detection accuracy. Therefore, detailed evaluation needs to be carried out in the level of data points, which requires the second round of data scan. Yet, two full data scans may be not satisfactorily efficient to deal with large datasets. Some existing methods are designed to prune away dense cells. But it is possible that some outliers are embedded in those pruned cells and therefore cannot be detected. Finally, those methods using clustering analysis will have to perform clustering before outliers can be detected. Yet, the clustering analysis itself may be complicated, expensive and sensitive to various clustering parameters, posing challenges for efficient and effective detection of outliers.

To solve the aforementioned limitations, we propose in this paper an innovative grid-based outlier detection method, called **GO-PEAS** (stands for Grid-based Outlier detection with Pruning Searching technique), to enhance the detection efficiency without compromising detection accuracy. The technical contributions of this paper are summarized as follows. First, GO-PEAS is equipped with innovative pruning searching mechanism to noticeably improve its efficiency. The correctness of these techniques are also proven theoretically to offer a performance guarantee that loss of detection accuracy will be impossible. Second, irrespective of how the data space is partitioned, GO-PEAS is guaranteed to detect outliers even when they are embedded in dense cells, thereby effectively reducing the sensitivity of GO-PEAS to partitioning granularity. Furthermore, the outlier-ness metric used in GO-PEAS, called k-WODF, is able to produce accurate modeling of data abnormality that leads to a good detection accuracy. No clustering analysis needs to be performed before outliers can be detected. Finally, the experimental evaluation demonstrates enhanced speed performance and good detection accuracy of GO-PEAS.

2   Outlier-ness Measurement and Method Framework

The outlier-ness metric, called k-Weighted Outlying Degree Factor (k-WODF), is devised and used in GO-PEAS. k-WODF measures the strength of outlierness of data in the dataset. k-WODF of a data object p is defined as the averaged distance between p and its k nearest representative data which are the centroids of dense cells in the grid, weighted by the portion of data in the cells. The dense cells are those whose density is above the average density level of the populate cells in the grid. k-WODF is mathematically defined as

$$k - WODF(p) = \frac{\sum_{i=1}^{k} \frac{Dist(p,r_i)}{w_i}}{k}$$

where r_i is the centroid of dense cell c_i and $w_i = \frac{density(c_i)}{N}$.

The basic detection framework of Go-PEAS, also referred to as the *baseline method*, takes the following three major steps:

Step 1: Assigning data into the grid structure. The data space is partitioned and a grid of cells is superimposed. Data in the dataset D are read in sequentially and assigned into the cells in the grid. Instead of physically creating the grid structure whose number of cells will explode for high-dimensional data, only the list of populated cells is maintained. The major purpose for assigning data into the grid structure is to obtain the density information (i.e., the number of data points) for the populated cells in the grid;

Step 2: Generating the representative data. Based on the density information of the grid cells, dense cells are selected and the centroids of the dense cells are extracted as the representative data. The set of representative data is the representation of the dense regions formed by the whole dataset;

Step 3: Generating the top n outliers. After the representative data are extracted, another full scan of the dataset D is performed and the k-WODF of each data is calculated. The top n outliers will be picked up which have the highest k-WODF values and returned to users.

3   Speed Enhancements Techniques of GO-PEAS

For large datasets, it would be a computationally expensive task to perform two full data scans, as in the baseline method, to achieve accurate detection result. Outliers are normally located in low-density data regions. It is therefore reasonable to prune away the data located in dense regions and only evaluate the data scattered in sparse areas to reduce the computational cost. Nevertheless, more complicated situations may exist that there may be a (very) small amount of outliers that are embedded in some relatively dense cells which cannot be successfully detected. This is because those outliers are masked by other data in the cell. These cells need be evaluated closely for detecting the outliers within them.

We first present the following lemma which establishes the upper bound of k-WODF of data points in a cell.

Lemma 1. *Let p denote a given data point in a cell c and $center(c)$ is the geometric center (called center for short) of c. The k-WODF of p satisfies the following inequation*

$$kWODF(p) \leq \frac{\sum_{i=1}^{k} Dist(center(c), r_i)}{k} + \frac{l_{diagonal}}{2}$$

where r_i is one of the k nearest representative data of p and $l_{diagonal}$ represents the length of the diagonal line of c.

Proof. For any nearest representative data of $p, r_i (1 \leq i \leq k)$, we have $Dist(p, r_i) < Dist(center(c), r_i) + Dist(center(c), p)$ based on triangular inequality. Since $Dist(center(c), p) \leq \frac{l_{diagonal}}{2}$, thus $Dist(p, r_i) < Dist(centerc), r_i) + \frac{l_{diagonal}}{2}$. This leads to k-$WODF(p) = \frac{\sum_{i=1}^{k} Dist(p, r_i)}{k} < \frac{\sum_{i=1}^{k} Dist(center(c), r_i)}{k} + \frac{l_{diagonal}}{2}$, as required.   □

Lemma 1 can be utilized to prune away those cells in the grid structure which definitely do not contain any data points that can possibly become the top n outlier. Specifically, all the data points in a cell can be safely pruned away if the following inequation is satisfied:

$$\frac{\sum_{i=1}^{k} Dist(center(c), r_i)}{k} + \frac{l_{diagonal}}{2} < Min_{kWODF} \qquad (1)$$

The pruned cells are mostly densely populated ones (containing a large number of data points) because they are generally close to their nearby representative data. Therefore, this pruning strategy contributes to a significant saving of computational cost for our method.

Please note that in Lemma 1, $r_1, r_2, \ldots, r_k$ are the k nearest representative data of p, but are not necessarily those of the cell center. The technical difficulty here is that, without individual evaluation, it is impossible to know in advance which representative data are the k nearest ones for a given data point in the cell. This will impede the direct use of the pruning strategy. In order to solve this problem, we develop a method to effectively find a set of representative data for a given cell such that this set contains the k nearest representative data for any data points in the cell. The concept of dominance is employed to help achieve this.

Definition 1. *(Dominance): A representative data r_1 is defined as dominating another representative data r_2, with regard to a given cell c, denoted as $r_1 \underset{c}{\succ} r_2$, iff the distance between r_1 and any data point in c is less than or equal to that of r_2, i.e.,*

$$r_1 \underset{c}{\succ} r_2 \text{ iff } \forall p \in c, Dist(r_1, p) \leq Dist(r_2, p)$$

Lemma 2. *Let r_1 and r_2 be two representative data, if $Dist(r_1, center(c)) + l_{diagonal} < Dist(r_2, center(c))$, then it is guaranteed that the distance between r_1 and any data points in c is no greater than that of r_2, i.e. $r_1 \succ r_2$.*

Proof. Based on triangular inequality again, for any data point $p \in c$, we have the following inequations:

$$Dist(r_1, p) < Dist(r_1, center(c)) + \frac{l_{diagonal}}{2}$$

$$Dist(r_2, p) > |Dist(r_2, center(c)) - \frac{l_{diagonal}}{2}|$$

So if we have $Dist(r_1, center(c)) + \frac{l_{diagonal}}{2} < |Dist(r_2, center(c)) - \frac{l_{diagonal}}{2}|$, which can be simplified as $Dis(r_1, center(c)) + l_{diagonal} < Dist(r_2, center(c))$, then it is guaranteed that $Dist(r_1, p) < Dist(r_2, p)$, as required.   □

For any particular cell, we can always find a subset of the representative data such that its members are not mutually dominated but any other representative data not in this subset is dominated by at least one member in this subset. This subset is called *non-dominant set* of the representative data for this cell, a.k.a *Pareto optimal set* in multi-objective optimization. By using the non-dominant set, we can calculate the upper bound of k-WODF of data points in a cell without the need to know their respective k nearest representative data, as required in Lemma 1. This makes it possible to directly employ the pruning strategy. Based on the non-dominant set of representative data of a given cell, we can establish a new upper bound of the value of k-WODF for data points inside the cell.

Lemma 3. *Let p denote a given data point in the cell c. The k-WODF of p satisfies the following new upper bound:*

$$kWODF(p) \leq \frac{\sum_{i=1}^{k} Dist(center(c), r_i^*)}{k} + \frac{l_{diagonal}}{2}$$

where $r_i^* \in R^*$ and R^* is the top k non-dominant representative data of c that have the largest distance from the center of c.

Proof. Since it is evident $\frac{\sum_{i=1}^{k} Dist(center(c), r_i)}{k} + \frac{l_{diagonal}}{2} \leq \frac{\sum_{i=1}^{k} Dist(center(c), r_i^*)}{k} + \frac{l_{diagonal}}{2}$ because r_i^* is the top k representative data of c that has the largest distance from c. This leads to k-$WODF(p) < \frac{\sum_{i=1}^{k} Dist(center(c), r_i^*)}{k} + \frac{l_{diagonal}}{2}$, as required.   □

The advantage of Lemma 3 is that we can easily find the upper bound of the k-WODF values of any data point in a given cell without the need to know exactly its k nearest representative data. Based on Lemma 3, Inequation (1) can be amended slightly to lead to the following updated pruning strategy that can be used directly: all the data points in a cell c can be safely pruned away if the following inequation is satisfied:

$$\frac{\sum_{i=1}^{k} Dist(center(c), r_i^*)}{k} + \frac{l_{diagonal}}{2} < Min_{kWODF} \tag{2}$$

4   Experimental Evaluation

Experimental evaluation is conducted to evaluate the speed and accuracy performance of GO-PEAS and the recent grid-based outlier detection and clustering methods (which can assist outlier detection) including DISTROD [10],

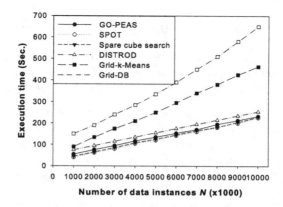

Fig. 1. Scalability with regard to N for different methods

the sparse cube search method [1], SPOT [11], Grid-k-Means [6] and Grid-DB [3]. Synthetic datasets are generated using a dataset generator which can produce datasets with desired number of instances and dimensions. They feature various dense and sparse regions in the data space, which offers an ideal testbed for our experiments. Five real-life datasets from the UCI machine learning repository are also used, i.e., Machine, Breast cancer, Segmentation, Ionosphere and Musk.

We start with the scalability study that investigates how efficient GO-PEAS is when the number of instances N in the dataset increases. The result is shown in Fig. 1 where N is increased from 1,000k to 10,000k. The result reveals that GO-PEAS, the sparse cube search method, SPOT and DISTROD are more scalable with respect to N than Grid-k-Means and Grid-DB. The sparse cube search method and SPOT boast the best efficiency performance. This is because that they use very simple outlier detection mechanism, that is, outliers are those data in located in low-density cells. As the result, they sacrifice detection accuracy for efficiency. GO-PEAS is ranked in the 3rd position in the comparison and is noticeably faster than DISTROD thanks to the use of the pruning searching technique we devised. GO-PEAS is also significantly faster than Grid-k-Means and Grid-DB because no expensive clustering or local outlier evaluation using $DB(pct; d_{min})$ metric is needed.

We also evaluate the scalability of different methods under varying number of dimensions d and the result is presented in Fig. 2. Since our method and all the competitive methods leverage a grid structure and deal with the same number of populated cells in the grid for the same dataset, thus dimensional scalability of all the methods is very similar. The difference in their exact execution time under different d mainly comes from the different detection mechanisms they use. All their execution time grows in a super-linear manner but it is much lower than the exponential order of d, showing the efficacy of using only populated cells in boosting the detection efficiency for grid-based outlier detection methods.

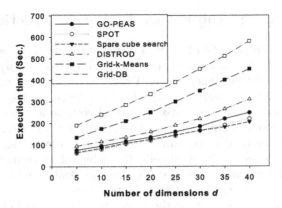

Fig. 2. Scalability with regard to d

Table 1. Outlier quality of different methods (The lower the better)

	GO-PEAS	SPOT	Sparse cube	DISTROD	Grid-k-Means	Grid-DB
Synthetic	0.63	1	0.96	0.65	0.67	0.86
Machine	0.75	0.95	1	0.75	0.71	0.94
Breast cancer	0.52	1	0.94	0.54	0.58	0.94
Segmentation	0.62	0.89	0.92	0.62	0.60	1
Innosphere	0.70	0.88	1	0.71	0.67	0.89
Musk	0.57	0.77	0.98	0.59	0.62	1

In the effectiveness study, Table 1 shows the quality of outliers detected by GO-PEAS and the competitive methods when dealing with different datasets including the synthetic datasets and the five real-life datasets from UCI. We do not need to compare GO-PEAS with its baseline version as their detection results are identical. The quality of outliers are measured by the Standard Deviation of Clusters (SDC) after outliers are removed. The result of the synthetic datasets are the averaged SDC value obtained by running GO-PEAS on 10 different synthetic datasets to minimize bias. To better present the results, the SDC values of different methods are normalized and converted to a value in the range from 0 to 1. GO-PEAS, DISTROD and Grid-k-Means enjoy the best SDC performance because all of them evaluate the outlier-ness of data points relative to the nearby dense regions (either dense cells or clusters). The sparse cube search method, SPOT and Grid-DB feature inferior SDC performance because they evaluate the outlier-ness of data points from a more local perspective.

5   Conclusion and the Future Research Directions

In this paper, we propose GO-PEAS, a scalable yet accurate grid-based outlier detection method. Innovative pruning techniques are incorporated to significantly improve the efficiency of GO-PEAS while maintaining a very good detection accuracy. The detection result of GO-PEAS is also less sensitive to the granularity of space partitioning. Experimental results demonstrate that GO-PEAS enjoys a good and balanced speed and accuracy performance.

In GO-PEAS, we need to maintain the mapping information between data points and their corresponding grid cells, i.e., which data belong to which cell. This requires extra storing space and I/O cost for dealing with large datasets. In our future work, we are interested in reducing the space requirement of our method to minimize the storage of the mapping information between data and grid cells, whereby effectively reducing space complexity and I/O cost.

Also, we will further extend the experimental evaluation in the future by evaluating the effectiveness of different outlier detection methods using other measurements for outlier quality such as precision-at-n and AUC. We will also investigate the impact of the granularity of partitioning on the performance of our and other grid-based detection methods.

Acknowledgement. The authors would like to thank the support from National Science Foundation of China through the research projects (No. 61370050, No. 61572036 and No. 61363030) and Guangxi Key Laboratory of Trusted Software (No. kx201527).

References

1. Aggarwal, C.C., Yu, P.S.: Outlier detection in high dimensional data. In: SIGMOD 2001 (2001)
2. Barnett, V., Lewis, T.: Outliers in Statistical Data, 3rd edn. Wiley, Chichester (1994)
3. Elahi, M., Lv, X., Nisar, M.W., Wang, H.: Distance based outlier for data streams using grid structure. Inf. Technol. J. **8**(2), 128–137 (2009)
4. Knorr, E.M., Ng, R.T.: Finding intentional knowledge of distance-based outliers. In: VLDB 1999, Edinburgh, Scotland, pp. 211–222 (1999)
5. Koh, J.L.Y., Lee, M.-L., Hsu, W., Ang, W.T.: Correlation-based attribute outlier detection in XML. In: ICDE 2008, pp. 1522–1524 (2008)
6. Ma, L., Gu, L., Li, B., Zhou, L., Wang, J.: An improved grid-based k-means clustering algorithm. Adv. Sci. Technol. Lett. **73**, 1–6 (2014)
7. Gupta, M., Gao, J., Aggarwal, C.C., Han, J.: Outlier detection for temporal data: a survey. IEEE Trans. Knowl. Data Eng. **25**(1), 1–20 (2014)
8. Schubert, E., Zimek, A., Kriegel, H.-P.: Generalized outlier detection with flexible kernel density estimates. In: SDM 2014, pp. 542–550 (2014)
9. Vijayarani, S., Jothi, P.: An efficient clustering algorithm for outlier detection in data streams. Int. J. Adv. Res. Comput. Commun. Eng. **2**(9), 3657–3665 (2013)
10. Zhang, J., Tao, X., Wang, H.: Outlier detection from large distributed databases. World Wide Web J. **17**(4), 539–568 (2014)

11. Zhang, J., Gao, Q., Wang, H., Liu, Q., Xu, K.: Detecting projected outliers in high-dimensional data streams. In: Bhowmick, S.S., Küng, J., Wagner, R. (eds.) DEXA 2009. LNCS, vol. 5690, pp. 629–644. Springer, Heidelberg (2009)
12. Su, L., Han, W., Yang, S., Zou, P., Jia, Y.: Continuous adaptive outlier detection on distributed data streams. In: HPCC 2007, Houston, TX, USA, pp. 74–85 (2007)
13. Tang, J., Chen, Z., Fu, A., Cheung, D.W.: Enhancing effectiveness of outlier detections for low density patterns. In: PAKDD 2002, Taipei, Taiwan, pp. 535–548 (2002)
14. Sheng, B., Li, Q., Mao, W., Jin, W.: Outlier detection in sensor networks. In: MobiHoc 2007, Montral, Qubec, Canada, pp. 219–228 (2007)
15. Otey, M., Ghoting, A., Parthasarathy, S.: Fast distributed outlier detection in mixed attribute data sets. Data Min. Knowl. Discov. **12**(2), 203–228 (2006)
16. Ramaswamy, S., Rastogi, R., Shim, K.: Efficient algorithms for mining outliers from large data sets. In: SIGMOD 2000, Dallas, Texas, pp 427–438 (2000)
17. Jin, W., Tung, A.K.H., Han, J.: Finding Top n Local Outliers in Large Database. In: SIGKDD 2001, San Francisco, CA, pp 293–298 (2001)
18. Ester, M., Kriegel, H-P., Sander, J., Xu, X.: A density-based algorithm for discovering clusters in large spatial databases with noise. In: SIGKDD 1996, Portland, Oregon, USA, pp 226–231 (1996)
19. Chhabra, P., Scott, C., Kolaczyk, E.D., Crovella, M.: Distributed spatial anomaly detection. In: INFOCOM 2008, Phoenix, AZ, pp 1705–1713 (2008)

Multi-objective Genetic Programming for Figure-Ground Image Segmentation

Yuyu Liang[(✉)], Mengjie Zhang, and Will N. Browne

School of Engineering and Computer Science, Victoria University of Wellington,
P.O. Box 600, Wellington 6140, New Zealand
{yuyu.liang,mengjie.zhang,will.browne}@ecs.vuw.ac.nz

Abstract. Figure-ground segmentation is a crucial preprocessing step in areas of computer vision and image processing. As an evolutionary computation technique, genetic programming (GP) can evolve algorithms automatically for complex problems and has been introduced for image segmentation. However, GP-based methods face a challenge to control the complexity of evolved solutions. In this paper, we develop a novel exponential function to measure the solution complexity. This complexity measure is utilized as a fitness evaluation measure in GP in two ways: one method is to combine it with the classification accuracy linearly to form a weighted sum fitness function; the other is to treat them separately as two objectives. Based on this, we propose a weighted sum GP method and a multi-objective GP (MOGP) method for segmentation tasks. We select four types of test images from bitmap, Brodatz texture, Weizmann and PASCAL databases. The proposed methods are compared with a reference GP method, which is single-objective (the classification accuracy) without considering the solution complexity. The results show that the new approaches, especially MOGP, can significantly reduce the solution complexity and the training time without decreasing the segmentation performance.

Keywords: Figure-ground segmentation · Genetic programming · Solution complexity · Multi-objective optimisation

1 Introduction

Figure-ground image segmentation is the process of separating foreground objects or regions of interest from their background. It is considered a crucial preprocessing step, as the results can be input to many higher-level computer vision and image processing tasks, such as object recognition, object tracking and image editing [26]. There are several problems in the existing approaches that include bottom-up [10] and top-down methods [8,9]. Bottom-up methods rely on continuity principles, which are sensitive to factors, such as illumination variations, noise and image contrast [10]. In contrast, top-down methods can learn from prior knowledge, so they can adapt to different image domains. As the figure-ground segmentation often needs certain rules for specific images to achieve accurate

© Springer International Publishing Switzerland 2016
T. Ray et al. (Eds.): ACALCI 2016, LNAI 9592, pp. 134–146, 2016.
DOI: 10.1007/978-3-319-28270-1_12

performance, top-down methods are more preferable. However, top-down methods often require heavy human guidance/work [8,9], making them difficult to be applied in diverse image domains. Moreover, the more human work required, the higher probability of introducing human bias.

Genetic programming (GP) is an evolutionary computation technique inspired by biological evolution [12]. It can handle user-defined tasks automatically by evolving computer programs, and does not require users to specify the form or structure of solutions [19]. Therefore, GP has the potential to evolve good performing segmentors without requiring much human work. Actually, GP has been introduced in the area of image segmentation by several works [15,20,23,24], which show that GP-evolved segmentors can deal with a wide range of images and achieve accurate segmentation results in certain domains [15,20,23,24]. For evolutionary algorithms [14], particularly GP, it is difficult to control the complexity of evolved solutions [22]. Program sizes can grow without (significant) corresponding increases in fitness, which is known as bloat [19].

Parsimony pressure is a simple and widely-used way to control bloat [5]. One kind of parsimony pressure methods is to penalize the fitness of programs based on the program size, and combine multiple objectives to form a single fitness function (known as weighted sum methods). For example, $f = \sum_i w_i * f_i$, where w_i represent the weight of the ith fitness function f_i. Zhang et al. [25] propose a fitness function in GP for object detection problems. This fitness function is a linear combination of detection rate, false alarm rate and false alarm area. The false alarm area is defined as the number of false alarm pixels which are incorrectly detected as object centres without clustering. Results show that this fitness function can reflect the smoothness of evolved programs, and this GP based method performs well on small and regular objects with uncluttered backgrounds. Alternative parsimony pressure methods modify the selection process to lean towards individuals with smaller sizes among individuals with equal fitnesses or rank (known as lexicographic parsimony pressure methods) [16]. In this paper, we propose a weighted sum method with a new fitness function.

The solution complexity can also be treated as a separate objective to tackle the bloat problem. They are multi-objective optimisation algorithms, which aim to evolve a Pareto front of tradeoff solutions based on all the objectives. Shao et al. [22] utilize multi-objective GP (MOGP) to develop global feature descriptors for image classification tasks. There are two objectives in this paper, which are the classification error and the tree complexity. The proposed method achieves better classification accuracies than many state-of-the-art feature extraction techniques, including local binary patterns (LBP) and Gabor filters. One problem is that the MOGP method requires a long time for evolution (e.g. 7.6 h on Caltech-101 dataset). Sarro et al. [21] formulate the effort estimation problem as an optimisation problem. They compare single-objective GP with five different fitness functions (e.g. mean magnitude of relative error) and the multi-objective GP considering the five functions simultaneously. It is concluded that single-objective GP with certain fitness functions can achieve comparable results with those produced by MOGP.

This paper aims to develop two new figure-ground image segmentation methods based on weighted sum GP and MOGP respectively. Both of them take the classfication accuracy and the solution complexity into account. One conducts a weighted sum of them to form a single fitness function, while the other keeps them separately and optimises the two objectives simultaneously using the Pareto front approach. To investigate whether the new approaches can perfrom well, we will test them on a sequence of figure-ground segmentation problems with increasing difficulties, and compare them with a reference GP-based approach, which takes the classfication accuracy as the single objective. Specifically, we investigate the following objectives:

1. whether the new complexity control weighted sum and multi-objective methods can outperform the reference GP method that does not control the complexity, and
2. which of the two new approaches can better perform the image segmentation tasks.

The rest of this paper is organized as follows. Section 2 introduces the reference GP-based method, which includes the algorithm framework, GP settings and the fitness function. Section 3 introduces the two new approaches: the weighted sum and multi-objective GP methods. Section 4 describes experiment preparations, including image datasets and three evaluation measures. In Sect. 5, results on four datasets produced by two new methods are analyzed and compared with that of the reference GP. Conclusions are drawn in Sect. 6.

2   Reference GP Method

As shown in Fig. 1, the segmentation system of the reference method has three major phases. Firstly, a binary classifier is evolved by GP. In this step, an equal number of sub-images, labeled as class A (objects) or B (background), are captured from objects and background in the training images. Features are extracted from these sub-images, which are raw pixel values in this paper. Based on the training samples, GP evolves binary classifiers that can classify sub-images as objects or background. Secondly, a shifting window is utilized to sweep across test images, capturing sub-images that have the same size as those in the first step. Next, the feature extraction is conducted to form the test samples, which can be categorized as class A or B by the evolved classifier. Finally, since the shifting window has overlaps, pixels in test images may have more than one assigned label. We apply a majority voting scheme to determine the estimated label of each pixel and produce the segmentation results.

2.1   GP Settings

In this paper, raw pixel values are directly used as input to the system, which makes the feature extraction phase simpler and time-saving. Table 1 displays the function set. It consists of four standard arithmetic operators and five conditional

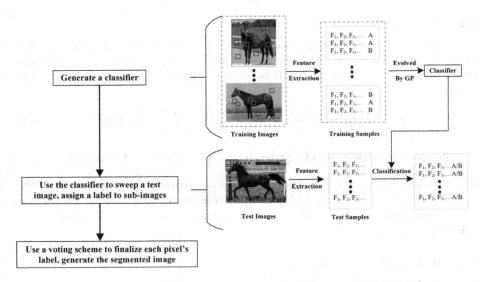

Fig. 1. The framework of GP based figure-ground segmentation method.

Table 1. Function set.

Function Name	Definition
$\text{Add}(a_1, a_2)$	$a_1 + a_2$
$\text{Sub}(a_1, a_2)$	$a_1 - a_2$
$\text{Mul}(a_1, a_2)$	$a_1 * a_2$
$\text{Div}(a_1, a_2)$	$\begin{cases} a_1/a_2 \text{ if } a_2 ! = 0 \\ 0 \quad\quad \text{ if } a_2 == 0 \end{cases}$
$\text{IF}(a_1, a_2, a_3)$	$\begin{cases} a_2 \text{ if } a_1 \text{ is true} \\ a_3 \text{ if } a_1 \text{ is false} \end{cases}$
$<= (a_1, a_2)$	$\begin{cases} true \quad \text{if } a_1 <= a_2 \\ false \text{ if otherwise} \end{cases}$
$>= (a_1, a_2)$	$\begin{cases} true \quad \text{if } a_1 >= a_2 \\ false \text{ if otherwise} \end{cases}$
$== (a_1, a_2)$	$\begin{cases} true \quad \text{if } a_1 == a_2 \\ false \text{ if otherwise} \end{cases}$
$\text{Between}(a_1, a_2, a_3)$	$\begin{cases} true \quad \text{if } a_2 <= a_1 <= a_3 \\ false \text{ if otherwise} \end{cases}$

operators, all of which are simple and easy to be calculated. We set the population size to 500, and use crossover and mutation as reproduction operators, whose rates are 90 % and 10 % respectively. The other GP set-up parameters follow the settings used by Koza [12].

2.2   Fitness Function

As a simple and effective evaluation measure, the classification accuracy (shown in Eq. 1) is commonly used as the fitness function for evolutionary algorithms based classification problems [4]. It is employed in our reference method as the single objective.

$$f_1 = \frac{Number.of.correctly.classified.samples}{Number.of.total.training.samples} * 100\,\%. \qquad (1)$$

3   New Methods with Solution Complexity Control

Based on the reference GP method, two new approaches are introduced to control the solution complexity. The solution complexity is measured by a novel exponential function. The difference between these two approaches is how to use this complexity measure.

3.1   Weighted Sum Method

To control the complexity/size of evolved solutions, this problem is considered along with the classification accuracy (f_1). The function selected to measure the solution size can be added to f_1, which means both of them should be monotonic and have the same value range. In this paper, we apply an expontional function $p(x) = exp(-\beta * x)$, where β is a scaling factor. For GP, the solution size ($size$) can be calculated by adding the number of terminals and functions in a program. $p(size)$ belongs to the range $(0, 1]$ and is monotonically decreasing, the same as f_1. Therefore, they meet the above requirements.

For the weighted sum GP method, $p(size)$ is combined with the accuracy linearly as a size penalty part to adjust the original individual's fitness evaluation (shown in Eq. 2). Based on our observation, the size of solutions evolved by the reference GP method can be dozens or hundreds. Due to the fact that $exp(-x)$ is close to 0 with the increase of x, which makes complexity control meaningless. Therefore, we introduce a weighting factor (β) and set it to 0.01.

$$f_2 = \alpha * Accuracy + (1 - \alpha) * exp(-\beta * size). \qquad (2)$$

where α is a weight factor between the classification accuracy and the size penalty part ($\alpha\epsilon(0, 1]$). $size$ represents the size of a program or solution.

3.2   Multi-objective Method

For the multi-objective method, $p(size) = exp(-\beta * size)$ is utilized as an independent objective from the classification accuracy. It aims to find a set of the best trade-off solutions, called Pareto front, between the two objectives. Nondominated sorting genetic algorithm II (NSGA-II) [11] is a well-known technique for multi-objective optimisation. It employs a genetic algorithm (GA) as the search algorithm to evolve Pareto fronts using multiple objectives. Based on NSGA-II, we develop nondominated sorting genetic programming (NSGP), in which GP replaces GA as the evolutionary algorithm to search for Pareto fronts.

4   Experiment Preparation

4.1   Datasets

Four types of images are selected to test the evolved segmentors in this paper. These images have different difficulty levels for the segmentation task. As described in Table 2, they include bitmap, texture and object images. Specifically, the bitmap image, named as "Rectangular", is sythesized from two bitmap patterns (P14 and P24) [3], and is a binary image. The texture image, D24vs34, is a grayscale image that is synthesized from two Brodatz textures (D24 and D34) [1]. In addition, the horse images from the Weizmann dataset [7] and the passenger air-plane images from the PASCAL dataset [2] are images containing certain objects and complex backgrounds. The Weizmann images contain one horse object per image and the objects vary in the position (standing, running and eating). The passenger air-plane images have the largest sizes and vary in object shapes and sizes. Moreover, some air-plane images contain multiple objects. Empirically, object images with larger sizes and complex variations are more difficult to be segmented accurately than binary or texture images [18]. Therefore, PASCAL images are considered as the most difficult images for segmentation tasks; while bitmap images are the simplest ones.

Table 2. Four types of images used in this paper.

Database	Images				Descriptions
Bitmap	P14	P24	Rectangular		Size: 256*256 Synthetic, binary images
Brodatz	D24	D34	D24vs34		Size: 320*160 Grayscale images
Weizmann	horse006 horse010 horse027		horse110 horse119		Average Size:248*211 Real images Varing horse positions One object per image
	horse121 horse122 horse159		horse165 horse317		
PASCAL (Name prefix: 2007_00)	0033	0256 0738	1288		Average Size:500*350 Real images Varing object sizes
	1761	2099 2266	2376		Multiple objects per image

4.2   Evaluation Measures

The segmentation accuracy (Eq. 3) is applied as an evaluation measure in this paper, as it is simple and commonly-used. However, it may not be sufficient to reflect the real segmentation performance in all cases. For example, when the background takes up a large proportion of an image, even though all the objects are incorrectly segmented as background, the segmentation accuracy would still be quite high. Therefore, another two evaluation methods, F_1 measure (Eq. 4) and NRM (negative rate metric, Eq. 5), are considered here to compensate it. F_1 combines precision and recall together; while NRM takes mismatches between a prediction and the ground truth into account [6].

The segmentation accuracy and F_1 reach its worst at 0 and best at 1; while NRM is worst at 1 and best at 0. To make it easy to analyze the result values obtained from the evaluation measures, we derive CNRM (complementary negative rate metric, shown in Eq. 5) from the NRM. In this way, all the values are the higher the better.

$$SegmentationAccuracy = \frac{TP + TN}{Total.Pixel.Number.In.An.Image} \tag{3}$$

$$F_1 = \frac{2 * Precision * Recall}{Precision + Recall} \tag{4}$$

$$NRM = (FNR + FPR)/2; \; CNRM = 1 - NRM \tag{5}$$

where $FNR = \frac{FN}{TP+FN}$, $FPR = \frac{FP}{FP+TN}$, $Precision = \frac{TP}{TP+FP}$, $Recall = \frac{TP}{TP+FN}$. TP, TN, FP and FN stand for true positives, true negatives, false positives and false negatives respectively. In the context of segmentation, TP represents the pixel number of desired objects that are correctly segmented as objects; TN means the pixel number of non-objects are correctly segmented as background; FP and FN represent the number of non-objects and objects that are incorrectly segmented respectively. FPR and FNR mean false positive rate and false negative rate respectively.

5   Results

In this section, we analyse the results of segmentors evolved by the proposed two approaches. In addition, results are also compared with the reference GP method. We set the size of sliding window to 4 for bitmap images and 16 for other test images; therefore, the feature dimensions are 16 for bitmap images and 256 for other images. Both the shifting step in horizontal and vertical direction are set to 2.

For bitmap and texture images, the training set has 1000 samples, in which there are 500 samples for each bitmap (or texture) patterns. The test images are shown in Table 2, named as Rectangular (the bitmap image) and D23vs34 (the texture image). Due to the limited number of the Weizmann and PASCAL images, the leave-one-out (LOO) cross-validation [13] is employed. Two hundred samples are extracted from each Weizmann image (1800 in total). Considering PASCAL images are much larger, 500 sampels are extracted from each PASCAL image (3500 in total). Each experiment has 30 independent runs, and final results are the average of those from 30 runs.

5.1   The Weighted Sum GP Method

As shown in Fig. 2, evaluation measures reach the highest when the weights are between 0.95 to 1.0 on all the datasets, except the CNRM measure on texture images. Since we attach more importance to the segmentation performance than the solution size, even though weights less than 0.95 may lead to lower solution sizes, we will focus on the weight range [0.95,1.0] in the following experiments.

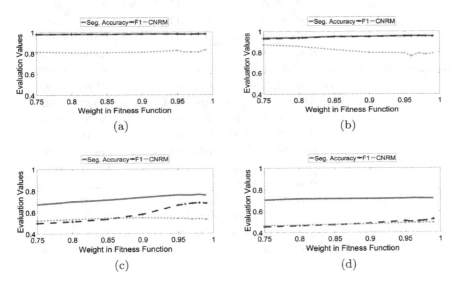

Fig. 2. Performance with different weights in The Fitness Function. (a) on a bitmap image; (b) on a texture image; (c) on Weizmann images; (d) on PASCAL images.

Results on different datasets are displayed in Table 3. In the tables, $TrainTime(s)$ means the average training time (second) for one GP run, which is determined by the number of training samples, the dimension of features and specific learning algorithms; $TestTime(s)$ represents the average time cost to segment one test image determined by the size of test images and specific algorithms used.

When testing on the bitmap image, the proposed weighted sum methods reduce the program size from 76 to around 12, which costs less than one-third training time per run of that of the reference method. For texture images, the fitness function with weight 0.95 performs best among the weighted sum functions. Compared with the reference method, both the size of solutions and training

Table 3. Statistical results of weighted sum method (Acc. represents accuracy).

Dataset	Fitness Measure		Segmentation Acc. (%)	F_1	CNRM	Size	Train Time (s)	Test Time (s)
Bitmap	Reference: f_1		98.12 ± 0.22	0.98	0.82	76	15.24	0.012
		$\alpha = 0.99$	98.07 ± 0.28	0.98	0.83	13	4.46	0.009
	Weighted	$\alpha = 0.98$	98.05 ± 0.24	0.98	0.81	12	4.14	0.009
	Sum:	$\alpha = 0.97$	97.94 ± 0.20	0.98	0.81	12	4.18	0.009
	f_2	$\alpha = 0.96$	97.96 ± 0.18	0.98	0.81	12	4.04	0.009
		$\alpha = 0.95$	98.06 ± 0.22	0.98	0.83	12	3.93	0.009
Texture	Reference: f_1		94.98 ± 2.75	0.95	0.81	343	23.86	0.042
		$\alpha = 0.99$	95.44 ± 0.93	0.95	0.79	260	21.40	0.036
	Weighted	$\alpha = 0.98$	95.55 ± 0.95	0.96	0.78	202	18.48	0.033
	Sum:	$\alpha = 0.97$	95.39 ± 1.70	0.95	0.78	163	15.85	0.030
	f_2	$\alpha = 0.96$	95.54 ± 1.19	0.95	0.78	132	14.48	0.029
		$\alpha = 0.95$	95.61 ± 0.87	0.96	0.79	127	13.38	0.030
Weizmann	Reference: f_1		75.76 ± 8.37	0.67	0.54	303	49.74	0.036
		$\alpha = 0.99$	75.75 ± 7.48	0.68	0.53	225	37.80	0.032
	Weighted	$\alpha = 0.98$	76.46 ± 7.10	0.69	0.54	175	30.29	0.029
	Sum:	$\alpha = 0.97$	75.89 ± 6.94	0.68	0.53	133	25.51	0.026
	f_2	$\alpha = 0.96$	75.87 ± 7.11	0.67	0.54	103	21.18	0.025
		$\alpha = 0.95$	76.01 ± 6.91	0.66	0.54	80	18.07	0.022
PASCAL	Reference: f_1		71.84 ± 10.63	0.51	0.49	321	129.82	0.129
		$\alpha = 0.99$	72.10 ± 8.26	0.52	0.49	176	93.45	0.103
	Weighted	$\alpha = 0.98$	72.14 ± 8.59	0.51	0.49	100	80.29	0.090
	Sum:	$\alpha = 0.97$	72.24 ± 8.35	0.51	0.49	77	55.19	0.072
	f_2	$\alpha = 0.96$	72.10 ± 9.16	0.50	0.49	59	50.32	0.073
		$\alpha = 0.95$	72.01 ± 8.68	0.51	0.49	43	44.24	0.063

time almost halved. On Weizmann images, the weighted sum methods with the weight factor of 0.98 and 0.96 perform better than the reference function in all the three measures, especially the one with 0.98. They also spend less training and test time. On PASCAL images, they achieve generally better performance under all the three evaluation measures than the reference method. For example, the function with the weight of 0.95 achieves a little higer accuracy and the same F_1 and CNRM values. However, the training time per GP run only takes up one third of that for the reference method.

Compared with the reference GP method, the proposed weighted sum approach, which adds penalty to the program complexity in the fitness function, produces similar or even better results. More importantly, as the sizes of evolved programs dereases significantly, both the training time and the test time are reduced. Since the test time is quite low already, the changes of the training time are much more obvious.

5.2   The NSGP Method

In this section, we conduct segmentation experiments using the proposed multi-objective approach – NSGP. Considering if the size of an evolved program is too small (e.g. 5), this solution is normally too simple and not effective to solve the complex segmentation task, so we set an restriction to the objective of the complexity measure ($p(size)$). Specifically, if an individual's size is less than 10, this objective will be given the lowest value 0. Fig. 3a shows the Pareto front produced in one GP run using texture samples. The Pareto front provides insights into the tradeoff of the two objectives (the classfication accuracy and the solution complexity) for the segmentation problem. As there is normally a large number of solutions on the Pareto front generated in the training process, solutions need to be selected based on our preference to segment the test images.

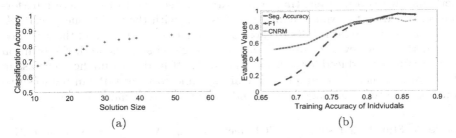

(a)   (b)

Fig. 3. (a) NSGP Pareto front evolved using texture training samples; (b) Performance of solutions from this pareto front on texture image.

Table 4. Result examples of NSGP method (G.T. means ground truth; Bitmap, Texture, W. and P. represent result examples of Bitmap, Texture, Weizmann and PASCAL images respectively).

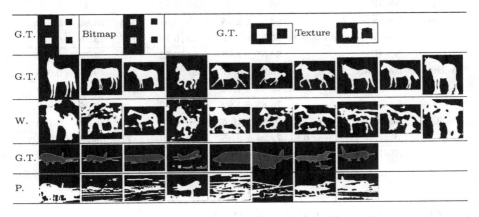

Between the classification accuracy and the solution complexity, we lean towards the former one. We assume that front solutions, generated on the training set, with higher classfication accuracies produce better results on the test dataset. This assumption can be testified by Fig. 3b, which shows that the values of three evaluation measures on the test dataset grow as the increase of front solutions' accuracies. Therefore, we select 20 solutions with the highest accuracies along the front in each GP run of the training process, and use them to segment test images. The best one of the 20 results is used to represent the algorithm's performance of this GP run. After 30 runs, we calculate the average performance.

Table 4 displays one example result of each test image using the NSGP approach. It can be seen that for bitmap and texture images, different patterns/textures have been accurately separated. For Weizmann and PASCAL images, even though some examples do not have clear object boundaries, objects are located accurately and the results are promising. Table 5 compares NSGP with the weighted sum method and the reference method. The weighted sum methods with certain weighting factors are selected due to their better performance. Based on the Mann-Whitney U-Test [17] with the significance level 5 %, NSGP achieves similar results to those of the reference method and the weighted sum method. However, compared with the weighted sum mentod, the solution sizes are further reduced for segmentation tasks. It leads to a further decrease in the training time. For example, the training time cost per GP run reduces two thirds on the texture image and around half on the Weizmann images.

Table 5. Statistical results of NSGP method (Seg. Acc. represents segmentation accuracy).

Dataset	Fitness Measure	Seg. Acc. (%)	F_1	CNRM	Size	Train Time (s)	Test Time (s)
Bitmap	Reference: f_1	98.12 ± 0.22	0.98	0.82	76	15.24	0.012
	WeightedSum:$\alpha = 0.95$	98.06 ± 0.22	0.98	0.83	12	3.93	0.009
	NSGP	98.12 ± 0.23	0.98	0.82	12	2.47	0.029
Texture	Reference: f_1	94.98 ± 2.75	0.95	0.81	343	23.86	0.042
	WeightedSum:$\alpha = 0.95$	95.61 ± 0.87	0.96	0.79	127	13.38	0.030
	NSGP	94.57 ± 2.67	0.94	0.82	38	4.72	0.033
Weizmann	Reference: f_1	75.76 ± 8.37	0.67	0.54	303	49.74	0.036
	WeightedSum:$\alpha = 0.98$	76.46 ± 7.10	0.69	0.54	175	30.29	0.029
	NSGP	76.83 ± 5.92	0.65	0.56	39	16.36	0.039
PASCAL	Reference: f_1	71.84 ± 10.63	0.51	0.49	321	129.82	0.129
	WeightedSum:$\alpha = 0.97$	72.24 ± 8.35	0.51	0.49	77	55.19	0.072
	NSGP	73.31 ± 8.09	0.51	0.49	49	28.78	0.140

6   Conclusions and Future Work

This paper developed a weighted sum GP method and a multi-objective GP method (NSGP) for the figure-ground image segmentation. To control solution complexity, an exponential function was designed as an additional objective to the function of the classification accuracy. The two functions were combined linearly in the weighted sum method, and treated separately as two objectives in NSGP.

A GP method, which took the classfication accuracy as the single objective, was employed as a reference method. Compared with it, the two proposed approaches with the complexity control achieved similar results in terms of three evaluation measures (the segmentation accuracy, F_1 and CNRM). However, both of them reduced the size of evolved solutions, leading to a significant decrease in the training time. In particular, the NSGP produced even smaller solutions than that of weighted sum method with similar segmentation performance. This indicates that considering the solution complexity the two new approaches outperformed the reference GP. Moreover, NSGP is more powerful in reducing solution complexity than the weighted sum method without reducing the segmentation performance.

In this paper, we used raw pixel values as input of GP directly. Since certain image features, such as Gabor filters, are powerful image descriptors, we will consider more powerful image features in the future, from which GP may evolve segmentors with better performance.

References

1. Brodatz texture database. http://multibandtexture.recherche.usherbrooke.ca/original_brodatz.html
2. The pascal visual object classes homepage. http://pascallin.ecs.soton.ac.uk/challenges/VOC/
3. Song, V.C.A.: Texture segmentation by genetic programming. Evol. Comput. **16**(4), 416–481 (2008)
4. Al-Sahaf, H., Song, A., Neshatian, K., Zhang, M.: Extracting image features for classification by two-tier genetic programming. In: 2012 IEEE Congress on Evolutionary Computation (CEC), pp. 1–8. IEEE (2012)
5. Alex, A.: Summary of parsimony pressure made easy. https://wiki.umn.edu/pub/UmmCSci4553s09/ResearchPaperGroupsAndTopics/ppMadeEzSummary.pdf
6. Ashburner, J., Friston, K.J.: Unified segmentation. Neuroimage **26**(3), 839–851 (2005)
7. Borenstein, E.: Weizmann horse database. http://www.msri.org/people/members/eranb/
8. Borenstein, E., Sharon, E., Ullman, S.: Combining top-down and bottom-up segmentation. In: Proceedings IEEE Workshop on Perceptual Organization in Computer Vision, pp. 1–8 (2004)
9. Borenstein, E., Ullman, S.: Class-specific, top-down segmentation. In: Heyden, A., Sparr, G., Nielsen, M., Johansen, P. (eds.) ECCV 2002, Part II. LNCS, vol. 2351, pp. 109–122. Springer, Heidelberg (2002)
10. Cote, M., Saeedi, P., et al.: Hierarchical image segmentation using a combined geometrical and feature based approach. J. Data Anal. Inf. Process. **2**(04), 117 (2014)
11. Deb, K., Pratap, A., Agarwal, S., Meyarivan, T.: A fast and elitist multiobjective genetic algorithm: NSGA-II. IEEE Trans. Evol. Comput. **6**(2), 182–197 (2002)

12. Koza, J.R.: Genetic Programming: On the Programming of Computers by Natural Selection. MIT Press, Cambridge (1992)
13. Kuhn, M.: Futility analysis in the crossvalidation of machine learning models, pp. 1–22 (2014). arXiv:1405.6974
14. Liang, Y., Zhang, M., Browne, W.N.: Image segmentation: a survey of methods based on evolutionary computation. In: Dick, G., Browne, W.N., Whigham, P., Zhang, M., Bui, L.T., Ishibuchi, H., Jin, Y., Li, X., Shi, Y., Singh, P., Tan, K.C., Tang, K. (eds.) SEAL 2014. LNCS, vol. 8886, pp. 847–859. Springer, Heidelberg (2014)
15. Liang, Y., Zhang, M., Browne, W.N.: A supervised figure-ground segmentation method using genetic programming. In: Mora, A.M., Squillero, G. (eds.) Applications of Evolutionary Computation. Lecture Notes in Computer Science, vol. 9028, pp. 491–503. Springer, Heidelberg (2015)
16. Luke, S., Panait, L.: Lexicographic parsimony pressure. In: Proceedings of GECCO-2002, pp. 829–836. Morgan Kaufmann Publishers (2002)
17. Mann, H.B., Whitney, D.R.: On a test of whether one of two random variables is stochastically larger than the other. Ann. Math. Stat. **18**, 50–60 (1947)
18. Poli, R.: Genetic programming for feature detection and image segmentation. Evol. Comput. **1143**, 110–125 (1996)
19. Poli, R., Langdon, W.B., McPhee, N.F.: A Field Guide to Genetic Programming. Published via http://lulu.com and freely available at http://www.gp-field-guide. org.uk, UK (2008)
20. Poli, R.: Genetic Programming for feature detection and image segmentation. In: Fogarty, T.C. (ed.) AISB-WS 1996. LNCS, vol. 1143, pp. 110–125. Springer, Heidelberg (1996)
21. Sarro, F., Ferrucci, F., Gravino, C.: Single and multi objective genetic programming for software development effort estimation. In: Proceedings of the 27th Annual ACM Symposium on Applied Computing, pp. 1221–1226. ACM (2012)
22. Shao, L., Liu, L., Li, X.: Feature learning for image classification via multiobjective genetic programming. IEEE Trans. Neural Netw. Learn. Syst. **25**(7), 1359–1371 (2014)
23. Singh, T., Kharma, N., Daoud, M., Ward, R.: Genetic programming based image segmentation with applications to biomedical object detection. In: Proceedings of the 11th Annual conference on Genetic and evolutionary computation, pp. 1123–1130. ACM (2009)
24. Song, A., Ciesielski, V.: Texture segmentation by genetic programming. Evol. Comput. **16**(4), 461–481 (2008)
25. Zhang, M., Andreae, P., Pritchard, M.: Pixel statistics and false alarm area in genetic programming for object detection. In: Raidl, G.R., Cagnoni, S., Cardalda, J.J.R., Corne, D.W., Gottlieb, J., Guillot, A., Hart, E., Johnson, C.G., Marchiori, E., Meyer, J.-A., Middendorf, M. (eds.) EvoIASP 2003, EvoWorkshops 2003, EvoSTIM 2003, EvoROB/EvoRobot 2003, EvoCOP 2003, EvoBIO 2003, and Evo-MUSART 2003. LNCS, vol. 2611, pp. 455–466. Springer, Heidelberg (2003)
26. Zou, W., Bai, C., Kpalma, K., Ronsin, J.: Online glocal transfer for automatic figure-ground segmentation. IEEE Trans. Image Process. **23**(5), 2109–2121 (2014)

A New Modification of Fuzzy C-Means via Particle Swarm Optimization for Noisy Image Segmentation

Saeed Mirghasemi$^{(\boxtimes)}$, Ramesh Rayudu, and Mengjie Zhang

School of Engineering and Computer Science,
Victoria University of Wellington, Wellington, New Zealand
{saeed.mirghasemi,ramesh.rayudu,mengjie.zhang}@ecs.vuw.ac.nz

Abstract. This paper presents a new clustering-based algorithm for noisy image segmentation. Fuzzy C-Means (FCM), empowered with a new similarity metric, acts as the clustering method. The common Euclidean distance metric in FCM has been modified with information extracted from a local neighboring window surrounding each pixel. Having different local features extracted for each pixel, Particle Swarm Optimization (PSO) is utilized to combine them in a weighting scheme while forming the proposed similarity metric. This allows each feature to contribute to the clustering performance, resulting in more accurate segmentation results in noisy images compared to other state-of-the-art methods.

Keywords: Particle swarm optimization · Fuzzy C-means · Noisy image segmentation · Clustering-based segmentation · Similarity metrics

1 Introduction

Image segmentation, a mid-level ill-posed image processing technique, is a mandatory preprocessing step for many high-level vision applications like object detection [1,2], image recognition [3,4], image retrieval [5], image compression [6], and video control/surveillance [7,8]. It is a procedure in which an image is partitioned into meaningful homogeneous regions. Based on the utilized technique and features these regions could be different. The technique has been widely studied since 1950s in the literature, and emerges with different definitions and interpretations in different applications. As the technology evolves, so are the demands for more accurate segmentation. Image segmentation algorithms could roughly be categorized into five groups [9,10]: clustering-based methods, graph-based methods, histogram thresholding-based methods, edge detection-based methods, and spatial-based methods. Noisy image segmentation is another inevitable related domain in computer vision due to environmental noise and noise caused by capturing devices. Utilization of fuzzy clustering-based approaches for noisy image segmentation has become an interesting field in recent years. Fuzzy C-means (FCM),

© Springer International Publishing Switzerland 2016
T. Ray et al. (Eds.): ACALCI 2016, LNAI 9592, pp. 147–160, 2016.
DOI: 10.1007/978-3-319-28270-1_13

as one of the most interesting clustering methods, has received a lot of attention over the years. It is known to have reasonable performance in case of overlapped regions, poor contrast, noise, and inhomogeneities in intensity [11]. The fuzzy membership property of FCM which allows each datapoint to belong to each cluster with different degrees of membership, is an interesting element when dealing with noisy data.

Particle swarm optimization (PSO) also as an effective evolutionary algorithm has become popular recently for image processing problems [12]. It is fast, easy to implement, and effective when solving NP-hard problems. The proposed algorithm in this paper introduces a new similarity metric as a substitution to the common Euclidean similarity metric utilizing PSO. The most interesting property of the algorithm is that it is parameter-free, and has considerable performance when dealing with severe noise corruption. The new similarity metric uses feature information from a local neighboring window around each pixel to adaptively use them for noise suppression according to image properties and volume of noise. There are coefficients involved with the new similarity criterion that need to be determined, and PSO does this task by searching within the specified space in an iterative manner.

This paper has been organized as follows. Section 2 gives a brief illustration on the existing literature, and related work. Section 3 describes the new proposed method. Section 4 is devoted to experiments and discussions, and Sect. 5 provides conclusions and future work.

2   Background

This section starts with the introduction of the primary FCM and its variants. We then introduce PSO as the evolutionary algorithm which we have utilized in this paper, and then related work will be presented.

2.1   FCM and Its Modifications

The FCM was first introduced by Dunn [13], and then extended by Bezdek [14]. As a clustering method it looks for c partitions by minimizing the following objective function:

$$J = \sum_{i=1}^{N} \sum_{j=1}^{c} u_{ji}^{m} d^2(x_i, v_j) \tag{1}$$

where considering an image as the input data which has to be clustered, and pixels as datapoints, $X = x_1, x_2, ..., x_N$ represents a p-dimensional vector associated with each pixel, N and c are the number of pixels and clusters respectively, u_{ij} is a value specifying the degree of membership pixel i to cluster j which needs to satisfy: $u_{ij} \in [0, 1]$ and $\sum_{i=1}^{C} u_{ij} = 1$, and m is the weighting exponent. $d^2(x_i, v_j)$ is the distance metric between pixel x_i and cluster centre v_j which is set to Euclidean metric in classic FCM. Using the Lagrange multipliers the two following equations are obtained which are necessary but not enough to have (1) at its minimum:

$$v_j^k = \frac{\sum_{i=1}^{N} \left(u_{ji}^k\right)^m x_i}{\sum_{i=1}^{N} \left(u_{ji}^k\right)^m} \quad (2)$$

$$u_{ji}^{k+1} = \frac{1}{\sum_{l=1}^{c} \left(\frac{d_{ji}}{d_{li}}\right)^{2/m-1}} \quad (3)$$

v and u are updating iteratively using (2) and (3) respectively where k is the iteration index. These equations repeat till the algorithm converges, meaning a certain degree of accuracy is obtained.

FCM does not provide satisfactory results for noisy image segmentation mainly because it does not include any spatial information. This has led to a number of research works for noisy image segmentation using the core concept of FCM [11,15–19]. They all introduce a modification to the objective function of FCM to include some spatial information. The first notable try in this way is FCM_S proposed in [15]. The method is designed to deal with the segmentation of magnetic images posing intensity inhomogeneities. The new objective function allows clustering of a pixel being affected by neighboring pixels. Based on FCM_S two modifications were introduced in [16] mainly trying to reduce the computation of FCM_S. The two algorithms named as FCM_S1 and FCM_S2 use a pre-formed mean and median-filter of the noisy image respectively to substitute the procedure that collects information from neighboring pixels to increase the efficiency. Then EnFCM [17] is proposed in which a linearly weighted filter is applied to the noisy image, and then the image is clustered using the gray-level histogram of the filtered image. Since the number of gray levels is much smaller than the number of pixels in an average-sized image, EnFCM performs quite fast.

One disadvantage of FCM_S, FCM_S1, FCM_S2, and EnFCM is that they all have a tunning parameter named α. α makes a trade-off between preserving the details of an image, and the ability to remove the noise. More clearly, α needs to be large enough to suppress the noise, and should be small enough to preserve the details. Being α-dependent, makes these algorithms effective only when a prior knowledge from the volume of noise is available. FGFCM was proposed in [11] to fix the problem with the trade-off tuning parameter, α. A new non-linear filtering factor was proposed in this algorithm incorporating spatial and gray information. As in EnFCM, the new filter, does preprocessing on the image, and then the clustering is performed using the histogram information. FGFCM also has two parameters named as λ_s and λ_g. These parameters function similar to the α [18], despite that FGFCM is less parameter-dependent. The same authors also proposed two modifications of FGFCM in [11] named as FGFCM_S1 and FGFCM_S2. Two specific generalizations of the non-linear filter lead to mean and median filtering of the neighboring window for FGFCM_S1 and FGFCM_S2 respectively. Motivated by strengths of the previous methods, FLICM was proposed in [18] to introduce a powerful parameter-free method for noisy image segmentation. A new fuzzy factor has been embedded into the objective function to replace the α, λ_s, and λ_g parameters in previous methods. The new fuzzy factor incorporates both spatial and gray level information at the same time in a fuzzy way. One problem with FLICM is that it tends to act very local, and in the case of multi-intensity noisy images it comes up with no accurate results [20]. It also has a problem identifying the class of boundary pixels, and in case of severe noise the performance degrades [19]. To cover the boundary pixels clustering, and also better performance in heavy noise distribution, ESFLICM was proposed [19] using a kernel induced distance instead of the common Euclidean metric.

2.2 Particle Swarm Optimization (PSO)

Particle Swarm optimization was first introduced in [21,22] motivated by social behaviors of animals like fish and bird. It is efficient, robust, and simple to implement [23]. Since its emergence it has been revolutionized a lot to cope with technical engineering problems, and many new modified versions have been proposed for a better performance. As an evolutionary computational search algorithm, it finds the solution of a problem which is hard to solve. Assuming that the problem is modeled with an objective function, PSO bombards the objective function with many solutions (the number of solutions is called the population size), evaluate the goodness of each solution, and then selects the best solution. This keeps going till the number of iterations are finished or the required accuracy is achieved. Each solution is represented with particles which have the ability to move in an specified n-dimensional space. Therefore, they need position, x, and velocity, v, which will be represented with $X_i = (x_{i1}, x_{i2}...x_{in})$ and $V_i = (v_{i1}, v_{i2}, ..., v_{in})$ for particle i in the n-dimensional space respectively. The best solution in each iteration is called *pbest*, and the best solution so far is *gbest*. The evaluation step is done with an inevitable part of each evolutionary algorithm, the *fitness* function. Fitness function will be defined with respect to the application, and conducts the searching direction. x and v will be updated in each iteration using the following equations:

$$v_{id}^{k+1} = wv_{id}^k + c_1 r_1(x_{pbest,id} - x_{id}) + c_2 r_2(x_{gbest,id} - x_{id}) \quad (4)$$

$$x_{id}^{k+1} = x_{id}^k + v_{id}^{k+1} \quad (5)$$

where $d = 1, 2, ..., n$ is the space dimension cardinality, $i = 1, 2, ..., N$ is the population size, c_1 and c_2 are positive constants, r_1 and r_2 are random numbers, uniformly distributed in the interval [0,1], and $k = 1, 2, ...$, denotes the number of iteration. x_{pbest} is the position of *pbest* and x_{gbest} is the position of *gbest*. w is the inertia weight which controls v, and reduces as the iteration increases according to:

$$w = (w_{initial} - w_{final}) \times \frac{(k_{max} - k)}{k_{max}} + w_{final} \quad (6)$$

where $w_{initial}$, is the preliminary value of w, w_{final} is the final value of w, k is the iteration number, and k_{max} is the maximum number of iterations.

2.3 Related Work

Not many research works exist in the literature incorporating PSO and FCM for noisy image segmentation. Among them, the main trend is that PSO searches for the optimum cluster centres when using an FCM-based method [24–26]. That is, each solution represents potential cluster centres, and the objective function of the FCM derivatives is taken as the fitness function. This approach, uses the objective function directly, and omits the updating formula for cluster centres from the clustering procedure. Since the FCM is already an optimization procedure itself, most often, only optimizing it with PSO does not yield to a significantly better performance. Contributions of other techniques are required to boost the performance like in [24] where the post-segmentation step refines the final results greatly, or in [25] where the authors have borrowed ideas from other FCM-based segmentation methods to modify the membership values when minimizing the objective function introduced in FGFCM.

Unlike the common approach, this paper proposes a noisy image segmentation in which the effort is put to optimize FCM while optimizing the similarity metric using different neighboring features. For this mean, PSO has been utilized to obtain the optimal weights for the contribution of each feature, according to the image properties. This algorithm not only produces good results by itself as demonstrated in Sect. 4, but also puts forward an algorithm that has the potential ability to fuse a variety of texture/spatial features for a better performance.

3 The Proposed Method

The presented algorithm in this paper introduces a new PSO-based similarity measure for the FCM clustering method which is parameter-free, gets adaptively tuned for noise removal according to the volume of the noise, and has promising performance in noisy image segmentation. The algorithm, unlike the existing trend, uses different features extracted from a local neighboring window to create an optimum weighted Euclidean distance for FCM clustering. This algorithm composes of three main stages as depicted in Fig. 1. The first stage is a preprocessing composed of two steps: a feature matrix construction and an initial FCM clustering. The second stage is a PSO search procedure in which the optimum similarity criterion is formed to replace the traditional Euclidean distance metric in FCM. The last stage, uses the best produced similarity measure from the second stage to do a final clustering followed by a segmentation procedure.

3.1 Preprocessing

To make the algorithm fast and efficient, a feature matrix is constructed in advance which will be used throughout the PSO search. This 3-D matrix is made of four simple statistical-based features which are extracted from a neighboring window centred at pixel i. The features which are mean (i_m), median (i_M), variance (i_v), and standard deviation (i_{sd}), make the feature vector, f_i, for each pixel, i, as $f_i = [i_m, i_M, i_v, i_{sd}]$. When referred to a pixel for clustering, f_i is easily accessible from the feature matrix. The size of this neighboring window along with all other parameters for the proposed algorithm are determined in Sect. 4. For an image of $m \times n$, the feature matrix size is $m \times n \times 4$.

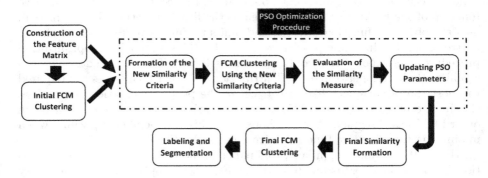

Fig. 1. Block diagram of the proposed method

After allocating a feature vector to each pixel with features extracted from the intensity information of its neighboring pixels, an FCM clustering is performed to obtain initial values for cluster centers to be used in the next stage, the PSO search. This primary FCM clustering has two advantages. First, it initializes PSO for a more meaningful search while looking for the optimum similarity metric, as cluster centres play a key role in forming the new metric. Second, it makes the final segmentation results stable. This clustering is carried out by the classic FCM using (2) and (3), and the formed feature matrix as the input.

3.2   The Proposed Similarity Measure

Creating the new Euclidean-based similarity metric is done within a PSO search procedure. The aim is to create a feature-weighted similarity criterion which takes advantages of each feature, and PSO provides the search space to find the optimum weights. The new similarity metric is created according to:

$$d^2(f_i, v_j) = \| f_i - v_j \| (1 - S_{ij}) \tag{7}$$

in which $d^2(f_i, v_j)$ is the similarity metric as in (1), $\| f_i - v_j \|$ is Euclidean-based distance, f_i is the feature vector of pixel i, v_j is the cluster centre of the jth cluster, and S_{ij} is a parameter that entangles each feature with its corresponding cluster centre as:

$$S_{ij} = \sum_{i=1}^{N} \sum_{j=1}^{4} \frac{\alpha_j \parallel (f_{ij} - v_j) \parallel}{\sum_{j=1}^{4} \parallel (f_{ij} - v_j) \parallel} \tag{8}$$

subjected to the two following criteria:

$$\begin{aligned} 0 < \alpha_j <&= 1 \\ S_{ij} <&= 1 \end{aligned} \tag{9}$$

where N is the number of pixels, and f_{ij} is the jth feature value of pixel i. The term $\sum_{i=1}^{N} \sum_{j=1}^{4} \parallel (f_{ij} - v_j) \parallel$ normalizes the S_{ij} to have reasonable values for α_js in the optimization procedure.

In the proposed S_{ij}, each feature property from each feature vector is only affiliated to one cluster centre, and this allows to consider each pixel's feature and the corresponding cluster centre coordinate individually while calculating the term $(1 - S_{ij})$. Overall, we have two phenomenons contributing to the better performance of the new similarity metric. One is that the proposed similarity metric reduces the original distance between each pixel and the corresponding cluster centre in (1), based on the mentioned information from a neighboring window around the pixel. This fusion of different features allows the metric to model noise and texture more accurately compared to each individual feature. The other, is the parameter α which controls the contribution of each feature. The determination of α values is being taken care of by the PSO procedure.

3.3   PSO Encoding

There are general (see Subsect. 2.2) and specific motivations to use PSO. Simplicity of representing our problem in form of the particles in PSO makes the encoding/decoding procedure quite straightforward. Nevertheless, this is something that could be done with other optimization/evolutionary techniques but probably at a different computational expense. PSO, as an evolutionary computation technique, searches for optimal values of α in the introduced similarity metric. The space that PSO does the search is 4-D as we have four features for each pixel, and thus four α values. Therefore, each potential solution in PSO is a vector of four values as $[\alpha_1, \alpha_2, \alpha_3, \alpha_4]$. Starting with random values for each particle, each solution gets evaluated in the course of PSO iterative procedure, and the best solution in each iteration gets conveyed to the next iteration. The best solution so far is also recorded. As stated before, PSO needs a fitness function which examines the goodness of each solution. The objective function of FCM introduced in (1) replaced with the new similarity metric is taken as the fitness function here. Minimizing this fitness function determines the values for optimum solutions locally and globally.

3.4   Summary of the Algorithm

The proposed algorithm summarizes as described in Fig. 2:

---

1. Construct the feature matrix according to mean, median, variance, and standard deviation of local neighboring windows.
2. Initialize the FCM parameters to be used throughout the algorithm.
3. Perform an initial FCM clustering to achieve initial values for the membership matrix U and cluster centres V.
4. Set the parameters for the PSO algorithm including the number of particles, iteration number, and initial values for position (x) and velocity (v).
5. Start the PSO search with random initial values for each particle.
6. Form the new similarity metric as (7).
7. Cluster the noisy pixels according to the similarity metric from the previous step.
8. Check the goodness of the solution using (1).
9. Select out **pbest** and **gbest** from the solutions based on the fitness evaluation results.
10. Update x and v values using (4) and (5).
11. Go back to step 6 for the next iteration unless it is the end of iterations.
12. Use the values obtained for α parameters to do steps 6 and 7 for the last time.
13. Utilize the membership matrix, U, to segment the image.

Fig. 2. The step-by-step elaborated structure of the proposed algorithm.

4   Experiments and Analysis

In this section we elaborate the results obtained from the proposed algorithm, and compare them with some of the state-of-the-art methods qualitatively and quantitatively. All the images in this section have been degraded by Gaussian noise with the variance of 20 %.

4.1   Datasets and Evaluation

To test the method we use images of two types. The first type is a dataset of synthetic images that has been created completely digitally. Using this dataset gives a clear intuition on how segmentation of simple images of limited-intensity works when it comes to partitioning compact and homogeneous regions. The second database is the Berkeley dataset [27] specifically created for image segmentation and boundary detection with ground-truths that comes handy when doing a quantitative evaluation. Using this dataset offers an insight on how the proposed method can act on real images of multi-intensity.

The proposed method is compared against several state-of-the-art methods to prove effectiveness. These methods include the hard clustering method K-means, the FCM itself [14], FCM_S1 and FCM_S2 [16], EnFCM [17], FGFCM, FGFCM_S1, and FGFCM_S2 [11]. The comparison is made both qualitatively and quantitatively. For quantitative comparison the Segmentation Accuracy (SA) [15] is utilized as follows:

$$SA = \sum_{i=1}^{c} \frac{A_i \cap C_i}{\sum_{j=1}^{c} C_j} \tag{10}$$

where A_i is the number of segmented pixels from the cluster i and, C_i is the number of pixels belonging to the ith cluster in the groundtruth image.

4.2   Parameter Setting

Both PSO and FCM algorithms have parameters to set intrinsically. Other than the size of local neighboring window, our algorithm does not have any specific parameters to set. As mentioned before, parameters related to the new similarity criterion get tuned automatically according to the properties of each noisy image. Table 1 shows all the parameters and their corresponding values.

Table 1. Parameter setting

Parameter	Value
Neighboring window for filtering	7×7
Weighting exponent (m)	2
Termination threshold for FCM	0.001
Maximum number of iterations for FCM	100
Particles number	20
Iterations number	50
Initial value for the first solution	0.001
c_1 and c_2 in PSO	1

In regards to other state-of-the-art methods, FCM_S1, FCM_S2, and EnFCM needs tuning for α, and FGFCM, FGFCM_S1, and FGFCM_S2 need tuning for λ_g according to the type and volume of noise. We take $\alpha = 1.8$, $\lambda_s = 3$, and $\lambda_g = 6$ according to the best performance analysis presented in [18].

4.3   Results

Figure 3 shows the segmentation results of the proposed method along other mentioned methods for some synthetic images. These four images named S1, S2, S3, and S4 are of size 256×256 pixels except for S1 which is of 128×128 pixels size. The number of clusters are fixed as 2, 3, 3, and 3 for them respectively. The qualitative comparison from this figure clearly states that one of the four FGFCM, FGFCM_S1, FGFCM_S2, and our method comes with the best

Table 2. Quantitative comparison according to SA metric for Fig. 3. Bold numbers indicate the first two best performances for each image

Algorithm	S1	S2	S3	S4
K-means	66.5283	59.1019	40.9424	46.5927
FCM	66.5161	59.0363	42.0914	46.7850
FCMS1	93.9270	92.7338	68.5333	75.0351
FCMS2	94.9280	95.6512	76.7303	79.2480
EnFCM	93.9697	92.8787	69.3192	75.4379
FGFCM_S1	96.7285	**98.1827**	**95.3308**	**86.6135**
FGFCM_S2	95.9045	97.3083	94.6289	83.4442
FGFCM	**97.0459**	97.8058	93.3075	84.3811
Our method	**97.0947**	**98.1934**	**95.4849**	**85.9497**

Table 3. Quantitative comparison according to SA metric for Fig. 3. Bold numbers indicate the first two best performances for each image

Algorithm	B1	B2	B3	B4
K-means	77.2042	52.8092	66.5896	59.8785
FCM	77.2042	52.8092	66.5896	60.1810
FCMS1	95.8426	59.0715	77.3136	68.9788
FCMS2	96.4689	62.1965	81.0241	72.1887
EnFCM	96.3653	60.5313	79.7793	71.0216
FGFCM_S1	97.1127	**73.0546**	**91.5473**	78.5111
FGFCM_S2	**97.3251**	72.8946	89.5713	**78.9367**
FGFCM	97.0343	68.0041	89.5486	76.7754
Our method	**98.1101**	**73.6083**	**90.7403**	**78.9464**

performance. This cuts off K-means, FCM, FCMS1, FCMS2, and EnFCM from the list of candidates for the most accurate segmentation. Quantitative evaluation is then performed based on SA metric to introduce the best segmentation performance. Table 2 shows the SA evaluation values for the sample images in Fig. 3 in which the two best performances are in bold. The numbers indicate that three out of four best segmentation performances belongs to our algorithm. Also, the performance difference between our method and FGFCM_S1 is quite minor and this is repeated for all other synthetic images in our dataset as well. There is one exception to this however, which is image S1 in which the second-best performance belongs to FGFCM method. That is, due to the simplicity of image S1 where there is only one edge in the existing spatial domain of the image, and other edges are actually image bordering pixels. Poor segmentation of FGFCM_S1 in these bordering pixels results in better performance of FGFCM compared to FGFCM_S1. Overall, in all images which are not simple as image S1, if the best results are from our algorithm, then the second-best results are from FGFCM_S1 and vise versa. This is not the case in real images which will be discussed next. In images S1, S2, and S3 our method performs better, and in image S4 the proposed method acts as the second-best method after FGFCM_S1.

The segmentation results of the Berkeley dataset in Fig. 4 compares our method against other methods visually. The four sample images from this dataset named B1, B2, B3, and B4 are of the size 481×321 pixels and they have different levels of gray intensity. This causes more difficulties in detecting the main regions, and therefore the SA accuracy drops down generally. The number of clusters for all four images is determined as 2. Here again our method obtains the best or second-best performance as the quantitative evaluation shows in Table 3. Having said that, when our method performs as the most accurate algorithm for B1, B2, and B4, the second-best performance goes to either FGFCM_S2 or FGFCM_S1.

Overall, the proposed method acts as the most stable algorithm compared to others testing on two different datasets. While other methods can loose their place among the first two best performances, our method always comes with the results as the best or second-best performance in image segmentation of heavy variance noises.

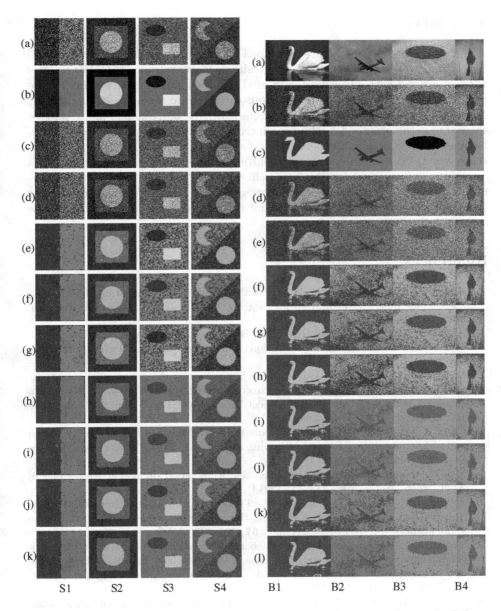

S1   S2   S3   S4   B1   B2   B3   B4

Fig. 3. Segmentation results on synthetic dataset. Rows (a) through (k) are the noisy corrupted images, the groundtruthes, K-means, FCM, FCM_S1, FCM_S2, EnFCM, FGFCM_S1, FGFCM_S2, FGFCM, and our methods segmentation results, respectively.

Fig. 4. Segmentation results on Berkeley dataset. Rows (a) through (l) are the noisy corrupted images, the groundtruthes, K-means, FCM, FCM_S1, FCM_S2, EnFCM, FGFCM_S1, FGFCM_S2, FGFCM, and our methods segmentation results, respectively.

5   Conclusion

A new similarity metric was proposed for FCM clustering using PSO with application in noisy image segmentation. Four simple features from a neighboring local window around each pixel were extracted to be combined in a weighted manner. This helped to take advantage from each feature for noise suppression in each image adaptively. Experiments on one synthetic and one real image dataset showed that the proposed method produced stable results in case of heavy distribution Gaussian noise while being ranked among the first two best performances compared to some of the state-of-the-arts methods. Two possible future work directions are assumed for this research. One is to use the neighboring information while forming the new similarity metric for a better normalization. The other is to use other texture and spatial features for even more effective noise suppression.

References

1. Zhuang, H., Low, K.-S., Yau, W.-Y.: Multichannel pulse-coupled-neural-network-based color image segmentation for object detection. IEEE Trans. Ind. Electron. **59**(8), 3299–3308 (2012)
2. Antúnez, E., Marfil, R., Bandera, J.P., Bandera, A.: Part-based object detection into a hierarchy of image segmentations combining color and topology. Pattern Recogn. Lett. **34**(7), 744–753 (2013)
3. Ferrari, V., Tuytelaars, T., Van Gool, L.: Simultaneous object recognition and segmentation by image exploration. In: Ponce, J., Hebert, M., Schmid, C., Zisserman, A. (eds.) Toward Category-Level Object Recognition. LNCS, vol. 4170, pp. 145–169. Springer, Heidelberg (2006)
4. Kang, Y., Yamaguchi, K., Naito, T., Ninomiya, Y.: Multiband image segmentation and object recognition for understanding road scenes. IEEE Trans. Intell. Transp. Syst. **12**(4), 1423–1433 (2011)
5. Mei, X., Lang, L.: An image retrieval algorithm based on region segmentation. Appl. Mech. Mater. **596**, 337–341 (2014)
6. Zhang, J.-Y., Zhang, W., Yang, Z.-W., Tian, G.: A novel algorithm for fast compression and reconstruction of infrared thermographic sequence based on image segmentation. Infrared Phys. Technol. **67**, 296–305 (2014)
7. Mahalingam, T., Mahalakshmi, M.: Vision based moving object tracking through enhanced color image segmentation using haar classifiers. In: Proceedings of the 2nd International Conference on Trendz in Information Sciences and Computing, TISC-2010, pp. 253–260 (2010)
8. Zhang, Q., Kamata, S., Zhang, J.: Face detection and tracking in color images using color centroids segmentation. In: 2008 IEEE International Conference on Robotics and Biomimetics, ROBIO 2008, pp. 1008–1013 (2009)
9. Unnikrishnan, R., Pantofaru, C., Hebert, M.: Toward objective evaluation of image segmentation algorithms. IEEE Trans. Pattern Anal. Mach. Intell. **29**(6), 929–944 (2007)
10. Wang, X.-Y., Wang, Q.-Y., Yang, H.-Y., Bu, J.: Color image segmentation using automatic pixel classification with support vector machine. Neurocomputing **74**(18), 3898–3911 (2011)

11. Cai, W., Chen, S., Zhang, D.: Fast and robust fuzzy c-means clustering algorithms incorporating local information for image segmentation. Pattern Recogn. **40**(3), 825–838 (2007)
12. Mirghasemi, S., Sadoghi Yazdi, H., Lotfizad, M.: A target-based color space for sea target detection. Appl. Intell. **36**(4), 960–978 (2012)
13. Dunn, J.C.: A fuzzy relative of the ISODATA process and its use in detecting compact well-separated clusters. J. Cybern. **3**(3), 32–57 (1973)
14. Hathaway, R., Bezdek, J., Hu, Y.: Generalized fuzzy c-means clustering strategies using LP norm distances. IEEE Trans. Fuzzy Syst. **8**(5), 576–582 (2000)
15. Ahmed, M.N., Yamany, S.M., Mohamed, N.A., Farag, A.A.: A modified fuzzy c-means algorithm for MRI bias field estimation and adaptive segmentation. In: Taylor, C., Colchester, A. (eds.) MICCAI 1999. LNCS, vol. 1679, pp. 72–81. Springer, Heidelberg (1999)
16. Chen, S., Zhang, D.: Robust image segmentation using FCM with spatial constraints based on new kernel-induced distance measure. IEEE Trans. Syst. Man Cybern. Part B: Cybern. **34**(4), 1907–1916 (2004)
17. Szilagyi, L., Benyo, Z., Szilagyi, S., Adam, H.: Mr brain image segmentation using an enhanced fuzzy C-means algorithm. In: 2003 Proceedings of the 25th Annual International Conference of the IEEE Engineering in Medicine and Biology Society, **1**, pp. 724–726. September 2003
18. Krinidis, S., Chatzis, V.: A robust fuzzy local information C-means clustering algorithm. IEEE Trans. Image Process. **19**(5), 1328–1337 (2010)
19. Wang, X., Lin, X., Yuan, Z.: An edge sensing fuzzy local information C-means clustering algorithm for image segmentation. In: Huang, D.-S., Jo, K.-H., Wang, L. (eds.) ICIC 2014. LNCS, vol. 8589, pp. 230–240. Springer, Heidelberg (2014)
20. Feng, J., Jiao, L., Zhang, X., Gong, M., Sun, T.: Robust non-local fuzzy C-means algorithm with edge preservation for SAR image segmentation. Signal Process. **93**(2), 487–499 (2013)
21. Eberhart, R., Kennedy, J.: A new optimizer using particle swarm theory. In: 1995 Proceedings of the Sixth International Symposium on Micro Machine and Human Science, MHS 1995, pp. 39–43 (1995)
22. Kennedy, J., Eberhart, R.: Particle swarm optimization. In: Proceedings of the IEEE International Conference on Neural Network, vol. 4, pp. 1942–1948 (1995)
23. Engelbrecht, A.P.: Computational Intelligence: An Introduction, 2nd edn. Wiley Publishing, Hoboken (2007)
24. Benaichouche, A., Oulhadj, H., Siarry, P.: Improved spatial fuzzy C-means clustering for image segmentation using PSO initialization, mahalanobis distance and post-segmentation correction. Digital Signal Process. **23**(5), 1390–1400 (2013)
25. Tran, D.C., Wu, Z., Tran, V.H.: Fast generalized fuzzy C-means using particle swarm optimization for image segmentation. In: Loo, C.K., Yap, K.S., Wong, K.W., Teoh, A., Huang, K. (eds.) ICONIP 2014, Part II. LNCS, vol. 8835, pp. 263–270. Springer, Heidelberg (2014)
26. Zhang, Q., Huang, C., Li, C., Yang, L., Wang, W.: Ultrasound image segmentation based on multi-scale fuzzy C-means and particle swarm optimization. In: IET International Conference on Information Science and Control Engineering 2012, ICISCE 2012, pp. 1–5. December 2012
27. Martin, D., Fowlkes, C., Tal, D., Malik, J.: A database of human segmented natural images and its application to evaluating segmentation algorithms and measuring ecological statistics. In: Proceedings of the 8th International Conference on Computer Vision, vol. 2, pp. 416–423 (2001)

Competitive Island Cooperative Neuro-evolution of Feedforward Networks for Time Series Prediction

Ravneil Nand[✉] and Rohitash Chandra

School of Computing Information and Mathematical Sciences,
University of South Pacific, Suva, Fiji
ravneiln@yahoo.com, c.rohitash@gmail.com

Abstract. Problem decomposition, is vital in employing cooperative coevolution for neuro-evolution. Different problem decomposition methods have features that can be exploited through competition and collaboration. Competitive island cooperative coevolution (CICC) implements decomposition methods as islands that compete and collaborate at different phases of evolution. They have been used for training recurrent neural networks for time series problems. In this paper, we apply CICC for training feedforward networks for time series problems and compare their performance. The results show that the proposed approach has improved the results when compared to standalone cooperative coevolution and shows competitive results when compared to related methods from the literature.

Keywords: Cooperative coevolution · Feedforward network · Problem decomposition · Neuron level · Synapse level

1 Introduction

Cooperative coevolution (CC) is an evolutionary algorithm that divides a large problem into subcomponents that are implemented as sub-populations [1]. CC applied to neuro-evolution is referred to as cooperative neuro-evolution that has been used for training feedforward and recurrent neural networks [2] for time series prediction [2]. Problem decomposition is vital for cooperative neuro-evolution. The two major decomposition methods are synapse level (SL) and neuron level (NL) methods. In synapse level problem decomposition, the sub-components are defined by the weight connection which is known as synapse [2–4]. In neuron level problem decomposition, the neural network gets decomposed by the number of hidden and output neurons as reference neurons in the network [5].

Competition and collaboration are vital components in the evolution of species in nature and motivated recent trend in design of evolutionary algorithms. The competitive coevolution technique was proposed for genetic algorithm where populations called host and parasite contested with each other

© Springer International Publishing Switzerland 2016
T. Ray et al. (Eds.): ACALCI 2016, LNAI 9592, pp. 160–170, 2016.
DOI: 10.1007/978-3-319-28270-1_14

with different mechanisms that enable fitness sharing and selection [6]. The competition characteristic in cooperative coevolution has also been used for multi-objective optimization that exploited connection and inter-dependencies between the components of the problem [7].

Cooperative island cooperative coevolution (CICC) employs problem decomposition strategies as islands that compete and collaborate during different phases of evolution [8,9]. It was initially proposed for training recurrent neural networks for time series problems [8] and later extended for global optimization [9] where it showed very promising results. The islands evolve in phases that is defined by evolution time. At the end of each phase of evolution, the best solutions from participating islands are compared and the best solution is copied to the rest of the islands.

In this paper, we employ CICC for training feedforward networks on chaotic time series problems. The proposed approach takes advantage of the different problem decomposition methods during evolution of feedforward neural network for time series prediction problems. The performance of the proposed approach is compared with recurrent neural networks used for chaotic time series problems [8].

The rest of the paper is organized as follows. In Sect. 2, the proposed method is discussed in detail while Sect. 3 reports on experimental setup and results. Section 4 reports on discussion and Sect. 5 concludes the paper with discussion of future work.

2   CICC for Feedforward Neural Networks

In this section, the details of Competitive Island Cooperative Coevolution (CICC) for training feedforward neural network is given. The proposed method employs the strengths of different problem decomposition methods that reflects on the different degrees of separability and diversity [5].

The proposed method is given in Algorithm 1 where a problem decomposition method is defined as an *island* that has distinct features in terms of how the problem is decomposed and encoded. There are two islands which have distinct problem decomposition methods as given below:

1. SL Island: Decomposes the neural network in its lowest level where each synapse becomes a subcomponent. The number of subcomponents depends on the number of synapse [3].
2. NL Island: Neuron level problem decomposition employs hidden and output neurons as reference point for each subcomponent. The number of subcomponents depends on the number of hidden and output neurons [5].

The subcomponents are implemented as sub-populations which are implemented using an evolutionary algorithm. Initially, all the sub-populations of each island is initialized and then evaluated.

Algorithm 1. Competitive Two-Island Cooperative Coevolution for training Feedforward Neural Networks

---

Step 1: Initialisation:
i. Cooperatively evaluate Neuron level Island
ii. Cooperatively Evaluate Synapse level Island
Step 2: Evolution:
while $FuncEval \leq GlobalEvolutionTime$ **do**
$\quad$ **while** $FuncEval \leq Island\text{-}Evolution\text{-}Time$ **do**
$\quad\quad$ **foreach** $Sub\text{-}population\ at\ Synapse\ level$ **do**
$\quad\quad\quad$ **foreach** $Depth\ of\ n\ Generations$ **do**
$\quad\quad\quad\quad$ Create new individuals using genetic operators
$\quad\quad\quad\quad$ Cooperative Evaluation
$\quad\quad\quad$ **end**
$\quad\quad$ **end**
$\quad$ **end**
$\quad$ **while** $FuncEval \leq Island\text{-}Evolution\text{-}Time$ **do**
$\quad\quad$ **foreach** $Sub\text{-}population\ at\ Neuron\ level$ **do**
$\quad\quad\quad$ **foreach** $Depth\ of\ n\ Generations$ **do**
$\quad\quad\quad\quad$ Create new individuals using genetic operators
$\quad\quad\quad\quad$ Cooperative Evaluation
$\quad\quad\quad$ **end**
$\quad\quad$ **end**
$\quad$ **end**
$\quad$ **Step 3:** Competition: Compare and mark the island with best fitness.
$\quad$ **Step 4:** Collaboration: Exchange the best fitness individual from the island into the other island.
end

In Step 2, the evolution of the islands take place where each island is evolved for a predefined time given by the number of fitness evaluations in a round-robin fashion. This is called *island evolution time* that is given by the number of function evaluations in the respective islands. Once both islands have been evolved for the island evolution time, the algorithm proceeds and checks if the best solution of the particular island is better. If the solution is better, then the *collaboration*, procedure takes place where the solution is copied to the other island.

Each island is evolved using genetic operators until the local evolution time has been reached as shown in Fig. 1. In the collaboration procedure, the method takes into account how the best solution from one island is copied into the other since both have different number of sub-populations.

The best individuals from each of the subcomponents needs to be carefully concatenated into an individual and transferred without losing any genotype (subcomponents in cooperative coevolution) to phenotype (feedforward neural network) mapping. When one island wins, the best solution is transferred to the other island as shown in Fig. 2.

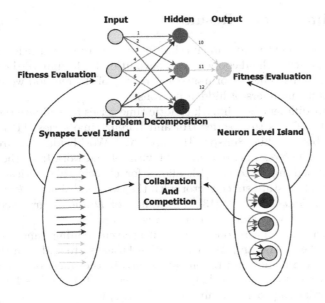

Fig. 1. The two islands compete with each other and the best solution is transferred to the losing Island.

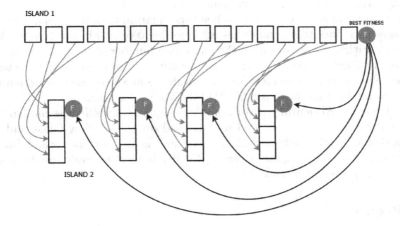

Fig. 2. The transfer of the best solution mapped between the islands (SL to NL).

As shown in Step 4 of Algorithm 1, the island that contains an individual with better solution needs to be shared with the other island. Synapse level island employs the highest number of sub-populations that are defined by number of weights in the network, whereas, neuron level island depends on the number of neurons in the hidden and output layer. Both islands have varied number of sub-populations with varied size, therefore, the transfer of the best solution needs to be mapped correctly between the islands which is shown in Fig. 2.

3   Experiments and Results

This section presents the experiments that feature neuron synapse level islands in proposed competitive island cooperative coevolution for feedforward networks for time series problems. The performance and results of the method were evaluated by using different numbers of hidden neurons.

We use four different benchmark chaotic time series to evaluate the proposed method. Mackey-Glass time series [10] and Lorenz time series [11] are the two simulated problems while Sunspot [12] and ACI Worldwide Inc. are the real-world problems. The results are compared with related work from the literature.

Taken's embedding theorem [13] allows for chaotic time series data to be reconstructed into a state space vector with the two conditions of *time delay (T)* and *embedding dimension (D)* [13]. The values of D and T are used as in the literature in order to provide a fair comparison [2,8].

All the data set used is reconstructed with the embedding dimensions as used in [2]. The Mackey-Glass and ACI time series datasets are scaled in the range of [0,1] whereas the Sunspot and Lorenz are scaled in the range of [−1,1].

The four time series are scaled in the range of [0,1] and [−1,1] as in the literature in order to provide a fair comparison [2,8].

The Generalized Generation Gap with Parent Centric Crossover (G3-PCX) evolutionary algorithm was used to evolve all the sub-populations with a pool size of 2 parents and 2 offspring as done in literature [2].

The number of generations for each sub-population known as *depth of search* and is kept as 1 since this number has achieved good results in previous work [2].

The algorithm terminates once the maximum number of function evaluations has been reached by the respective cooperative neuro-evolutionary methods. CICC employs a total of 100 000 function evaluations where each island employs 50 000. Standalone methods use 50 000 function evaluations.

The feedforward neural network employs sigmoid units in the hidden layer and in the output layer a sigmoid unit is used for the Mackey-Glass and ACI Worldwide Inc., while the hyperbolic tangent unit is used for Lorenz and Sunspot time series. Root mean squared error (RMSE) is used to evaluate the performance of the proposed method [2].

3.1   Results

This section reports on the performance of CICC for training the feedforward network on four different benchmark problems of the chaotic time series.

In Tables 1, 2, 3 and 4, the results are shown for different number of hidden neurons using the CICC method which is compared with the results of standalone cooperative coevolution based on feedforward network.

The results in the Tables 1, 2, 3 and 4 report the RMSE for training and generalisation performance. They are given by the mean and 95 percent confidence interval for 50 experimental runs for different number of hidden neurons (H).

Table 1 shows experimental results of the Mackey-Glass time series problem where CICC has outperformed the standalone methods (SL and NL). All the

Table 1. The prediction training and generalisation performance (RMSE) of NL and SL Mackey-Glass time series

Prob.	H	Training	Generalisation	Best
NL	3	0.0107 ± 0.00131	0.0107 ± 0.00131	0.0050
	5	0.0089 ± 0.00097	0.0088 ± 0.00097	0.0038
	7	0.0078 ± 0.00079	0.0078 ± 0.00079	0.0040
SL	3	0.0237 ± 0.0023	0.0237 ± 0.0023	0.0125
	5	0.0195 ± 0.0012	0.0195 ± 0.0012	0.0124
	7	0.0177 ± 0.0009	0.0178 ± 0.0009	0.0121
CICC	3	0.00950 ± 0.0013	0.0947 ± 0.0013	0.0043
	5	0.00690 ± 0.0005	0.0068 ± 0.0005	0.0035
	7	0.0063 ± 0.0005	0.0063 ± 0.0005	0.0026

Table 2. The prediction training and generalisation performance (RMSE) of NL and SL for the Lorenz time series

Prob.	H	Training	Generalisation	Best
NL	3	0.0170 ± 0.0031	0.0176 ± 0.0031	0.0043
	5	0.0249 ± 0.0062	0.0271 ± 0.0067	0.0021
	7	0.0379 ± 0.0093	0.0416 ± 0.0092	0.0024
SL	3	0.0680 ± 0.0325	0.0452 ± 0.0229	0.0153
	5	0.0526 ± 0.0084	0.0546 ± 0.0084	0.0082
	7	0.0574 ± 0.0075	0.0605 ± 0.0074	0.0079
CICC	3	0.0191 ± 0.00328	0.0198 ± 0.00359	0.0022
	5	0.0212 ± 0.00569	0.0225 ± 0.00611	0.0012
	7	0.0254 ± 0.00701	0.0281 ± 0.00748	0.0023

methods produced better generalization performance with seven hidden neurons. The overall performance increased for all the methods as the number of hidden neurons increased.

In Table 2, the CICC method has performed better than SL method and closer to the NL method in terms of generalization for the Lorenz time series problem. The generalization performance of the CICC and the other two methods deteriorates as the number of the hidden neuron increases. The best result was seen for three hidden neurons for CICC.

Table 3 shows results for the Sunspot time series problem where three hidden neurons have given the best performance for CICC and also for the other two methods. The generalization performance of all the methods deteriorates as the number of the hidden neuron increases.

The ACI Worldwide Inc. time series problem is evaluated in Table 4. It shows that the CICC has performed much better than the other two standalone

Table 3. The prediction training and generalisation performance (RMSE) of NL and SL Sunspot time series

Prob.	H	Training	Generalisation	Best
NL	3	0.0207 ± 0.0035	0.0538 ± 0.0091	0.015
	5	0.0289 ± 0.0039	0.0645 ± 0.0093	0.017
	7	0.0353 ± 0.0048	0.0676 ± 0.0086	0.021
SL	3	0.0539 ± 0.0261	0.04998 ± 0.0238	0.210
	5	0.0560 ± 0.0208	0.05210 ± 0.0177	0.302
	7	0.0568 ± 0.0178	0.05250 ± 0.0132	0.344
CICC	3	0.0193 ± 0.00351	0.0480 ± 0.00722	0.017
	5	0.0216 ± 0.00321	0.0549 ± 0.00993	0.014
	7	0.0316 ± 0.00488	0.0719 ± 0.00924	0.018

Table 4. The prediction training and generalisation performance (RMSE) of NL and SL for ACI time series

Prob.	H	Training	Generalisation	Best
NL	3	0.0214 ± 0.00039	0.0215 ± 0.00039	0.020
	5	0.0203 ± 0.00047	0.0212 ± 0.00041	0.019
	7	0.0201 ± 0.00038	0.0208 ± 0.00033	0.019
SL	3	0.0466 ± 0.0039	0.0411 ± 0.0036	0.080
	5	0.0413 ± 0.0038	0.0390 ± 0.0038	0.042
	7	0.0449 ± 0.0028	0.0424 ± 0.0027	0.134
CICC	3	0.0301 ± 0.0115	0.0332 ± 0.0197	0.0150
	5	0.0240 ± 0.0036	0.0227 ± 0.00566	0.0148
	7	0.0202 ± 0.00020	0.0178 ± 0.00088	0.0150

methods (SL and NL). The generalization performance of the CICC and the other two methods gets better as the number of the hidden neuron increases. The best result was seen for seven hidden neurons for all the methods.

Figures 3 and 4 show that a typical experimental run from the CICC method was able to cope with the noise from the real-world datasets. The error graph is also given which indicates the challenges for the chaotic nature of these time series problems at certain time intervals.

Table 5, compares the best results from Tables 1, 2, 3 and 4 with some of the related methods from the literature. The RMSE of the best run together with NMSE (Normalized Mean Squared Error) are used for the comparison. The proposed method has given better performance when compared to some of the methods in the literature.

Table 5, Mackey-Glass time series shows that CICC has outperformed all of the methods except for Auto Regressive Moving Average with Neural Network

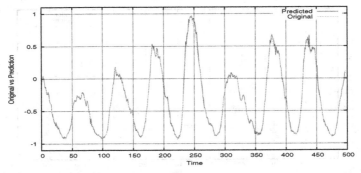

(a) Performance given by CICC on the testing set for Sunspot Worldwide.

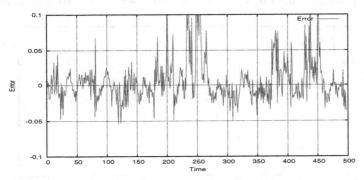

(b) Error on the test data set given by CICC for the Sunspot time series.

Fig. 3. Typical mean prediction given by CICC for Sunspot time series.

(ARMA-NN), Radial Basis Network with Orthogonal Least Squares (RBF-OLS) and Locally Linear Neuro-Fuzzy Model (LLNF).

In Lorenz problem given in the Table 5, the proposed method outperformed all the methods. In Table 5, for the Sunspot time series problem, the proposed method was able to outperform the rest of the methods from the literature. As for ACI Worldwide Inc. problem in Table 5, the proposed method outperforms majority of the methods.

4   Discussion

Competitive island cooperative coevolution enables competition of diversity enforced through the number of sub-populations. The collaboration feature allows to improve diversity through injection of the best materials from the winning island after a predefined time. These features seem to improve the results of the standalone methods. Synapse level problem decomposition method seems to enable better global search features through higher diversity that is useful during the early stages of evolution. Collaboration and competition take advantages

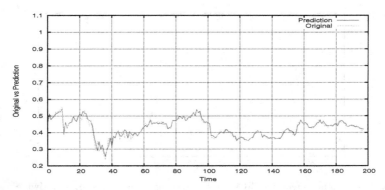

(a) Performance given by CICC on the testing set for ACI Worldwide Inc.

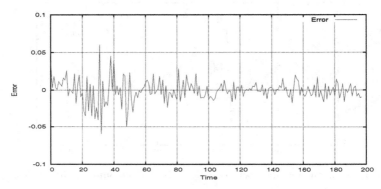

(b) Error on the test data set given by CICC for the ACI Worldwide Inc time series.

Fig. 4. Typical mean prediction given by CICC for ACI Worldwide Inc time series.

of these features during evolution. The proposed method takes advantage of solutions produced by two problem decomposition methods after each phase of competition.

The comparison of results with literature has shown that the proposed method performs better than cooperative co-evolutionary recurrent neural networks (CCRNN-SL and CCRNN-NL). We note that the performance also depends on the neural network architecture, hence, we cannot make strict comparison and only use the results from the literature of the related methods as a baseline to evaluate the proposed method. This is also the case when comparing the performance of proposed CICC-FNN with its counterpart CICC-RNN for the same problems. We also note that CICC was unable to outperform some of the related methods since they have additional enhancements such as the optimization of the embedding dimensions and strength of architectural properties [15].

Table 5. A comparison with the results from literature for all time series

Problem	Prediction method	RMSE	NMSE
Mackey	Auto regressive moving average (ARMA-NN)(2008) [14]	2.5E-03	
	Radial basis network (RBF-OLS)(2006) [15]	1.02E-03	
	Locally linear neuro-fuzzy model (LLNF) (2006) [15]	9.61E-04	
	Neural fuzzy network (PS0) (2009) [4]	2.10E-02	
	Neural fuzzy network (CPS0) (2009) [4]	1.76E-02	
	Synapse level-CCRNN (SL-CCRNN) (2012) [2]	6.33E-03	2.79E-04
	Neuron level-CCRNN (NL-CCRNN) (2012) [2]	8.28E-03	4.77E-04
	Competitive island cooperative coevolution (CICC-RNN) (2014) [8]	3.99E-03	1.11E-04
	Proposed CICC-FNN	2.61E-03	1.29E-05
Lorenz	Radial basis network (RBF-OLS)(2006) [15]		1.41E-09
	Locally linear neuro-fuzzy model (LLNF) (2006) [15]		9.80E-10
	Auto regressive moving average (ARMA-ANN)(2008) [14]	8.76E-02	
	Backpropagation neural network and genetic algorithms (2011) [16]	2.96E-02	
	Synapse level-CCRNN (SL-CCRNN) (2012) [2]	6.36E-03	7.72E-04
	Neuron level-CCRNN (NL-CCRNN) (2012) [2]	8.20E-03	1.28E-03
	Competitive island cooperative coevolution (CICC-RNN) (2014) [8]	3.55E-03	2.41E-04
	Proposed CICC-FNN	1.16E-03	2.80E-05
Sunspot	Radial basis network (RBF-OLS)(2006) [15]		4.60E-02
	Locally linear neuro-fuzzy model (LLNF) (2006) [15]		3.20E-02
	Synapse level-CCRNN (SL-CCRNN) (2012) [2]	1.66E-02	1.47E-03
	Neuron level-CCRNN (NL-CCRNN) (2012) [2]	2.60E-02	3.62E-03
	Competitive island cooperative coevolution (CICC-RNN) (2014) [8]	1.57E-02	1.31E-03
	Proposed CICC-FNN	1.44E-02	5.84E-04
ACI	Competitive island cooperative coevolution (CICC-RNN) (2014) [8]	1.92E-02	
	Synapse level (FNN-SL) (2014) [17]	1.92E-02	
	Neuron level (FNN-NL) (2014) [17]	1.91E-02	
	MOCCFNN with 2-objectives (T=2)(MO-CCFNN-T=2) (2014)[18]	1.94E-02	
	MOCCFNN with 2-objectives (T=3)(MO-CCFNN-T=3) (2014)[18]	1.47E-02	
	Proposed CICC-FNN	1.48E-02	1.19E-03

5   Conclusion

In this paper, we applied competitive island-based cooperative coevolution of feedforward neural networks for chaotic time series prediction. The proposed approach employed two island competitive method where the islands were defined by neuron level and synapse level problem decomposition methods. The results have shown good results on the different benchmark problems and has given competitive performance with the majority of the methods in the literature. It can be concluded that sharing of resources between the different islands that have different features helps in achieving better solutions.

In future work, the proposed method can be improved by exploring other problem decomposition methods that can provide more competition. A multi-threaded version of the algorithm can be developed to reduce the computation time. The method can be used to evolve other neural network architectures for similar problems and those that involve pattern classification and control.

References

1. Potter, M.A., De Jong, K.A.: A cooperative coevolutionary approach to function optimization. In: Davidor, Y., Schwefel, H.-P., Männer, R. (eds.) PPSN III. LNCS, vol. 866, pp. 249–257. Springer, Heidelberg (1994)
2. Chandra, R., Zhang, M.: Cooperative coevolution of Elman recurrent neural networks for chaotic time series prediction. Neurocomputing **186**, 116–123 (2012)
3. Gomez, F., Schmidhuber, J., Miikkulainen, R.: Accelerated neural evolution through cooperatively coevolved synapses. J. Mach. Learn. Res. **9**, 937–965 (2008)
4. Lin, C.-J., Chen, C.-H., Lin, C.-T.: A hybrid of cooperative particle swarm optimization and cultural algorithm for neural fuzzy networks and its prediction applications. IEEE Trans. Syst., Man, Cybern., Part C: Appl. Rev. **39**(1), 55–68 (2009)
5. Chandra, R., Frean, M., Zhang, M.: On the issue of separability for problem decomposition in cooperative neuro-evolution. Neurocomputing **87**, 33–40 (2012)
6. Rosin, C.D., Belew, R.K.: New methods for competitive coevolution. Evol. Comput. **5**(1), 1–29 (1997)
7. Goh, C.K., Tan, K.C., Liu, D.S., Chiam, S.C.: A competitive and cooperative coevolutionary approach to multi-objective particle swarm optimization algorithm design. Eur. J. Oper. Res. **202**, 42–54 (2010)
8. Chandra, R.: Competition and collaboration in cooperative coevolution of Elman recurrent neural networks for time-series prediction. IEEE Trans. Neural Networks Learn. Syst. (2015, in Press)
9. Chandra, R., Bali, K.: Competitive two island cooperative coevolution for real parameter global optimization. In: IEEE Congress on Evolutionary Computation, Sendai, Japan (May 2015, in Press)
10. Mackey, M., Glass, L.: Oscillation and chaos in physiological control systems. Science **197**(4300), 287–289 (1977)
11. Lorenz, E.: Deterministic non-periodic flows. J. Atmos. Sci. **20**, 267–285 (1963)
12. SILSO World Data Center, The International Sunspot Number (1834–2001), International Sunspot Number Monthly Bulletin and Online Catalogue. Royal Observatory of Belgium, Avenue Circulaire 3, 1180 Brussels, Belgium. Available http://www.sidc.be/silso/ Accessed 02 February 2015
13. Takens, F.: Detecting strange attractors in turbulence. In: Rand, D., Young, L.-S. (eds.) Dynamical Systems and Turbulence, Warwick 1980. Lecture Notes in Mathematics, vol. 898, pp. 366–381. Springer, Heidelberg (1981)
14. Rojas, I., Valenzuela, O., Rojas, F., Guillen, A., Herrera, L., Pomares, H., Marquez, L., Pasadas, M.: Soft-computing techniques and arma model for time series prediction. Neurocomputing **71**(4–6), 519–537 (2008)
15. Gholipour, A., Araabi, B.N., Lucas, C.: Predicting chaotic time series using neural and neurofuzzy models: a comparative study. Neural Process. Lett. **24**, 217–239 (2006)
16. Ardalani-Farsa, M., Zolfaghari, S.: Residual analysis and combination of embedding theorem and artificial intelligence in chaotic time series forecasting. Appl. Artif. Intell. **25**, 45–73 (2011)
17. Chand, S., Chandra, R.: Cooperative coevolution of feed forward neural networks for financial time series problem. In: International Joint Conference on Neural Networks (IJCNN), pp. 202–209, Beijing, China, July 2014
18. Chand, S., Chandra, R.: Multi-objective cooperative coevolution of neural networks for time series prediction. In: 2014 International Joint Conference on Neural Networks (IJCNN) , pp. 190–197 (2014). doi:10.1109/IJCNN.2014.6889442

Reverse Neuron Level Decomposition for Cooperative Neuro-Evolution of Feedforward Networks for Time Series Prediction

Ravneil Nand[✉] and Rohitash Chandra

School of Computing Information and Mathematical Sciences,
University of South Pacific, Suva, Fiji
ravneiln@yahoo.com, c.rohitash@gmail.com

Abstract. A major challenge in cooperative neuro-evolution is to find an efficient problem decomposition that takes into account architectural properties of the neural network and the training problem. In the past, neuron and synapse Level decomposition methods have shown promising results for time series problems, howsoever, the search for the optimal method remains. In this paper, a problem decomposition method, that is based on neuron level decomposition is proposed that features a reverse encoding scheme. It is used for training feedforward networks for time series prediction. The results show that the proposed method has improved performance when compared to related problem decomposition methods and shows competitive results when compared to related methods in the literature.

Keywords: Cooperative coevolution · Feedforward networks · Problem decomposition · Time series prediction

1 Introduction

A time series dataset is a chronological series of the past and present data is involved that are measured regularly at progressive intervals [1,2]. Time series prediction uses past data to predict future occurrence of events using robust methods such as neural networks [3].

Cooperative neuro-evolution employs cooperative coevolution for training neural networks [3–5]. Cooperative coevolution solves a large problem by breaking it down into sub-components and implements them as sub-population using evolutionary algorithms [4]. The sub-populations are evolved in a round-robin fashion while cooperation takes place for fitness evaluation.

Cooperative neuro-evolution has shown to be effective for training feedforward [6,7] and recurrent neural networks [3,8] with applications in classification [6,9], control [8] and time series prediction [3]. In cooperative neuro-evolution, problem decomposition depends on the structural properties of the network that

© Springer International Publishing Switzerland 2016
T. Ray et al. (Eds.): ACALCI 2016, LNAI 9592, pp. 171–182, 2016.
DOI: 10.1007/978-3-319-28270-1_15

have inter-dependencies [9]. The efficiency of a problem decomposition method depends on the training problem and the neural network architecture [9].

The two established problem decomposition methods for cooperative neuro-evolution are synapse level (SL) [3,5] and neuron level (NL) [8–10]. In SL, the network is decomposed to its lowest level of granularity where the number of subcomponents depends on the number of weight-links or synapses in the neural network. In NL, the number of subcomponents consists of the total number of hidden and output neurons.

Synapse level ensures global search and provides the most diversity. However, this level of decomposition works best if there are less interacting variables or synapses in the neural network training problem. Synapse level decomposition has shown good performance for time series and control problems [3,5], howsoever, it performed poorly for pattern classification problems [9]. It seems that time series prediction does not feature a high level of interactions when compared to pattern classification problems.

Neuron level decomposition has less diversity and enables grouping the interacting variables. In cooperative neuro-evolution, the problem is to balance diversity and interacting variables. A study of grouping interacting variables motivated the grouping of synapses with reference to hidden in output neurons [9].

In this paper, we introduce *reverse neuron level* (RNL) decomposition, which essentially features reverse encoding of neuron level decomposition. Neuron level decomposition takes hidden and output layer neurons as reference for each subcomponent, whereas RNL uses hidden and input layer. RNL is used for training feedforward networks for chaotic time series problems.

The rest of the paper is organized as follows. In Sect. 2, the proposed method is discussed in detail while in Sect. 3, experiments and results are given. Section 4 concludes the paper with a discussion of future work.

2   Proposed Problem Decomposition

An ideal problem decomposition method efficiently decomposes the network in a way where the interacting variables or synapses are grouped into separate subcomponents [9]. In this way, a deep greedy search for the subcomponents will not be problematic for partially separable problems such as training neural networks. Analysis of the degree of separability of the neural network training problem showed that neuron level is an efficient way for decomposition [9]. Howsoever, other strategies for effectively decomposing the network can also be explored that are related to neuron level (Figs. 1 and 2).

2.1   Reverse Neuron Level Decomposition

Reverse neuron level (RNL) decomposition encodes the neural network in a way where the input and hidden neurons are used as reference points rather than the hidden and output neurons as in the case of neuron level. Each subcomponents in RNL consists of outgoing synapse connected linked with neurons in the input

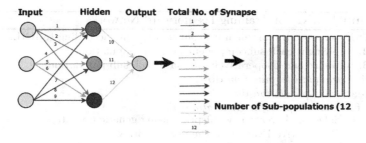

Fig. 1. Synapse level decomposition of the neural network training problem. Note that the subcomponents are implemented as sub-populations.

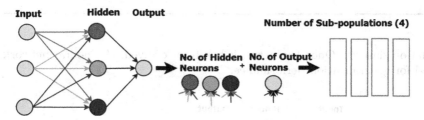

Fig. 2. Neuron level decomposition of neural network training problem. Note that the subcomponents are implemented as sub-populations.

and hidden layers. Therefore, each subcomponent for a layer is composed as follows:

1. For a given neuron i in the input layer, the input layer subcomponents consists of all the synapses that are connected from input neuron i to the hidden layer. The bias of i is also included.
2. For a given neuron j in the hidden layer, the hidden layer subcomponents consists of all synapses that are connected from hidden neuron j to the output layer. The bias of j is also included.

The total number of subcomponents is the total number of hidden and input neurons along with biases within hidden and input layer neurons as shown in Fig. 3. RNL is used to train the feedforward network and is shown in Algorithm 1. In Step 1, the network is encoded using RNL problem decomposition.

In Step 2, subcomponents are encoded as sub-populations. In Step 3, each sub-population is evolved using the designated evolutionary algorithm. Evaluation of the fitness of each individual in a particular sub-population is done cooperatively [4]. This is done by concatenating the best individuals from the rest of the sub-populations and encoding them into the neural network for fitness evaluation.

All the sub-populations are evolved for a fixed number of generations. The evolution continues until the termination criteria is met which is either the total number of function evaluations or the desired fitness for the network based on

---

Algorithm 1. RNL for Training Feedforward Networks

Step 1: Decompose the problem into subcomponents according to RNL.
Step 2: Implement each subcomponent in a sub-population.
Step 3: Initialize and cooperatively evaluate each sub-population.
foreach *Cycle until termination* **do**
    foreach *Sub-population* **do**
        foreach *Depth of n Generations* **do**
            Select and create new offspring using genetic operators
            Cooperative Evaluation the new offspring
        end
    end
end

---

validation dataset. Once the network has been evolved, the neural network is tested for generalization performance.

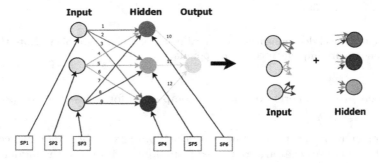

Fig. 3. Reverse neuron level problem decomposition. Note that the number of sub-population are based on the number of input and hidden neurons.

The proposed decomposition creates fewer subcomponents when compared to synapse level decomposition. It creates more subcomponents when compared to neuron level decomposition for problems with one output neuron that are used for single dimensional time series problems.

3   Experiments and Results

This section presents the experiments using the proposed RNL cooperative neuro-evolution method for training feedforward neural networks. NL and SL problem decomposition methods are used for comparison. The performance and results of the method were evaluated using different number of hidden neurons.

Four different benchmark chaotic time series datasets are used to evaluate the proposed method. Mackey-Glass time series [11] and Lorenz time series [12] are the two simulated time series. The real-world problems include the Sunspot [13] and ACI Worldwide Inc. [14] time series. The results are compared with related work from the literature.

3.1 Experimental Setup

All the datasets are reconstructed using Taken's embedding theorem [15]. Taken's embedding theorem allows chaotic time series dataset to be reconstructed into a state space vector using *time delay (T)* and *embedding dimension (D)* [15].

The differential equation used to generate the Mackey Glass time series is given below in Eq. 1.

$$\frac{dx}{dt} = \frac{ax(t - \tau)}{[1 + x^c(t - \tau)]} - bx(t) \tag{1}$$

1000 sample points are used and the phase space of the original time series is reconstructed with the embedding dimensions $D = 3$ and $T = 2$. The first half of samples are used for training while the rest for testing. This time series data set is scaled in the range [0,1].

The *Lorenz time series* is simulated time series, which is chaotic in nature that was proposed by Edward Lorenz along with the principles of Chaos theory [12]. This dataset is scaled in the range of [-1,1]. The first half of the 1000 sample points are used for training while the rest for testing. The phase space of the original time series is reconstructed with the embedding dimensions $D = 3$ and $T = 2$, similar as previous time series data.

The *Sunspot time series* gives good indication of the solar activities for solar cycles which impacts Earth's climate [16]. The monthly smoothed Sunspot time series has been obtained from the *World Data Center* for the Sunspot Index [13]. This time series is scaled in the range [-1,1] and first is used for training while the second half for testing. Embedding dimension of $D = 5$ and $T = 2$ is used.

The *ACI Worldwide Inc. time series* [14] is taken from the NASDAQ stock exchange and contains 800 sample points from December 2006 to February 2010 [14]. It is scaled in the range [0,1]. The first half is used for training and the second half for testing. Embedding dimension of $D = 5$ and $T = 2$ is used.

The feedforward network employs sigmoid units in the hidden and the output layer for the Mackey-Glass and ACI Worldwide Inc. problems. However, the hyperbolic tangent unit is used in the output layer for the Lorenz and Sunspot time series. Root mean squared error (RMSE) is used to evaluate the performance of the proposed method as done in previous work [3]. The G3-PCX evolutionary algorithm is employed to evolve all the sub-populations [17]. It uses specific parameters for creation of new solutions such as the pool size of 2 parents and 2 offspring [3].

The number of generations for each sub-population known as *depth of search* is kept as 1 as done in [3]. The algorithm terminates once the maximum number of function evaluations (50 000) have been reached by the respective cooperative neuro-evolutionary methods (RNL, NL and SL).

3.2   Results

In Tables 1, 2, 3, and 4 the results are shown for different number of hidden neurons using RNL, NL and SL. The RMSE and 95 percent confidence interval along with the best run are reported for 50 independent experimental runs. We evaluate the best results for each case with lowest RMSE in training and generalization performance irrespective of number of hidden neurons used.

In the Mackey-Glass problem shown in Table 1, it was observed that RNL gives better training and generalization performance when compared to SL. RNL was unable to outperform NL.

In Table 2, for the Lorenz problem, it was observed that the RNL has performed much better than SL, however, it was unable to outperform NL in terms of training or generalization. Unlike for the Mackey-Glass problem, it was seen that the generalization and training performance of all the methods deteriorates when the number of the hidden neuron increases.

Table 1. Training and generalisation performance for Mackey-Glass time series problem

Method	H	Training	Generalisation	Best
NL	3	0.0107 ± 0.00131	0.0107 ± 0.00131	0.0050
	5	0.0089 ± 0.00097	0.0088 ± 0.00097	0.0038
	7	0.0078 ± 0.00079	0.0078 ± 0.00079	0.0040
SL	3	0.0237 ± 0.0023	0.0237 ± 0.0023	0.0125
	5	0.0195 ± 0.0012	0.0195 ± 0.0012	0.0124
	7	0.0177 ± 0.0009	0.0178 ± 0.0009	0.0121
RNL	3	0.0151 ± 0.00087	0.0151 ± 0.00087	0.0076
	5	0.0132 ± 0.00064	0.0132 ± 0.00064	0.0088
	7	0.0133 ± 0.00066	0.0133 ± 0.00066	0.0092

The performance of the Sunspot time series problem in Table 3 shows that RNL was able to outperform SL and NL in generalisation performance.

The ACI Worldwide Inc. in Table 4 shows similar performance when compared to Sunspot time series as both are real world applications that contain noise. RNL outperformed SL and gave close performance to NL.

Tables 5, 6, 7, and 8, compares the best results from Tables 1, 2, 3, and 4 with some of the related methods from the literature. The RMSE of the best experimental run together with NMSE (normalized mean squared error) are used for the comparison. The proposed RNL method has given good performance when compared to some of the methods in the literature.

The best result of Mackey-Glass time series problem was compared to methods from the literature in Table 5. The proposed method was able to outperform some of the methods.

Table 2. Training and generalisation performance for the Lorenz time series problem

Method	H	Training	Generalisation	Best
NL	3	0.0170 ± 0.0031	0.0176 ± 0.0031	0.0043
	5	0.0249 ± 0.0062	0.0271 ± 0.0067	0.0021
	7	0.0379 ± 0.0093	0.0416 ± 0.0092	0.0024
SL	3	0.0680 ± 0.0325	0.0452 ± 0.0229	0.0153
	5	0.0526 ± 0.0084	0.0546 ± 0.0084	0.0082
	7	0.0574 ± 0.0075	0.0605 ± 0.0074	0.0079
RNL	3	0.0263 ± 0.0051	0.027 ± 0.0051	0.0062
	5	0.0309 ± 0.0087	0.0333 ± 0.0087	0.0075
	7	0.0395 ± 0.0083	0.0435 ± 0.0083	0.0058

Table 3. Training and generalisation performance for Sunspot time series

Method	H	Training	Generalisation	Best
NL	3	0.0207 ± 0.0035	0.0538 ± 0.0091	0.015
	5	0.0289 ± 0.0039	0.0645 ± 0.0093	0.017
	7	0.0353 ± 0.0048	0.0676 ± 0.0086	0.021
SL	3	0.0539 ± 0.0261	0.04998 ± 0.0238	0.210
	5	0.0560 ± 0.0208	0.05210 ± 0.0177	0.302
	7	0.0568 ± 0.0178	0.05250 ± 0.0132	0.344
RNL	3	0.0411 ± 0.0051	0.0472 ± 0.0048	0.031
	5	0.0390 ± 0.0044	0.0467 ± 0.0039	0.030
	7	0.0414 ± 0.0069	0.0533 ± 0.0060	0.030

Table 4. Training and generalisation performance for ACI Worldwide Inc. time series

Method	H	Training	Generalisation	Best
NL	3	0.0214 ± 0.00039	0.0215 ± 0.00039	0.020
	5	0.0203 ± 0.00047	0.0212 ± 0.00041	0.019
	7	0.0201 ± 0.00038	0.0208 ± 0.00033	0.019
SL	3	0.0466 ± 0.0039	0.0411 ± 0.00360	0.080
	5	0.0413 ± 0.0038	0.0390 ± 0.00378	0.042
	7	0.0449 ± 0.0028	0.0424 ± 0.00270	0.134
RNL	3	0.0250 ± 0.00097	0.0228 ± 0.00077	0.019
	5	0.0236 ± 0.00075	0.0220 ± 0.00059	0.019
	7	0.0232 ± 0.00072	0.0219 ± 0.00063	0.019

The Table 6 shows the best result of Lorenz time series problem being compared to works in literature. It was seen that the proposed method outperformed all the methods except for co-evolutionary recurrent neural networks (CICC-RNN) which cannot be strictly compared due to difference in network architectures.

Table 5. A comparison with the results from literature on the Mackey-Glass time series

Prediction method	RMSE	NMSE
Locally linear neuro-fuzzy model (LLNF-LoLiMot) (2006) [18]	9.61E-04	
Neural fuzzy network and PS0 (2009) [19]	2.10E-02	
Neural fuzzy network and CPS0 (2009) [19]	1.76E-02	
Neural fuzzy network and DE (2009) [19]	1.62E-02	
Neural fuzzy network and GA (2009) [19]	1.63E-02	
Synapse Level-CCRNN (SL-CCRNN) (2012) [3]	6.33E-03	2.79E-04
Neuron Level-CCRNN (NL-CCRNN) (2012) [3]	8.28E-03	4.77E-04
Competitive Island Cooperative Coevolution (CICC-RNN) (2014) [20]	3.99E-03	1.11E-04
Proposed FNN-RNL	7.59E-03	1.09E-04

Table 6. A comparison with the results from literature on the Lorenz time series

Prediction method	RMSE	NMSE
Auto regressive moving average (ARMA-ANN)(2008) [21]	8.76E-02	
Backpropagation neural network and GA (2011) [22]	2.96E-02	
Synapse Level-CCRNN (SL-CCRNN) (2012) [3]	6.36E-03	7.72E-04
Neuron Level-CCRNN (NL-CCRNN) (2012) [3]	8.20E-03	1.28E-03
Competitive Island Cooperative Coevolution (CICC-RNN) (2014) [20]	3.55E-03	2.41E-04
Proposed FNN-RNL	5.81E-03	1.77E-04

The best result of the Sunspot time series problem was compared to the literature in Table 7. The proposed method was unable to outperform different co-evolutionary recurrent neural networks (SL-RNN, NL-RNN and CICC-RNN) which cannot be strictly compared due to difference in neural network architecture.

The best result of the ACI Worldwide Inc. problem was compared to the literature in Table 8. The proposed method outperformed all the methods except for multi-objective method with T=3. The results are better when compared to other works from the literature.

Table 7. A comparison with the results from literature on the Sunspot time series

Prediction method	RMSE	NMSE
Radial basis network (RBF-OLS)(2006) [18]		4.60E-02
Locally linear neuro-fuzzy model (LLNF-LoLiMot) (2006) [18]		3.20E-02
Synapse Level-CCRNN (SL-CCRNN) (2012) [3]	1.66E-02	1.47E-03
Neuron Level-CCRNN (NL-CCRNN) (2012) [3]	2.60E-02	3.62E-03
Competitive Island Cooperative Coevolution (CICC-RNN) (2014) [20]	1.57E-02	1.31E-03
Proposed FNN-RNL	2.96E-02	2.68E-03

Table 8. A comparison with the results from literature on the ACI time series

Prediction method	RMSE	NMSE
Competitive Island Cooperative Coevolution CICC-RNN [23]	1.92E-02	
Synapse Level (FNN-SL) (2014) [24]	1.92E-02	
Neuron Level (FNN-NL) (2014) [24]	1.91E-02	
MOCCFNN with 2-objectives (T=2)(MO-CCFNN-T=2) (2014) [25]	1.94E-02	
MOCCFNN with 2-objectives (T=3)(MO-CCFNN-T=3) (2014) [25]	1.470E-02	
Proposed FNN-RNL	1.91E-02	2.00E-03

Figure 4 show that a typical experimental run from the RNL method was able to cope with the noise from one of the real-world dataset. The error graph is also given which indicates the challenges for the chaotic nature of these time series problems at certain time intervals.

4   Discussion

In general, the results of the experiments showed that proposed reverse neuron level is better than synapse level and gives close performance when compared to neuron level for given time series problems. Reverse neuron level gives a competitive performance when compared to other methods from the literature.

Reverse neuron level employs fewer subcomponents when compared to synapse level and more subcomponents when compared to neuron level according to the network topology with one output neuron used for one step ahead time series problems. The results showed that reverse neuron level has been able to achieve similar performance when compared to other methods in terms of the generalization.

Reverse neuron level groups subcomponents similar to synapse level for the hidden-output layer. It seems that due to more interaction between hidden to output layer, where more decision making takes place, it was unable to have better performance when compared to neuron level. Reverse neuron level seems to
.

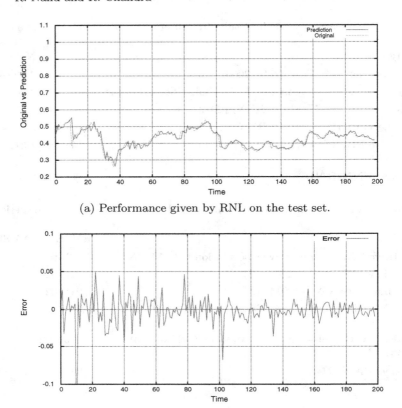

(a) Performance given by RNL on the test set.

(b) Error on the test data set.

Fig. 4. Typical train prediction given by RNL for ACI Worldwide Inc time series.

perform better than synapse level mainly due to the weight connections between input-hidden layer. It is better to combine the weights together, which is the case in reverse neuron level and neuron level.

5 Conclusion and Future Work

In this paper, we proposed reverse neuron level decomposition for the cooperative neuro-evolution of feedforward neural networks applied to time series problems. The results of the experiments have given a better understanding of decomposition of neural network in terms of interacting variables. The proposed method has also outperformed some of the methods from the literature. In general, the proposed method is much better than synapse level decomposition and produces competitive results with neuron level decomposition.

In future work, the proposed method can be further tested on other problems, including multi-dimensional time series. The method can be used to evolve other neural network architectures for pattern classification and control.

References

1. Stephen, H.K.: In the Wake of Chaos: Unpredictable Order in Dynamical Systems. University of Chicago Press, Chicago (1993)
2. Parras-Gutierrez, E., Rivas, V., Garcia-Arenas, M., del Jesus, M.: Short, medium and long term forecasting of time series using the L-Co-R algorithm. Neurocomputing **128**, 433–446 (2014). http://www.sciencedirect.com/science/article/pii/S0925231213008990
3. Chandra, R., Zhang, M.: Cooperative coevolution of Elman recurrent neural networks for chaotic time series prediction. Neurocomputing **186**, 116–123 (2012)
4. Potter, M., De Jong, K.: A cooperative coevolutionary approach to function optimization. In: Davidor, Y., Schwefel, H.-P., Mnner, R. (eds.) Parallel Problem Solving from Nature PPSN III. LNCS, vol. 866, pp. 249–257. Springer, Berlin Heidelberg (1994)
5. Gomez, F., Schmidhuber, J., Miikkulainen, R.: Accelerated neural evolution through cooperatively coevolved synapses. J. Mach. Learn. Res. **9**, 937–965 (2008)
6. García-Pedrajas, N., Ortiz-Boyer, D.: A cooperative constructive method for neural networks for pattern recognition. Pattern Recogn. **40**(1), 80–98 (2007)
7. Chandra, R., Frean, M.R., Zhang, M.: Crossover-based local search in cooperative co-evolutionary feedforward neural networks. Appl. Soft Comput. **12**(9), 2924–2932 (2012)
8. Gomez, F., Mikkulainen, R.: Incremental evolution of complex general behavior. Adapt. Behav. **5**(3–4), 317–342 (1997)
9. Chandra, R., Frean, M., Zhang, M.: On the issue of separability for problem decomposition in cooperative neuro-evolution. Neurocomputing **87**, 33–40 (2012)
10. Chandra, R., Frean, M., Zhang, M.: An encoding scheme for cooperative coevolutionary feedforward neural networks. In: Li, J. (ed.) AI 2010. LNCS, vol. 6464, pp. 253–262. Springer, Heidelberg (2010)
11. Mackey, M., Glass, L.: Oscillation and chaos in physiological control systems. Science **197**(4300), 287–289 (1977)
12. Lorenz, E.: Deterministic non-periodic flows. J. Atmos. Sci. **20**, 267–285 (1963)
13. SILSO World Data Center, The International Sunspot Number (1834–2001), International Sunspot Number Monthly Bulletin and Online Catalogue, Royal Observatory of Belgium, Avenue Circulaire 3, 1180 Brussels, Belgium (2015). Accessed on 02 February 2015. http://www.sidc.be/silso/
14. NASDAQ Exchange Daily: 1970–2010 Open, Close, High, Low and Volume (2015). Accessed on 02 February 2015. http://www.nasdaq.com/symbol/aciw/stock-chart
15. Takens, F.: Detecting strange attractors in turbulence. In: Rand, D., Young, L.-S. (eds.) Dynamical Systems and Turbulence, Warwick 1980. LNCS, vol. 898, pp. 366–381. Springer, Heidelberg (1995)
16. Sello, S.: Solar cycle forecasting: a nonlinear dynamics approach. Astron. Astrophys. **377**, 312–320 (2001)
17. Deb, K., Anand, A., Joshi, D.: A computationally efficient evolutionary algorithm for real-parameter optimization. Evol. Comput. **10**(4), 371–395 (2002)
18. Gholipour, A., Araabi, B.N., Lucas, C.: Predicting chaotic time series using neural and neurofuzzy models: a comparative study. Neural Process. Lett. **24**, 217–239 (2006)
19. Lin, C.-J., Chen, C.-H., Lin, C.-T.: A hybrid of cooperative particle swarm optimization and cultural algorithm for neural fuzzy networks and its prediction applications. IEEE Trans. Syst. Man Cybern. Part C: Appl. Rev. **39**(1), 55–68 (2009)

20. Chandra, R.: Competition and collaboration in cooperative coevolution of Elman recurrent neural networks for time-series prediction. IEEE Transactions onNeural Networks and Learning Systems (2015). (In Press)
21. Rojas, I., Valenzuela, O., Rojas, F., Guillen, A., Herrera, L., Pomares, H., Marquez, L., Pasadas, M.: Soft-computing techniques and arma model for time series prediction. Neurocomputing **71**(4–6), 519–537 (2008)
22. Ardalani-Farsa, M., Zolfaghari, S.: Residual analysis and combination of embedding theorem and artificial intelligence in chaotic time series forecasting. Appl. Artif. Intell. **25**, 45–73 (2011)
23. Chandra, R.: Competitive two-island cooperative coevolution for training Elman recurrent networks for time series prediction. In: International Joint Conference on Neural Networks (IJCNN), Beijing, China, pp. 565–572, July 2014
24. Chand, S., Chandra, R.: Cooperative coevolution of feed forward neural networks for financial time series problem. In: International Joint Conference on Neural Networks (IJCNN), Beijing, China, pp. 202–209, July 2014
25. Chand, S., Chandra, R.: Multi-objective cooperative coevolution of neural networks for time series prediction. In: International Joint Conference on Neural Networks (IJCNN), Beijing, China, pp. 190–197. July 2014

A Delaunay Triangulation Based Density Measurement for Evolutionary Multi-objective Optimization

Yutao Qi[1(✉)], Minglei Yin[1], and Xiaodong Li[2]

[1] School of Computer Science and Technology, Xidian University, Xi'an, China
ytqi@xidan.edu.cn
[2] School of Computer Science and IT, RMIT University, Melbourne, Australia

Abstract. Diversity preservation is a critical issue in evolutionary multi-objective optimization algorithms (MOEAs), it has significant influence on the quality of final solution set. In this wok, a crowding density measurement is developed for preserving diversity in MOEAs by using the Delaunay triangulation mesh built on the population in the objective space. Base on the property of the Delaunay triangulation, the new density measurement considers both the Euclidean distance and the relative position between individuals, and thus provide a more accurate estimation of the density around a specific individual within the population. Experimental results indicate that the suggested density measurement help to improve the performance of MOEAs significantly.

Keywords: Evolutionary multi-objective optimization · Diversity preservation · Delaunay triangulation · Density measurement

1 Introduction

Multi-objective optimization problem (MOP) is a category of problems that optimize two or more conflicting objectives simultaneously [1]. Different from single-objective optimization problems, a MOP usually has no unique solution that meets all the objectives. Instead, there exist some trade-off solutions which are known as the Pareto optimal solutions. The collection of all the Pareto optimal solutions in the decision space is termed as the Pareto set (PS) whose image in the objective space is called the Pareto front (PF). As it is time-consuming or even impossible to obtain the whole PF, the aim of a multi-objective optimizer is to find a representative set of non-dominated solutions that approximates the PF as closely as possible and spreads evenly along the PF. Provided with an approximated set of the PF, a decision maker would have a better understanding of the target MOP and thus make more reasonable decisions.

Among existing multi-objective optimization approaches, multi-objective optimization evolutionary algorithms (MOEAs) are recognized as one of the most successful techniques. By evolving a population of solutions, MOEAs can provide a required set of non-dominated solutions in a single run, which is significant advantage over traditional approaches [2]. Since the pioneer work by Schaffer [3] who first combined the traditional multi-objective optimization technique with evolutionary computation, many

© Springer International Publishing Switzerland 2016
T. Ray et al. (Eds.): ACALCI 2016, LNAI 9592, pp. 183–192, 2016.
DOI: 10.1007/978-3-319-28270-1_16

research efforts have been devoted to this area, and many MOEAs have been developed. These MOEAs can be roughly divided into two categories. One is the Pareto-dominance based MOEAs in which NSGAII [4] and SPEA2 [5] are the most representative ones. The other is the Non-Pareto-dominance based MOEAs, including decomposition-based MOEAs like MOEA/D [6] and indicator-based MOEAs like IBEA [7].

Diversity preservation is considered to be an important technique in an evolutionary algorithm to prevent it from premature convergence and thus yields good performance. It is especially critical in MOEAs, because MOP presents more challenges to optimizers in terms of the coverage and uniformity of the Pareto optimal solutions [8]. Existing studies on diversity preservation in MOEAs can be classified into the following four categories: (1) Crowding: including Niching techniques [9, 10] and crowding density based sorting [4, 11]. (2) Hyper-grid: dividing the objective space into uniform grid cells and emphasizing solutions in less crowded hyper-boxes [12]. (3) Clustering: extracting density information by using clustering techniques and reducing the non-dominated set without destroying its characteristics [5, 13]. (4) Entropy: making use of the entropy information to measure the population diversity and guide the selection [14, 15]. Among these diversity preservation techniques, the crowding method is widely used especially in Pareto-dominance based MOEAs.

In the crowding method, the density measurement of a specific individual in the population is determined by the distances between the individual and its k-nearest neighbors [4, 16]. Here, the parameter k is usually assigned to a predetermined value that equal to the number of objectives. Such density measurement is reasonable when the k-nearest neighbors of a specific individual scatter surround it in the objective space, however, when it is not the case, this measurement will be inaccurate. According to our observation, such inaccuracy comes from the ignorance of the information of relative position between individuals. On the other hand, the parameter k is not necessary equal to the number of objectives, it should be assigned to an appropriate value.

In this work, a new density measurement based on Delaunay triangulation is developed for diversity preservation in the Pareto-dominance based MOEAs. The main contributions of this work are as follows:

- A neighborhood relationship between individuals in the population is designed by constructing the Delaunay triangulation mesh of the points in the decision space where the parameter k is adaptively determined.
- A novel density measurement based on the Delaunay triangulation mesh, which considers both the Euclidean distance and the relative position between individuals, is developed for diversity preservation in MOEAs.

The remainder of this paper is organized as follows. Section 2 describes the motivation and the main idea of this work. Section 3 presents the proposed density measurement base on Delaunay triangulation. Section 4 shows some experimental results which compares the suggested density measurement with existing ones under the same algorithmic framework. Section 5 concludes this paper.

2   Motivation

As we have mentioned before, the k-nearest-neighbor density measurement is not always accurate. Figure 1 illustrates an elaborate example to show its drawbacks. Given a population with eight individuals in a three-dimensional objective space, as shown in Fig. 1(a), let's focus on individuals A and B in the population. Individual A has its three nearest neighbors C, B and D. While C, A and D are the three nearest neighbors of B. Now we assume that individuals C and D are located on the midperpendicular line of the line segment between A and B, in other words, we have |AC| = |BC| and |AD| = |BD|. In this case, A and B have the same density measurement according to the k-nearest-neighbor density measurement. Let's further assume that we move the individual B along line AB to a new position B′ and keep the three nearest neighbors of the two individuals unchanged, as shown in Fig. 1(b). Then, individual B′ should have higher density measurement than A. If we have to remove one individual from the population at this time, then A will be chosen according to the k-nearest-neighbor density measurement. However, it is obvious that the population will achieve better uniformity by removing the individual B′ rather than A. The main reason of this inaccuracy is that the three nearest neighbors of individual A do not spread surrounding it in the objective space as it is assumed by the density measurement.

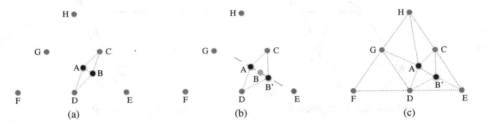

Fig. 1. An example to show the inaccuracy of the k-nearest-neighbor density measurement. (a) The population in the objective space. (b) Changing the population density by moving B to a new position B′. (c) The neighborhood relationship based on Delaunay Triangulation.

Figure 1(c) shows the Delaunay triangulation mesh of the individuals in the population. It can be seen that, in this mesh, A has five neighbors and B′ has four neighbors. That is to say, the parameter k is adaptively determined. The Delaunay triangulation mesh constructs a new neighborhood relationship between individuals in the population, and if a specific individual in the mesh is not a boundary individual, the mesh guarantees that the neighbors of the individual scatter surrounding it. In addition, the area bounded by A's neighbors is larger than that bounded by neighbors of B′ which implies that B′ can be removed as we expect if a density measurement is appropriately designed based on the Delaunay triangulation mesh. With this aim, the Delaunay triangulation technique, which will be introduced in the next subsection, is employed to model and describe the relative positions between solutions, giving rise to a new density measurement for diversity preservation in MOEAs.

3   The Delaunay Triangulation Based Density Measurement

In this section, the definition of Delaunay triangulation is introduced at first. Then, the suggested Delaunay triangulation based density measurement is presented. At last, the selection operator using the newly developed density measurement for MOEAs is described and analyzed.

3.1   Definition of Delaunay Triangulation

Triangulation is one of the main topics in the field of computational geometry. Given a point set P, the Delaunay triangulation [17] built on P is a particular triangulation, noted as DT(P), such that every triangle in DT(P) contains no point from P in its interior (points are permitted on the circumcircle). In other words, every triangle of a Delaunay triangulation has an empty circumcircle. Figure 2 compares a Delaunay triangulation with a non-Delaunay triangulation built on four points. It has been proved that, the Delaunay triangulation is unique if no more than three points are located on the same cycle.

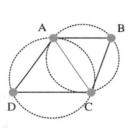   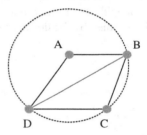

(a) Delaunay Triangulation   (b) Non-Delaunay Triangulation

Fig. 2.   Delaunay triangulation and non-Delaunay triangulation

Delaunay triangulation has certain nice properties. The most important one is that the Delaunay triangulation maximizes the minimum angle of all the angles of the triangles in the triangulation. To put it simply, the Delaunay triangulation tend to avoid skinny triangles and generate triangles in regular shape. Due to this property, points in the Delaunay triangulation mesh are more likely to connect with their nearest neighbors. As shown in Fig. 2, the edge DB which connects two points with long distance is not likely to appear in the Delaunay triangulation. To conclude, a specific point in the Delaunay triangulation mesh, if not a boundary point, keeps connections with several nearest neighbors surrounding it. That is what we need in the definition of the density measurement.

3.2   Definition of the Proposed Density Measurement

The proposed density measurement takes advantage of the property of the Delaunay triangulation mentioned before. The density measurement of a specific individual x_i in population P, noted as $D\left(x_i\right)$, is determined by its connected neighbors $\left\{x_j | x_j \in N\left(x_i\right)\right\}$ in the Delaunay triangulation mesh, in which $N\left(x_i\right)$ denotes the neighbor set of individual x_i with size k_i. The boundary individuals in the Delaunay triangulation mesh are assigned with an infinite density measurement to guarantee that those boundary individuals will always be selected to survive as done in most MOEAs [2, 4, 11]. Therefore, the density measurement of individual x_i can be calculated by the following formula (1):

$$D\left(x_i\right) = \begin{cases} INF & x_i \in B\left(DT\left(P\right)\right) \\ \left(\displaystyle\prod_{x_j \in N(x_i)} \left|x_i x_j\right|\right)^{1/k_i} & \text{otherwise} \end{cases} \tag{1}$$

where, $B\left(DT\left(P\right)\right)$ means the set of boundary individuals in the Delaunay triangulation mesh $DT\left(P\right)$. INF denotes an infinite number. $\left|x_i x_j\right|$ is the Euclidean distance between individual x_i and x_j in the objective space.

Given a point set P with n individuals, its Delaunay triangulation mesh $DT\left(P\right)$ can be built by using a divide-and-conquer based Delaunay generation algorithm with time complexity of $O\left(nlogn\right)$ [18]. Using convex hull detecting algorithm, the boundary individual set $B\left(DT\left(P\right)\right)$ can be determined. The convex hull has been extensively studied in computational geometry. Currently, many convex hull detecting algorithms for both two-dimensional [19] and general-dimensional [20] point sets have been developed with time complexity from $O\left(nlogn\right)$ to $O\left(n^2\right)$. In this work, the Graham algorithm with $O\left(nlogn\right)$ time complexity [19] is employed to identify the boundary individuals in the population.

3.3   Selection Operator with the New Density Measurement for MOEAs

In this section, a selection operator which combines the fast non-dominated sorting method [4] and the diversity preservation technique based on the newly developed density measurement is presented for MOEAs. The main idea of the suggested selection is the same as that in NSGA-II [4]. More specifically, the selection operator is carried out base on the non-domination rank and the density measurement of individuals. All the individuals in the population are sorted by using a crowded-comparison-operator at first, and then a binary tournament selection is applied to reduce the population into a predefined size. The crowded-comparison-operator works as following: if two individuals have different non-domination ranks, the one with lower rank will win. Otherwise, the one with larger density measurement will be ranked higher.

In the proposed selection operator, the density measurement in NSGA-II, which is the crowding distance measurement, is replaced by the newly developed density measurement when the objective number is greater than two. All the other parts are kept unchanged. With regard to time complexity, constructing the Delaunay triangulation mesh is $O\left(nlogn\right)$ and the convex hull detecting is $O\left(nlogn\right)$, therefore, the total time complexity of the proposed selection operator will not be larger than $O\left(n^2\right)$ which is the time complexity of the original selection operator in NSGA-II.

3.4 Workflow of the NSGAII-DT

Following the algorithmic framework of NSGA-II, the proposed NSGAII-DT replaces the crowding distance based density measurement in NSGA-II with the Delaunay triangulation based density measurement. In the following Algorithm 1, the flowchart of NSGAII-DT is described in detail. In which, the statement in line 8 is the only difference between NSGAII-DT and the original NSGAII.

Algorithm 1: NSGAII-DT	
1. $t=0$, P_t=*Initialization*(N);	Initialize a population of N individuals at random.
2. *While* stop criteria not met *do*	Main loop
3. Q_t= *Evolve* (P_t);	Evolve and create offspring set Q_t.
4. R_t= $P_t \cup Q_t$;	Combine parent and offspring population.
5. P_{t+1}=$\emptyset$ and i=1;	
6. F= *FastNondominatedSort*(R_t);	$F = (F_1, F_2, ...)$ all nondominated fronts of R_t.
7. *While* $|P_{t+1}|+|F_i| \leq N$	Until the parent population is filled.
8. *DT-density-assignment*(F_i);	Calculate DT based density measurement in F_i.
9. $P_{t+1} = P_{t+1} \cup F_i$;	Include i-th nondominated front
10. i= i+1;	Check the next front for inclusion.
11. *End while*	
12. *Sort* (F_i, $\prec_n$);	Sort using crowded-comparison-operator $\prec_n$.
13. P_{t+1}=$P_{t+1} \cup F_i[1:(N - |P_{t+1}|)]$;	Choose the first $N - |P_{t+1}|$ elements of F_i.
14. $t = t$+1;	Go to the next iteration
15. *End while*	

4   Experimental Studies

In this part, the proposed density measurement is compared with the crowding distance based density measurement [4] and the vicinity distance based density measurement [16] by implementing the three density measurements in the same algorithmic framework of NSGA-II. For ease of discussion, the three compared algorithms are noted as NSGA-II, NSGA-II-DT and NSGA-II-VD, which means the original NSGA-II with crowding distance based measurement, NSGA-II with our Delaunay triangulation based density measurement, and NSGA-II with the vicinity distance based measurement respectively. The compared algorithms are applied on four benchmark functions with three objectives, including DTLZ1, DTLZ2, DTLZ6 problems [21] with linear, spherical and discrete PF respectively, and the WFG1 problem [22] with a convex PF.

The inverted generational distance (IGD) metric [23] is employed to evaluate the performances of the compared algorithms. IGD is a comprehensive metric which considers both convergence and diversity of the final non-dominated solution set obtained by the compared algorithms. Given a set of evenly scattered points P^* over the PF of the target problem and the final non-dominated solution set P obtained by MOEAs, the IGD value of P can be determined by formula (2).

$$\text{IGD}\,(P, P^*) = \frac{\sum_{v \in P^*} d\,(v, P)}{|P^*|} \qquad (2)$$

where $d(v, P)$ denotes the minimum Euclidean distance between a specific point v from P^* and the solutions in P. $|P^*|$ is the size of the reference set P^*. The IGD metric has a nonnegative value and the lower the better.

In the following experimental studies, the size of the reference set is set as 2500. The parameter setting of all the compared algorithms follows the original NSGA-II [4]. All the compared algorithms stop when the number of function evaluations reaches 75000 for DTLZ1, DTLZ2 and DTLZ6 problems, and 200000 for WFG1 problem. The experimental data are calculated over 30 independent runs.

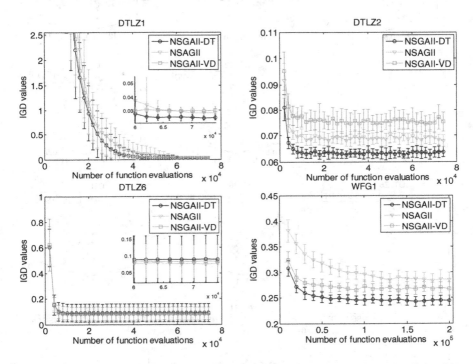

Fig. 3. Comparisons on the convergence of the IGD values for the three compared algorithms on the four benchmarks over 30 independent runs. Median (line), the first quartile (top error-bar) and the third quartile (bottom error-bar).

Figure 3 illustrates the IGD metric values over time obtained by the three compared algorithms on the four benchmarks. The bottom and top error-bars are the first and third quartiles, and points on the line are the median points. It can be seen that NSGA-II-DT significantly outperforms NSGA-II and NSGA-II-VD on DTLZ1, DTLZ2 and WFG1 problems, its performance is unstable on DTLZ6. The reason is that the DTLZ6 problem has a discrete PF with four disconnected regions, when detecting the boundary individuals in the population, the inner breakpoints that located on the inner edge of each PF region are not considered by the NSGA-II-DT method, as they are not the boundary individuals on the convex hull of the population. On the other hand, there is some degree of randomness in the shape of the triangles associated with those inner breakpoints in the Delaunay Triangulation mesh. These triangles might provide inaccurate neighborhood relationship between individuals and thus degrade the stability of the algorithm (Fig. 4).

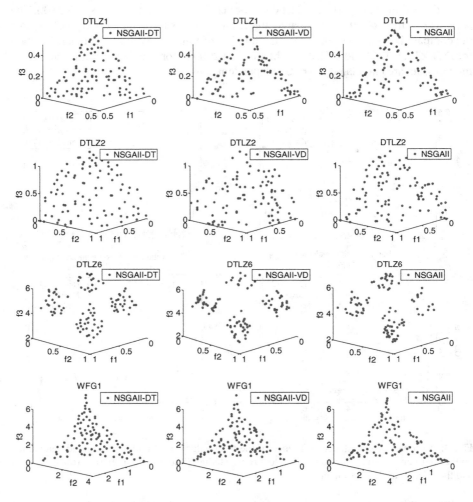

Fig. 4. The distribution of the final non-dominated solutions with the lowest IGD values obtained by the three compared algorithms on the four benchmarks.

To conclude, NSGAII-DT performs better than NSGAII and NSGAII-VD on benchmarks with continuous PFs, however it performs unstably on benchmarks with disconnected regions. These results indicate that the suggested density measurement based on the Delaunay triangulation mesh does help the MOEAs preserve diversity and obtain better uniformity of the resulting non-dominated solutions.

5 Conclusions

Base on the Delaunay triangulation mesh built on the population in the objective space, a crowding density measurement has been developed for diversity preservation in multi-objective optimization evolutionary algorithms (MOEAs). Experimental results indicate that MOEAs with the suggested density measurement can obtain significantly better uniformity of the resulting non-dominated solutions on multi-objective optimization problems (MOPs) with continuous Pareto fronts (PFs).

Although the suggested density measurement helps to improve the performances of MOEAs, it might make the algorithm perform unstably on MOPs with discontinuous PFs. Because the proposed density measurement might provide inaccurate neighborhood relationship between individuals which are located on the inner edge of each sub-region of PF. How to refine the density measurement for MOPs with discontinuous PFs will be the subject of future investigations.

References

1. Deb, K.: Multi-objective optimization. Search methodologies, pp. 403–449. Springer, US (2014)
2. Zhou, A., Qu, B.-Y., Li, H., Zhao, S.-Z., Suganthan, P.N., Zhang, Q.: Multiobjective evolutionary algorithms: a survey of the state of the art. Swarm Evol. Comput. **1**, 32–49 (2011)
3. Schaffer, J.D.: Multiple objective optimization with vector evaluated genetic algorithms. In: Proceedings of the 1st International Conference on Genetic Algorithms, pp. 93–100. L. Erlbaum Associates Inc. (1985)
4. Deb, K., Pratap, A., Agarwal, S., Meyarivan, T.: A fast and elitist multiobjective genetic algorithm: NSGA-II. IEEE Trans. Evol. Comput. **6**, 182–197 (2002)
5. Zitzler, E., Laumanns, M., Thiele, L.: SPEA2: improving the strength pareto evolutionary algorithm for multiobjective optimization Evolutionary methods for design, optimisation, and control, pp. 95–100. CIMNE, Barcelona Spain (2002)
6. Zhang, Q., Li, H.: MOEA/D: a multiobjective evolutionary algorithm based on decomposition. IEEE Trans. Evol. Comput. **11**, 712–731 (2007)
7. Zitzler, E., Künzli, S.: Indicator-based selection in multiobjective search. In: Yao, X., et al. (eds.) PPSN 2004. LNCS, vol. 3242, pp. 832–842. Springer, Heidelberg (2004)
8. Chen, B., Lin, Y., Zeng, W., Zhang, D., Si, Y.-W.: Modified differential evolution algorithm using a new diversity maintenance strategy for multi-objective optimization problems. Appl. Intell. **43**, 49–73 (2015)
9. Li, X.: Niching without niching parameters: particle swarm optimization using a ring topology. IEEE Trans. Evol. Comput. **14**, 150–169 (2010)
10. Kim, H., Liou, M.-S.: New fitness sharing approach for multi-objective genetic algorithms. J. Global Optim. **55**, 579–595 (2013)
11. Biao, L., Jinhua, Z., Jiongliang, X., Jun, W.: Dynamic crowding distance? A new diversity maintenance strategy for MOEAs. In: Fourth International Conference on Natural Computation, ICNC 2008, pp. 580–585 (2008)
12. Knowles, J.D., Corne, D.W.: Approximating the nondominated front using the Pareto archived evolution strategy. Evol. Comput. **8**, 149–172 (2000)

13. Tahernezhad, K., Lari, K.B., Hamzeh, A., Hashemi, S.: A multi-objective evolutionary algorithm based on complete-linkage clustering to enhance the solution space diversity. In: 2012 16th CSI International Symposium on Artificial Intelligence and Signal Processing (AISP), pp. 128–133. IEEE (2012)

14. Tan, K.C., Goh, C.K., Mamun, A., Ei, E.: An evolutionary artificial immune system for multi-objective optimization. Eur. J. Oper. Res. **187**, 371–392 (2008)

15. Pires, E.J.S., Machado, J.A.T., de Moura Oliveira, P.B.: Entropy diversity in multi-objective particle swarm optimization. Entropy **15**, 5475–5491 (2013)

16. Kukkonen, S., Deb, K.: A fast and effective method for pruning of non-dominated solutions in many-objective problems. In: Runarsson, T.P., Beyer, H.-G., Burke, E.K., Merelo-Guervós, J.J., Whitley, L., Yao, X. (eds.) PPSN 2006. LNCS, vol. 4193, pp. 553–562. Springer, Heidelberg (2006)

17. Lee, D.T., Schachter, B.J.: Two algorithms for constructing a Delaunay triangulation. Int. J. Comput. Inform. Sci. **9**, 219–242 (1980)

18. Dwyer, R.A.: A faster divide-and-conquer algorithm for constructing Delaunay triangulations. Algorithmica **2**, 137–151 (1987)

19. Graham, R.L.: An efficient algorithm for determining the convex hull of a finite planar set. Inf. Process. Lett. **1**, 132–133 (1972)

20. Barber, C.B., Dobkin, D.P., Huhdanpaa, H.: The quickhull algorithm for convex hulls. ACM Trans. Math. Softw. (TOMS) **22**, 469–483 (1996)

21. Deb, K., Thiele, L., Laumanns, M., Zitzler, E.: Scalable multi-objective optimization test problems. In: Proceedings of the 2002 Congress on Evolutionary Computation, pp. 825–830 (2002)

22. Huband, S., Barone, L., While, L., Hingston, P.: A scalable multiobjective test problem toolkit. In: Proceedings of the International Conference on Multi-Criterion Optimization, pp. 280–294 (2005)

23. Zitzler, E., Thiele, L., Laumanns, M., Fonseca, C.M., Da Fonseca, V.G.: Performance assessment of multiobjective optimizers: an analysis and review. IEEE Trans. Evol. Comput. **7**, 117–132 (2003)

Use of Infeasible Solutions During Constrained Evolutionary Search: A Short Survey

Hemant Kumar Singh$^{(\boxtimes)}$, Khairul Alam, and Tapabrata Ray

School of Engineering and Information Technology, University of New South Wales,
Canberra, Australia
{h.singh,k.alam,t.ray}@adfa.edu.au
http://www.unsw.adfa.edu.au, http://www.mdolab.net

Abstract. Most real world optimization problems involve constraints and constraint handling has long been an area of active research. While older techniques explicitly preferred feasible solutions over infeasible ones, recent studies have uncovered some shortcomings of such strategies. There has been a growing interest in the efficient use of infeasible solutions during the course of search and this paper presents of short review of such techniques. These techniques prefer *good infeasible* solutions over feasible solutions during the course of search (or a part of it). The review looks at major reported works over the years and outlines how these *preferences* have been dealt in various stages of the solution process, *viz*, problem formulation, parent selection/recombination and ranking/selection. A tabular summary is then presented for easy reference to the work in this area.

Keywords: Constraint handling · Review · Evolutionary algorithms · Optimization · Infeasible solutions

1 Introduction

Real life optimization problems involve constraints arising out of design requirements, physical laws, statutory norms, etc. The performance of population based stochastic optimization algorithms (e.g. evolutionary algorithms) is known to be largely dependent on the underlying mechanisms of constraint handling [37]. Broadly, the term *constraint handling* refers to all mechanisms that are used to deal with infeasible solutions, either in problem formulation or during the run. Let us start by illustrating why *feasibility-first* schemes might not be always the best. Consider, for example the landscape of a constrained function shown in Fig. 1(a). Explicit preference of feasible solutions over infeasible ones would result in a search trajectory via the feasible region towards the optimum (Fig. 1(b)). On the other hand, if some selected infeasible solutions near the constraint boundary (i.e. good infeasible solutions) were allowed to exist in the population, the search trajectory could have been much shorter thus resulting in significant savings on the number of function evaluations (Fig. 1(c)). Furthermore, for a

© Springer International Publishing Switzerland 2016
T. Ray et al. (Eds.): ACALCI 2016, LNAI 9592, pp. 193–205, 2016.
DOI: 10.1007/978-3-319-28270-1_17

problem with disconnected feasible regions, explicit preference of feasible solutions over infeasible ones could lead to a premature convergence to a local optimum of a feasible region, where the global optimum lies on a different feasible region (Fig. 1(d)). Several recent algorithms have implicitly or explicitly preferred/preserved *good infeasible solutions* via novel problem formulation, recombination and ranking/selection strategies. This short paper provides a review of major works in this area.

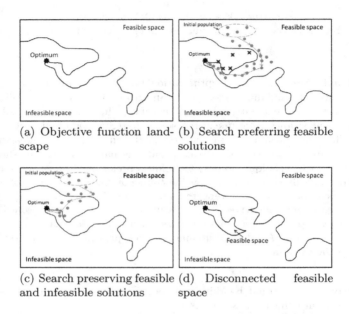

(a) Objective function landscape

(b) Search preferring feasible solutions

(c) Search preserving feasible and infeasible solutions

(d) Disconnected feasible space

Fig. 1. Traversal of objective function landscape using feasible/infeasible solution preference

2   Review

A number of methods have been proposed in literature to deal with constraints within a population based stochastic optimization algorithms. Some of the key review papers [8,35,37] have discussed and classified constraint handling techniques into a few broad categories, namely, penalty function based methods, decoders, special operators, separation of objectives and constraints, and hybrid methods. Although there is extensive volume of work in the constraint handling domain as evident from the list of references assembled in [7], the review presented here focuses only on those techniques which incorporate preference of infeasible solutions over feasible in some form to aid the search.

In this paper, an overview of methods that tend to prefer infeasible solutions during the course of search as opposed to conventional methods that indiscreetly prefer feasible solutions, is presented. In recent years, such methods have shown immense promise and offered significant boost in the efficiency over feasibility first techniques. A canonical stochastic optimization algorithm is used in the context of this discussion and the issue of constraint handling is discussed in the context of (re-)formulation, parent selection/recombination and ranking/selection strategies.

2.1   Re-formulation

Formulation of objectives and constraints is the first step of any optimization exercise. In the absence of specific constraint handling mechanisms, reformulating the problem to eliminate the constraints (and then solving it using an unconstrained optimizer) is one of the most common approaches that has been used over the years. More recently, reformulation is used in conjunction with other constraint handling techniques for further enhancements.

One of the most widely used re-formulation scheme relies on the use of penalty functions. In this approach, the problem is reformulated by adding a weighted penalty to the objective function whenever a solution violates its constraint(s). The weights/penalty parameters dictate the severity of the penalty. If a very large penalty factor is used, feasible solutions are likely to be always preferred. Use of controlled/adaptive penalty parameters [13, 22, 23] often scale the objectives and constraints to similar orders of magnitude and offers the possibility of preferring infeasible solutions over feasible ones. Such schemes are likely to reach the constrained optimum faster if the optimum lies on constraint boundaries.

There are also reports on constraint transformation, wherein the constraints (or measures based on constraint violations) as used as additional objectives and nondominance based schemes are used for the solution of the problem [6, 24, 53, 58, 59]. In such approaches, infeasible solutions have a chance of being preserved. Since transforming each constraint to an objective results in too many objectives, a number of infeasibility measures have been used instead. In [28], the number of constraint violations were treated as an objective, while a rank-sum measure was used in [42, 46, 48–50]. Some recent approaches have also used a combination of penalty functions *and* additional objectives [10–14, 17].

Yet another form of re-formulation appears in algorithms employing *two populations* [29–31]. In such approaches, the first population is evolved to improve the objective function values while the second is evolved to minimize constraint violations. Though a new objective is not introduced in this case, consideration of objectives and constraints in isolation (i.e. in two separate populations), constitutes a formulation different from the original.

2.2   Parent Selection/Recombination

At each generation of a population based stochastic algorithm, a new set of offspring solutions are generated via the process of recombination. The offspring solutions inherit the properties of the parent solutions, and hence parent selection can be used as a control measure to influence the search. *Fitter* parents are allowed to participate in recombination and often such parents are identified using binary tournaments or roulettes based on rank/fitness. If the fitness comparison rules favor feasible solutions over infeasible ones, the feasible solutions would actively participate in recombination e.g. [19]. On the other hand, if the comparison rules allow for feasible-infeasible recombinations along with feasible-feasible ones, the algorithm is likely to find solutions near the constraint boundary quicker (if the optimum lies on the constraint boundary). In [42,46,49], a percentage of marginally infeasible solutions were explicitly preserved and ranked higher than the feasible solutions to initiate infeasible-infeasible and infeasible-feasible recombinations.

There are also reports on matching strategies [26,39], wherein two different solutions satisfying different set of constraints were used in recombination to generate an offspring satisfying the union of the constraints. In [40,41], different parent matching schemes for unconstrained, moderately constrained and highly constrained problems have been suggested. Constraint driven crossovers [22,23], constraint driven mutation and gradient based local search strategies [10–14,48, 50] have also been reported in literature. Such strategies aim to induce good solutions relatively early in the course of search.

2.3 Ranking and Selection

Ranking is arguably the most prominent phase where the preferences can be categorically enforced. In *feasibility first* schemes, the feasible solutions are ranked using their objective values and infeasible solutions are ranked based on their constraint violations. Thereafter, the infeasible solutions are placed below the feasible set of solutions [16,19,32,36,38]. In the context of a generational model, the use of such a scheme would select M feasible solutions as members of the population for the next generation (if there are at least M feasible solutions in the pool consisting of $2M$ solutions (M parents and M offspring)). However, as mentioned in Sect. 1, such an explicit preference may delay convergence. To overcome this drawback, various ranking/selection strategies have been proposed. Stochastic ranking was proposed in [43], where infeasible solutions were preferred over feasible solutions with a finite probability. The classical meta-heuristic Simulated Annealing was also extended along similar lines [24,47,52]. In [22,23], a target proportion of feasible and infeasible solutions was maintained in the population by adjusting the penalty parameters. In [33], a probability factor S_r was introduced to prefer a solution based on its objective function value regardless of its feasibility, in order to promote infeasible solutions in promising regions. This probability was reduced over generations to a minimal value in order to reject infeasible solutions in the later half of the search. Similar preference for infeasible solutions was incorporated in a PSO algorithm in [60]. In [25], an *objective-first* scheme was introduced in contrary to *feasibility-first* scheme, where the objective values of the solutions were improved before improving their feasibility. The scheme allows for infeasible solutions to remain longer in the population, with an expectation that good infeasible solutions will generate good feasible solutions during the search.

Epsilon level constraint method is another recent method for constraint handling, where an infeasible solution is preferred over a feasible solution if its constraint violation is less than certain value, and its objective value is superior. This technique has been used in [2,4,55,56]. The scheme allows for the preservation of marginally infeasible solutions.

Lastly, there have been recent efforts to explicitly preserve some fraction of infeasible solutions in the population *irrespective* of how many feasible solutions are available or stage of evolution. This translates to an active search through the infeasible (in addition to feasible) space while simultaneously delivering marginally infeasible solutions for trade-off studies. In [28], a user defined percentage of solutions was maintained as infeasible and ranked above feasible solutions. Number of constraint violations was used as an additional objective. This additional objective was subsequently modified to incorporate constraint violation rank, which focuses on solutions closer to the constraint boundaries [21,42,46,49,51]. This ranking scheme was also used in conjunction with local search in [48,50]. In [44,45], the top ranked infeasible solutions were preserved and selected for repair. In [29–31], two separate populations were evolved, one for improving the objective values and the other for improving constraint violations. Both, feasible and infeasible solutions were preserved in the process. In another approach, solutions were evaluated and ranked with respect to different sequences of constraints [1,3,5]. This approach is particularly beneficial for problems in multi-disciplinary design, where each constraint evaluation may be computationally expensive.

The discussion presented here is summarized in Table 1. The tables include selected references and list details of the baseline algorithm, phase of preference articulation and the nature of the underlying scheme (i.e. deterministic or stochastic). As evident from the tables, different preference schemes have been used in various stages of the algorithms.

3   Conclusion and Future Directions/Opportunities

This paper provides a short review of major reported works in the area of evolutionary search, where infeasible solutions have been preferred/preserved over feasible solutions to improve the efficiency of the search process. Various forms of *preference articulation schemes* have been used in various stages of the solution process i.e. problem formulation, parent selection/recombination and ranking/selection schemes. The review brings forth a new perspective to the important area of constraint handling and provide the researchers with a succinct classification of various schemes.

While extensive research has been done in several areas of constraint handling, there are a number of areas which still need research attention. One of them relates to the development of novel and more efficient methods to deal with equality constrained optimization problems. Treatment of equalities as a pair of inequalities may not be the most efficient scheme. Other areas which have been less explored include the development of strategies to identify the best sequence

Table 1. Summary (Abbreviations used: Evolutionary Algorithm ≡ EA, Evolutionary Strategy ≡ ES, Differential Evolution ≡ DE, Particle Swarm Optimization ≡ PSO, Local Search ≡ LS, Sequential Quadratic Programming ≡ SQP, Artificial Immune System ≡ AIS)

Reference	Algorithm capability: Discrete/Continuous/Mixed (D or C or M)	Algorithm capability: Single/Multi/Both (S or M or C)	Baseline algorithm (EA, ES, DE, PSO etc.)	Phase (where an infeasible solution is preferred over feasible solution) Reformulation (RF), Recombination (RE), Ranking (RA)	Method (of preference) Deterministic/ Stochastic	Problems reported Benchmark or Engineering
Isaacs et al. [28]	M	M	EA	RF, RE, RA	Det.	Benchmark: CTP-series
Singh et al. [49]	M	C	EA	RF, RE, RA	Det.	Benchmark: g-series, CTP-series; Engineering: Car side impact, Bulk carrier design
Ray et al. [42]	M	C	EA	RF, RE, RA	Det.	Benchmark: g-series, CTP-series
Singh et al. [48]	C	S	EA, SQP	RF, RE, RA	Det.	Benchmark: C01–C18
Singh et al. [50]	C	S	EA, SQP	RF, RE, RA	Det.	Engineering: Belleville spring, Welded beam design, Car side impact, Bulk carrier design
Asafuddoula et al. [2]	C	M	EA	RE	Det.	Benchmark: CTP2–CTP8, SRN, TNK, OSY; Engineering: Toysub design problem
Mezura-Montes and Coello [32]	C	S	ES	RE	Det.	Benchmark: g01–g13
Mezura-Montes and Coello [34]	M	S	ES	RE	Det.	Engineering: Welded beam design, Pressure vessel, Tension/Compression string, Speed reducer
Hamida and Schoenauer [22]	C	S	EA	RF, RE, RA	Det.	Benchmark: g01–g11
Hamida and Schoenauer [23]	C	S	EA	RF, RE, RA	Det.	Benchmark: g01–g11
Wei and Wang [60]	C	M	PSO	RE, RA	Det.	Benchmark: CTP1–CTP7, CONSTR, SRN, TNK
Runarsson and Yao [43]	C	S	ES	RA	Stoc.	Benchmark: g01–g13

Table 1. (*Continued*)

Reference	Algorithm capability: Discrete/Continuous/Mixed (D or C or M)	Algorithm capability: Single/Multi/Both (S or M or C)	Baseline algorithm (EA, ES, DE, PSO etc.)	Phase (where an infeasible solution is preferred over feasible solution) Reformulation (RF), Recombination (RE), Ranking (RA)	Method (of preference) Deterministic/Stochastic	Problems reported (Benchmark or Engineering)
Xiao and Zu [61]	C	M	EA/AIS	RA	Stoc.	Benchmark: CTP2-CTP7
Hingston et al. [25]	C	M	EA	RA	Stoc.	Benchmark: TNK, OSY, REV; Engineering: Communication circuit design
Kimbrough et al. [29]	D	S	EA	RF, RA	Stoc.	Benchmark: 14 knapsack test problems (e.g. hp, pb, pet, sento, weing, weish)
Kimbrough et al. [31]	D	S	EA	RF, RA	Det.	Benchmark: 21 test problems from literature
Singh et al. [47]	C	M	SA	RA	Det.	Benchmark: CTP2-CTP8
Hedar and Fukushima [24]	C	S	SA	RA	Det.	Benchmark: g01-g13; Engineering: Welded beam design, Pressure vessel design, Tension/Compression string
Takahama et al. [56]	C	S	Hybrid (EA, PSO)	RA	Det.	Benchmark: Himmelblau's problem; Engineering: Welded beam design, Pressure vessel design
Takahama and Sakai [55]	C	S	DE	RA	Det.	Benchmark: g03, g05, g11, g13
Yu and Zhou [62]	C	S	EA	RA	Det.	Benchmark: Subset Sum Problem
Hinterding and Michalewicz [26]	C	S	EA	RE	Det.	Benchmark: g01-g05
Surry et al. [54]	C	S	EA	RA	Det.	Engineering: gas-network pipe-sizing problem

Table 1. (*Continued*)

Reference	Algorithm capability: Discrete/ Continuous/ Mixed (D or C or M)	Algorithm capability: Single/ Multi/ Both (S or M or C)	Baseline algorithm (EA, ES, DE, PSO etc.)	Phase (where an infeasible solution is preferred over feasible solution) Reformulation (RF), Recombination (RE), Ranking (RA)	Method (of preference) Deterministic/ Stochastic	Problems reported Benchmark or Engineering
Farmani and Wright [20]	M	S	EA	RF, RA	Det.	Benchmark: g01–g11, one test problem with discontinuous search space
Tessema and Yen [57]	C	S	EA	RF, RA	Det.	Benchmark: g01–g19, g21, g23, g24
Coello and Mezura-Montes [9]	C	S	EA	RA	Det.	Benchmark: g02, g04, g11, g12
Kimbrough et al. [30]	M	S	EA	RF	Det.	Benchmark: Yuan
Ho and Shimizu [27]	C	S	ES	RA	Stoc.	Benchmark: g01–g14, g16, g19, g21, g22; Engineering: Welded beam design
Deb and Datta [15]	C	S	Hybrid (EA, LS)	RF, RA	Det.	Benchmark: a mathematical test function, TP3–TP6, TP8; Engineering: Welded beam design
Datta and Deb [14]	C	S	Hybrid (EA, LS)	RF, RA	Det.	Benchmark: g03, g05, g11, g13–g15, g17, g21
Datta and Deb [12]	C	S	Hybrid (EA, LS)	RF, RA	Det.	Benchmark: 2 mathematical test functions, TP3–TP6, TP8; Engineering: Welded beam design, Three-bar truss design
Deb and Datta [17]	C	S	Hybrid (EA, LS)	RF, RA	Det.	Benchmark: g01–g19, g21, g23–g24; Engineering: Welded beam design
Datta et al. [10]	C	S	Hybrid (EA, LS)	RF, RA	Stoc.	Benchmark: g01, g07, g18, g24; Engineering: Welded beam design, Robotics problem

Table 1. (*Continued*)

Reference	Algorithm capability: Discrete/Continuous/Mixed (D or C or M)	Algorithm capability: Single/Multi/Both (S or M or C)	Baseline algorithm	Phase (where an infeasible solution is preferred over feasible solution) Reformulation (RF), Recombination (RE), Ranking (RA)	Method (of preference) Deterministic/Stochastic	Problems reported Benchmark or Engineering
Datta et al. [11]	C	S	Hybrid (EA, PS)	RF, RA	Det.	Benchmark: TP3–TP6, TP8
Datta and Deb [13]	C	S	Hybrid (EA, LS)	RF, RA	Det.	Benchmark: a mathematical test function, TP3-TP6, TP8; Engineering: Welded beam design
Deb et al. [18]	C	S	Hybrid (EA, SQP)	RF, RA	Det.	Benchmark: 13 test problems from CEC-06, Rastrigin's test problem
Asafuddoula et al. [1]	C	S	DE	RE, RA	Stoc.	Benchmark: g01, g02, g04, g06-g10, g12, g18, g24
Asafuddoula et al. [3]	C	S	DE	RE, RA	Stoc.	Benchmark: g01, g02, g04, g06-g10, g12, g18, g24
Asafuddoula et al. [5]	C	M	DE	RE, RA	Stoc.	Engineering: OSY, Welded beam design, Car-side impact, Speed reducer design
Ray et al. [39]	C	S	PSO	RE	Det.	Benchmark: 3 mathematical test functions; Engineering: Welded beam design
Ray et al. [40]	C	M	EA	RE	Stoc.	Engineering: Two bar truss, Four bar truss, Vibration platform design, Water resource planning
Saha and Ray [45]	C	M	EA	RA	Det.	Benchmark: modified ZDT-series (termed as constrained-ZDT or czdt)
Saha and Ray [44]	C	C	EA	RA	Det.	Benchmark: g2, g6, g10, g24; Engineering: Welded beam design

of constraint evaluation. While complete evaluation of a solution is the current norm, evaluating a solution till it violates a constraint can offer significant savings for computationally expensive optimization problems. From a practitioners point of view, research on constraint handling has been heavily skewed towards the identification of best feasible solution. Constraints other than ones arising out of statutory requirements or physical laws are often open for negotiation and users are keen to know about such trade-offs. Hopefully infeasibility based techniques can be developed further to deliver practical solutions with a greater efficiency in the future.

References

1. Asafuddoula, M., Ray, T., Sarker, R.: A differential evolution algorithm with constraint sequencing. In: 2012 Third Global Congress on Intelligent Systems (GCIS), pp. 68–71 (2012)
2. Asafuddoula, M., Ray, T., Sarker, R., Alam, K.: An adaptive constraint handling approach embedded MOEA/D. In: IEEE Congress on Evolutionary Computation (CEC), pp. 1–8 (2012)
3. Asafuddoula, M., Ray, T., Sarker, R.: A self-adaptive differential evolution algorithm with constraint sequencing. In: Thielscher, M., Zhang, D. (eds.) AI 2012. LNCS, vol. 7691, pp. 182–193. Springer, Heidelberg (2012)
4. Asafuddoula, M., Ray, T., Sarker, R.: A decomposition based evolutionary algorithm for many objective optimization with systematic sampling and adaptive epsilon control. In: Purshouse, R.C., Fleming, P.J., Fonseca, C.M., Greco, S., Shaw, J. (eds.) EMO 2013. LNCS, vol. 7811, pp. 413–427. Springer, Heidelberg (2013)
5. Asafuddoula, M., Ray, T., Sarker, R.: Evaluate till you violate: A differential evolution algorithm based on partial evaluation of the constraint set. In: 2013 IEEE Symposium on Differential Evolution (SDE), pp. 31–37 (2013)
6. Coello, C.A.C.: Treating constraints as objectives for single-objective evolutionary optimization. Eng. Optimization $32(3)$, 275–308 (2000)
7. Coello, C.A.C., Zacatenco, C.S.P.: List of references on constraint-handling techniques used with evolutionary algorithms. Power $80(10)$, 1286–1292 (2010)
8. Coello, C.A.C.: Theoretical and numerical constraint-handling techniques used with evolutionary algorithms: a survey of the state of the art. Comput. Methods Appl. Mech. Eng. $191(11–12)$, 1245–1287 (2002)
9. Coello, C.A.C., Mezura-Montes, E.: Handing constraints in genetic algorithms using dominance-based tournaments. In: Proceedings of the fifth International Conference on Adaptive Computing Design and Manufacture (ACDM 2002) (2002)
10. Datta, R., Bittermann, M.S., Deb, K., Ciftcioglu, O.: Probabilistic constraint handling in the framework of joint evolutionary-classical optimization with engineering applications. In: IEEE Congress on Evolutionary Computation (CEC), pp. 1–8 (2012)
11. Datta, R., Costa, M.F.P., Deb, K., Gaspar-Cunha, A.: An evolutionary algorithm based pattern search approach for constrained optimization. In: IEEE Congress on Evolutionary Computation (CEC), pp. 1355–1362 (2013)
12. Datta, R., Deb, K.: An adaptive normalization based constrained handling methodology with hybrid bi-objective and penalty function approach. In: IEEE Congress on Evolutionary Computation (CEC), pp. 1–8 (2012)

13. Datta, R., Deb, K.: Individual penalty based constraint handling using a hybrid bi-objective and penalty function approach. In: IEEE Congress on Evolutionary Computation (CEC), pp. 2720–2727 (2013)
14. Datta, R., Deb, K.: A bi-objective based hybrid evolutionary-classical algorithm for handling equality constraints. In: Takahashi, R.H.C., Deb, K., Wanner, E.F., Greco, S. (eds.) EMO 2011. LNCS, vol. 6576, pp. 313–327. Springer, Heidelberg (2011)
15. Deb, K., Datta, R.: A fast and accurate solution of constrained optimization problems using a hybrid bi-objective and penalty function approach. In: IEEE Congress on Evolutionary Computation (CEC), pp. 1–8 (2010)
16. Deb, K.: An efficient constraint handling method for genetic algorithms. Comput. Methods Appl. Mech. Eng. **186**(2–4), 311–338 (2000)
17. Deb, K., Datta, R.: A bi-objective constrained optimization algorithm using a hybrid evolutionary and penalty function approach. Eng. Optim. **45**(5), 503–527 (2013)
18. Deb, K., Lele, S., Datta, R.: A hybrid evolutionary multi-objective and sqp based procedure for constrained optimization. In: Kang, L., Liu, Y., Zeng, S. (eds.) ISICA 2007. LNCS, vol. 4683, pp. 36–45. Springer, Heidelberg (2007)
19. Deb, K., Pratap, A., Agarwal, S., Meyarivan, T.: A fast and elitist multiobjective genetic algorithm: NSGA-II. IEEE Trans. Evol. Comput. **6**(2), 182–197 (2002)
20. Farmani, R., Wright, J.A.: Self-adaptive fitness formulation for constrained optimization. IEEE Trans. Evol. Comput. **7**(5), 445–455 (2003)
21. Filipiak, P., Michalak, K., Lipinski, P.: Infeasibility driven evolutionary algorithm with ARIMA-based prediction mechanism. In: Yin, H., Wang, W., Rayward-Smith, V. (eds.) IDEAL 2011. LNCS, vol. 6936, pp. 345–352. Springer, Heidelberg (2011)
22. Hamida, S.B., Schoenauer, M.: An adaptive algorithm for constrained optimization problems. In: Deb, K., Rudolph, G., Lutton, E., Merelo, J.J., Schoenauer, M., Schwefel, H.-P., Yao, X. (eds.) PPSN 2000. LNCS, vol. 1917, pp. 529–538. Springer, Heidelberg (2000)
23. Hamida, S.B., Schoenauer, M.: ASCHEA: New results using adaptive segregational constraint handling. In: Proceedings of the 2002 Congress on Evolutionary Computation, vol. 1, pp. 884–889 (2002)
24. Hedar, A.R., Fukushima, M.: Derivative-free filter simulated annealing method for constrained continuous global optimization. J. Global Optim. **35**(4), 521–549 (2006)
25. Hingston, P., Barone, L., Huband, S., While, L.: Multi-level ranking for constrained multi-objective evolutionary optimisation. In: Runarsson, T.P., Beyer, H.-G., Burke, E.K., Merelo-Guervós, J.J., Whitley, L.D., Yao, X. (eds.) PPSN 2006. LNCS, vol. 4193, pp. 563–572. Springer, Heidelberg (2006)
26. Hinterding, R., Michalewicz, Z.: Your brains and my beauty: Parent matching for constrained optimisation. In: Proceedings of the 5th International Conference on Evolutionary Computation (CEC), pp. 810–815 (1998)
27. Ho, P.Y., Shimizu, K.: Evolutionary constrained optimization using an addition of ranking method and a percentage-based tolerance value adjustment scheme. Inf. Sci. **177**(14), 2985–3004 (2007)
28. Isaacs, A., Ray, T., Smith, W.: Blessings of maintaining infeasible solutions for constrained multi-objective optimization problems. In: IEEE Congress on Evolutionary Computation (CEC), pp. 2780–2787 (2008)
29. Kimbrough, S.O., Lu, M., Wood, D.H., Wu, D.J.: Exploring a two-market genetic algorithm. In: Proceedings of the Genetic and Evolutionary Computation Conference (GECCO), pp. 415–421. Morgan Kaufmann (2002)

30. Kimbrough, S.O., Koehler, G.J., Lu, M., Wood, D.H.: On a feasible-infeasible two-population (FI-2Pop) genetic algorithm for constrained optimization: Distance tracing and no free lunch. Eur. J. Oper. Res. **190**(2), 310–327 (2008)
31. Kimbrough, S.O., Lu, M., Wood, D.H., Wu, D.J.: Exploring a two-population genetic algorithm. In: Cantú-Paz, E., et al. (eds.) GECCO 2003. LNCS, vol. 2723, pp. 1148–1159. Springer, Heidelberg (2003)
32. Mezura-Montes, E., Coello, C.A.C.: A simple multimembered evolution strategy to solve constrained optimization problems. IEEE Trans. Evol. Comput. **9**(1), 1–17 (2005)
33. Mezura-Montes, E., Velazquez-Reyes, J.,Coello, C.A.C.: Modified differential evolution for constrained optimization. In: IEEE Congress on Evolutionary Computation (CEC), pp. 25–32 (2006)
34. Mezura-Montes, E., Coello, C.A.C.: Useful infeasible solutions in engineering optimization with evolutionary algorithms. In: Gelbukh, A., Albornoz, Á., Terashima-Marín, H. (eds.) MICAI 2005. LNCS (LNAI), vol. 3789, pp. 652–662. Springer, Heidelberg (2005)
35. Mezura-Montes, E., Coello, C.A.C.: Constraint-handling in nature-inspired numerical optimization: Past, present and future. Swarm Evol. Comput. **1**(4), 173–194 (2011)
36. Mezura-Montes, E., Coello, C.A.C.: An improved diversity mechanism for solving constrained optimization problems using a multimembered evolution strategy. In: Deb, K., Tari, Z. (eds.) GECCO 2004. LNCS, vol. 3102, pp. 700–712. Springer, Heidelberg (2004)
37. Michalewicz, Z.: A survey of constraint handling techniques in evolutionary computation methods. In: Proceedings of the Fourth Annual Conference on Evolutionary Programming, pp. 135–155. MIT Press, Cambridge (1995)
38. Powell, D., Skolnick, M.M.: Using genetic algorithms in engineering design optimization with non-linear constraints. In: Proceedings of the 5th International Conference on Genetic Algorithms, pp. 424–431. Morgan Kaufmann Publishers Inc. (1993)
39. Ray, T., Liew, K.M., Saini, P.: An intelligent information sharing strategy within a swarm for unconstrained and constrained optimization problems. Soft Comput. **6**(1), 38–44 (2002)
40. Ray, T., Tai, K., Seow, K.C.: Multiobjective design optimization by an evolutionary algorithm. Eng. Optim. **33**(4), 399–424 (2001)
41. Ray, T., Kang, T., Chye, S.K.: An evolutionary algorithm for constrained optimization. In: Genetic and Evolutionary Computation Conference (GECCO), pp. 771–777 (2000)
42. Ray, T., Singh, H.K., Isaacs, A., Smith, W.: Infeasibility driven evolutionary algorithm for constrained optimization. In: Mezura-Montes, E. (ed.) Constraint-Handling in Evolutionary Optimization. SCI, vol. 198, pp. 145–165. Springer, Heidelberg (2009)
43. Runarsson, T.P., Yao, X.: Stochastic ranking for constrained evolutionary optimization. IEEE Trans. Evol. Comput. **4**(3), 284–294 (2000)
44. Saha, A., Ray, T.: A repair mechanism for active inequality constraint handling. In: IEEE Congress on Evolutionary Computation (CEC), pp. 1–8 (2012)
45. Saha, A., Ray, T.: Equality constrained multi-objective optimization. In: IEEE Congress on Evolutionary Computation (CEC), pp. 1–7 (2012)

46. Singh, H.K., Isaacs, A., Nguyen, T.T., Ray, T., Yao, X.: Performance of infeasibility driven evolutionary algorithm (IDEA) on constrained dynamic single objective optimization problems. In: IEEE Congress on Evolutionary Computation (CEC), pp. 3127–3134 (2009)

47. Singh, H.K., Isaacs, A., Ray, T., Smith, W.: A simulated annealing algorithm for constrained multi-objective optimization. In: IEEE Congress on Evolutionary Computation (CEC), pp. 1655–1662 (2008)

48. Singh, H.K., Ray, T., Smith, W.: Performance of infeasibility empowered memetic algorithm for CEC 2010 constrained optimization problems. In: IEEE Congress on Evolutionary Computation (CEC), pp. 1–8 (2010)

49. Singh, H.K., Isaacs, A., Ray, T., Smith, W.: Infeasibility driven evolutionary algorithm (IDEA) for engineering design optimization. In: Wobcke, W., Zhang, M. (eds.) AI 2008. LNCS (LNAI), vol. 5360, pp. 104–115. Springer, Heidelberg (2008)

50. Singh, H.K., Ray, T., Smith, W.: Performance of infeasibility empowered memetic algorithm (IEMA) on engineering design problems. In: Li, J. (ed.) AI 2010. LNCS, vol. 6464, pp. 425–434. Springer, Heidelberg (2010)

51. Singh, H.K., Ray, T., Sarker, R.: Optimum oil production planning using infeasibility driven evolutionary algorithm. Evol. Comput. 21(1), 65–82 (2013)

52. Singh, H.K., Ray, T., Smith, W.: C-PSA: Constrained pareto simulated annealing for constrained multi-objective optimization. Inf. Sci. 180(13), 2499–2513 (2010)

53. Surry, P.D., Radcliffe, N.J.: The COMOGA method: Constrained optimisation by multi-objective genetic algorithms. Control Cybern. 26(3), 391–412 (1997)

54. Surry, P.D., Radcliffe, N.J., Boyd, I.D.: A multi-objective approach to constrained optimisation of gas supply networks: The COMOGA method. In: Fogarty, T.C. (ed.) AISB-WS 1995. LNCS, vol. 993, pp. 166–180. Springer, Heidelberg (1995)

55. Takahama, T., Sakai, S.: Constrained optimization by ϵ constrained differential evolution with dynamic ϵ-level control. In: Chakraborty, U.K. (ed.) Advances in Differential Evolution 2008. SCI, vol. 143, pp. 139–154. Springer, Heidelberg (2008)

56. Takahama, T., Sakai, S., Iwane, N.: Constrained optimization by the ϵ constrained hybrid algorithm of particle swarm optimization and genetic algorithm. In: Zhang, S., Jarvis, R.A. (eds.) AI 2005. LNCS (LNAI), vol. 3809, pp. 389–400. Springer, Heidelberg (2005)

57. Tessema, B., Yen, G.G.: An adaptive penalty formulation for constrained evolutionary optimization. IEEE Trans. Syst. Man Cybern. Part A: Syst. Hum. 39(3), 565–578 (2009)

58. Vieira, D.A.G., Adriano, R., Vasconcelos, J.A., Krahenbuhl, L.: Treating constraints as objectives in multiobjective optimization problems using niched Pareto genetic algorithm. IEEE Trans. Magn. 40(2), 1188–1191 (2004)

59. Vieira, D.A.G., Adriano, R.L.S., Krahenbuhl, L., Vasconcelos, J.A.: Handling constraints as objectives in a multiobjective genetic based algorithm. J. Microwaves Optoelectron. 2(6), 50–58 (2002)

60. Wei, J., Wang, Y.: An infeasible elitist based particle swarm optimization for constrained multiobjective optimization and its convergence. Int. J. Pattern Recogn. Artif. Intell. 24(3), 381–400 (2010)

61. Xiao, H., Zu, J.W.: A new constrained multiobjective optimization algorithm based on artificial immune systems. In: Proceedings of the 2007 IEEE International Conference on Mechatronics and Automation, Harbin, China, pp. 3122–3127 (2007)

62. Yu, Y., Zhou, Z.H.: On the usefulness of infeasible solutions in evolutionary search: A theoretical study. In: IEEE Congress on Evolutionary Computation (CEC), pp. 835–840 (2008)

Planning and Scheduling

A Differential Evolution Algorithm for Solving Resource Constrained Project Scheduling Problems

Ismail M. Ali[✉], Saber Mohammed Elsayed, Tapabrata Ray, and Ruhul A. Sarker

School of Engineering and Information Technology, University of New South Wales,
Canberra, Australia
Ismail.Ali@student.adfa.edu.au,
{S.Elsayed,T.Ray,R.Sarker}@adfa.edu.au

Abstract. The resource constrained project scheduling problem is considered as a complex scheduling problem. In order to solve this NP-hard problem, an efficient differential evolution (DE) algorithm is proposed in this paper. In the algorithm, improved mutation and crossover operators are introduced with an aim to maintain feasibility for generated individuals and hence being able to converge quickly to the optimal solutions. The algorithm is tested on a set of well-known project scheduling problem library (PSPLIB), with instances of 30, 60, 90 and 120 activities. The proposed DE is shown to have superior performance in terms of lower average deviations from the optimal solutions compared to some of the state-of-the-art algorithms.

1 Introduction

The resource constrained project scheduling problem (RCPSP) is a challenging research topic due to its importance in real life and as similar problems arises in many fields, such as production planning [1], course and classroom scheduling [2], aircrew-scheduling [3], control system [4]. In general, the objective of these problems is to generate schedule, with minimum possible makespan, subject to the satisfaction of a number of constraints. For detail description of the problem, and it modelling and solution approaches, the interested readers are referred to Brucker et al. [5] and Kolisch and Padman [6].

In classical RCPSPs, a project consists of a set of activities, where each activity has to be executed only once and each activity has its own pre-known resource requirement and execution time. RCPSP aims to schedule project activities in such a way that minimizes the makespan or the total duration of the project subject to two constraints that must be strictly satisfied, the first one is the precedence relationship (i.e., the relationship between each activity with its predecessor and successor activities), while the second constraint is the resource availability. The resources used by the activities of projects are generally of two types: renewable and non-renewable. Renewable resources are available with their full capacity in every time period that can be repeatedly used, such as available manpower and machines. On the other hand, non-renewable resources are available with limited capacities, such as the budget of the project [7].

In the literature, many exact methods have been proposed for solving RCPSP. However, they are not applicable for solving instances with large dimensions, as the

© Springer International Publishing Switzerland 2016
T. Ray et al. (Eds.): ACALCI 2016, LNAI 9592, pp. 209–220, 2016.
DOI: 10.1007/978-3-319-28270-1_18

computational complexity of these approaches are significantly increased with the number of activities increased. Demeulemeester and Herroelen [8] have developed a branch and bound based algorithm, which was able to find the optimal solutions for some RCPSP. In contrast, other algorithms can solve the problem in a reasonable computational time, but it is hard to satisfy all problem constraints, such as priority scheduling [9] and greedy-based [10]. Xu and Cheng [11] combined branch-and-bound procedure with heuristic algorithms to present a hybrid algorithm and constructed a project scheduling model using a time constraint and the hybrid algorithm.

Also, several meta-heuristic approaches, which are commonly begin with random solutions and can search very large spaces of candidate solutions without having pre-assumptions about the problem being optimized, have been developed for solving RCPSP, such as simulated annealing algorithm (SA), tabu search (TS), ant colony optimization (ACO), practical swarm intelligence (PSO), differential evolution (DE) and genetic algorithm (GA). Recently, Zheng et al. [12] proposed a multi-agent optimization algorithm for RCPSP. In their work, each feasible solution was represented by an agent and the agents were evolved according to four main elements including social behavior, autonomous behavior, self-learning, and environment adjustment. The objective function was to minimize the total duration of the project by replacing a classical SA search scheme with a new design that considered the specificity and features of the solution space of project scheduling problems. Nonobe and Ibaraki [13] extended the definition of RCPSP further to include various complicated constraints and objective functions. Then, they developed a TS based heuristic algorithm, which contained improvements in representing solutions and in constructing neighborhood. Fang and Wang [14] proposed a heuristic based on the framework of the shuffled frog-leaping algorithm (SFLA) for solving RCPSP. Chen and Ni [15] proposed a new optimization method based on chaotic DE (CDE) algorithm for solving the RCPSP by using improved logistic chaotic map and penalty function. Results showed that their algorithm was competitive and stable in performance with other optimization methods. Damak et al. [16] proposed a DE based algorithm to solve RCPSP by improving the performance of DE to solve the problem within reasonable time. Recently, Cheng and Tran [17] integrated the fuzzy c-means clustering technique and the chaotic technique into the DE algorithm to develop an innovative method for solving complex optimization problems. Experimental results showed that their proposed algorithm obtained optimal results more reliably and efficiently than the benchmark algorithms considered.

Despite the well-known advantages of DE, it has several drawbacks. DE does not guarantee the convergence to the global optimum [18]. Also, it does not guarantee the new offspring are always feasible.

Motivated by these facts, this research uses a new strategy to improve the DE performance. This strategy incorporates a developed validation procedure, which provides feasible solutions within the initial population, and improved DE operators, which force the direction of DE search towards the feasibility. Moreover, the population size is adaptively reduced in order to increase the exploration process at the begging and then adaptively focus on the exploitation process by excluding the worst individuals from the population.

The numerical experiments on a well-known benchmark (with 30, 60, 90 and 120 activities) show that the proposed algorithm is able to achieve the optimal solutions for the entire J30 instances and obtain very low average deviation values for J60, J90 and J120 instances.

The remainder of this paper is organized as follows: Sect. 2 gives a brief description to RCPSP and its mathematical model; Sect. 3 provides a brief overview of DE algorithm; Sect. 4 provides a detailed description of the proposed algorithm; Sect. 5 demonstrates the performance of the proposed algorithm using numerical experiments and results comparisons and, finally, Sect. 6 discuss the conclusions and future work.

2   Resource Constrained Project Scheduling Problem

In the description of RCPSP, the objective function of RCPSPs is to finish the project with minimum total duration by optimizing the execution order of the activities subject to the non-renewable resources limitation and predecessor-successor relationships (or dependency) constraints. In this paper, as we consider a single project, let N be the dimension of the problem (number of activities to be scheduled), R is the number of available resources to be assigned, d_j the time required by j activity to be finished, and r_k be the number of resource k required by a single activity. Generally, the activities of the project are represented by a set $0, 1, \ldots, N, N + 1$ where activities 0 and $N + 1$ are dummy activities which present the start and end of the project, respectively. Dummy activates have no resource or time costs so, $d_0 = d_{n+1} = 0$ and $r_{0,k} = r_{n+1,k} = 0, \forall k \in K$. Furthermore, the set of resources can be defined by $0, 1, \ldots, r$ and Pre_j denotes the predecessor activities of any activity j. Two types of resources are commonly used by the activities of projects renewable and non-renewable. Renewable resources are available with their full capacity every period of time without limitations, such as available manpower and machines. In contrast, the non-renewable resources which can be available with a limited capacity and are allowed for one time use only such as the budget of the project [7].

In RCPSP, the feasibility of the solution is the main factor for the acceptance of that solution. Feasibility can be determined according to the satisfaction of two main constraints. Firstly, precedence constraints or predecessor-successor relationships as an activity j cannot be started until all its predecessor activities Pre_j are scheduled. Secondly, resource availability as the resources, in a specific time, can be used by the activities with availability limit.

For more clarify, RCPSP with total 13 activities is considered. In Fig. 1, each activity is presented by a number inside each circle. Numbers above each circle are presenting the time (d_j) and resources (r_j) requirements of each activity, respectively. Maximum number of resource of type k available per time (R_k) is 5. Moreover, arrows between circles are shown the predecessors-successors relationships between the activities. Obviously that d_j and r_j for both dummy activities $j = 0, 1, 2$ equal to zero. Figure 2 shows the optimal way to schedule the activities of the project to be finished in minimum total duration equal to 17.

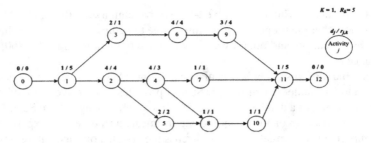

Fig. 1. Example of a project with 13 activities

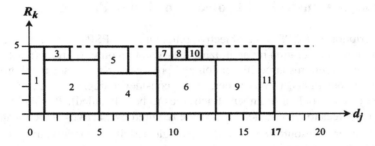

Fig. 2. The optimal schedule for the activities of the project

Mathematical model of the RCPSP is developed and described by Christofides et al. [19] and Kolisch and Hartmann [20] as follows:

$$Minimize\ F_{j+1} \tag{1}$$

Subject to:

$$F_j \leq F_{j+1} - d_{j+1}, \quad j = 1, \dots, n \tag{2}$$

$$\sum_{j \in A(t)} r_{j,k} \leq R_k, \quad k \in K; \ t \geq 0 \tag{3}$$

$$F_j \geq 0, \quad j = 1, \dots, N \tag{4}$$

The first equation shows the objective function that is to minimize the finish time of the last activity N which in turn leads to minimize the total completion time of the project. The first constraint assures that none of the dependency constraints is violated. The second constraint ensures that the number of non-renewable resources k used by all activities does not exceed its limitation in any time period t. $A(t)$ is the set of current activities at t. The last constraint enforces that the last times of all activities are non-negative.

3   Differential Evolution

DE [21] is a stochastic, population based search technique, which uses selection, cross-over and mutation operators to guide the search to find the (near) optimal solutions. So, it can be classified as an evolutionary algorithm (EA) [22]. Among EAs, DE was considered to be a powerful algorithm for solving optimization problems.

In DE, an initial population, with a pre-determined size (PS), is generated. Each individual, $\vec{x}_i$ consists of N variables, is evolved using three operators that are mutation, crossover and selection. In the simplest form of the *mutation operator*, for each target vector, $\vec{x}_i$ a mutant vector is generated according to

$$\vec{v}_i = \vec{x}_{r_1} + F \times (\vec{x}_{r2} - \vec{x}_{r3}) \tag{5}$$

where F is a scaling factor, $\vec{x}_{r_1}, \vec{x}_{r2}, \vec{x}_{r3}$ are three vectors selected randomly, and also they are not equal to each another, or to the target vector $\vec{x}_i$.

In the *crossover operator*, a combination between the target vectors and mutant vectors, according to a pre-determined probability is occurred in order to generate trail vectors. In the binomial crossover, the trial vector is generated as follows:

$$u_i^j = \begin{cases} v_i^j, rnd\,(j) \le CR & or\ j = N_j \\ x_{i,}^j & otherwise \end{cases} \tag{6}$$

where $j = 1, 2, \ldots, N; CR$ is the crossover rate within a range $[0,1]$, rnd a uniform random number generated within $[0,1]$, and N_j a randomly selected dimension to make sure that at least one element of the mutant vectors in v_i^j exists in the new generated vector.

For the selection operator, the greedy selection can be applied to determine which vectors will survive to the next generation by comparing each trial vector with its corresponding target vector, based on the fitness value and/or constraint violation.

4   Improved DE Algorithm

In this paper, a DE based approach is proposed to solve RCPSPs. Details of the proposed algorithm's components are briefly discussed in this section.

4.1   Chromosome Representation

In the proposed algorithm, each individual is represented by a vector of integer values, where the length of the vector equals to the number of activities within the project. In Fig. 3, an example of one individual representation with start and end dummy activities is shown.

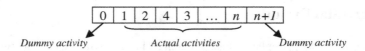

Fig. 3. Representation of one solution or chromosome

As DE was originally proposed to deal with continuous space, the following is proposed to adapt it to solve RCPSPs, in which random vectors of continuous numbers are generated. So that, each integer value, which represents the activity number, has a corresponding continuous value as a sequence and determines the appearance of this activity in the schedule, as shown in Fig. 4.

Chromosome	0	1	2	4	3	...	N	N+1
Sequence	0	0.05	0.1	0.14	0.25	...	0.95	1

Fig. 4. Random generated sequence for one individual

Since the feasibility of any solution is measured by the violation of the constraints, it is very important to propose a simple representation of constraints which makes it easy to be accessed and checked within a reasonable time. So, an incidence matrix is used to represent the predecessors-successors relationships between activities in the project. As described in Fig. 5, the incidence matrix is used to represent the dependency between the four activities shown in the graph, where each row represents the predecessor activities of the row number activity and each column shows the successor activities of the column number activity.

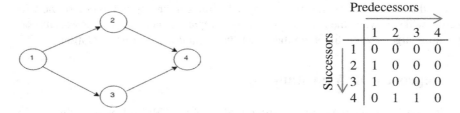

Fig. 5. An incidence matrix to represent the dependency between four activities

4.2   Individuals Evaluations

In the beginning, individuals of the initial population, of a size PS, are generated randomly. Also, sequences for the individuals are generated randomly within the range [0, 1]. Sequences are used to represent the execution order of each activity in the schedule.

The fitness value and/or constraints violations are used to evaluate any solution. The fitness value is calculated under a restriction of the resource availability constraint.

In the mechanism, the activities of the candidate solutions are scheduled by their orders (sequences) in the generated schedule. Each activity can be processed if and only if its required number of resources does not exceed the available amount of resources at specific time so the produced schedule is guaranteed to satisfy the resource availability constraint. In general, the objective function is to minimize the finish time of the final scheduled activity. While, the violation value of each solution is determined by calculating the number of violations of the dependency constraint by each activity within the schedule. Moreover, for calculating the total duration of the project, we do an activity by activity schedule and after each insertion of a new activity, the finish time of the new processed activity is cumulatively calculated.

4.3   Proposed Repairing Method

As RCPSPs are complex optimization problems, it was noticed that the evolutionary process takes long time to converge to the optimal solutions, if there are no feasible solutions in the initial population. So, in order to speed up the convergence rate of the algorithm, a heuristic repairing method is developed that finds feasible solutions from infeasible ones. This is achieved by satisfying the second constraint (predecessors-successors relationships constraint). In its process, the position of each activity is modified to fit its predecessors and successors activates according to the incidence matrix, which represents the dependencies between the activities. Unfortunately, starting with all feasible solutions may significantly reduce the population diversity and hence increase the probability of getting stuck in a local optimum. Therefore, the repairing method is applied to a certain percent of the population (R_m). The steps of the proposed repairing method and violation calculation are shown in Fig. 6.

```
Set i=1; feas_count=1;violation(S_i)=0;
While i < PS
   Generate a random solution S_i
   While feas_count<R_m
     Find Pre_j of each gene j in S_i
       If all (Pre_j) is already scheduled, then
           j is feasible
       else
           violation(S_i) = violation(S_i)+1
           Rearrange activities positions in Pre_j
           Add activity j to the schedule
           feas_count= feas_count +1
       end
   end
   i =i +1
end
```

Fig. 6. Scheme for the proposed repairing method

4.4 Improved DE Operators

DE begins directly to apply its different operators (mutation, crossover, and selection) to the generated sequence of the individuals to evolve the solutions. The proposed mutation and crossover operators guarantee the feasibility of any new generated individual.

In the proposed mutation, the mutant vectors are produced using the sequences of the activities according to the following formula:

$$\vec{v}_i = \vec{x}_\lambda + F \times (\vec{x}_{r1} - \vec{x}_{r2}) \tag{7}$$

which is same as in Eq. (5), but here, $\vec{x}_\lambda$ is selected from the top 10 % solutions within the current population, $r_1, r_2 \in [1, PS]$ are randomly chosen integer numbers, and they neither equal to one another, nor to the target individual i. The produced mutant vectors are guaranteed to produce feasible solution by changing the sequence of each activity within the individual to satisfy its predecessors and successors activities conditions.

After that, the binomial crossover is used to produce trail vectors depending on Eq. (6). Besides, the sequence of each activity is re-arranged to satisfy the predecessors and successors activities constraints. The proposed approach is described using the Pseudo-code in Fig. 7.

```
For j=1 to N
    Find Pre_j; the predecessors of current gene (j)
    Calc. new_{seq(j)}; the new sequence value of j
    If all(Pre_j) are already scheduled, then
        seq_j(the current sequence value of j) ←new_{seq(j)}
    Else
        For i = 1 to end of Pre_j
            If seq(Pre_j)>= new_{seq(j)}, then
                Swap seq(Pre_j) with new_{seq(j)}
            end
        end
    end
end
```

Fig. 7. Proposed approach to obtain feasible solutions from the mutation and crossover

Lastly, for the selection process, the greedy selection strategy is adopted to the individuals to decide which individuals can survive to the next generation.

5   Experimental Results

In this section, the computational results for instances of J30 (each with 30 activities), J60 (each with 60 activities), J90 (each with 90 activities) and J120 (each with 120 activities), taken from a standard benchmark from the well-known test set library PSPLIB created by Kolisch et al. [23], are shown. The data set, we considered here, include 16 instances from J30, 15 instances from J60, 15 instances from J90 and 15 instances from J120. Four types of resources are used in each instance. Also, in order to judge the performance of our proposed algorithm, comparisons with the state-of-art algorithms are conducted.

The proposed DE algorithm has been coded using Matlab R2013b, and was implemented on a PC with a 3.4 GHz CPU and Windows 7. Usually, the average percentage deviations ($AvgDev(\%)$) from the optimal solutions, if it is available as for J30 instances which is reported by Stinson et al. [24], or from the lower bound as for J60, J90 and J120, which are available on PSPLIB, are considered to be a performance metric for comparison. Generally, a lower $AvgDev(\%)$, as shown in Eq. (8), means a better solution

$$AvgDev\,(\%\,) = \frac{1}{S} \times \sum_{s=1}^{S} \frac{BS_s - LB_s}{LB_s} \times 100 \tag{8}$$

where S is the total number of instances used, BS_s is the best solution achieved by an algorithm for S instance and LB_s is the pre-known lower bound of s instance.

5.1 Parameters Setting

The parameters of the proposed algorithm are set as follows: cfe is the number of calling the fitness function. Fit_{Max}, the maximum cfe, is set to a value of 5000 and 50,000. R_m, which is the number of the individuals that will be repaired to be feasible using the proposed repairing method explained in Sect. 4.3, is set to a value of 25 % of PS. PS is adaptively reduced from 150 to 50 using Eq. (9) in order to increase the exploration at early stages of the search process, and the exploitation capability at the end.

$$PS_{new} = \frac{PS_{LB} - PS_{UB}}{Fit_{Max}} \times cfe + PS_{UB} \tag{9}$$

$F = 0.9$ [25]. In [21], it was mentioned that $CR = 0.1$ is a good initial choice for crossover rate while $CR = 0.9$ or 1.0 can be tried to increase the convergence speed. Based on the above, we set CR to be calculated adaptively using Eq. (10) where $CR_{LB} = 0.1$ and $CR_{UB} = 0.8$ to make some balance between a good initial value and the speed of convergence.

$$CR = CR_{LB} + CR_{UB} \times \frac{cfe}{Fit_{Max}} \tag{10}$$

5.2 Computational Results

For each test problem, 30 independent runs were executed. There were two stopping criteria: (1) run the algorithm for up to reach Fit_{Max}; or (2) no improvement in fitness value during 150 consecutive generations was achieved. In Table 1, the $AvgDev(\%)$) from the optimal solutions for J30 and from the lower bound for J60, J90 and J120, and the average CPU time in seconds for each instances are given with 5000 and 50,000 maximum number of generations.

Table 1. Results of the proposed DE algorithm

Max. no. of schedule	5000				50,000			
Instances	J30	J60	J90	J120	J30	J60	J90	J120
AvgDev(%)	0	0.98	4.04	19.62	0	2.07	8.81	31.68
Avg. CPU time (S)	12.46	41.86	72.12	106.71	46.22	192.26	306.89	453.56

The results show that the proposed DE algorithm has achieved the optimal solutions for all J30 test problems with deviations from the optimal solution equal to zero with both 5000 and 50,000 number of schedules. For the J60 instances, the proposed algorithm obtained the optimal solutions for 80 % of test problems. Moreover, the algorithm was able to reach the optimality for 67 % of test problems for J90 instances. Finally, however, only 6.7 % of test problems have been reached to the optimal solution for J120 instances, the algorithm showed a very low average deviation value compared with other algorithms from literature.

5.3   Comparison with the Art-of-State Algorithms

In this sub-section, the proposed algorithm is compared with six existing algorithms selected from the literature. The comparison is based on the AvgDev(%).

In Table 2, the AvgDev(%) values of all the comparative algorithms for data sets J30, J60 and J120 are listed. From these tables, for 5000 maximum number of schedules, it is clear that the proposed algorithm has the first rank among all 7 algorithms used with very low values of average deviation for all instances. For 50,000, our algorithm achieves very low average deviation values for J30 and J60.

Table 2. Average deviation (%) for J30, J60 and J120

Algorithms	J30		J60		J120	
Max no. of schedules	5000	50,000	5000	50,000	5000	50,000
Proposed DE	0.00	0.00	0.98	2.07	19.6	31.68
CDE [15]	0.19	-	11.36	-	35.17	-
Multi-agent optimization algorithm [12]	0.06	0.01	10.84	10.64	32.64	31.02
PSO [26]	0.05	0.02	11.19	10.85	33.78	32.4
Magnet-based GA [27]	0.04	0.00	10.94	10.65	32.89	31.30
Shuffled frog-leaping [14]	0.21	0.18	10.87	10.66	33.2	31.11
TS [13]	0.16	0.05	11.17	10.74	33.36	32.06

6 Conclusions and Future Work

During the last few decades, many heuristic and meta-heuristic algorithms have been introduced to solve resource constrained project scheduling problems. The main contributions in this paper can be summarized as following: (1) proposing a repairing procedure for finding feasible solutions within the initial population; (2) proposing a simple representation for chromosomes and predecessors-successors relationships between activities; (3) improving DE operators to produce feasible mutant and trail vectors which guarantee the feasibility of any individual generated by the mutation and crossover operators.

The proposed DE has been used to solve instances J30, J60, J90 and J120 from PSPLIB. The results showed that the proposed DE could achieve the optimal solutions for the entire J30 instances and obtain very low average deviation values for J60, J90 and J120 instances.

In the future work, the proposed algorithm will be extended to solve problems with multiple mode resource. Also, we will work on improving the algorithm's performance to achieve better computational results and time. Finally, more detailed analysis regarding the effect of each parameter in the algorithm will be performed.

References

1. Zhai, X., Tiong, R.L.K., Bjornsson, H.C., Chua, D.K.H.: A simulation-GA based model for production planning in precast plant. In: Proceedings of the 38th Conference on Winter Simulation, pp. 1796–1803. Winter Simulation Conference (2006)
2. Mathaisel, D.F., Comm, C.L.: Course and classroom scheduling: an interactive computer graphics approach. J. Syst. Softw. **15**, 149–157 (1991)
3. Chang, S.C.: A new aircrew-scheduling model for short-haul routes. J. Air Transp. Manag. **8**, 249–260 (2002)
4. Fleming, P.J., Fonseca, C.M.: Genetic algorithms in control systems engineering: a brief introduction. In: IEE Colloquium on Genetic Algorithms for Control Systems Engineering, pp. 1/1–1/5. IET (1993)
5. Brucker, P., Drexl, A., Möhring, R., Neumann, K., Pesch, E.: Resource-constrained project scheduling: notation, classification, models, and methods. Eur. J. Oper. Res. **112**, 3–41 (1999)
6. Kolisch, R., Padman, R.: An integrated survey of deterministic project scheduling. Omega **29**, 249–272 (2001)
7. Hartmann, S., Briskorn, D.: A survey of variants and extensions of the resource-constrained project scheduling problem. Eur. J. Oper. Res. **207**, 1–14 (2010)
8. Demeulemeester, E., Herroelen, W.: A branch-and-bound procedure for the multiple resource-constrained project scheduling problem. Manag. Sci. **38**, 1803–1818 (1992)
9. Li, C., Bettati, R., Zhao, W.: Static priority scheduling for ATM networks. In: Proceedings of the 18th IEEE Real-Time Systems Symposium, pp. 264–273. IEEE (1997)
10. Lupetti, S., Zagorodnov, D.: Data popularity and shortest-job-first scheduling of network transfers. In: ICDT 2006 International Conference on Digital Telecommunications, pp. 26–26. IEEE (2006)
11. Cheng, X., Wu, C.: Hybrid algorithm for complex project scheduling. Comput. Integr. Manuf. Syst. Beijing **12**, 585 (2006)

12. Zheng, X.-L., Wang, L.: A multi-agent optimization algorithm for resource constrained project scheduling problem. Expert Syst. Appl. **42**, 6039–6049 (2015)
13. Nonobe, K., Ibaraki, T.: Formulation and tabu search algorithm for the resource constrained project scheduling problem. Essays and Surveys in Metaheuristics, pp. 557–588. Springer, Berlin (2002)
14. Fang, C., Wang, L.: An effective shuffled frog-leaping algorithm for resource-constrained project scheduling problem. Comput. Oper. Res. **39**, 890–901 (2012)
15. Chen, W., Ni, X.: Chaotic differential evolution algorithm for resource constrained project scheduling problem. Int. J. Comput. Sci. Math. **5**, 81–93 (2014)
16. Damak, N., Jarboui, B., Siarry, P., Loukil, T.: Differential evolution for solving multi-mode resource-constrained project scheduling problems. Comput. Oper. Res. **36**, 2653–2659 (2009)
17. Cheng, M.Y., Tran, D.H.: An efficient hybrid differential evolution based serial method for multimode resource-constrained project scheduling. KSCE J. Civil Eng. 1–11 (2015)
18. Jia, D., Zheng, G., Khan, M.K.: An effective memetic differential evolution algorithm based on chaotic local search. Inf. Sci. **181**, 3175–3187 (2011)
19. Christofides, N., Alvarez-Valdés, R., Tamarit, J.M.: Project scheduling with resource constraints: a branch and bound approach. Eur. J. Oper. Res. **29**, 262–273 (1987)
20. Kolisch, R., Hartmann, S.: Heuristic algorithms for the resource-constrained project scheduling problem: classification and computational analysis. In: Weglarz, J. (ed.) Project Scheduling, vol. 14, pp. 147–178. Springer, Berlin (1999)
21. Storn, R., Price, K.: Differential evolution–a simple and efficient heuristic for global optimization over continuous spaces. J. Global Optim. **11**, 341–359 (1997)
22. Blum, C., Chiong, R., Clerc, M., De Jong, K., Michalewicz, Z., Neri, F., Weise, T.: Evolutionary Optimization. Variants of Evolutionary Algorithms for Real-World Applications, pp. 1–29. Springer, Berlin (2012)
23. Kolisch, R., Schwindt, C., Sprecher, A.: Benchmark instances for project scheduling problems. In: Weglarz, J. (ed.) Project Scheduling, vol. 14, pp. 197–212. Springer, Berlin (1999)
24. Stinson, J.P., Davis, E.W., Khumawala, B.M.: Multiple resource–constrained scheduling using branch and bound. AIIE Trans. **10**, 252–259 (1978)
25. Ronkkonen, J., Kukkonen, S., Price, K.V.: Real-parameter optimization with differential evolution. In: Proceedings of IEEE CEC, Vol. 1, pp. 506–513 (2009)
26. Fahmy, A., Hassan, T.M., Bassioni, H.: Improving RCPSP solutions quality with stacking justification-application with particle swarm optimization. Expert Syst. Appl. **41**, 5870–5881 (2014)
27. Zamani, R.: A competitive magnet-based genetic algorithm for solving the resource-constrained project scheduling problem. Eur. J. Oper. Res. **229**, 552–559 (2013)

A Hybrid Imperialist Competitive Algorithm for the Flexible Job Shop Problem

Behrooz Ghasemishabankareh[1(✉)], Nasser Shahsavari-Pour[2],
Mohammad-Ali Basiri[3], and Xiaodong Li[1]

[1] School of Computer Science and IT, RMIT University, Melbourne, Australia
{behrooz.ghasemishabankareh,xiaodong.li}@rmit.edu.au
[2] Department of Industrial Management, Vali-e-Asr University, Rafsanjan, Iran
shahsavari_n@alum.sharif.edu
[3] Department of Industrial Engineering, Science and Research Branch,
Islamic Azad University, Kerman, Iran
mohammadali.basiri@yahoo.com

Abstract. Flexible job shop scheduling problem (FJSP) is one of the hardest combinatorial optimization problems known to be NP-hard. This paper proposes a novel hybrid imperialist competitive algorithm with simulated annealing (HICASA) for solving the FJSP. HICASA explores the search space by using imperial competitive algorithm (ICA) and use a simulated annealing (SA) algorithm for exploitation in the search space. In order to obtain reliable results from HICASA algorithm, a robust parameter design is applied. HICASA is compared with the widely-used genetic algorithm (GA) and the relatively new imperialist competitive algorithm (ICA). Experimental results suggest that HICASA algorithm is superior to GA and ICA on the FJSP.

Keywords: Flexible job shop scheduling problem · Imperialist competitive algorithm · Genetic algorithm · Simulated annealing algorithm · Taguchi parameter design

1 Introduction

The classical job shop problem (CJSP) deals with scheduling n jobs on m machines, which is known as a NP-hard Problem [1]. Each job involves a set of operations with their pre-specified sequences as well as processing times. However, in today's competitive businesses, companies often need to apply more flexible and efficient production systems in order to satisfy their requirements. More specifically, not only automation and flexible machines need to be used, but also a flexible scheduling should be designed as well.

Flexible job shop scheduling problem (FJSP) extends CJSP which does not restrict the operations to be processed on pre-specified machines [2, 3]. Flexibility allows the problem to be modeled in a more realistic manner, however, exact methods are unable to solve the problem efficiently. The FJSP scheduling encompasses two sub-problems: assigning an operation to a machine through existing machines and specifying the sequence of the jobs' operations. Brucker and Schlie [4] studied the FJSP for the first time.

© Springer International Publishing Switzerland 2016
T. Ray et al. (Eds.): ACALCI 2016, LNAI 9592, pp. 221–233, 2016.
DOI: 10.1007/978-3-319-28270-1_19

They introduced a polynomial algorithm for the problem with two jobs. Although in some cases the exact methods can in theory find the optimal solution for the problems, computational time is so long that it is not practical to use them. Researchers have been trying to find ways in which optimal or near optimal solutions can be obtained in reasonable computational time. In recent years, some heuristic and meta-heuristic methods have shown to be promising in achieving this goal, including tabu search (TS), simulated annealing (SA), ant colony optimization (ACO), genetic algorithm (GA) [5–8].

A new evolutionary algorithm named imperialist competitive algorithm (ICA), has been proposed recently by Atashpaz and Lucas [9]. This meta-heuristic algorithm has shown promising results on several engineering problems and industrial engineering field [10–15]. Combining two or more meta-heuristic methods seem to help achieve good efficiency that is not possible by applying each one alone. Here, TS, SA and variable neighborhood search (VNS) play an important role. Tavakkoli-Moghaddam et al. [16] and Naderi et al. [17] presented a hybridization of electromagnetic-like mechanism and SA. Some other hybrid meta-heuristics for solving the abovementioned problem are also available [18–22]. Furthermore, Shahsavari-pour and Ghasemishabankareh [23] presented a novel hybrid GA and SA algorithm to solve the FJSP, where for the first time, an efficient hybrid ICA and SA has been applied for solving the FJSP.

As mentioned earlier, since the FJSP is well-known to be NP-hard, meta-heuristic algorithms have significant advantages to solve the problem over exact methods. Hybridization of meta-heuristic methods has attracted much attention of many researchers. This paper proposes a new hybridized algorithm named as hybrid imperialist competitive algorithm with Simulated Annealing (HICASA), where SA is applied as a local search algorithm, while ICA does global search in the solution space. In this study the FJSP is considered as a single-objective problem and the proposed algorithm is applied to minimize the makespan. The robust parameter setting procedure is applied to set all parameters for HICASA, GA and ICA. By solving the same benchmarks, our results show that HICASA is superior to GA and ICA.

The remaining sections of the paper are organized as follow: Sect. 2 gives problem representation. Section 3 describes solution methodologies for solving the FJSP. The experimental design and computational results are provided in Sect. 4. Finally the conclusions are presented in Sect. 5.

2   Problem Representation

The FJSP includes n jobs which are scheduled on m machines. The jobs are represented by the set $J = \{1, 2, ..., n\}$ and the set $M = \{1, 2, ..., m\}$ indicates the machines. The purpose of the optimization task is to generate a feasible schedule consistent with minimization of the objective function and satisfying problem constraints at the same time. In this FJSP problem, all machines are assumed to be available at time zero, all jobs can be processed at time zero, each machine can have only one operation at a time, each job can be processed by only one machine at a time and transportation times are not considered. Notations and variables of the FJSP are presented as follows:

J	Indices of jobs, $j = 1, 2, ..., n$
i, p	Indices of machines, $i, p = 1, 2, ..., m$
e	Indices of jobs which operate exactly before job j on the same machine, $e = 1, 2, ..., n$
K	The set of numbers of each job's operations. For example $K(j) = L$ means that the jth job has L operations.
l, q	Indices of numbers of operations, $l, q = 1, 2, ..., K(j)$
C_{lji}	Completion time of the lth operation of job j on machine i
P_{lji}	Processing time of the lth operation of job j on machine i

The mathematical model of the FJSP is given as follows:

$$Z = Min\{\max\{C_{K(j)ji}\}\}; K(j) \in K; j \in J; i \in M \tag{1}$$

s.t:

$$C_{lji} - P_{lji} \geq C_{l-1jp} \quad l = 1, 2, ..., K(j) \quad j = 1, 2, ..., n \quad i, p = 1, 2, .., m \tag{2}$$

$$C_{lji} - P_{lji} \geq C_{qei} \quad q, l = 1, 2, ..., K(j) \quad e, j = 1, 2, ..., n \quad i = 1, 2, ..., m \tag{3}$$

$$C_{lji} \geq 0 \quad l = 1, 2, ..., K(j) \quad j = 1, 2, ..., n \quad i = 1, 2, ..., m, \tag{4}$$

where Eq. (1) implies the objective function (makespan), which should be minimized. As noted above, the problem contains two basic restrictions: the first one is precedence constraint belonging to the operations of a job. It means that the operation 1 of job j, cannot be started until the whole previous operations (operation 1 to $l - 1$) to be completed (Eq. (2)). The second restriction is non-overlapping constraint of the operations on a machine which is specified by Eq. (3). It means that the machine does not start to process the next operation until the current operation is finished completely.

3 Solution Procedure

3.1 Proposed *HICASA* Algorithm

The imperialist competitive algorithm is one of the efficient evolutionary algorithms in solving discrete optimization problems [9]. In this algorithm, there are some countries (or colonies) which are divided into two categories, imperialists and colonies. The imperialist with its colonies, is called an empire. Competition among imperialists continues and the most powerful imperialist has a higher chance to take the weakest colony of the weakest imperialist. This process continues until just one imperialist remains. Finally all the imperialists and colonies become the same.

HICASA is a novel meta-heuristic algorithm that integrates ICA with the SA algorithm. SA has functions as a neighborhood search process and improves the convergence of the solutions. During this process, some colonies are chosen randomly from each empire and the SA algorithm is used as neighborhood search to alter chosen colonies. The altered colonies replace the previous ones in each empire and the algorithm goes on. The structure of HICASA is as follows (all equations of ICA are captured from Atashpaz and Lucas [9]):

Establishing Initial Empires. In ICA the initial population, which is generated randomly, as colonies, is located in the form of array. Each individual in the population is equivalent to the chromosomes in GA. Each array in the FJSP consists of two strings [24]. The first ordered string represents the number of machines and the second string represents the order of the job operations. Figure 1 shows an example of an array for our experiments in Sect. 4. Note that the fifth element in the first string is 2 and the counterpart element in the second one is 3. It means the second operation of job 3 should be performed on machine 2 (O_{ij}: operation j from job i). The number of initial population is considered as NC (number of countries) in this paper.

String A (Machines)   `3 4 2 1 2 1 4 1 5 3 4 2`
String B (Operations) `3 1 1 2 3 4 1 3 2 2 3 4`
                       O_{31} O_{32} O_{33} O_{34}

Fig. 1. Array structure of a country (colony).

Calculating Objective Function and Generating Colonies. In order to evaluate the colonies' power, a cost function should be calculated. In the FJSP, the cost function is equivalent to the value of makespan (C_{max}). For each colony the value of C_{max} is equal to:

$$C_{max} = \max\{C_{K(j)ji}\}; \quad K \in K(j); j = 1, 2, \ldots, n; \quad i = 1, 2, \ldots, m \qquad (5)$$

Then N_{imp} (number of empires) of the best members are chosen as imperialists. N_{col} is the number of remaining countries which should be distributed between the imperialists. The number of colonies for each imperialist depends on the imperialists' power. In order to calculate their power, first the normalized cost should be computed according to Eq. (6) (i.e., normalized makespan):

$$C_O = c_O - \max_{i=1,2,\ldots,N_{imp}} \{c_i\}; \forall O = 1, 2, \ldots, N_{imp}, \qquad (6)$$

where c_O is the makespan of the Oth imperialist and C_O is its normalized value. Now the relative power of each imperialist (P_O) is calculated through the following:

$$p_O = \left| \frac{C_O}{\sum_{i=1}^{N_{imp}} C_i} \right|; \forall O = 1, 2, \ldots, N_{imp} \qquad (7)$$

Obviously, each imperialist's power is the portion of colonies that should be possessed by that imperialist. Hence the number of colonies of each imperialist is computed by Eq. (8):

$$N.C._O = round\{p_O \times N_{col}\}; \forall O = 1, 2, \ldots, N_{imp}, \qquad (8)$$

where $N.C._O$ is the initial number of *Oth* imperialist's colonies. *round* is a function which rounds a decimal number into the nearest integers. So each imperialist in an empire, has $N.C._O$ colonies, which are chosen from the remained initial countries randomly.

Assimilating. The empires attempt to increase their power by improving their colonies. In other words, they propel their colonies to become similar to their imperialist through making constructive changes in their structures. This changing process is similar to the crossover process in GA. The assimilating process in the FJSP is shown as a designed algorithm in Fig. 2.

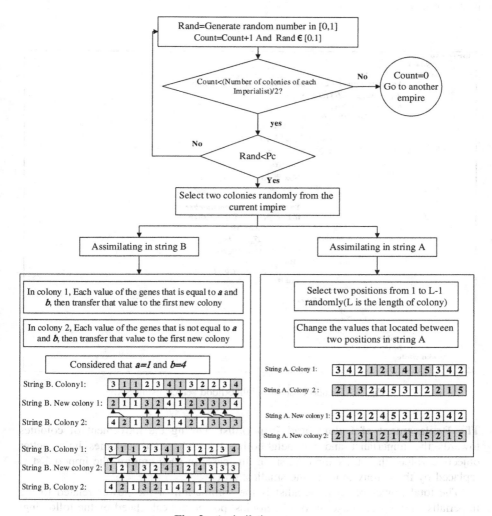

Fig. 2. Assimilating process.

Now the cost function (makespan) for the colonies resulting from assimilating process is calculated by Eq. (1).

Neighborhood Search Through SA Algorithm. As mentioned before, neighborhood search is suitable for further fine-tuning solutions produced by global optimization methods. In this paper, SA is integrated with ICA to deal with the FJSP problem. The algorithm works as follows: *NSA* colonies are chosen randomly from each empire and SA is carried out for each chosen colony. At first the neighborhood search algorithm works with the second string of each array, if it does not get improved after *NI* iterations, it goes to the first string (machines string) of that array. The ultimate array replaces the current solution. The function of SA algorithm in this neighborhood search is shown in Fig. 3.

```
for i=1 to Nimp
        NSO=0
    while NSO<NSA do
        XB=Select one colony from current empire randomly
        F_XB = C_max (XB) ;(Eq. 5)
        for RO= 1 to R do
            for SO=1 to S do
                XN=Modify selected colony
                F_XN = C_max (XN) ;(Eq. 5)
                if F_XB ≥ F_XN then
                    XB=XN
                    F_XB = F_XN
                    NCO=0
                else
                    Y=Generate random number in [0,1]
                    if Y<exp(-(FXN-FXB))/T then
                        XB=XN
                        F_XB = F_XN
                        NCO=NCO+1
                    else
                        NCO=NCO+1
                    end if
                end if
                SO=SO+1
            end for
            T=T*α
            RO=RO+1
        end for
        NSO=NSO+1
    end while
end for
```

Fig. 3. Pseudo code of neighborhood search using SA.

The Replacement of Colony and Imperialist. During the movement of colonies towards the imperialist and the neighborhood search, some colonies have better objective values than their imperialist. In this case, in each empire, the imperialist is replaced by the colony that has the smallest cost.

The total power of an imperialist is the summation of the power related to the imperialist and a percentage of its all colonies' power and calculated by the following:

$$T.C._n = C_n(imperialist_n) + \xi \cdot mean\{C_n(\ colonies\quad of\quad impire_n\ )\},\qquad (9)$$

where $T.C._n$ is the total cost of the nth empire and ζ is a positive value, which shows the level of influence of colonies' power in calculating the total power of the empire.

During an algorithm run, each empire that cannot increase its power loses its competition power gradually. There is always competition among empires and the stronger empires have the higher chance to seize the colony, and for this purpose the chance of possession is defined by possession probability. Total normalized cost of each empire ($N.T.C._o$) is calculated by Eq. (10) and the possession probability of each empire is calculated by Eq. (11):

$$N.T.C_O = T.C._O - \max_{i=1,2,\ldots,N_{imp}}\{T.C._i\}; \forall O = 1, 2, \ldots, N_{imp}\qquad (10)$$

$$P_{Po} = \left| \frac{N.T.C._O}{\sum\limits_{i=1}^{N_{imp}} N.T.C._i} \right|; \forall O = 1, 2, \ldots, N_{imp}\qquad (11)$$

The colonies are divided among empires randomly and with regards to the probability of acquiring each empire. To do this, first P vector is formed as follows: $P = [p_{P_1}, p_{P_2}, p_{P_3}, \ldots, p_{PN_{imp}}]$. Then vector R should be generated randomly in the closed interval [0,1] with the same size as P ($R = [r_1, r_2, r_3, \ldots, r_{N_{imp}}]$). Finally we calculate vector D ($D = P - R = [D_1, D_2, D_3, \ldots, D_{N_{imp}}] = [p_{P_1} - r_1, p_{P_2} - r_2, p_{P_3} - r_3, \ldots, p_{PN_{imp}} - r_{N_{imp}}]$) and a colony belongs to the empire which has the maximum index in D vector.

In each iteration, the algorithm eliminates the empire which has no colonies. In the algorithm's each iteration, all the empires collapse gradually except for the strongest one. The algorithm stops when just one empire is remained. Notations of parameters for HICASA are as follows: NC is the number of countries, N_{imp} is the number of empires, Pc is assimilation rate, ζ is constant value, S and R are the number of internal and external loop in SA respectively, NSA is the number of local search performed by SA algorithm and α is decreasing rate for temperature.

3.2 Genetic Algorithm

GA is one of the most widely-used population-based stochastic search algorithms proposed by Holland [25]. GA begins with an initial population and improves the solutions based on the evolutionary process. In this regard, GA utilizes two important operators to modify solutions and produce offspring. A selection procedure is used to generate offspring in the next generation. In the selection procedure better solutions have higher probability to be chosen. This process continues until the termination condition is satisfied. The crossover and mutation are captured from [23, 24].

4 Design of Experiments

In this paper, to evaluate the proposed algorithm, the FJSP has been considered. The problem includes 4 jobs and 5 machines. Data containing processing times have been extracted from [26] and shown here in Table 1. The objective function of the above-mentioned FJSP problem has been treated as a single-objective through minimizing the makespan. The results of HICASA, ICA and GA have been compared.

Table 1. Processing time of 4 × 5 problem.

Job	Operation	Processing time for machine MI				
		M1	M2	M3	M4	M5
J1	1	2	5	4	1	2
	2	5	4	5	7	5
	3	4	5	5	4	5
J2	1	2	5	4	7	8
	2	5	6	9	8	5
	3	4	5	4	54	5
J3	1	9	8	6	7	9
	2	6	1	2	5	4
	3	2	5	4	2	4
J4	4	4	5	2	1	5
	1	1	5	2	4	12
	2	5	1	2	1	2

4.1 Taguchi Parameter Design

Since the three algorithms are population-based and their parameters' values affect the final solution qualities significantly. There are different methods to calibrate the parameters of algorithms [14]. In this paper Taguchi method is used. Taguchi method has been utilized for optimization [27, 28] including evolutionary algorithms [29, 30]. Taguchi method has three phases: system design, parameter design and tolerance design. In this paper, Taguchi method is used as a robust parameter design. In this approach parameters' design is used to define factors which provide the best performance of processes/products.

In Taguchi method, instead of doing full factorial trails, an orthogonal array is used to carry out fewer experiments which examine the effect of noise. The orthogonal array suggests a definite number of combinations of factor levels which have the same results as full factorial trails. A robust parameter design tries to minimize the effect of noise factor through achieving a higher ratio of signal-to-noise (S/N). In other words, a higher value of S/N causes less effect of uncontrollable and noise factors in the performance of the algorithm. The value of the S/N is calculated as [28]:

$$S/N = -10 \times \log_{10}(objective function)^2 \qquad (12)$$

In this study, we select crucial factors of the algorithms (GA, ICA) according to the previous researches. Three factors of HICASA are the same as ICA but we add NSA parameter to show the effect of neighborhood search in the proposed algorithm. Interested readers can refer to [14, 30, 31]. By using the Taguchi method the best combination of the factors and their levels can be obtained for each algorithm. This process is used to compare the performance of the algorithms. The factors and their levels for the algorithms are shown in Table 2. Notations for GA algorithm are as follows: *GN* is the number of generation, *Pop_size* is the number of individuals, *Pc* and *Pm* are the probabilities of crossover and mutation respectively.

Table 2. Factors and their level in GA, HICASA and ICA.

	Factors in GA			
	A(GN)	*B(Pop_size)*	*C(Pc)*	*D(Pm)*
Levels	A1:100	B1:50	C1:0.9	D1:0.1
	A2:150	B2:100	C2:0.95	D2:0.15
	A3:200	B3:200	C3:.98	D3:0.2
	Factors in *HICASA*			
	A(NSA)	*B(NC)*	*C(Pc)*	*D(ζ)*
Levels	A1:4	B1:40	C1:0.9	D1:1.4
	A2:5	B2:50	C2:0.94	D2:1.5
	A3:8	B3:35	C3:0.91	D3:1.6
	Factors ICA			
	A(NC)	*B(Pc)*	*C(ζ)*	
Levels	A1:40	B1:0.9	C1:1.4	
	A2:50	B2:0.94	C2:1.5	
	A3:35	B3:0.91	C3:1.6	

As shown in Table 2 for GA there are four 3-level factors, for ICA three 3-level factors and for HICASA four 3-level factors. In order to facilitate and decrease the number of the experiments, the orthogonal array is used. Appropriate orthogonal arrays assigned for GA and HICASA is L9 and for ICA is L9 [14]. Table 3 shows the orthogonal arrays.

Table 3. Orthogonal array L9 for GA and HICASA.

Trail	L9 for GA and HICASA				L9 for ICA		
	A	B	C	D	A	B	C
1	1	1	1	1	1	1	1
2	1	2	2	2	1	2	2
3	1	3	3	3	1	3	3

(Continued)

Table 3. (*Continued*)

Trail	L9 for GA and HICASA				L9 for ICA		
	A	B	C	D	A	B	C
4	2	1	2	3	2	1	2
5	2	2	3	1	2	2	3
6	2	3	1	2	2	3	1
7	3	1	3	2	3	1	3
8	3	2	1	3	3	2	1
9	3	3	2	1	3	3	2

The mean value of S/N is calculated and shown in Figs. 4, 5 and 6 for all algorithms.

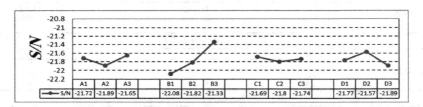

Fig. 4. Mean S/N ratio for each level of factors in GA.

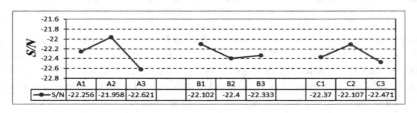

Fig. 5. Mean S/N ratio for each level of factors in ICA.

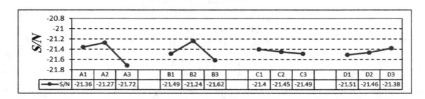

Fig. 6. Mean S/N ratio for each level of factors in HICASA.

According to the Figs. 4, 5 and 6 the optimal levels of the factors are the set {A3, B3, C1 and D2}, the set {A2, B1 and C2} and the set {A2, B2, C1 and D3} for GA, ICA and HICASA respectively.

4.2 Experimental Results

The algorithms are implemented in Visual Basic Application (VBA) and run on PC 2 GHz with 512 MB RAM. According to the parameters set in the previous section, the problem presented in Table 1 is solved by the proposed HICASA, ICA and GA. Each algorithm has been run 50 times and the averaged value was recorded as the final results. As shown in Fig. 7, the objective function values (makespan) for HICASA in all 50 runs converged to the optimal value of 11 but for GA and ICA the objective function values (makespan) did not converge to the optimal makespan in most of the runs. Clearly, the proposed algorithm (HICASA) obtains better solution in solving the same benchmark. Figure 8 illustrates the solution obtained by HICASA for the problem presented in Table 1. The numbers in the Gantt chart (Fig. 8) illustrate jobs' number.

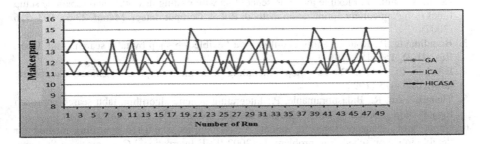

Fig. 7. Results of GA, ICA and HICASA.

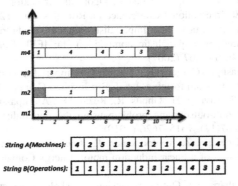

Fig. 8. Gantt chart of the obtained solution by HICASA for 4 × 5 Problem.

5   Conclusions

In this paper a novel hybrid meta-heuristic method (HICASA) has been developed to solve the FJSP. The proposed algorithm is a hybridization of ICA and SA algorithm which attempts to minimize makespan as the objective function. HICASA algorithm is compared with ICA and GA. Results from calculating and comparing between these three algorithms demonstrate that HICASA algorithm performs better than GA and ICA. By using the neighborhood search in the procedure of HICASA algorithm, it is able to solve the FJSP optimization problems effectively. HICASA can be used for solving different scheduling problems. It is also possible to integrating this algorithm with other meta-heuristic algorithms.

References

1. Gary, M.R., Johnson, D.S., Sethi, R.: The complexity of flow shop and job shop scheduling. Math. Oper. Res. **1**(2), 117–129 (1976)
2. Rossi, A., Dini, G.: Flexible job-shop scheduling with routing flexibility and separable setup times using ant colony optimization method. Robot. Comput. Integr. Manuf. **23**(5), 503–516 (2007)
3. Brandimarte, P.: Routing and scheduling in a flexible job shop by tabu search. Ann. Oper. Res. **41**(3), 157–183 (1993)
4. Brucker, P., Schlie, R.: Job-shop scheduling with multi-purpose machines. Computing **45**(4), 369–375 (1990)
5. Thamilselvan, R., Balasubramanie, P.: Integrating genetic algorithm, tabu search approach for job shop scheduling. Int. J. Comput. Sci. Inf. Secur. **2**(1), 1–6 (2009)
6. Najid, N.M., Dauzere-Peres, S., Zaidat, A.: A modified simulated annealing method for flexible job shop scheduling problem. In: 2002 IEEE International Conference on Systems, Man and Cybernetics, vol. 5 (2002)
7. Colorni, A., Dorigo, M., Maniezzo, V., Trubian, M.: Ant system for job-shop scheduling. Belg. J. Oper. Res. Statist. Comput. Sci. **34**, 39–54 (1994)
8. Chen, H., Ihlow, J., Lehmann, C.: A genetic algorithm for flexible job-shop scheduling. In: Proceeding of IEEE International Conference on Robotics, pp. 1120–1125 (1999)
9. Atashpaz-Garagari, E., Lucas, C.: Imperialist competitive algorithm: an algorithm for optimization inspired by imperialistic competition. In: IEEE Congress on Evolutionary Computation, pp. 4661–4667 (2007)
10. Khabbazi, A., Atashpaz-Gargari, E., Lucas, C.: Imperialist competitive algorithm for minimum bit error rate beam forming. Int. J. Bio-Inspired Comput. **1**(1–2), 125–133 (2009)
11. Nazari-Shirkouhi, S., Eivazy, H., Ghods, R., Rezaie, K., Atashpaz-Gargari, E.: Solving the integrated product mix-outsourcing problem using the imperialist competitive algorithm. Expert Syst. Appl. **37**(12), 7615–7626 (2010)
12. Lucas, C., Nasiri-Gheidari, Z., Tootoonchian, F.: Application of an imperialist competitive algorithm to the design of a linear induction motor. Energy Convers. Manag. **51**(7), 1407–1411 (2010)
13. Kaveh, A., Talatahari, S.: Optimum design of skeletal structures using imperialist competitive algorithm. Comput. Struct. **88**(21–22), 1220–1229 (2010)

14. Shokrollahpour, E., Zandieh, M., Dorri, B.: A novel imperialist competitive algorithm for bi-criteria scheduling of the assembly flow shop problem. Int. J. Prod. Res. **49**(11), 3087–3103 (2011)
15. Attar, S.F., Mohammadi, M., Tavakkoli-moghaddam, R.: A novel imperialist competitive algorithm to solve flexible flow shop scheduling problem in order to minimize maximum completion time. Int. J. Comput. Appl. **28**(10), 27–32 (2011)
16. Tavakkoli-Moghaddam, R., Khalili, M., Naderi, B.: A hybridization of simulated annealing and electromagnetic-like mechanism for job shop problems with machine availability and sequence-dependent setup times to minimize total weighted tardiness. Soft. Comput. **13**(10), 995–1006 (2009)
17. Naderi, B., Tavakkoli-Moghaddam, R., Khalili, M.: Electromagnetism-like mechanism and simulated annealing algorithms for flow shop scheduling problems minimizing the total weighted tardiness and makespan. Knowl. Based Syst. **23**(2), 77–85 (2010)
18. Soke, A., Bingul, Z.: Hybrid genetic algorithm and simulated annealing for two-dimensional non-guillotine rectangular packing problems. Eng. Appl. Artif. Intel. **19**(5), 557–567 (2006)
19. Li, W.D., Ong, S.K., Nee, A.Y.C.: Hybrid genetic algorithm and simulated annealing approach for the optimization of process plans for prismatic parts. Int. J. Prod. Res. **40**(8), 1899–1922 (2002)
20. Osman, I.H., Christofides, N.: Capacitated clustering problems by hybrid simulated annealing and tabu search. Int. Trans. Oper. Res. **1**(3), 317–336 (1994)
21. Swarnkar, R., Tiwari, M.K.: Modeling machine loading problem of FMSs and its solution methodology using a hybrid tabu search and simulated annealing-based heuristic approach. Robot. Comput. Integr. Manuf. **20**(3), 199–209 (2004)
22. Behnamian, J., Zandieh, M., Fatemi Ghomi, S.M.T.: Parallel-machine scheduling problems with sequence-dependent setup times using an ACO, SA and VNS hybrid algorithm. Expert. Syst. Appl. **36**(6), 9637–9644 (2009)
23. Shahsavari-pour, N., Ghasemishabankareh, B.: A novel hybrid meta-heuristic algorithm for solving multi objective flexible job shop scheduling. J. Manuf. syst. **32**(4), 771–780 (2013)
24. Zhang, G.H., Shao, X.Y., Li, P.G., Gao, L.: An effective hybrid particle swarm optimization algorithm for multi-objective flexible job shop scheduling problem. Comput. Ind. Eng. **56**(4), 1309–1318 (2009)
25. Holland, J.: Adaptation in Natural and Artificial Systems. University of Michigan Press, Ann Arbor (1975)
26. Kacem, I., Hammadi, S., Borne, P.: Pareto-optimality approach for flexible job-shop scheduling problems: hybridization of evolutionary algorithms and fuzzy logic. Math. Comput. Simul. **60**(3–5), 245–276 (2002)
27. Taguchi, G.: Introduction to Quality Engineering. Asian Productivity Organization/ UNIPUB, White Plains (1986)
28. Phadke, M.S.: Quality Engineering Using Robust Design. Prentice-Hall, New Jersey (1986)
29. Molla-Alizadeh-Zavardehi, S., Hajiaghaei-Keshteli, M., Tavakoli-Moghaddam, R.: Solving a capacitated fixed-charge transportation problem by artificial immune and genetic algorithms with a Prüfer number representation. Expert Syst. Appl. **38**(8), 10462–10474 (2011)
30. Hajiaghaei-Keshteli, M., Molla-Alizadeh-Zavardehi, S., Tavakoli-Mogaddam, R.: Addressing a nonlinear fixed-charge transportation problem using a spanning tree-based genetic algorithm. Comput. Ind. Eng. **59**(2), 259–271 (2010)
31. Behnamian, J., Zandieh, M.: A discrete colonial competitive algorithm for hybrid flowshop scheduling to minimize earliness and quadratic tardiness penalties. Expert Syst. Appl. **38**(13), 14490–14498 (2011)

Parallel Multi-objective Job Shop Scheduling Using Genetic Programming

Deepak Karunakaran[✉], Gang Chen, and Mengjie Zhang

School of Engineering and Computer Science, Victoria University of Wellington,
Wellington, New Zealand
{deepak.karunakaran,aaron.chen,mengjie.zhang}@ecs.vuw.ac.nz

Abstract. In recent years, multi-objective optimization for job shop scheduling has become an increasingly important research problem for a wide range of practical applications. Aimed at effectively addressing this problem, the usefulness of an evolutionary hyper-heuristic approach based on both genetic programming and island models will be thoroughly studied in this paper. We focus particularly on evolving energy-aware dispatching rules in the form of genetic programs that can schedule jobs for the purpose of minimizing total energy consumption, makespan and total tardiness in a job shop. To improve the opportunity of identifying desirable dispatching rules, we have also explored several alternative topologies of the island model. Our experimental results clearly showed that, with the help of the island models, our evolutionary algorithm could outperform some general-purpose multi-objective optimization methods, including NSGA-II and SPEA-2.

Keywords: Job shop scheduling · Genetic programming · Island model · Multi-objective optimization · Energy-aware scheduling

1 Introduction

Job shop scheduling (JSS) is an NP-hard problem with a wide range of practical applications in industrial processes, airline scheduling, distributed computing systems, and many other domains. Various evolutionary computation (EC) technologies, including genetic algorithms citepezzella2008genetic, simulated annealing [15], ant colony optimization algorithms [6], etc., have been extensively utilized to address this problem. Meanwhile, effective heuristics such as IFT-UIT+NPT [2], ASP2013-Rule#6 [10], etc. have also been developed with considerable success to scheduling.

A study of the literature shows that many existing research works feature the use of sequential scheduling methods and focus primarily on optimizing a single performance objective, such as the makespan or the total tardiness. In practice, however, it is frequently shown that multi-objective optimization is essential for successful job shop scheduling especially when useful schedules must meet multiple performance criteria. Moreover the objectives to be optimized are usually conflicting in nature. As a result, not a single optimal solution but

© Springer International Publishing Switzerland 2016
T. Ray et al. (Eds.): ACALCI 2016, LNAI 9592, pp. 234–245, 2016.
DOI: 10.1007/978-3-319-28270-1_20

a collection of *Pareto optimal solutions* will need to be identified in order to properly schedule jobs in a job shop.

Despite of its practical significance, energy-aware job shop scheduling has received relatively less attention from the research community [1]. Driven by the fast improvement of EC-based scheduling technologies over the last decade, we believe it is now the right time for us to start considering energy consumption as a major optimization factor.

A key technology to achieve this goal lies on the use of *island models* [7,14]. Some island models have been proposed in recent years for tackling a variety of multi-objective optimization problems. For instance, Xiao et al. [17] demonstrated the effectiveness of using various topological structures in island models. Their work motivated our research in this paper. We will investigate the usefulness of island models towards parallel evolution of dispatching rules for multiobjective job shop scheduling. In particular, several alternative topologies of the island model will be experimentally studied and analyzed in order to develop an in-depth understanding of their practical usefulness. Our results will also pave the way for future development of more effective island models that can solve difficult JSS problems.

In addition to the island models, Genetic Programming (GP) will be substantially exploited in this paper as well. GP has been widely used as hyper-heuristic methods for automated design of dispatching rules with prominent success [2]. In comparison with other EC techniques for job shop scheduling, GP enjoys the clear advantage thanks to its flexible representation and its global search ability. Specifically, different from genetic algorithms or ant colony optimization methods, dispatching rules can be more straightforwardly represented as genetic programs in GP. GP also enables efficient search through all possible dispatching rules at a global scale. Due to these reasons, a GP-based EC approach for evolving useful dispatching rules will be developed and experimentally evaluated in this paper.

The remainder of this paper is organised as follows. We give a brief overview of job shop scheduling in Sect. 2. We introduce the objectives used in our experiments specifically the energy objective. The different topologies for the island model are discussed in the Sect. 3 with our approach to use genetic programming for scheduling. In the Sects. 4 and 5, we describe our experiments and the results.

2   The Job Shop Scheduling Problem

In a nutshell, the JSS problem aims at identifying suitable ways of scheduling a set of jobs $\{\mathcal{J}_1, \mathcal{J}_2 \ldots \mathcal{J}_n\}$ on a set of machines $\{\mathcal{M}_1, \mathcal{M}_2, \ldots, \mathcal{M}_m\}$. Each job consists of several operations which must each be processed sequentially on specific machines for a job to complete. Let the processing times of the jobs be $\{p_1, p_2 \ldots p_n\}$. Meanwhile, a schedule S specifies the starting times of all requested operations to be performed on individual machines in order to complete all jobs.

It is generally desirable for a schedule S to minimize its *makespan*. For any job $\mathcal{J}_i$, let's use $\mathcal{C}_i$ to refer to its completion time according to schedule S.

The makespan of schedule $\mathcal{S}$ can hence be determined as the maximum completion time over all jobs, i.e.

$$\mathcal{C}_{max} = \max_{\mathcal{J}_i} \mathcal{C}_i. \tag{1}$$

Besides the makespan, the *tardiness* of any job $\mathcal{J}_i$ in a schedule $\mathcal{S}$, i.e. $\mathcal{T}_i$, is defined as $\max\{0, \mathcal{C}_i - \mathcal{D}_i\}$, where $\mathcal{D}_i$ is the *due-date* of job $\mathcal{J}_i$. Thus, the *total tardiness* becomes

$$total\,tardiness = \sum_{\mathcal{J}_i} \mathcal{T}_i \tag{2}$$

Energy-aware scheduling is considered strictly harder than constructing schedules that minimize merely the makespan [1]. In this paper, we consider energy optimization for JSS problems. We will adopt an energy consumption model that is fundamentally identical to the one presented in [8]. Specifically, it is assumed in the model that total energy consumption (equivalent to energy cost if we assume constant power tariff) of any working machine is completely independent from the schedule to be used in a job shop. Moreover, the machines have constant working and idle power consumption rates. Thus the total energy could be considered as the sum of the idle energy and the working energy.

$$\mathcal{E}_{price}^{total} = \mathcal{E}_{price}^{idle} + \mathcal{E}_{price}^{work} \tag{3}$$

The total idle energy cost across all machines is defined in (4), where S_k^r and C_k^r stand for the start and completion time of an operation m_k^r performed on machine M_k respectively. P_k^{idle} indicates the machine's idle power rate.

$$\mathcal{E}_{price}^{idle} = \sum_{M_k} \left\{ P_k^{idle} \times \left(\max_{m_k^r}(C_k^r) - \min_{m_k^r}(S_k^r) - \sum_{m_k^r}(C_k^r - S_k^r) \right) \right\} \tag{4}$$

The total working energy cost across all machines is defined in (5), where P_k^{work} indicates machine's working power rate.

$$\mathcal{E}_{price}^{work} = \sum_{M_k} \left\{ P_k^{work} \times \left(\sum_{m_k^r}(C_k^r - S_k^r) \right) \right\} \tag{5}$$

3   Evolving Dispatching Rules for JSS by Using GP and Island Models

One key step towards building effective island models for multi-objective optimzation is to determine the suitable communication topologies to be applied to these models. In [17], three topologies have been demonstrated to be highly effective in practice. They are depicted respectively as *Topology I*, *Topology II* and *Topology III* in Fig. 1. In this paper, the real usefulness of these topologies for tackling JSS problems will be further examined experimentally by using a

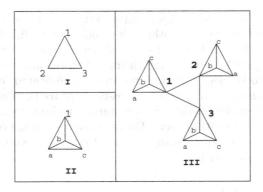

Fig. 1. Island topologies

GP-based algorithm. Before presenting our GP algorithm in detail, it is necessary to develop a clear technical understanding of the three topologies first.

Every topology shown in Fig. 1 is represented as a graph with a collection of nodes which are further connected with each other through edges. Every node refers to a separate *island* that will be processed by a different computing node. Therefore the number of islands in a topology determines the level of parallelism of the corresponding EC algorithm. We can easily distinguish two types of islands in a topology: (1) type 1 islands which are indicated with numbers and (2) type 2 islands which are indicated through alphabetic letters. Every type 1 island aims at optimizing all objectives. On the other hand, only a subset of objectives will be optimized in any type 2 islands.

Besides the islands, the edges in a topology enable direct communication in between any two connected islands. Following a common practice, communication through any edge is *bi-directional*, meaning that individual solutions can be freely migrated from both ends of an edge.

To further control the migration activities, every island $\mathcal{I}_i$ in a topology $\mathcal{G}$ has its own *migration policy*, denoted as Π_i. Hence, a complete island topology can be represented as a collection of tuples as shown below

$$\mathcal{G} = \{< \mathcal{I}_1, \Pi_1 >, \ldots, < \mathcal{I}_k, \Pi_k >\}$$

where k gives the total number of islands in topology $\mathcal{G}$. The policy Π_i for island $\mathcal{I}_i$ specifies how many individuals in island $\mathcal{I}_i$ should be migrated to other islands directly connected with island $\mathcal{I}_i$. It also specifies the migration frequency, i.e. the number of generations in between any two consecutive migrations. For example, if island $\mathcal{I}_i$ is connected with island $\mathcal{I}_m$ and island $\mathcal{I}_n$ in topology $\mathcal{G}$, then its policy Π_i can be defined as

$$\Pi_i = \left\{ \begin{array}{l} < \mathcal{I}_m, h_i^m, u_i^m >, \\ < \mathcal{I}_n, h_i^n, u_i^n > \end{array} \right\}$$

As clearly indicated in policy Π_i above, island $\mathcal{I}_i$ should send its u_i^m individuals to island $\mathcal{I}_m$ after every h_i^m generations. Similarly, island $\mathcal{I}_i$ should also send its u_i^n individuals to island $\mathcal{I}_n$ after every h_i^n generations.

Based on the island models described above, we are now ready to propose a GP-based hyper-heuristic algorithm for producing useful dispatching rules through parallel evolution. Detailed steps of our algorithm have been summarized through the pseudo code in Algorithm 1. Before running Algorithm 1, an island model has to be determined. After that, as indicated in Algorithm 1, a total of F iterations will run in order to closely capture the Pareto front of our multi-objective JSS problem. Here F is a number to be determined a priori by the experimenter (or algorithm user). During each iteration, every island in our island model will be evolved by using a general-purpose optimization algorithm denoted as $\mathcal{A}$ in Algorithm 1.

Input: $\mathcal{G}$, $\mathcal{D}ataset(train)$
Output: $\{\omega_1, \omega_2, \ldots, \omega_p\}$

```
 1  for s ← 1 : F do
 2      for k ← 1 : |G| do
 3          Run s^th iteration of A for < I_k, Π_k > (∈ G).
 4          for j ← 1 : |Π_k| do
 5              if s%h_j^k = 0 then
 6                  Transfer u_j^k fit individuals from I_k to I_j, where
                       < I_j, h_k^j, u_k^j >∈ Π_k.
 7              end
 8              if pop. I_j < pop. limit then
 9                  The individuals are added to I_j.
10              end
11          end
12      end
13      Wait for all the communication to complete.(synchronous)
14  end
15  Collect the genetic programs corresponding to the Pareto front :
       {ω_1, ω_2, . . . , ω_p}.
```

Algorithm 1. JSS using Island Model

According to lines 4–11 of Algorithm 1, for every neighboring island $\mathcal{I}_j$ (connected with island $\mathcal{I}_k$ through a direct edge), whenever a fixed number of iterations has passed since last migration from island $\mathcal{I}_k$ to island $\mathcal{I}_j$, i.e. $s\%h_j^k = 0$, u_j^k individuals will be selected from island $\mathcal{I}_k$ by using a tournament selection method. Finally, after F iterations have been completed, suppose there are p non-dominating dispatching rules identified through Algorithm 1, i.e. $\{\omega_1, \ldots, \omega_p\}$. These rules will jointly form a Pareto front which is treated as the final output from our algorithm.

4   Experiment Design

In this section, we explain our design of experiments for job shop scheduling and provide details about the experimental settings. The dispatching rules in our experiments are represented by genetic programs constructed from a list of function and terminal sets, as summarized in Table 1. We use the standard Koza parameters for evolution and conduct 51 iterations for all runs. We repeat each experiment 50 times using 50 independent random seeds.

Table 1. Functional and Terminal Sets for genetic programs.

Function Set	Meaning
+	Addition
−	Subtraction
*	Multiplication
/	Division
Max	Maximum
Min	Minimum
$If - then - else$	Conditional
Terminal Set	Meaning
DueDate	Due date of job (DD)
MachineIdlePower	Power consumed by idle machine(MWP)
MachineWorkPower	Power consumed by working machine(MIP)
ProcessingTime	Processing time of each operation(PR)
RemainingOperations	Remaining operations for each job(RO)
RemainingTime	Remaining processing time of each job(RT)
ERC	Ephemeral Random constant

In our present work, due to our primary focus on island topologies shown in Fig. 1, for simplicity only static migration policies are considered. Particularly, every island will exchange 40 individuals with each adjacent island after every 5 generations. The population sizes for different algorithms have been presented in Table 2. The values enclosed in brackets refer to population sizes of every island (or subpopulation) when island models and Algorithm 1 are used.

Table 2. Population size per island in braces

	NSGA-II	SPEA-2	Top-I	Top-II	Top-III
Bi objective	4096	4096	3072 {1024}	−	−
Multi objective	4096	4096	12288 {4096}	16384 {4096}	12288 {1024}

We use the dataset generated by Taillard et al. [13] for our experiments. This dataset consists of 8 subsets that together cover JSS problems with varied number of jobs and number of machines. The maximum number of jobs considered in any subset is 100 jobs, which will have to be scheduled on 20 separate machines. The JSS problem instances within each subset will be further divided into 60 : 40 train and test set. This division is completely random and all instances will have an equal probability of being used either for training or testing.

Since a maximum of 20 machines will be included in any problem instance, for all the 20 machines, their idle power rates and working power rates are further determined randomly under a general restriction that the working power rate of any machine must be greater than its idle power rate. The obtained power rates, organized in order according to the 20 machines, are given in Table 3. No specific models have been utilized in our experiments to determine these power rates. We believe this enables us to evaluate the power consumption of job shops without being restricted to specific type of machines and application domains. However, to further evaluate the usefulness of evolved dispatching rules in practical applications, realistic power consumption settings will need to be adopted. We are interested in addressing this issue in our future work. Meanwhile, in our experiments, we assume that the machines are always on. Even though temporary turn-off of machines is proposed to save energy [8], in general many machines used in real job shops cannot be powered down.

Table 3. Idle power and working power of machines.

Idle power	0.93	0.34	0.77	0.40	0.09	0.25	0.58	0.70	0.23	0.95
	0.66	0.51	0.48	0.22	0.48	0.88	0.13	0.78	0.19	0.28
Working power	0.94	0.74	0.95	0.87	0.61	0.56	0.77	0.97	0.55	0.99
	0.88	1.0	0.72	0.47	0.8	0.97	0.39	0.8	0.85	0.44

In order to determine the due dates we use a job specific assignment procedure [3]. This follows the procedure of endogenously finding due date by using total work content (TWK) [3]. The due date is assigned with a tightness of 1.25 with all jobs released at the outset.

In order to evaluate a dispatching rule and calculate its fitness values a simulation framework for job shop scheduling is required. We use the java library, jasima [5] which provides an environment to create and run computer experiments for manufacturing and logistics. We have extended the library to calculate energy fitness values for the dispatching rules during evolution. For every individual (dispatching rule) the fitness values corresponding to the three objectives discussed earlier are calculated with respect to each job shop instance in the train (test) dataset by simulating the use of the dispatching rule. The fitness values for each objective are then obtained by summing across all the problem instances.

5   Experimental Results

We conduct our experiments using ECJ [9], a Java based evolutionary computation research system. In order to compare the Pareto fronts obtained for each run we use hypervolume indicator [18], generational distance [18] and generalized spread [4] as the three metrics. These metrics need a true Pareto front for evaluation which is not known to us. Because of that, following a simple strategy demonstrated in [4], we combine the individual Pareto fronts obtained by NSGA-II, SPEA-2 and our Algorithm 1 together and jointly determine an approximated Pareto front. Separate approximated fronts are created with respect to the train and the test

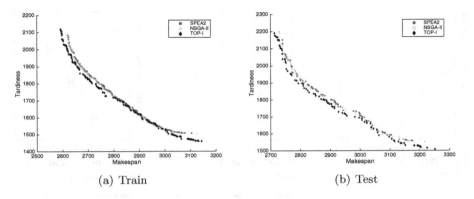

(a) Train   (b) Test

Fig. 2. Bi objective: combined Pareto fronts.

sets. A higher value of hypervolume indicator means better performance while for generational distance and generalized spread a lower value is better. We use the Wilcoxon signed-rank test [16] to verify the significance of our results.

In order to understand whether Algorithm 1 can outperform NSGA-II and SPEA-2 even with commonly used optimization objectives, including both the makespan and total tardiness, a series of experiments have been conducted and the results obtained have been presented in Subsect. 5.1. Inspired by these encouraging results, further experiments that include energy as the third optimization objective have been conducted and reported in Subsect. 5.2.

5.1 Experiments on Bi-objective JSS Problems

In this experiment, we consider only the optimization of makespan and total tardiness. Since Topologies II and III in Fig. 1 involve the use of multiple type 2 islands which are not necessary for bi-objective optimization, we conduct the experiment using only Topology I. In Topology I each island will consider both the makespan and total tardiness.

We compare our work against the standard implementation of SPEA-2 and NSGA-II. We combine Pareto fronts from all the runs and generate a single Pareto front from the combined solutions for each algorithm. The combined Pareto fronts are shown in Fig. 2. The Pareto front of Topology I dominates the fronts from SPEA-2 and NSGA-II. We show the box-plot comparisons from the runs in Fig. 3. For the Wilcoxon test to be significant we need the p-value to be lower than 0.05. The hypervolume indicator shows Topology I to outperform NSGA-II and SPEA-2 for the train set. For the hypervolume indicator and generalized spread we obtained the p-values of $7e - 15$ and 0.09 (not significant) respectively against NSGA-II. For the generational distance the Algorithm 1 shows no improvement. For the test set we observe similar performance, with the p-values of $7e - 15$ and 0.02 for hypervolume indicator and generalized spread respectively against NSGA-II.

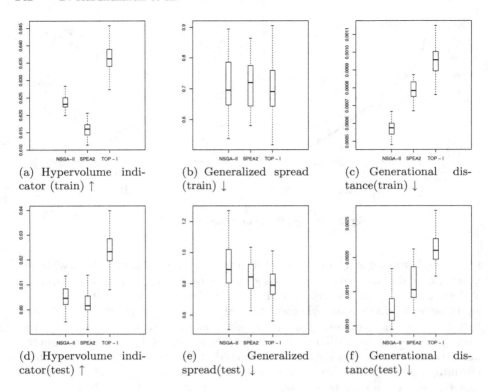

Fig. 3. Bi-objective optimization (up arrow indicates higher the better (vice versa))

More importantly the total population size used for Topology I is less than for the other two methods. As shown in Table 2, the population used for Topology I is 1024 per island which sums to 3072 individuals for the topology. In our experiments we observed that NSGA-II took close to 3.8 h for completion against approximately 0.76 h for Topology I. The increased performance and saving in time comes at the price of some communication complexity (Sect. 3).

5.2   Experiments on Multi-objective JSS Problems

In this set of experiments, we evolve solutions to the multi-objective optimization problem and use all the proposed topologies in Fig. 1.

Algorithm 1 again shows improvement over NSGA-II. The pairs plot of the pareto front is shown in Fig. 4. The training set shows that there is significant difference in the quality of solutions generated from the different methods. This is more clear when we show the results using the box plots (Fig. 5). But we do not observe a significant difference in the test case, as the solutions represented by different methods are not visually distinguishable in the plot.

We again use the metrics of hypervolume indicator, generalized spread and generational distance to compare the different methods and the Wilcoxon

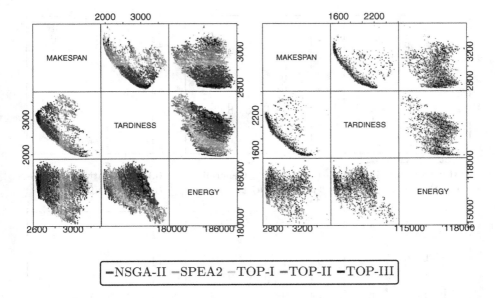

−NSGA-II −SPEA2 −TOP-I −TOP-II −TOP-III

Fig. 4. Multi-objective pareto fronts. (left: train, right: test)

signed-rank test to determine the significance (0.05) of our results. The box plot of the results is shown in Fig. 5. For the train set, Topology I outperformed NSGA-II with a p-value of $2.4e - 06$ and 0.0002 for the hypervolume indicator and generational distance respectively. For the test set Topology I and Topology II outperformed NSGA-II, with respect to the hypervolume indicator, showing p-values of $3e - 8$ and $1e - 14$ respectively. The Topology II also outperformed Topology I with a p-value of 0.02 for the same metric. There is no significant difference for performance based on generational distance in the test set.

Though Topology III outperformed SPEA-2 but not NSGA-II, it must be noted that the computation time needed in Topology III is much lower than that of NSGA-II. On average, the processing times of 5.2 h, 5.5 h, 6.4 h and 2.7 h were needed for NSGA-II and Topologies I, II and III respectively per run. For the population sizes as indicated in Table 2, although Topology I and II required longer processing time than NSGA-II due to the communication and synchronization overhead, they can achieve significantly better performance.

To summarize, of the three island topologies used with Algorithm 1, Topology I generally performed better than both NSGA-II and SPEA-2, as confirmed particularly by the hypervolume indicator. Though Topology II also performed well in Subsect. 5.2, it did not outperform Topology I significantly. Because only simple and static migration policies have been utilized in our island models, useful individuals cannot be effectively exchanged among multiple islands in Topology III. As a result Topology III failed to perform as we hoped. However, considering the fact that Topology III could potentially reduce the total time required for evolving useful dispatching rules, its practical usefulness should be further investigated in the future.

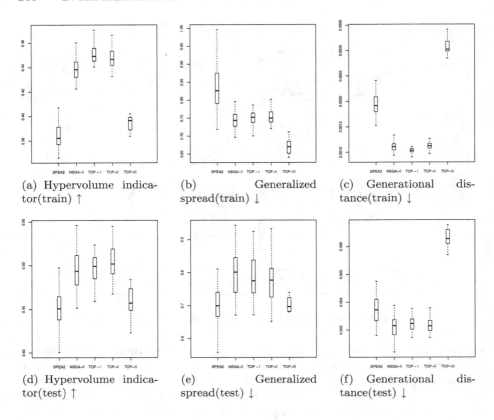

(a) Hypervolume indicator(train) ↑

(b) Generalized spread(train) ↓

(c) Generational distance(train) ↓

(d) Hypervolume indicator(test) ↑

(e) Generalized spread(test) ↓

(f) Generational distance(test) ↓

Fig. 5. Multi-objective optimization (up arrow indicates higher the better (vice versa))

6   Conclusion

In this paper, we focused on investigating the potential usefulness of island models for multi-objective job shop scheduling. Island models serve as an important technology for parallel evolution of dispatching rules that can effectively optimize multiple performance objectives. We have particularly considered total energy consumption as an important objective for optimization. Despite of its practical significance, energy consumption in job shops has not been substantially studied in the literature.

By using a GP-based hyper-heuristic algorithm, we experimentally studied several different communication topologies and island models in many benchmark JSS problems. Our experimental results showed that, with the help of these island models, we can achieve significantly better Pareto fronts based on some standard performance metrics, in comparison with widely used optimization algorithms such as NSGA-II and SPEA-2. Moreover, island models also enable us to obtain desirable dispatching rules much faster than conventional methods that can only run on a single computing node.

References

1. Agrawal, P., Rao, S.: Energy-aware scheduling of distributed systems. IEEE Trans. Autom. Sci. Eng. **11**(4), 1163–1175 (2014)
2. Branke, J., Pickardt, C.W.: Evolutionary search for difficult problem instances to support the design of job shop dispatching rules. Eur. J. Oper. Res. **212**(1), 22–32 (2011)
3. Cheng, T., Gupta, M.: Survey of scheduling research involving due date determination decisions. Eur. J. Oper. Res. **38**(2), 156–166 (1989)
4. Deb, K., Pratap, A., Agarwal, S., Meyarivan, T.: A fast and elitist multiobjective genetic algorithm: NSGS-II. IEEE Trans. Evol. Comput. **6**(2), 182–197 (2002)
5. Hildebrandt, T.: Jasima-an efficient java simulator for manufacturing and logistics. Last accessed 16 (2012)
6. Huang, K.-L., Liao, C.-J.: Ant colony optimization combined with taboo search for the job shop scheduling problem. Comput. Oper. Res. **35**(4), 1030–1046 (2008). Elsevier
7. Lin, S.C., Goodman, E.D., Punch III, W.F.: Investigating parallel genetic algorithms on job shop scheduling problems. In: Angeline, P.J., McDonnell, J.R., Reynolds, R.G., Eberhart, R. (eds.) EP 1997. LNCS, vol. 1213, pp. 383–393. Springer, Heidelberg (1997)
8. Liu, Y.: Multi-objective optimisation methods for minimising total weighted tardiness, electricity consumption and electricity cost in job shops through scheduling. Ph.D. thesis, University of Nottingham (2014)
9. Luke, S.: ECJ evolutionary computation system (2002)
10. Nguyen, S., Zhang, M., Johnston, M., Tan, K.C.: Dynamic multi-objective job shop scheduling: a genetic programming approach. In: Uyar, A.S., Ozcan, E., Urquhart, N. (eds.) Automated Scheduling and Planning. SCI, vol. 505, pp. 251–282. Springer, Heidelberg (2013)
11. Pezzella, F., Morganti, G., Ciaschetti, G.: A genetic algorithm for the flexible job-shop scheduling problem. Comput. Oper. Res. **35**(10), 3202–3212 (2008). Elsevier
12. Potts, C.N., Strusevich, V.A.: Fifty years of scheduling: a survey of milestones. J. Oper. Res. Soc. **60**, S41–S68 (2009)
13. Taillard, E.: Benchmarks for basic scheduling problems. Eur. J. Oper. Res. **64**(2), 278–285 (1993)
14. Tomassini, M.: Spatially Structured Evolutionary Algorithms: Artificial Evolution in Space and Time (Natural Computing Series). Springer-Verlag New York Inc., Secaucus (2005)
15. Van Laarhoven, P.J.M., Aarts, E.H.L., Lenstra, J.K.: Job shop scheduling by simulated annealing. Oper. Res. **40**(1), 113–125 (1992). INFORMS
16. Wilcoxon, F.: Individual comparisons by ranking methods. Biometrics Bull. **1**, 80–83 (1945)
17. Xiao, N., Armstrong, M.P.: A specialized island model and its application in multiobjective optimization. In: Cantú-Paz, E., et al. (eds.) GECCO 2003. LNCS, vol. 2724, pp. 1530–1540. Springer, Heidelberg (2003)
18. Zitzler, E., Thiele, L., Laumanns, M., Fonseca, C.M., Da Fonseca, V.G.: Performance assessment of multiobjective optimizers: an analysis and review. IEEE Trans. Evol. Comput. **7**(2), 117–132 (2003)

Optimization of Location Allocation of Web Services Using a Modified Non-dominated Sorting Genetic Algorithm

Boxiong Tan[✉], Hui Ma, and Mengjie Zhang

School of Engineering and Computer Science, Victoria University of Wellington,
Wellington, New Zealand
{Boxiong.Tan,Hui.Ma,Mengjie.Zhang}@ecs.vuw.ac.nz

Abstract. In recent years, Web services technology is becoming increasingly popular because of the convenience, low cost and capacity to be composed into high-level business processes. The service location-allocation problem for a Web service provider is critical and urgent, because some factors such as network latency can make serious effect on the quality of service (QoS). This paper presents a multi-objective optimization algorithm based on NSGA-II to solve the service location-allocation problem. A stimulated experiment is conducted using the WS-DREAM dataset. The results are compared with a single objective genetic algorithm (GA). It shows NSGA-II based algorithm can provide a set of best solutions that outperforms genetic algorithm.

1 Introduction

Web Services are considered as self-contained, self-describing, modular applications that can be published, located, and invoked across the Web [20]. With the ever increasing number of functional similar Web services being available on the Internet, the Web service providers (WSPs) are trying to improve the quality of service (QoS) to become competitive in the market.

Service response time is a critical measurement in QoS. It has two components: transmission time and network latency [14]. Study [13] shows that network latency is a significant component of service response delay. Ignoring network latency will underestimate response time by more than 80 percent [21]. To reduce the network latency WSPs need to allocate services to a location where has the lower latency to the user center that access the services. User center denotes a geometric location (e.g., a city) that is encompassed by a service area.

Ideally, WSPs could deploy their services to each user center in order to provide the best quality. However, the more services deployed, the higher deployment cost will be.

The Web service location-allocation problem is essentially a multi-objective optimization problem [2], for which there are two conflict objectives, to provide optimal QoS to Web service users and to consume minimal deployment cost. This problem can be classified as a multidimensional knapsack problem (MKP).

© Springer International Publishing Switzerland 2016
T. Ray et al. (Eds.): ACALCI 2016, LNAI 9592, pp. 246–257, 2016.
DOI: 10.1007/978-3-319-28270-1_21

Therefore, it is considered NP-hard due to the combinatorial explosion of the search space [22].

[1,21] try to solve the problem by using integer linear programming techniques. In particular, [21] solved this problem by employing greedy and linear relax-ations of Integer transportation problem. However, integer programming (IP) is very effective for small-scale or mid-scale MKP but suffers from large memory requirement for large-scale MKP [11]. Huang [9] proposes an enhanced genetic algorithm (GA)-based approach on Web service location allocation. He models the problem as a single objective problem with respect to network latency. In particular, the position of a web service in a Web service composition workflow is considered in his model.

Evolutionary multi-objective optimization (EMO) methodologies is ideal for solving multi-objective optimization problems [6], since EMO works with a pop-ulation of solutions and a simple EMO can be extended to maintain a diverse set of solutions. With an emphasis for moving toward the true Pareto-optimal region, an EMO can be used to find multiple Pareto-optimal solutions in one single simulation run [15]. Among numerous EMO algorithms, Non-dominated sorting GA (NSGA-II) [3], Strength Pareto Evolutionary Algorithm 2 (SPEA-2) [4] have become standard approaches.

NSGA-II is one of the most widely used methods for generating the Pareto front, because it can keep diversity without specifying any additional parameters [5]. In this paper, we propose to use NSGA-II to solve the Web service location-allocation problem, which has two objectives, to minimize cost and network latency.

The aim of this project is to propose a NSGA-II based approach to produce a set of near optimal solutions of service location-allocation, so that cost and overall network latency are close to minimum. Then, the WSPs could use the algorithm which is proposed by this paper, to select an optimal plan based on their fund constraints. The main objectives are:

- To model the Web service location-allocation problem so that it can be tackled by NSGA-II.
- To develop a NSGA-II based approach to the Web service location-allocation problem.
- To evaluate our proposed approach using some existing datasets.

In Sect. 2 we introduce the background of NSGA-II and GA. In Sect. 3 we provide models of the service location allocation problems. Section 4 develops a NSGA-II based algorithm. Section 5 presents a GA based algorithm. The exper-iment design and results evaluation are shown in Sect. 6. Section 7 provides a brief summary.

2   Background

GA [17] is a method to solve combinatorial optimization problems. It is an iter-ative procedure based on a constant-size population. In GA, a population of strings (called chromosomes), which are encoded as candidate solutions (called individuals) to an optimization problem, evolves towards better solutions. Each genome is associated with a fitness value based on a fitness function that indicates how close it comes to meet the overall specification, when compared with other genomes in the population. The fitness value of an individual is also an indication of its chances of survival and reproduction in the next generation. A typical genetic algorithm requires a genetic representation of the solution domain and a fitness function to evaluate the solution domain. Since a chromosome from the population represents a solution, when the algorithm starts, the whole population moves like one group towards an optimal area. Integer scalarization technique [2] is used to solve multi-objective problems with GA, by predefining a weight for each objective.

NSGA-II is a multi-objective algorithm based on GA. When it is used for problems with two or three objectives, NSGA-II performs well in both convergence and computing speed. NSGA-II permits a remarkable level of flexibility with regard to performance assessment and design specification. It assumes that every chromosome in the population has two attributes: a non-domination rank in the population and a local crowding distance in the population. The goal of NSGA-II is to converge to the Pareto front as much as possible and with even spread of the solutions on the front by controlling the two attributes.

3   Problem Description and Modeling

3.1   Problem Description and Assumptions

Web service location-allocation problem is to determine reasonable locations for Web services so that the deployment cost of WSP can be minimized while service performance can be optimized. In this paper, to optimize service performance we consider to minimize network latency.

The task of service location allocation has two objectives:

- To minimize the total cost of the services.
- To minimize the total network latency of the services.

In the mean time, service providers have cost constraints which limit the total cost of services deployment.

Stakeholder Web Service Providers. Assume the historical information of Web service usage has been collected. WSPs wish to allocate services to servers in candidate locations in order to maximum their profit.

The WSP must decide on services locations from a finite set of possible locations. In order to make a decision, the WSP must obtain data of service usages. Based on these data, the WSP could summarize several customer demands concentrated on n discrete nodes [1], namely user centers. We assume that the WSP has already done this step and a list of user centers and candidate locations are given. A candidate location is the geometric location that is suitable to deploy services. User centers and candidate locations are very likely overlapping when

Web service are deployed locally to user centers. In addition to deciding locations of the services, information about network latency between user centers and candidate locations are needed.

The list below shows some critical information that should be provided by the WSPs.

1. A list of user centers.
2. A list of candidate locations
3. 3. Service invocation frequencies from user centers to services
4. Average network latencies from user centers to candidate locations
5. Web service deployment cost for each candidate location

These are the main input data that the decision making is dependent on. The details of these input data and modelling are introduced in Sect. 3.2. Worth noting that service invocation frequencies are changing over time.

Network latency highly depends on the network traffic and may be very different during periods of a day. However, as long as there is no significant changes in the network topology, the average network latency remain stable. Therefore, the average network latency for a period of time should be representative.

Although dynamic service deployment is possible [16], the static deployment is still the mainstream [8]. In this paper, we made an assumption that WSPs periodically change the Web service deployment.

3.2   Model Formulation

To model service location-allocation problem, we need to make use of a set of matrices, to present input information and output solutions.

Assume a set of $S = \{s_1, s_2, ...s_s, s_x\}$ services are requested from a set of locations $I = \{i_1, i_2, ...i_i, i_y\}$. The service providers allocate services to a set of candidate facility locations $J = \{j_1, j_2, ...j_j, j_z\}$.

Service invocation frequency matrix, $F = [f_{is}]$, is used to record services invocation frequencies from user centers, where f_{is} is an integer that indicates the number of invocations in a period of time from a user center i to a service s. For example, $f_{31} = 85$ denotes service s_1 is called 85 times in a predefined period of time from user center i_3.

$$F = \begin{array}{c} \\ i_1 \\ i_2 \\ i_3 \end{array} \begin{array}{ccc} s_1 & s_2 & s_3 \\ \left[\begin{array}{ccc} 120 & 35 & 56 \\ 14 & 67 & 24 \\ 85 & 25 & 74 \end{array}\right] \end{array} \qquad L = \begin{array}{c} \\ i_1 \\ i_2 \\ i_3 \end{array} \begin{array}{ccc} j_1 & j_2 & j_3 \\ \left[\begin{array}{ccc} 0 & 5.776 & 6.984 \\ 5.776 & 0 & 2.035 \\ 0.984 & 1.135 & 2.3 \end{array}\right] \end{array}$$

Network latency matrix $L = [l_{ij}]$, is used to record network latencies from user centers to candidate locations. For example, the network latency between user center i_2 with candidate location j_1 is 5.776s. These data could be collected by monitoring network latencies [26, 27].

The cost matrix, $C = [c_{sj}]$, is used to record the cost of deployment of services to candidate locations, where c_{sj} is an integer that indicates the cost of deploying a service to a location. For example, $c_{12} = 80$ denotes the cost of deploying service s_1 to location j_2 is 80 cost units.

$$
C = \begin{array}{c} \\ s_1 \\ s_2 \\ s_3 \end{array}
\begin{array}{ccc} j_1 & j_2 & j_3 \\ \left[\begin{array}{ccc} 130 & 80 & 60 \\ 96 & 52 & 86 \\ 37 & 25 & 54 \end{array}\right] \end{array}
\qquad
A = \begin{array}{c} \\ s_1 \\ s_2 \\ s_3 \end{array}
\begin{array}{ccc} j_1 & j_2 & j_3 \\ \left[\begin{array}{ccc} 0 & 1 & 0 \\ 0 & 0 & 1 \\ 1 & 1 & 0 \end{array}\right] \end{array}
$$

Service location-allocation matrix $A = [a_{sj}]$ represents the actual service location-allocation, where a_{sj} is a binary value 1 or 0 to indicate whether a service is allocate to a location or not.

Using service location allocation matrix $A = [a_{sj}]$ and network latency matrix $L = [l_{ij}]$, we can compute user response time matrix $R = [r_{is}]$,

$$
r_{is} = MIN\{l_{ij} \mid j \in \{1, 2, ..., z\} \text{ and } a_{sj} = 1\} \tag{1}
$$

For example, we can use the two example matrices L and A presented above to construct the response time matrix R. For each service s, by checking matrix A, we can find out which location the service has been deployed. Then we check matrix L, to find out its corresponding latency to each user center i. If there is more than one location, then the smallest latency is selected. Therefore, we can construct the response time matrix R as:

$$
R = \begin{array}{c} \\ i_1 \\ i_2 \\ i_3 \end{array}
\begin{array}{ccc} s_1 & s_2 & s_3 \\ \left[\begin{array}{ccc} 5.776 & 6.984 & 0 \\ 0 & 2.035 & 0 \\ 1.135 & 2.3 & 0.984 \end{array}\right] \end{array}
$$

4 NSGA-II for Web Services Location Allocation

4.1 Chromosome Representation and Constraints

In our approach, we model the service location matrix $A = [a_{sj}]$ as a chromosome. The constraint setting is based on service providers' needs. In our case, we need set two constraints. The first constraint, *service number constraints*, requires that each service is deployed in at least one location.

$$
\sum_{x \in S} a_{xj} \geq 1 \tag{2}
$$

The second constraint, *cost constraint*, which sets up the upper boundary of the total cost. An integer number *CostLimitation* is decided by the WSP.

$$
\sum_{s \in S} \sum_{j \in J} c_{sj} \times a_{sj} \leq CostLimitation \tag{3}
$$

4.2 Genetic Operators

Our problem is discretized, therefore we use the binary GA mutation and crossover operations [18]. The selection operator is the tournament selection [23], which allows the highest probability of being reproduced to next generation.

Fitness Function. In order to accomplish these two objectives, we design two fitness functions to evaluate how good each chromosome meets the objectives. We use *CostFitness* to calculate the overall cost of deploying services under an allocation plan

$$CostFitness = \sum_{s \in S} \sum_{j \in J} c_{sj} \times a_{sj} \qquad (4)$$

where c_{sj} is the cost of deploying service s at location j, a_{sj} represents the deployment plan. The sum of the multiplication of c_{sj} and a_{sj} is the total deployment cost.

We assume the latency is symmetrical between user center and candidate location. e.g., $l_{ij} = l_{ji}$. We use *Latency Fitness* to calculate overall latency of all service request over a period of time.

$$LatencyFitness = \sum_{i \in I} \sum_{s \in S} r_{is} \times f_{is} \qquad (5)$$

where r_{is} denotes the minimum network latency from user center i to service s. f_{is} denotes the invocation frequency from i to s.

Normalise Function. To indicate the goodness of an allocation solution we normalise *CostFitness* and *LatencyFitness* according to the largest and minimum values of *CostFitness* and *LatencyFitness*. Normalised fitness values can also be used to compare results from different approaches. Since the maximum and minimum values for total cost and total latency are deterministic, we use exhaustive search to find out the $Latency_{max}$. $Latency_{min}$ is zero for we assume each service could be deployed in each user center. $Cost_{min}$ is the cost of allocating each of services at a location that leads to the minimal cost and $Cost_{max}$ is the cost of allocating each service to all the locations.

$$CostFitness' = \frac{CostFitness - Cost_{min}}{Cost_{max} - Cost_{min}} \qquad (6)$$

$$LatencyFitness' = \frac{LatencyFitness - Latency_{min}}{Latency_{max} - Latency_{min}} \qquad (7)$$

4.3 NSGA-II Based Algorithm for Service Location-Allocation

In this section we present our NSGA-II based algorithm for service location-allocation as Algorithm 1, comparing with the original NSGA-II our proposed algorithm has three new features.

Firstly, in order to avoid repeatedly evaluating the fitness of chromosomes, after the first generation is initialized, it stores the nondominated solutions in the nondominated pool. In each generation, when evaluate the chromosomes, the chromosomes are checked to see they exist in the nondominated pool. If so,

---

Algorithm 1. NSGA-II for service location-allocation

Inputs: Cost Matrix C, Server network latency matrix L, Service invocation frequency matrix F

Outputs: Nondominated set:a set of service allocation matrix A

 1: Initialize a population of chromosome with random binary values and include a chromosome represents location with minimal cost
 2: Evaluate population with fitness functions
 3: Non-dominated sort and assign a ranking to each chromosome
 4: Evaluate the Crowding distance of each chromosome
 5: Initialize the Nondominated Pool
 6: **while** predefined generation **do**
 7:     Apply Tournament Selection
 8:     Apply Crossover
 9:     Apply Mutation
10:     **for** (**do** each chromosome)
11:         **while** violate service number constraint **do**
12:             random choose a location j and set $a_{sj} = 1$
13:         **end while**
14:         **while** violate cost constraint **do**
15:             random choose a location j and set $a_{sj} = 0$, as long as $\sum_{s \in S} a_{sj} \geq 1$
16:         **end while**
17:         **if** chromosome does not exist in the Nondominated Pool **then**
18:             Evaluate with the fitness functions
19:         **end if**
20:     **end for**
21:     Non-dominated sort and assign ranking
22:     Evaluate the Crowding distance
23:     Recombination and Selection
24:     Update the Nondominated Pool with the current Nondominated solutions
25: **end while**
26: Return the Nondominated Pool

---

then the calculation of fitness will be skipped. At the end of each iteration, the nondominated pool is replaced by current nondominated solutions.

Secondly, it uses general mutation and crossover operation instead of polynomial mutation and simulated binary crossover. It is important to note that the mutation and crossover operators can produce solutions that might violate the constraints. Therefore, repair operators are needed to maintain feasible solutions. The proposed algorithm checks the cost and service number constraint to avoid possible infeasible solutions.

Thirdly, we include a solution that leads to minimal cost as an individual in the initialized generation. To do that we expect that it could accelerate the convergence as well as keep the solutions diversity.

5   GA for Web Service Location Allocation

In order to show the performance of our multi-objective NSGA-II based approach, we extend the single-objective GA based approach in [10] to consider two objectives. We employ integer scalarization technique [7] to transform the multi-objective problem into a single objective problem. A weight w needs to be predefined in GA. The weight measures the importance of objectives. Therefore, it is used to balance which objective is more favourable to the service provider. Conventionally, the weight is in the range of $[0, 1]$. For example, if we define the weight equals 0.7. It denotes that we consider cost outweigh network latency. In our approach, we define the weight equals 0.5 since we consider both objectives equally important.

As in Sect. 3.2 we model an allocation matrix as a chromosome. Crossover and mutation operators are same as defined in Sect. 4.2. To evaluate the chromosomes of population. We use Integer Scalarization technique [7] to calculate the fitness value.

$$Fitness = w \times CostFitness' + (1 - w) \times LatencyFitness' \qquad (8)$$

w is a predefined value used to measure the important of cost and latency. Note that *CostFitness* and *LatencyFitness* are calculated using Formulas 6 and 7 in Sect. 4.2.

6   Experiment Evaluation

To evaluate the effectiveness and efficiency of our proposed NSGA-II based approach to service location-allocation, we compare our approach with the GA-based single objective approach in Sect. 5 using an existing dataset, WS-DREAM [26, 27], which is a historical dataset on QoS of Web services from different locations. It contains the data of latencies from 339 different user locations invoked 5824 Web services scattered over different locations. The algorithm was coded in R [19] using existed package: NSGA2R. The program was run on a 3.40 GHz desktop computer with 8 GB RAM. Four different service location-allocation problems are designed with different complexities (Table 1).

Table 1. Test cases

Problem	User location	Server location	Number of service
1	3	3	3
2	5	5	5
3	10	10	10
4	15	15	15

A cost matrix is randomly generated from a normal distribution with mean as 100 and standard deviation as 20. In addition, a frequency matrix, is randomly generated from a uniform distribution over $[1, 120]$.

In each dataset, algorithms are run under four different levels of cost constraints: Sufficient condition (indicating services were allocated to all candidate locations), good condition (70 %), pool condition (40 %) and minimum budget condition (0 %). We tried to stimulated a real world budget condition with these four scenarios. In the minimum budget condition, both algorithms exhaustively reduce the cost until it reaches the service number constraint. The NSGA-II based algorithm runs 40 independent times with different random seeds ranging from 1 to 40. To test the efficiency of the algorithms, we evaluate the average run time for each algorithm.

Parameter settings for the algorithms are as follow. The population size is 50, and the maximum number of generations is 50. The tournament size is 3. The crossover probability P_c is 0.8 and the mutation probability P_m is 0.2 as we found that this combination can produce good results. We use same parameter settings for GA.

To compare the result of Algorithm 1 with GA-based algorithm, we first derive the nondominated set by using the approach in [24,25], and then compare the results using approach in [12]. Under each cost constraint, our NSGA-II based algorithm was run 40 times to generate 40 sets of solutions, which are then combined into one set. Then we applied non-dominated sort over this set. In the mean time.

GA may also run 40 times to generates 40 sets of solutions. We select the best one based on its fitness value from each set and combine them into one set. The non-dominated solutions are presented to compare with the solutions achieved by GA.

In addition to the comparison between NSGA-II based algorithm and GA based algorithm, we conducted full experiments on NSGA-II without minimal cost initialisation and GA without minimal cost initialisation. We expect the initialized algorithms superior than the uninitialized algorithms.

6.1 Effectiveness Comparison

We conducted experiments on NSGA-II, GA, NSGA-II with initialisation and GA with initialisation respectively. We use cost fitness value and latency fitness value as x, y coordinates. Our goal is to minimize both cost and latency. Therefore, better solution should locate close to the origin.

Experiment results (Fig. 1) show that different cost constraints leads to similar result patterns. Due to page constraints, we show the results of one cost constraints.

From the above results we can see that for all the four problems, NSGA-II based approach produce results that dominate or overlap the results from GA based approach. Further, NSGA-II with an initialized chromosome that represents service location-allocation of the minimum cost dominate the results without a chromosome of the lower cost, though for problem 1 and problem 2 of small complexity size, this observation is not obvious.

In particular, for big problems, problem 3 and 4, results of NSGA-II based approaches dominate the results of GA-based approaches. We also notice that even though the population size is small as 50, including a chromosome of optimal cost can help to narrow down searching space and to converge to optimal solution faster (Table 2).

Table 2. Execution time (s)

	problem 1		problem 2		problem 3		problem 4	
	NSGA-II(s)	GA(s)	NSGA-II(s)	GA(s)	NSGA-II(s)	GA(s)	NSGA-II(s)	GA(s)
Sufficient	4.4 ± 0.3	1.6 ± 0.1 ↓	5.9 ± 0.1	3.2 ± 0.1 ↓	13.7 ± 0.1	11.0 ± 0.1	27.0 ± 0.1	23.9 ±0.5↓
Good	4.4 ± 0.2	1.6 ±0.1 ↓	6.0 ± 0.1	3.2 ± 0.1 ↓	13.9 ± 0.08	11.1 ± 0.3	27.2 ± 0.1	24.1 ± 0.27 ↓
Poor	4.6 ± 0.19	2.2 ±0.2 ↓	6.3 ± 0.07	4.29 ± 0.17 ↓	15.2 ± 0.16	14.8 ± 0.3	31.3 ± 0.28↓	33.6 ± 0.45
Minimum	4.6 ± 0.1	2.2 ± 0.1 ↓	7.2 ± 0.12	5.75 ±0.17 ↓	24.12 ± 0.5 ↓	25.8 ±0.5	56.72 ± 1.6 ↓	66.8±1.2

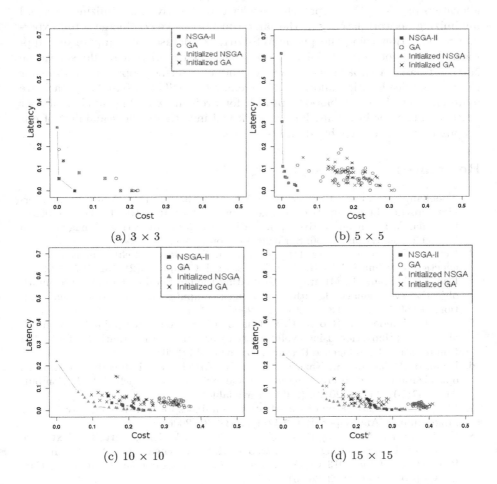

(a) 3 × 3   (b) 5 × 5

(c) 10 × 10   (d) 15 × 15

Fig. 1. Comparisons Between NSGA-II, GA, initialized-NSGA-II and initialized-GA

6.2   Efficiency Comparison

The results from initialized algorithms are similar with uninitialized algorithms, therefore we only present the uninitialized results. As shown in the table above for small problems GA based approach are faster. However for bigger problem (problem 3 and 4) NSGA-II based approach, are more efficient than GA-based approach. Also NSGA-II based approach produces a set of non-dominated solutions instead of one solution, which provide WSPs with more options.

7 Conclusion

In this paper, we proposed a NSGA-II based approach to Web service location-allocation problem. Our approach consider two objectives, minimizing cost and minimizing network latency at the same time. We have conducted a full experiment evaluation using the public WS-DREAM dataset to compare our approach to single-objective GA-based approach. The experiment results shows the NSGA-II based approach is effective to produce a set near-optima solutions for the Web service location-allocation problem. Also, NSGA-II based approach are more efficient than GA-based approach for problem with big number of user centers and server locations. Future work will investigate the scalability of our proposed approaches for big datasets.

References

1. Aboolian, R., Sun, Y., Koehler, G.J.: A locationallocation problem for a web services provider in a competitive market. Eur. J. Oper. Res. **194**(1), 64–77 (2009)
2. Caramia, M.: Multi-objective optimization. In: Multi-objective Management in Freight Logistics, pp. 11–36. Springer, London (2008)
3. Deb, K., Pratap, A., Agarwal, S., Meyarivan, T.: A fast and elitist multiobjective genetic algorithm: NSGA-II. IEEE Trans. Evol. Comput. **6**(2), 182–197 (2002)
4. Deb, K., Mohan, M., Mishra, S.: Evaluating the epsilon-domination based multi-objective evolutionary algorithm for a quick computation of pareto-optimal solutions. Evol. Comput. **13**(4), 501–525 (2005)
5. Deb, K., Sundar, J., Rao N, U.B., Chaudhuri, S.: Reference point based multi-objective optimization using evolutionary algorithms. In: International Journal of Computational Intelligence Research, pp. 635–642 (2006)
6. Desai, S., Bahadure, S., Kazi, F., Singh, N.: Article: Multi-objective constrained optimization using discrete mechanics and NSGA-II approach. Int. J. Comput. Appl. **57**(20), 14–20 (2012). (full text available)
7. Ehrgott, M.: A discussion of scalarization techniques for multiple objective integer programming. Ann. Oper. Res. **147**(1), 343–360 (2006)
8. He, K., Fisher, A., Wang, L., Gember, A., Akella, A., Ristenpart, T.: Next stop, the cloud: Understanding modern web service deployment in ec2 and azure. In: Proceedings of the 2013 Conference on Internet Measurement Conference, IMC 2013, pp. 177–190. ACM (2013)
9. Huang, H., Ma, H., Zhang, M.: An enhanced genetic algorithm for web service location-allocation. In: Decker, H., Lhotská, L., Link, S., Spies, M., Wagner, R.R. (eds.) DEXA 2014, Part II. LNCS, vol. 8645, pp. 223–230. Springer, Heidelberg (2014)
10. Huang, V.L., Suganthan, P.N., Liang, J.J.: Comprehensive learning particle swarm optimizer for solving multiobjective optimization problems: Research articles. Int. J. Intell. Syst. **21**(2), 209–226 (2006)
11. Hwang, J., Park, S., Kong, I.Y.: An integer programming-based local search for large-scale maximal covering problems. Int. J. Comput. Sci. Eng. **3**, 837–843 (2011)

12. Ishibuchi, H., Nojima, Y., Doi, T.: Comparison between single-objective and multi-objective genetic algorithms: Performance comparison and performance measures. In: IEEE Congress on Evolutionary Computation, CEC 2006, pp. 1143–1150 (2006)

13. Jamin, S., Jin, C., Kurc, A., Raz, D., Shavitt, Y.: Constrained mirror placement on the internet. In: INFOCOM 2001, Twentieth Annual Joint Conference of the IEEE Computer and Communications Societies, Proceedings, vol. 1, pp. 31–40. IEEE (2001)

14. Johansson, J.M.: On the impact of network latency on distributed systems design. Inf. Technol. Manag. **1**(3), 183–194 (2000)

15. Kanagarajan, D., Karthikeyan, R., Palanikumar, K., Davim, J.: Optimization of electrical discharge machining characteristics of wc/co composites using non-dominated sorting genetic algorithm (NSGA-II). Int. J. Adv. Manufact. Technol. **36**(11–12), 1124–1132 (2008)

16. Kemps-Snijders, M., Brouwer, M., Kunst, J.P., Visser, T.: Dynamic web service deployment in a cloud environment (2012)

17. Man, K.F., Tang, K.S., Kwong, S.: Genetic algorithms: concepts and applications. IEEE Trans. Ind. Electron. **43**(5), 519–534 (1996)

18. Mitchell, M.: An Introduction to Genetic Algorithms. MIT Press, Cambridge (1998)

19. Morandat, F., Hill, B., Osvald, L., Vitek, J.: Evaluating the design of the R language. In: Noble, J. (ed.) ECOOP 2012. LNCS, vol. 7313, pp. 104–131. Springer, Heidelberg (2012)

20. Ran, S.: A model for web services discovery with QoS. SIGecom Exch. **4**(1), 1–10 (2003)

21. Sun, Y., Koehler, G.J.: A location model for a web service intermediary. Decis. Support Syst. **42**(1), 221–236 (2006)

22. Vanrompay, Y., Rigole, P., Berbers, Y.: Genetic algorithm-based optimization of service composition and deployment. In: Proceedings of the 3rd International Workshop on Services Integration in Pervasive Environments, SIPE 2008, pp. 13–18. ACM (2008)

23. Xie, H., Zhang, M., Andreae, P., Johnson, M.: An analysis of multi-sampled issue and no-replacement tournament selection. In: Proceedings of the 10th Annual Conference on Genetic and Evolutionary Computation, GECCO 2008, pp. 1323–1330. ACM (2008)

24. Xue, B., Zhang, M., Browne, W.N.: Multi-objective particle swarm optimisation (pso) for feature selection. In: Proceedings of the 14th Annual Conference on Genetic and Evolutionary Computation, GECCO 2012, pp. 81–88. ACM (2012)

25. Xue, B., Zhang, M., Browne, W.: Particle swarm optimization for feature selection in classification: a multi-objective approach. IEEE Trans. Cybern. **43**(6), 1656–1671 (2013)

26. Zhang, Y., Zheng, Z., Lyu, M.: Exploring latent features for memory-based QoS prediction in cloud computing. In: 2011 30th IEEE Symposium on Reliable Distributed Systems (SRDS), pp. 1–10 (2011)

27. Zheng, Z., Zhang, Y., Lyu, M.: Distributed QoS evaluation for real-world web services. In: 2010 IEEE International Conference on Web Services (ICWS), pp. 83–90 (2010)

A Double Action Genetic Algorithm for Scheduling the Wind-Thermal Generators

Md Forhad Zaman[✉], Saber Mohammed Elsayed, Tapabrata Ray, and Ruhul A. Sarker

Department of School of Engineering and Information Technology,
The University of New South Wales, Canberra, Australia
md.zaman@student.adfa.edu.au,
{s.elsayed,t.ray,r.sarker}@adfa.edu.au

Abstract. Scheduling of wind-thermal electrical generators is a challenging constrained optimization problem, where the main goal is to find the optimal allocation of output power among various available generators to serve the system load. Over the last few decades, a large number of solution approaches, including evolutionary algorithms, have been developed to solve this problem. However, these approaches are usually ineffective and time consuming. In this paper, we apply two variants of genetic algorithm (GA) for solving the problem where the first variant is to optimize the allocation and the second one is to rank the generators for allocation. The proposed algorithm is applied to a recent wind-thermal benchmark that comprises five thermal and 160 wind farms. The model includes a stochastic nature of wind energy and gas emission effects of thermal plants. The simulation results show that the proposed method is superior to those results of different variants of GA and the state-of-the-art algorithms.

Keywords: Economic dispatch · Wind-thermal system · Genetic algorithm · Heuristic

1 Introduction

Over the last few decades, the use of fossil fuel in electricity generation has increased the environmental pollution and consequently fostered the growth and development of renewable energy generation systems. Wind energy is a promising alternative in power generation, because of its great environmental and social benefits. However, the availability of wind energy is highly fluctuating, which makes it difficult to know the exact wind power in advance. Hence, it is a challenging optimization problem to schedule the right mix of generation from a number of wind and thermal units to serve a daily load demand at minimum cost, which is known as dynamic economic dispatch (DED) problem [1]. Moreover, DED considers different level of load demands and an internal coupling of the power plants operations, at each time interval (which is called ramp limits), and higher variable dimensions [2].

Over the decades, various conventional optimization methods, such as Lagrange multiplier [3], interior point method [4], and iterative method [5], were used to solve this DED problem. The gradient-based optimization methods are usually faster, but sensitive to initial value and easy to get trapped in local optima. In addition, the valve

© Springer International Publishing Switzerland 2016
T. Ray et al. (Eds.): ACALCI 2016, LNAI 9592, pp. 258–269, 2016.
DOI: 10.1007/978-3-319-28270-1_22

point effect of large steam generators produces the cost function non-smooth and multi-modal characteristic. Therefore, the gradient based methods may not converge to optimal solutions for such complex problems.

Over the last few decades, several meta-heuristic optimization techniques have been effectively used to solve different real world problems [6]. In recent years, these approaches are applied to solve the high dimensions and complex DED problems, because they are flexible, efficient and have a stochastic searching feature, for example, genetic algorithm (GA) [7, 8] simulated annealing (SA) [9], particle swarm optimization (PSO) [10] and differential evolution (DE) [1]. Some hybrid methods that combine two or more approaches, such as evolutionary programming and sequential quadratic programming (EP-SQP) [11], PSO-SQP [12], and modified hybrid EP–SQP (MHEP-SQP) [12], have also been used. However, it was noticed that such techniques may have a slow convergence rate and computationally insufficient. The reasons for this is that in those approaches, the equality constraints were usually handled using the penalty-function technique, but the existence of many equality constraints makes it hard to generate feasible solutions and maintain feasibility after applying the evolutionary operators. Even if a feasible solution is obtained after a huge computational effort, the quality of that solution may be poor.

In this paper, a double action GA with a heuristic is proposed to solve the high dimensional constrained and complex wind-thermal DED problem. In it, two GAs are used in parallel, where one GA is used to optimize the overall operating cost by allocating the load demands among the committed units, while another GA is used to determine the best set of rank to help this allocation process. In this process, an iteration process is used to allocate the hourly load demands by providing more portions of demands to a higher ranked unit (*i.e.* a cheaper one) and least portion to a lower ranked unit (*i.e.* an expensive one). Once the reallocation process of first time interval is performed, the generation capacity limits of each unit are updated based on their ramp limits. Then, the iteration process is again applied to reallocate the generation according to their rank found from second GA, and the process is continued until the reallocation process for all intervals are performed. As the unit cost of a generator depends on amount of generation for a particular period, the rank of a generator is dynamically updated during the evolutionary process. In the first GA, the simulated binary crossover and non-uniform mutation are used, while the single point crossover and shift mutation are used in second GA. The proposed framework is applied for solving the wind-thermal DED problem with and without considering transmission power losses [2]. The stochastic features of wind energy at any given time are considered in terms of the overestimation and under-estimation cost [13]. Moreover, the environmental effect of thermal power plants is also included in the DED model. In order to demonstrate the performance of proposed algorithm, the test problem is also solved using a standard GA, and a GA with a heuristic that meets the load demands at random slack generation approach [1]. Their obtained results are compared with each other and recently published state-of-the-art algorithms. The analysis of results ensures that heuristics enhance the performance of GA, while our proposed heuristic outperforms all other algorithms considered in this paper.

The rest of this paper is organized as follows: Sect. 2 presents the problem formulation, Sect. 3 the proposed methodology, Sect. 4, the results from the optimization exercise, and Sect. 5 a summary of our findings.

2   Mathematical Formulation

In this section, the mathematical models of DED wind-thermal is presented, in which the objective function is to minimize the cost of thermal and wind generators. The cost function comprises the fuel and environmental cost of thermal generators, operating cost of wind turbines, and the overestimated and underestimated cost of wind energy due to stochastic nature of wind speeds. The Weibull probability density function is used to calculate the overestimate and underestimate cost in each interval. Taking into account these costs for a wind-thermal power system, the DED model in T time intervals is expressed as [2, 13].

$$\text{Minimize } F\left(P_{T_{i,t}}, W_{w_{i,t}}\right) = F_C\left(P_{T_{i,t}}\right) + F_E(P_{T_{i,t}}) + F_w\left(W_{w,t}\right) + F_U\left(W_{w,t}\right) + F_O\left(W_{w,t}\right) \tag{1}$$

$$F_C\left(P_{T_{i,t}}\right) = a_i + b_i P_{T_{i,t}} + c_i P_{T_{i,t}}^2 + \left| d_i \sin\left\{ e_i\left(P_{T_{i,t}}^{\min} - P_{T_{i,t}}\right)\right\}\right| \quad \forall i, t \in T \tag{2}$$

$$F_E(P_{T_{i,t}}) = \sum_{t=1}^{T}\sum_{i=1}^{N_T} 10^{-2}\left(\alpha_i + \beta_i P_{T_{i,t}} + \gamma_i P_{T_{i,t}}^2\right) + \eta_i e^{\lambda_i P_{T_{i,t}}} \tag{3}$$

$$F_w\left(W_{w,t}\right) = \sum_{t=1}^{T}\sum_{w=1}^{N_W} \delta_w W_{w,t} \tag{4}$$

$$W_{w,t} = \begin{cases} 0, \text{ if } v_{out_w} < v_{w,t} < v_{in_w} \\ W_{R_w} \frac{v_{w,t} - v_{in_w}}{v_{r_w} - v_{in_w}}, \text{ if } v_{in_w} < v_{w,t} < v_{r_w} \\ W_{R_w}, \text{ if } v_{r_w} < v_{w,t} < v_{out_w} \end{cases} \tag{5}$$

$$F_U\left(W_{w,t}\right) = \sum_{t=1}^{T}\sum_{w=1}^{N_W} k_{U_w} \int_{W_{w,t}}^{W_{R_w}} \left(w - W_{w,t}\right) f_{W_{w,t}}(w) dw \tag{6}$$

$$F_O\left(W_{w,t}\right) = \sum_{t=1}^{T}\sum_{w=1}^{N_W} k_{O_w} \int_{0}^{W_{R_w}} \left(W_{w,t} - w\right) f_{W_{w,t}}(w) dw \tag{7}$$

$$f_{W_{w,t}}(w) = \frac{K_t l v_{in}}{c_t} \varphi^{K_t - 1} e^{-\varphi^{K_t}}, 0 < W_t < W_R \tag{8}$$

$$K_t = \left(\sigma_t / \mu_t\right)^{-1.086}, c_t = \mu_t / \Gamma\left(1 + K_t^{-1}\right)$$
$$\phi = \left(\frac{(1 + \psi l) v_{in}}{c_t}\right), \psi = \frac{w}{W_R}, l = \frac{v_r - v_{in}}{v_{in}}, w \in W_{w,t} \tag{9}$$

$$\text{Subject to: } \sum_{i=1}^{N_T} P_{T_{i,t}} + \sum_{w=1}^{N_W} W_{w,t} = P_{D_t} + P_{loss_t} \tag{10}$$

$$P_{loss_t} = \sum_{i=1}^{N_T+N_W} \sum_{j=1}^{N_T+N_W} P_i B_{i,j} P_j, \quad P_i \in \left[P_{T_{i,t}}, W_{w,t} \right], \quad \nabla i, w, t \tag{10.1}$$

$$P_{T_i}^{\min} \leq P_{T_{i,t}} \leq P_{T_i}^{\max} \quad i \in N_T, t \in T \tag{11}$$

$$0 \leq W_{w,t} \leq W_{R_w} \quad w \in N_W, t \in T \tag{12}$$

$$\left[T_{t-1,i}^{on} - T_{\min_i}^{on} \right] \left[S_{t-1,i} - S_{t,i} \right] \geq 0$$
$$\left[T_{t-1,i}^{off} - T_{\min_i}^{off} \right] \left[S_{t,i} - S_{t,i-1} \right] \geq 0 \tag{13}$$

$$-DR_i \leq \left(P_{t,i} - P_{t-1,i} \right) \leq UR_i, \text{ if } P_{t-1,i} > P_i^{\min}$$
$$-DR_i^0 \leq \left| P_{t,i} - P_{t-1,i} \right| \leq UR_i^1, \text{ if } 0 < P_{t-1,i} < P_i^{\min} \tag{14}$$

The objective function (1) is to minimize the sum of all fuel (F_c) and gas emission costs (F_E) of thermal power plants (N_T), and operating (F_w), underestimated (F_U) and overestimated (F_O) cost of wind power plants (N_W) during the operational cycle (T). Where, a_i, b_i, c_i, d_i and e_i are the cost coefficients of ith thermal plant, and δ_w are the operational coefficients of wth wind farm, $P_{T_{i,t}}$ and $W_{w,t}$ are output power of ith thermal and wth wind unit at tth time interval. The underestimated (6) and overestimated (7) penalty cost is calculated from the probability density function (8), where K_{U_w} and K_{O_w} are the underestimated and overestimated cost coefficients. W_{R_w} is the rated power, v_{in_w}, v_{out_w} and v_{r_w} are cut-in, cut-out and rated wind speed, respectively of wth wind farm. In (9), Γ is a gamma function and μ_t and c_t are the mean value and standard deviation of wind speeds for a certain period.

Constraint (10) refers the power balance equation in each cycle. Using the transmission loss coefficients B, power loss (P_{loss}) of each period is expressed in (10.1). Constraint (11) and (12) are the capacity constraints of thermal and wind power plants, respectively, where P_i^{min} and P_i^{max} are the minimum and maximum output power of the ith thermal unit, respectively. Constraints (13) and (14) are the minimum on-off time, and ramp limits of thermal plants, respectively, where, $S, T^{on}, T_{min}^{on}, T^{off}$, and T_{min}^{off}, are the operation status, continuous online time and minimum on time, continuous offline time and minimum off time of conventional generator, respectively, and DR^0 and UR^1 upper limit and lower limit of variation rate while unit is in the process of startup or shutdown. Detailed descriptions of the mathematical model can be found in [2, 13].

3 Proposed Approach

As discussed earlier, the wind-thermal DED model is a single-objective constrained optimization problem involving non-differentiable and multimodal cost functions with many equality and inequality constraints. To effectively solve this problem using GA, in this paper, a double action GA under two populations are considered, one is used to evolve the decision variables associated with wind and thermal generators in order to minimize the overall cost, while the other one is used to determine the best set of sequences in order to allocate the load demands among those generators according to priority basis. The pseudo code of the proposed algorithm is outlined in Algorithm-1, and each component described in detail in the following sub-sections.

Algorithm 1: Pseudo code of proposed algorithm

---

1. Requires: $N_G, N_P \leftarrow$ number of maximum generations, and the population size.
2. Generate an initial population for the decision variables and sequences based on section 3.1.
3. ***for*** $i = 1: N_P$ ***do***
   - If the ith individual ($\vec{x}_i$) is infeasible, then apply the proposed heuristic (section 3.3) to it, considering a sequence set of $\overrightarrow{seq}_i$.
   - Calculate the fitness value (FV) and constraints violations (CVs) according to Eqns. (1), and (10) to (14), respectively.
   - Return FV, CVs, $\overrightarrow{seq}_i$ and updated $\vec{x}_i$

   end for
4. ***for*** $g = 2: N_G$ ***do***
5. Sort the parent individuals of decision variables ($\vec{x}_i \forall i$) and the corresponding sequences ($\overrightarrow{seq}_i \forall i$) according to their FVs and CVs.
6. Offspring generations of the decision variables ($\vec{y}_i \forall i$) and sequences ($\overrightarrow{Seq}_i \forall i$):

   for $i = 1: 2: N_P$ ***do***
   - Select r_1, r_2 individuals of $\vec{x}_i \forall i$ and $\overrightarrow{seq}_i \forall i$ based on tournament selection.
   - Apply a simulated binary crossover (section 3.2.1) and single point crossover (section 3.2.2) with a crossover rate of 0.9 among $\vec{x}_{r_1}, \vec{x}_{r_2}$ and $\overrightarrow{seq}_{r_1}, \overrightarrow{seq}_{r_2}$, and generate $\vec{y}_i, \vec{y}_{i+1}$, and $\overrightarrow{Seq}_i, \overrightarrow{Seq}_{i+1}$, respectively.
   - Apply a non-uniform mutation (section 3.2.3) and shift mutation (section 3.2.4) with a mutation rate of 0.1 to diversify the offspring $\vec{y}_i, \vec{y}_{i+1}$, and $\overrightarrow{Seq}_i, \overrightarrow{Seq}_{i+1}$, respectively.

   end for
7. Repeat step 3 to evaluate child' FV, CV and true $\vec{y}_i \forall i$.
8. Select the best N_P individuals of both decision variables and sequences from entire parents and child populations, based on section 3.4.
10. If stopping criterions are satisfied, terminate main (g) loop.
11. ***end for*** (g).

3.1 Representation and Initial Population

The representation of chromosome for the proposed algorithm can be expressed as:

$$X_i = [\vec{x}_i, \vec{seq}_i], \ i = 1, 2, \ldots, N_P \tag{15}$$

$$\vec{x}_i = \left[P_{T_{k,t}}, W_{w,t}\right], \ k = 1, 2, \ldots, N_T; w = 1, 2, \ldots, N_W; t = 1, 2, \ldots, T \tag{16}$$

$$\vec{seq}_i = \left[r_1, r_2, \ldots, r_{N_T + N_W}\right], \ \forall r \in N_T. \tag{17}$$

Here, $P_{T_{k,t}} \in \left[P_{T_k}^{min}, P_{T_k}^{max}\right]$, $W_{w,t} \in \left[0, W_{R_w}\right]$, and the number of control variables is $N_X = 2 \times T \times (N_T + N_W)$. The individuals in the initial population are generated as:

$$\vec{x}_i = \vec{x}_i^{min} + \left(\vec{x}_i^{max} - \vec{x}_i^{min}\right) \text{lhsdesign}(1, N_x)$$
$$\vec{seq}_i = \text{randperm}\,(T, N_T + N_W) \tag{18}$$

where x_i^{min} and x_i^{max} $\forall i$ are the upper and lower bounds of each variable that can be found from each power plant's limits, and *lhsdesign* and *randperm* are MATLAB functions used for Latin hypercube sampling and random permutation, respectively.

3.2 Genetic Operators

Among various GA search operators, simulated binary crossover (SBX), and non-uniform mutation (NUM) have been shown good performance for solving continuous problems [1], while single point crossover (SPX) and shift mutation (SM) have been found excellent performance in solving integer problems [14]. Hence in this research, those operators have been considered in which SBX and NUM are used to evolve the decision variables, while SPX and SM are employed for determining the best set of rank of each generator at each time interval. The each operator is described below.

3.2.1 Simulated Binary Crossover

In SBX, two random parents (r_1, r_2) are determined using a tournament pool, and consequently two child are evaluated as follow:

$$\vec{y}_i = 0.5 \left[(1 + \beta_q)\vec{x}_{r_1} + (1 - \beta_q)\vec{x}_{r_2}\right] \ i \in N_P \tag{19}$$

$$\vec{y}_{i+1} = 0.5 \left[(1 - \beta_q)\vec{x}_{r_1} + (1 + \beta_{q_k})\vec{x}_{r2}\right] \ i \in N_P \tag{20}$$

$$\text{where, } \beta_q = \begin{cases} (2u_i)^{1/\eta_c + 1} & u_i \leq 0.5, \\ \left(\dfrac{1}{2(1 - u_i)}\right)^{1/\eta_c + 1} & u_i > 0.5, \end{cases} \tag{21}$$

where $u_i \in [0, 1]$ is a random number, $i \in N_P$, and η_c a pre-defined parameter of distribution index.

3.2.2 Single-point Crossover

In SPX, a crossover point is firstly determined by randomly dividing of such two parents used in SBX, and two new offspring subsequently created by appending the first part of the first parent to the second part of the second parent, and the second part of the first parent to the first part of the second parent, as shown below.

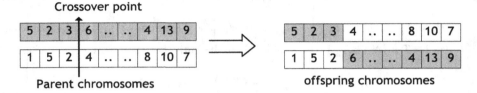

3.2.3 Non-uniform Mutation

In it, a child is diversified from its original value as:

$$\vec{y}_i = \vec{y}_i + \Delta\vec{y}_i \qquad (22)$$

$$\Delta\vec{y}_i = \begin{cases} \left(\vec{y}_i^{\max} - \vec{y}_i\right)\left(1 - u_g^{1-(g/N_G)^b}\right) & u_g \leq 0.5 \\ \left(\vec{y}_i^{\min} - \vec{y}_i\right)\left(1 - u_g^{1-(g/N_G)^b}\right) & u_g > 0.5 \end{cases} \qquad (23)$$

where $i \in N_P$ and $u_g \in [0, 1]$ is a random number, and g and N_G the current and maximum number of generations, respectively. The speed of the step length can be controlled by choosing different 'b' values and, in this research, is set to 5 [15].

3.2.4 Shift Mutation

In order to maintain diversity and avoid redundancy of the sequences after performing SPX, shift mutation is used whereby a random element is chosen from an offspring and shifted to the left or right. If any redundancy occurs in an offspring, the redundant element is replaced by a non-used element.

3.3 Heuristics for DED Constraints

As previously mentioned, the wind-thermal DED is a highly constrained optimization problem involving a number of equality and inequality constraints. The solutions generated by EAs may not satisfy all these constraints. Even a feasible solution may obtain in one generation, its child may be become infeasible in next generation. In order to overcome this deficiency, we propose a heuristic that transforms an infeasible solution into a good-quality feasible one. In the process, the T-hour load cycle is divided into T sub-problems, with production allocated to meet the load demand in each hour. The generators' allocations depend on their rank, with inferior ones given higher and costly ones lower ranks, and consequently higher ranked unit takes more load than lower one, and so on. As the fuel cost of a generator is not linear, we use another optimization approach to determine the best set of rankings for each period in each generation. The proposed priority based heuristic (PH) as shown in Algorithm 2.

Algorithm 2: Pseudo code of heuristic for DED constraints

1. Determine P and SEQ matrix from $\vec{x}_i$ and $\overrightarrow{seq}_i$, respectively as $T \times (N_T + N_W)$ size.

2. Calculate relaxation factor, ε for equality constraints, where ε_0 is the CVs at initial generation.

$$\varepsilon_g = \begin{cases} \varepsilon_0 \left(1 - \dfrac{g}{0.5N_G}\right), 0 < g < 0.5N_G \\ 1e - 6, otherwise; \end{cases}$$

3. Set, capacity limits, $P_{1,i}^{max} = x_i^{max}, P_{1,i}^{min} = x_i^{min}$ $i \in N; N = N_T + N_W$

4. **for** $t = 1:T$ **do**

5. Satisfy generation limits

$$P_{t,i} = \begin{cases} P_{t,i}^{max}, \ P_{t,i} > P_{t,i}^{max} \\ P_{t,i}^{min}, \ P_{t,i} < P_{t,i}^{max} \quad i = 1,2,..,N \\ P_{t,i}, \ otherwise; \end{cases}$$

6. Satisfy demand constraints by repairing cheaper unit (n_d) first,
   for $k = 1:N$ **do,**
   if $\left| \sum_{i=1}^N P_{t,i} - (P_{D_t} + P_{loss_t}) \right| \le \varepsilon$
   Terminate loop (k);
   elseif $\sum_{i=1}^N P_{t,i} > (P_{D_t} + P_{loss_t})$
   $n_d = SEQ_{t,(N+1)-k}$
   else
   $n_d = SEQ_{t,k}$
   end if

   $$P_{t,n_d} = max\left[P_{t,n_d}^{min}, min\left\{ \left(P_{D_t} - \sum_{\substack{i=1 \\ i \ne n_d}}^N P_{t,i} \right), P_{t,n_d}^{max} \right\} \right]$$

   end for (k)

7. Update capacity limits,
   $P_{t+1,i}^{max} = min[P_i^{max}, (P_{t,i} + UR_i)], i = 1,2,..,N_T$
   $P_{t+1,i}^{min} = max[P_i^{min}, (P_{t,i} - DR_i)], i = 1,2,...,N_T$
   end for (t)

8. Reconstruct $\vec{x}_i$ from updated P matrix.

9. Return $\vec{x}_i$.

3.4 Selection Process

Once the entire offspring are evaluated according to Eqs. (1) and (8)–(13), respectively, their FVs, CVs and the parents' FVs and CVs are sorted, where a greedy selection scheme is used so that a feasible solution is always considered better than an infeasible one, as:

$$
\vec{x}_{g+1} = \begin{cases}
\vec{y}_{g+1}, & \text{if } FV\left(\vec{y}_{g+1}\right) \leq FV\left(\vec{x}_g\right) \ \& \ CV\left(\vec{y}_{g+1}\right) \leq CV\left(\vec{x}_g\right) \\
\vec{x}_g, & \text{if } FV\left(\vec{y}_{g+1}\right) \leq FV\left(\vec{x}_g\right) \ \& \ CV\left(\vec{y}_{g+1}\right) \geq CV\left(\vec{x}_g\right) \\
\vec{x}_g, & \text{if } FV\left(\vec{y}_{g+1}\right) < FV\left(\vec{x}_g\right) \ \& \ CV\left(\vec{y}_{g+1}\right) > CV\left(\vec{x}_g\right) \\
\vec{y}_{g+1}, & \text{if } FV\left(\vec{y}_{g+1}\right) < FV\left(\vec{x}_g\right) \ \& \ CV\left(\vec{y}_{g+1}\right) < CV\left(\vec{x}_g\right)
\end{cases}
\tag{24}
$$

During the selection process, the selected individuals' sequences are also considered for next generation evaluation. As a result, at the end of the current generation, the only better-performing individuals and their corresponding sequences are placed for the next generation evaluation.

4 Experimental Results

The proposed algorithm has been tested on a wind-thermal DED problem, which contains five thermal and 160 wind farms for a 6-hour planning horizon with a one-hour long time period. The problem has been solved with and without considering power transmission loss (PTL). In order to demonstrate the effectiveness of proposed algorithm, the test problems have been solved using: (*i*) GA without any heuristic (GA), (*ii*) GA with a heuristic that meets the load demands in a random basis (RH-GA), and (*iii*) GA with the proposed heuristic that meets the load demands in priority basis (PH-GA), under the same platform. It is noted that the RH-GA is almost similar to PH-GA while the heuristic in RH-GA reallocates the hourly load demands to the committed generators in random basis [1]. The process of this heuristic is identical of Algorithm 2, but the n_d in step 6 is considered randomly from $n_d \in N$. However, the experimental results from these three algorithms are compared each other and with results found in [2]. For each case of illustration, we define the test problem as two cases.

Case 1: wind-thermal system with PTL [2];
Case 2: wind-thermal system without PTL [2].

The algorithm has been coded using MATLAB and run on a desktop computer with Intel Core i7 processor at 3.4 GHZ with 16 GB of RAM. The GA parameters, the probability of crossover, distribution index (η) and probability of mutation are set to 0.9, 3 and 0.1, respectively. For a fair comparison, each algorithm performs 30 runs, and the N_P and N_G are set to 100 and 1000, respectively for both cases. The algorithm runs until the number of generations is higher than N_G (criterion 1) or the best fitness value is no longer improved for 100 generations (criterion 2) or the average fitness value is no longer improved for 100 generations (criterion 3).

4.1 Wind-Thermal DED with Power Loss

As the PTL is very significant in the power system operation, the PTL is considered in this paper, while the loss coefficients (*B*) and generators data can be found in [2]. The results obtained by GA, RH-GA and PH-GA and those from literature [2] using DE, PSO, chaotic PSO (CPSO) and bi-population chaotic DE (BPCDE) are listed in Table 1. From the results, it is clear that PH-GA outperforms all the state-of-the-art algorithms. In addition, it is found that using a heuristic improves the performance of GA, while PH-GA consistently obtains the best results within reasonable computational times. Moreover, PH-GA produces quite stable results in all runs, as the standard deviation (STD) value is lower than that of RH-GA.

Table 1. Statistical analysis for the wind-thermal system with PTL

Method	Production cost ($)				CPU time (min)
	Minimum	Median	Maximum	STD	
DE [2]	798891	NR	NR	NR	NR
PSO [2]	802386	NR	NR	NR	NR
CPSO [2]	799258	NR	NR	NR	NR
BPCDE [2]	795194	NR	NR	NR	NR
GA	888130	956859	983831	32943.83	5.75
RH-GA	791077	791216	794888	1156.0	8.79
PH-GA	**790761**	**791111**	**791477**	**254.36**	8.93

NR-Not reported in the literature

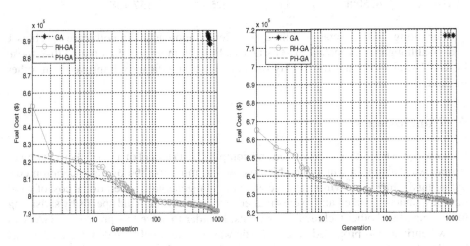

Fig. 1. Convergence characteristics of GA, RH-GA and PH-GA for case-1 (left one) and case -2 (right one)

Also, the convergence characteristics of GA, RH-GA and PH-GA are presented in Fig. 1. In this figure, GA without heuristic does not find a single feasible solution in first half of N_G, and after that, it although finds few feasible solutions, but their qualities are very poor. It is also noticed that GA in case-1 gets stuck and stops before reaching N_G, because the stopping criterion-2 is met. On the other hand, RH-GA and PH-GA both obtain feasible solutions quickly and run up to N_G, where PH-GA dominates RH-GA in terms of obtaining better solutions. A non-parametric statistical (Wilcoxon) test is also undertaken between PH-GA and both GA and RH-GA, as their results are available. The tests reveal that the PH-GA provides significant better results than both other methods.

4.2   Wind-Thermal DED Without Loss

In this section, we demonstrate our algorithm's performance on solving the test problem without considering PTL. Likely case-1, the test problem without PTL is also solved using GA, RH-GA and PH-GA. As the test problem without PTL has not been solved in the literature, the results obtained from GA, RH-GA and PH-GA are presented in Table 2. From this table, it is clear that PH-GA outperforms GA and RH-GA in terms of solutions quality and robustness.

Table 2. Statistical analysis for the wind-thermal system without PTL

Method	Production cost ($)				CPU time (min)
	Minimum	Median	Maximum	STD	
GA	716225	798045	940119	82040.51	5.68
RH-GA	625307	625547	625845	185.1668	8.60
PH-GA	**625000**	**625318**	**625499**	**157.1584**	8.85

Regarding the computational time, of different approaches in both cases (Tables 1 and 2), although the proposed PH-GA takes a little bit more simulation time than those in RH-GA, and GA, but the quality of solutions is significantly improved than other methods.

5   Conclusions

In this paper, a nonlinear, constrained and complex DED model of a wind-thermal power system was solved, in which the objective was to minimize the overall operation cost including the fuel and environmental cost of thermal generators, operational cost of wind turbines, underestimated and overestimated cost of uncertain wind speeds by satisfying load demand and other technical constraints. In order to solve this problem, a GA with a new heuristic was proposed. The heuristic was used to satisfy the demand constraints by allocating the generators in priority basis. As the rank of a unit depends on amount of generation producing that time, the priority of a unit was dynamically updated using another GA. The proposed algorithm was referred as PH-GA.

The algorithm was found better than other two GA variants (GA and RH-GA). To add to this, the algorithm was superior to other meta-heuristics, namely DE and PSO used in literature.

References

1. Zaman, M.F., Elsayed, S.M., Ray, T., Sarker, R.A.: Evolutionary algorithms for dynamic economic dispatch problems. IEEE Trans. Power Syst. **PP**(99), 1–10 (2015)
2. Peng, C., Sun, H., Guo, J., Liu, G.: Dynamic economic dispatch for wind-thermal power system using a novel bi-population chaotic differential evolution algorithm. Int. J. Electr. Power Energy Syst. **42**, 119–126 (2012)
3. Hindi, K.S., Ghani, M.R.A.: Dynamic economic dispatch for large scale power systems: a Lagrangian relaxation approach. Int. J. Electr. Power Energy Syst. **13**, 51–56 (1991)
4. Irisarri, G., Kimball, L.M., Clements, K.A., Bagchi, A., Davis, P.W.: Economic dispatch with network and ramping constraints via interior point methods. IEEE Trans. Power Syst. **13**, 236–242 (1998)
5. Chen, C.L., Lee, T.Y., Jan, R.M.: Optimal wind-thermal coordination dispatch in isolated power systems with large integration of wind capacity. Energy Convers. Manag. **47**, 3456–3472 (2006)
6. Chiong, R., Weise, T., Michalewicz, Z.: Variants of evolutionary algorithms for real-world applications. Springer, Berlin (2012)
7. Lee, J.C., Lin, W.M., Liao, G.C., Tsao, T.P.: Quantum genetic algorithm for dynamic economic dispatch with valve-point effects and including wind power system. Int. J. Electr. Power Energy Syst. **33**, 189–197 (2011)
8. Zaman, F., Sarker, R.A., Ray, T.: Solving an economic and environmental dispatch problem using evolutionary algorithm. In: IEEE International Conference on Industrial Engineering and Engineering Management (IEEM), pp. 1367–1371 (2014)
9. Panigrahi, C.K., Chattopadhyay, P.K., Chakrabarti, R.N., Basu, M.: Simulated Annealing Technique for Dynamic Economic Dispatch. Electric Power Compon. Syst. **34**, 577–586 (2006)
10. Aghaei, J., Niknam, T., Azizipanah-Abarghooee, R., Arroyo, J.M.: Scenario-based dynamic economic emission dispatch considering load and wind power uncertainties. Int. J. Electr. Power Energy Syst. **47**, 351–367 (2013)
11. Attaviriyanupap, P., Kita, H., Tanaka, E., Hasegawa, J.: A hybrid EP and SQP for dynamic economic dispatch with nonsmooth fuel cost function. IEEE Trans. Power Syst. **22**, 77 (2002)
12. Victoire, T.A.A., Jeyakumar, A.E.: A modified hybrid EP-SQP approach for dynamic dispatch with valve-point effect. Int. J. Electr. Power Energy Syst. **27**, 594–601 (2005)
13. Hetzer, J., Yu, D.C., Bhattarai, K.: An economic dispatch model incorporating wind power. IEEE Trans. Energy Convers. **23**, 603–611 (2008)
14. Deep, K., Singh, K.P., Kansal, M.L., Mohan, C.: A real coded genetic algorithm for solving integer and mixed integer optimization problems. Appl. Math. Comput. **212**, 505–518 (2009)
15. Elsayed, S.M., Sarker, R.A., Essam, D.L.: Adaptive configuration of evolutionary algorithms for constrained optimization. Appl. Math. Comput. **222**, 680–711 (2013)

Feature Selection

Investigating Multi-Operator Differential Evolution for Feature Selection

Essam Debie$^{(\boxtimes)}$, Saber Mohammed Elsayed, Daryl L. Essam, and
Ruhul A. Sarker

School of Engineering and Information Technology, University of New South Wales,
Canberra, Australia
{E.Debie,S.Elsayed,D.Essam,R.Sarker}@adfa.edu.au

Abstract. Performance issues when dealing with a large number of
features are well-known for classification algorithms. Feature selection
aims at mitigating these issues by reducing the number of features in
the data. Hence, in this paper, a feature selection approach based on
a multi-operator differential evolution algorithm is proposed. The algorithm partitions the initial population into a number of sub-populations
evolving using a pool of distinct mutation strategies. Periodically, the
sub-populations exchange information to enhance their diversity. This
multi-operator approach reduces the sensitivity of the standard differential evolution to the selection of an appropriate mutation strategy. Two
classifiers, namely decision trees and k-nearest neighborhood, are used
to evaluate the generated subsets of features. Experimental analysis has
been conducted on several real data sets using a 10-fold cross validation.
The analysis shows that the proposed algorithm successfully determines
efficient feature subsets, which can improve the classification accuracy
of the classifiers under consideration. The usefulness of the proposed
method on large scale data set has been demonstrated using the KDD
Cup 1999 intrusion data set, where the proposed method can effectively
remove irrelevant features from the data.

1   Introduction

High-dimensional data (data with a high number of features) analysis is gaining
increasing importance in the machine learning community. Many important data
analysis problems in fields like intrusion detection, finance, and satellite imagery,
are high-dimensional. Increasing the number of features could potentially provide
detailed information for classification. However, such high-dimensional feature
spaces cause scalability problems for classification algorithms. On the one hand,
the number of training instances linearly increases as a function of the number
of features for a linear classifier, and increases to square of the number of features for a quadratic classifier. For stochastic classifiers, the required number of
training instances increases exponentially as a function of the number of features
[12]. On the other hand, real-world data contains redundant and irrelevant features. Redundancy and noise degrade not only the computational efficiency of
classification algorithms, but also their classification accuracy [3].

© Springer International Publishing Switzerland 2016
T. Ray et al. (Eds.): ACALCI 2016, LNAI 9592, pp. 273–284, 2016.
DOI: 10.1007/978-3-319-28270-1_23

To deal with high-dimensional data, feature selection techniques are often applied to simplify a classification model. They merely identify a representative subset of features for the original high-dimensional data. By training classifiers with this representative feature subset, more accurate results can often be obtained, while reducing the computational costs. Different feature selection techniques have been studied in the literature, and they can be categorized into two main categories: (1) filter techniques [8]; and (2) wrapper techniques [9]. In filter techniques, a relevance score is calculated for each feature, and a predetermined number of high-scoring features are presented as input to the classification algorithm. Wrapper techniques explore the space of feature subsets for the optimal or near optimal feature subset. Evaluation of different feature subsets is obtained by training and testing a specific classification model using cross validation on the data set.

Finding the optimal feature subset is considered a NP hard optimisation problem and a search strategy is needed to explore the feature subset space. Various search algorithms have been proposed in the literature, such as sequential forward search and sequential backward search [6]. The forward and backward searches work by adding or removing one feature at a time, depending on the classification accuracy. The search stops when the classification accuracy declines. Evolutionary algorithms have also been investigated in feature subset selection and have provided competitive performance in this regard [1,15,17].

Differential evolution (DE) was originally proposed by Storn and Price [18]. It is a simple and fast population based evolutionary search technique that has been shown to perform well on a wide variety of problems. It has been used in the feature selection domain and showed encouraging results. Martinovic et al. [14] proposed a wrapper based feature selection approach. The classifier used was k-NN and a DE algorithm was adapted for binary spaces. Good quality solutions found during the DE run were stored in an archive. A final solution was then obtained from the archive by performing a k-fold cross-validation of its solutions and the best one was selected. DE was firstly used for finding informative gene subsets in Tasoulis et al. [19] used a version of DE for integer representation of genes (features of microarray data set). It applied a Feedforward Neural Network (FNN) as the classifier of selected subsets. Jose Garcia and Javier Apolloni [7] have proposed a binary version of DE for the efficient gene selection of high dimensional microarray datasets. Support vector machines (SVM) classifier was used to evaluate generated solutions. Khushaba et al. [10] have proposed a DE filter feature selection algorithm, where the desired number of features is determined by the user. Instead of using a binary variant of DE, the authors directly encoded the indices of the features into the DE population, i.e. the lower and upper boundaries of the entries of a given vector is 1 and the total number of features respectively.

Despite the encouraging results of DE in the feature selection domain, its performance is sensitive to the choice of mutation strategy and other parameter setup [13]. The best parameter setup can be different for different problems. Therefore, a time-consuming trial-and-error process is performed to select the most appropriate strategy and to tune its associated parameter to successfully solve a specific problem. Elsayed et al. [4] have proposed a multi-operator genetic algorithm (GA) for single objective optimization problems. The proposed app- roach partitions the initial population into a number of sub-populations that evolve using their own parameter setup. Their model overcame the manual selec- tion of parameter setup and provided better performance than the standard single operator GA.

The purpose of this paper is to investigate the effectiveness of using the multi-operator approach in DE based feature selection to search for the most representative feature subset, and subsequently its usefulness in enhancing the generalization capabilities of classification models. Our hypothesis is that uti- lizing the multi-operator approach can mitigate the DE sensitivity to using a specific mutation strategy for a given problem. The multi-operator approach can also yield a more refined subset selection and so can provide more accu- rate classification solutions in complex problems. To achieve this, we propose a new feature selection algorithm, based on multi-operator DE. The quality of generated solutions is evaluated using the classification accuracy of a specific classifier. A final solution is then obtained by selecting the best solution across all sub-populations. The different sub-populations evolve in parallel alongside with the 10-fold cross-validation attempts to ensure the selection of the most salient features from the set. In this paper, four variants of DE from the litera- ture are chosen and implemented. The performance of the proposed algorithm is compared with the original data set without feature selection and with two other popular feature selection algorithms on 12 real-world data sets taken from the UCI machine learning repository.

The remainder of this paper is organized as follows: Sect. 2 briefly discusses the feature selection problem, and DE is explained in Sect. 3. The proposed multi-operator DE based feature selection MODE-FS is presented in Sect. 4. Experimental setup, results and analysis on small-scale data sets are presented in Sect. 5. Results on large-scale intrusion detection data sets are discussed in Sect. 6. Finally, Sect. 7 summarizes the work presented in this paper, concludes, and discusses future work.

2 Feature Selection Problem

Feature selection is the process of removing irrelevant or redundant features from the classification task. Although an increasing number of features can improve the generalization capabilities of classification algorithms, the presence of fea- tures that are deemed to not be useful to the classification task degrades classi- fication performance in terms of both classification accuracy and computational complexity. This is due to the noise that is contributed by these additional fea- tures [2]. The goal of feature selection is therefore to search for the set of relevant features that produce comparable or better classification performance than the case when all the features are used.

Suppose, that the set of available features for a given classifier are denoted by $F = \{F_1, F_2, ..., F_D\}$ where D is the total number of features. The feature selection problem is then stated as follows: Find the appropriate subset of features $\bar{F} \subseteq F$ such that the classification accuracy of a classifier trained using $\bar{F}$ is maximized.

3   Differential Evolution

DE is an efficient and powerful population-based stochastic search technique for solving optimization problems. In comparison to other stochastic search algorithms, DE exhibits better performance in terms of accuracy and convergence speed, on a wide variety of single and multi-objective optimization problems [20].

Many variants of the standard differential evolution have been proposed in the literature. To differentiate among them, a notation is often used in the form of DE/x/y/z, where x denotes how the mutation of new offspring is performed, y denotes the number of vector differences added to the base vector, and z indicates the crossover method used. For example, the most popular strategy, denoted by DE/rand/1/bin, generates the point v by adding the weighted difference of two points and uses a binomial (uniform) crossover operator.

An initial population of N D-dimensional real-valued vectors is generated randomly. Each vector in the population (also known as an individual, or a chromosome in some rare cases) forms a candidate solution to the problem being solved. At any generation, the ith vector of the current generation $g \in [1 - G]$, where G is the total number of generations, is represented as follows:

$$\boldsymbol{X}_{i,g} = [x_{1,i,g}, x_{2,i,g}, ..., x_{D,i,g}] \tag{1}$$

where D is the dimensionality of the problem.

3.1   Evolutionary Process

For each ith vector from the current population (also known as the target vector or parent), three other distinct vectors, say $\boldsymbol{x}_{r_1}$, $\boldsymbol{x}_{r_2}$, $\boldsymbol{x}_{r_3}$, are sampled randomly from the current population. The indices r_1, r_2, and r_3 are mutually exclusive integers randomly chosen from the range $[1, N]$, which are also different from the base (target) vector index i. These indices are randomly generated once for each mutant vector. To obtain a new vector (referred to as the donor vector), one of the following mutation strategies is applied:

1. DE/rand/1: A new vector is obtained as follows:

$$\boldsymbol{Y}_{i,g} = \boldsymbol{X}_{r_1,g} + F.\left(\boldsymbol{X}_{r_2,g} - \boldsymbol{X}_{r_3,g}\right) \tag{2}$$

2. DE/best/1: A new vector is obtained as follows:

$$\boldsymbol{Y}_{i,g} = \boldsymbol{X}_{best,g} + F.\left(\boldsymbol{X}_{r_1,g} - \boldsymbol{X}_{r_2,g}\right) \tag{3}$$

3. DE/rand-to-best/1: A new vector is obtained by as follows:

$$\boldsymbol{Y}_{i,g} = \boldsymbol{X}_{i,g} + F.\,(\boldsymbol{X}_{best,g} - \boldsymbol{X}_{i,g}) + F.\,(\boldsymbol{X}_{r_1,g} - \boldsymbol{X}_{r_2,g}) \tag{4}$$

4. DE/Current-to-best/1: A new vector is obtained as follows:

$$\boldsymbol{Y}_{i,g} = \boldsymbol{X}_{i,g} + F.\,(\boldsymbol{X}_{best,g} - \boldsymbol{X}_{i,g} + \boldsymbol{X}_{r_1,g} - \boldsymbol{X}_{r_2,g}) \tag{5}$$

where F is a scaling number chosen in the range $[0, 2]$, and $\boldsymbol{X}_{best,g}$ is the individual with the best fitness value in the current generation.

A crossover operation is performed after generating the donor vector through mutation. The purpose of this step is to enhance the potential diversity in the new population. During crossover the donor vector exchanges its entries with the target vector $\boldsymbol{X}_{i,g}$ to form the trial vector $\boldsymbol{T}_{i,g} = [t_{1,i,g}, t_{2,i,g}, ..., t_{D,i,g}]$. Although various crossover methods have been proposed, the binomial crossover is widely used in DE in the literature [16]. In binomial crossover, the elements of the trial vector $T_{i,g}$ are chosen using the following formula:

$$T_{d,i,g} = \begin{cases} Y_{d,i,g} & \text{if}\,(rand_{i,j}\,[0,1] \leq Cr \text{ or } j = j_{rand}) \\ \mathrm{X}_{d,i,g} & \text{otherwise} \end{cases} \tag{6}$$

where $rand_{i,j}\,[0,1]$ is a uniformly distributed random number.

Algorithm 1. MODE-FS

1: Initialize IP;
2: $g \leftarrow 0$;
3: Partition IP into S sub populations;
4: **repeat**
5:     **for** $s = 1$ to S **do**
6:         Create a new generation into P_s;
7:     **end for**
8:     Increment g by 1;
9:     **if** $g\%W = 0$ **then**
10:       **for** $s = 1$ to S **do**
11:           Replace the worst $S - 1$ individuals in P_s;
12:       **end for**
13:     **end if**
14: **until** $g > G$ or optimal value reached

---

4 Multi-Operator Differential Evolution Based Feature Selection

The purpose of this section is to introduce the multi-operator DE for feature selection (MODE-FS). The proposed algorithm is initialized with a randomly generated population with a number (N) of individuals. The initial population is then partitioned into a number (S) of equal sized sub-populations P_s, where $s \in S$ is the index of the corresponding sub-population. Conventional DE employs one mutation strategy to generate new candidate solutions. To overcome the drawbacks of using a single mutation strategy, the proposed algorithm employs multiple mutation strategies. Each sub-population P_s employs a mutation strategy of choice and which is different from that employed by other sub-populations. Periodically, migration of solutions is performed where separately evolving sub-populations identify and exchange genetic information. After every W generations, the worst $S - 1$ individuals of each-sub population P_s are replaced by chosen individuals from the other $S - 1$ sub-populations. For each sub-population $P_i \mid i \in S$ and $i \neq s$, the population is sorted in descending order using the fitness values and an individual is chosen randomly from the top M individuals. The goal of this migration is to improve the diversity and the convergence speed of the set of DE sub-populations. The best individual across all sub-populations is returned as the solution for the feature selection problem. Algorithm 1 shows pseudo-code of the proposed algorithm MODE-FS.

4.1   Individual Encoding

The length of an individual equals the total number of features in the problem D. The entries of each individual are randomly initialized in the range $[0, 1]$, where a value less than 0.5 means that the corresponding feature does not participate in the feature subset. If the value of a particular entry is greater than or equal to 0.5, then the corresponding feature participates in the feature subset. An example of individual encoding with 10 entries is shown in Fig. 1.

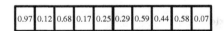

Fig. 1. An example of individual encoding with 10 features.

4.2   Fitness Calculation

To evaluate generated individuals, a fitness value is assigned to each individual in the sub-populations. The following steps are followed to calculate the fitness value.

1. Suppose, there are $\overline{D}$ features present in a particular individual (i.e., there are $\overline{D}$ entries whose values are greater than or equal to 0.5).
2. Construct a classifier with only these $\overline{D}$ features.
   (a) the data is divided into 3 sets: training set, test set, and validation set. Both the training and testing sets are used during individual evaluation, while the validation set is used to evaluate the final solution of the algorithm. The classifier is trained using the training set with the $\overline{D}$ features encoded in the current individual and are evaluated with the test set.

3. The classification accuracy of the classifier on the test set is assigned to the current individual as its fitness value.

4.3 Mutation

Each sub-population in MODE-FS employs its own mutation strategy. For each target vector in a given sub-population, a mutant vector (donor) is generated according to the mutation strategy of choice. The donor vector is then checked for boundary excess, i.e. if an entry falls outside the range [0,1] then it is approximated to remain in that range.

4.4 Crossover

Crossover is introduced in order to increase the diversity in the population of individuals. To this end, the trial vector is generated according to Eq. 6, where CR belongs to [0,1] and has to be determined by the user.

5 Experiments on Small Scale Data Sets

In this section, an experimental analysis of the performance of the proposed MODE-FS model is discussed. First, the experimental setup is presented, followed by an analysis and comparison of the performance of MODE-FS with two of the popular feature selection algorithms in the literature, namely RELIEF [11], and fast correlation-based filter (FCBF) [21].

5.1 Experimental Setup

A set of experiments were run on 12 real data sets that were extracted from the UCI repository [5], and are summarized in Table 1. All the data sets were partitioned using a stratified 10-fold cross-validation to generate training/testing data sets. Each generated training set is then repartitioned using a stratified 10-fold cross validation to generate training/validating data sets. The results represent the average of a total of 10 folds. The subset that achieves the highest classification accuracy is output as the final selected feature subset.

The parameters of MODE-FS were set as follows: $N = 100$, $S = 4$, the top number of individuals from which individuals were chosen for migration $M = 5$. The scaling factor F varies in the range [0.4, 1], the crossover probability $Cr = 0.95$. Four variants of the mutation operators were used in the sub-populations as follows: DE/rand/1/bin, DE/best/1, DE/rand-to-best/1, and DE/Current-to-best/1. The performance of the proposed feature selection algorithm was tested with two classifiers: K-nearest neighbor (KNN), and decision tree classifier (DT). Student t-tests with a confidence interval of 95 % were used to determine whether significant differences between the classification accuracy of MODE-FS and other algorithms were recognized over the 10 folds.

Table 1. Data set description. #inst represents the number of instances, #feat represents the total number of features, and #cls represents the number of classes.

Id.	Data set	#inst	#feat	#cls
win	Wine	178	13	3
h-s	Heart-s	270	13	2
vot	Vote	436	15	2
veh	Vehicle	846	18	4
hep	Hepatitis	155	19	2
seg	segmentation	2310	19	7
thy	Thyroid	7200	21	3
par	Parkinson	195	22	2
wpbc	Wisc. pronostic breast cancer	198	33	2
spt	Spectf	267	44	2
son	Sonar	208	60	2
old	Ozone level detection	2536	73	2

5.2 MODE-FS with K-Nearest Neighbor Classifier

Table 2 contains the results of the experiments performed to evaluate MODE-FS. In Table 2, each data set is represented by one row. The classification accuracy reported is the average over 10 folds along with their standard deviations. Original data set denotes the accuracies with the original data set before feature selection. MODE-FS denotes the classification accuracies with the feature subset generated by MODE-FS. RELIEF denotes the classification accuracies with the feature subset generated by RELIEF algorithm. FCBF denotes the classification accuracies with the feature subset generated by FCBF algorithm. All classification accuracies were obtained using KNN classifier algorithm. The best result for each data set is shown in bold, where significantly better results are marked by âĂŸ*âĂŸ.

It can be observed in Table 2, that for all data sets, the feature subset generated by the proposed MODE-FS algorithm produces higher accuracy than the original data set and the feature subsets generated by RELIEF and FCBF. Also, the accuracy difference was significant in 7 of the 12 data sets. The null hypothesis that all algorithms present similar classification accuracy was tested using a Friedman's test with 95 % confidence interval. The resulting p-value of (0.000075 < 0.05) indicates that the null hypothesis of equivalence was rejected. The last row in Table 2 shows the corresponding Friedman's rank of each algorithm.

5.3 MODE-FS with Decision Tree Classifier

Table 3 contains the results of the experiments performed to evaluate MODE-FS using a DT classifier. On the data sets under consideration, there was no significant difference between the feature subset generated by the proposed algorithm

Table 2. Classification comparison of MODE-FS with KNN classifier.

Id.	Original data set	MODE-FS	RELEIF	FCBF
win	96.93 ± 1.25	**97.47 ± 0.31**	96.81 ± 1.91	96.75 ± 0.93
h-s	75.27 ± 9.56	**92.48 ± 1.05** *	89.00 ± 1.16	90.52 ± 0.41
vot	77.78 ± 12.83	**82.72 ± 5.66**	79.78 ± 12.83	79.01 ± 14.97
veh	79.26 ± 14.31	**95.42 ± 0.06** *	88.26 ± 4.31	93.09 ± 0.09
hep	74.39 ± 4.30	**81.49 ± 2.03** *	76.39 ± 2.10	64.16 ± 3.80
seg	83.33 ± 14.09	**91.67 ± 7.22**	90.33 ± 6.09	91.67 ± 7.22
thy	96.97 ± 0.98	**98.12 ± 0.12** *	90.97 ± 1.11	88.02 ± 5.75
par	94.95 ± 0.79	**99.21 ± 0.21** *	94.95 ± 0.79	92.55 ± 0.08
wpbc	93.16 ± 2.93	**96.58 ± 0.97** *	90.24 ± 2.93	89.74 ± 4.90
spt	77.72 ± 6.61	**88.16 ± 2.75** *	78.63 ± 6.53	72.54 ± 7.42
son	84.90 ± 7.84	**88.75 ± 3.71**	79.19 ± 5.84	71.18 ± 6.24
old	85.32 ± 8.94	**95.16 ± 0.14** *	89.62 ± 3.94	90.32 ± 4.77
Friedman's rank	1.96	3.96	2.29	1.79

Table 3. Classification comparison of MODE-FS with DT classifier.

Id.	Original data set	MODE-FS	RELEIF	FCBF
win	97.16 ± 2.85	98.33 ± 1.68	92.68 ± 9.69	**99.41 ± 0.86**
h-s	**90.37 ± 7.65**	88.89 ± 4.28	90.37 ± 7.65	87.78 ± 6.99
vot	96.75 ± 3.83	97.69 ± 2.11	**98.10 ± 1.55**	95.61 ± 3.55
veh	90.65 ± 6.16	89.95 ± 3.69	**92.50 ± 7.54**	68.43 ± 4.51
hep	92.50 ± 7.54	**97.50 ± 2.27**	96.75 ± 3.83	95.00 ± 3.74
seg	98.44 ± 1.43	**99.00 ± 0.41**	95.10 ± 4.40	95.24 ± 1.88
thy	**99.83 ± 0.13**	99.71 ± 0.14	90.65 ± 6.16	92.58 ± 0.07
par	96.42 ± 3.50	**97.97 ± 2.52**	90.47 ± 7.69	90.63 ± 7.72
wpbc	92.68 ± 6.69	**94.84 ± 4.90**	90.37 ± 7.65	85.50 ± 13.00
spt	94.26 ± 5.76	95.88 ± 3.27	**99.83 ± 0.13** *	81.64 ± 4.49
son	95.10 ± 4.40	**98.55 ± 1.34**	94.83 ± 3.21	95.62 ± 3.38
old	98.37 ± 1.26	**98.43 ± 0.65**	96.42 ± 3.50	96.92 ± 0.26
Friedman's rank	2.21	4.00	2.21	1.58

and the original data set, except in the spectf data set where RELIEF was the best algorithm. Compared to the other feature selection algorithms, MODE-FS achieved similar results on all data sets in comparison to RELIEF algorithm where the difference in classification accuracy was not significant. MODE-FS provided significantly better results than FCBF on six data sets, it was outperformed on one data set (wbcd). On the remaining data sets, the difference in classification accuracies was not significant. To add to that, the proposed algorithm achieved more robust results which is shown by its lowest standard deviation among other techniques. The p-value of a Friedman's test with 95 % confidence interval indicates that the null hypothesis of equivalence is rejected with probability (0.000006 < 0.05). The last row in Table 3 shows the corresponding Friedman's rank of each algorithm. To sum up, the proposed algorithm has been shown to provide similar, if not better performance than the other feature selection algorithms considered in this study when using a DT classifier.

6   Experiments on Intrusion Detection Data Set

The problem of intrusion detection has been studied extensively in computer security and has received a lot of attention in machine learning and data mining. The KDD CUP 1999 data set is a popular data set to evaluate learning algorithms in the literature, it was extracted from the original 1998 DARPA intrusion detection data set. The KDD CUP data set contains 494,021 connection records as training data and 311,000 connection records for testing. Each record is described with 41 features and a label that specifies whether it is a normal record or a specific attack type. In this section, we investigate the applicability of MODE-FS in the intrusion detection domain. The parameters of MODE-FS are set as explained in Sect. 5. The reported results represent the average of the classification accuracy over 10 independent runs on the data set.

Table 4. Classification performance on KDD Cup 1999 data set. Clr refers to the classifier used, #feat refers to the number of features selected by each algorithm. Acc refers to the average accuracy rate achieved along with the corresponding standard deviation.

Clr	MODE-FS		RELEIF		FCBF	
	#feat	Acc	#feat	Acc	#feat	Acc
DT	10.4	98.92 ± 0.13	19	98.76 ± 0.28	21	97.33± 0.45
KNN	10.4	99.25 ± 0.15	19	98.94 ± 0.18	21	98.63± 0.29

Table 4 summarizes the results of the experiments obtained on the KDD CUP data set. There were variations among the feature selection algorithms used in the experiments. As to the number of selected features, MODE-FS resulted in the lowest number of relevant features when compared to both RELEIF and FCBF. In regard to the classification accuracy, a student t-test with a confidence interval of 95 % showed that MODE-FS presented significantly better classification accuracy compared to FCBF. On the other hand, there was no significant difference in the classification accuracy between MODE-FS and RELEIF.

7   Conclusion and Future Work

Different DE algorithms have been proposed to solve feature selection problems. Most of these algorithms were designed to use a single mutation operator. For a given data set, multiple DE mutation strategies may be more effective than a single mutation strategy, as in conventional DE. Based on this observation, a multi-operator DE feature selection algorithm was proposed in this paper. The performance of MODE-FS was evaluated on a set of benchmark classification data sets of varying sizes and numbers of features and was compared with two popular feature selection algorithms. The results of the analysis show the usefulness of the proposed approach. The results achieved by the proposed method were statistically evaluated using a student t-test. In the KNN classifier, it was shown that the differences in performance were in most cases statistically significant. MODE-FS has been also shown perform well on the large-scale KDD CUP 1999 data set. As future work, other advanced variants of DE will be investigated. In addition, controlling algorithm's parameters, such as the number of mutation variants and each sub-populations size can be adaptively based on convergence performance.

Acknowledgement. This work was supported by the Australian Centre for Cyber Security Research Funding Program, under a grant no. PS38135.

References

1. Bazi, Y., Melgani, F.: Toward an optimal SVM classification system for hyperspectral remote sensing images. IEEE Trans. Geosci. Remote Sens. **44**(11), 3374–3385 (2006). 00252
2. Caruana, R., Freitag, D.: Greedy Attribute Selection, pp. 28–36. Citeseer (1994). 00536
3. Debie, E., Shafi, K., Lokan, C., Merrick, K.: Performance analysis of rough set ensemble of learning classifier systems with differential evolution based rule discovery. Evol. Intell. **6**(2), 109–126 (2013). 00001
4. Elsayed, S.M., Sarker, R.A., Essam, D.L.: Multi-operator based evolutionary algorithms for solving constrained optimization problems. Comput. Oper. Res. **38**(12), 1877–1896 (2011). http://www.sciencedirect.com/science/article/pii/S030505481100075X.00072
5. Frank, A., Asuncion, A.: UCI Machine Learning Repository. University of California, Irvine, School of Information and Computer Sciences (2010). http://archive.ics.uci.edu/ml
6. Gadat, S., Younes, L.: A stochastic algorithm for feature selection in pattern recognition. J. Mach. Learn. Res. **8**, 509–547 (2007)
7. Garcia-Nieto, J., Alba, E., Apolloni, J.: Hybrid DE-SVM approach for feature selection: application to gene expression datasets, pp. 1–6. IEEE (2009)
8. Hall, M.A.: Correlation-based Feature Selection for Machine Learning. Ph.D. thesis (1999)
9. John, G.H., Kohavi, R., Pfleger, K.: Irrelevant Features and the Subset Selection Problem. In: Proceedings, pp. 121–129. Morgan Kaufmann (1994)

10. Khushaba, R.N., Al-Ani, A., Al-Jumaily, A.: Feature subset selection using differential evolution and a statistical repair mechanism. Expert Syst. Appl. **38**(9), 11515–11526 (2011). http://linkinghub.elsevier.com/retrieve/pii/S0957417411004362

11. Kononenko, I.: Estimating attributes: analysis and extensions of RELIEF. In: Bergadano, F., De Raedt, L. (eds.) ECML-94. LNCS, vol. 784, pp. 171–182. Springer, Heidelberg (1994). http://dx.doi.org/10.1007/3-540-57868-4_57

12. Maimon, O., Rokach, L.: Improving supervised learning by feature decomposition. In: Eiter, T., Schewe, K.-D. (eds.) FoIKS 2002. LNCS, vol. 2284, pp. 178–196. Springer, Heidelberg (2002)

13. Mallipeddi, R., Suganthan, P.N., Pan, Q.K., Tasgetiren, M.F.: Differential evolution algorithm with ensemble of parameters and mutation strategies. Appl. Soft Comput. **11**(2), 1679–1696 (2011)

14. Martinoyić, G., Bajer, D., Zorić, B.: A differential evolution approach to dimensionality reduction for classification needs. Int. J. Appl. Math. Comput. Sci. **24**(1), 111 (2014). http://www.degruyter.com/view/j/amcs.2014.24.issue-1/amcs-2014-0009/amcs-2014-0009.xml

15. Oh, I.S., Lee, J.S., Moon, B.R.: Hybrid genetic algorithms for feature selection. IEEE Trans. Pattern Anal. Mach. Intell. **26**(11), 1424–1437 (2004)

16. Price, K., Storn, R., Lampinen, J.: Differential Evolution: A Practical Approach to Global Optimization. Springer, New York (2005)

17. Raymer, M.L., Punch, W.F., Goodman, E.D., Kuhn, L., Jain, A.K.: Dimensionality reduction using genetic algorithms. IEEE Trans. Evol. Comput. **4**(2), 164–171 (2000)

18. Storn, R., Price, K.: Differential evolution-a simple and efficient heuristic for global optimization over continuous spaces. J. Global Optim. **11**(4), 341–359 (1997). 09676

19. Tasoulis, D.K., Plagianakos, V.P., Vrahatis, M.N.: Differential evolution algorithms for finding predictive gene subsets in microarray data. In: Maglogiannis, I., Karpouzis, K., Bramer, M. (eds.) AIAI. IFIP, vol. 204, pp. 484–491. Springer, New York (2006)

20. Tušar, T., Filipič, B.: Differential evolution versus genetic algorithms in multiobjective optimization. In: Obayashi, S., Deb, K., Poloni, C., Hiroyasu, T., Murata, T. (eds.) EMO 2007. LNCS, vol. 4403, pp. 257–271. Springer, Heidelberg (2007). http://dx.doi.org/10.1007/978-3-540-70928-2_22

21. Yu, L., Liu, H.: Feature selection for high-dimensional data: a fast correlation-based filter solution, pp. 856–863 (2003). http://citeseerx.ist.psu.edu/viewdoc/summary?doi=10.1.1.68.2975

Coevolutionary Feature Selection and Reconstruction in Neuro-Evolution for Time Series Prediction

Ravneil Nand[(✉)] and Rohitash Chandra

School of Computing Information and Mathematical Sciences,
University of South Pacific, Suva, Fiji
ravneiln@yahoo.com, c.rohitash@gmail.com

Abstract. Feature reconstruction of time series problems produces reconstructed state-space vectors that are used for training machine learning methods such as neural networks. Recently, much consideration has been given to employing competitive methods in improving cooperative neuro-evolution of neural networks for time series predictions. This paper presents a competitive feature selection and reconstruction method that enforces competition in cooperative neuro-evolution using two different reconstructed feature vectors generated from single time series. Competition and collaboration of the two datasets are done using two different islands that exploit their strengths while eradicating their weaknesses. The proposed approach has improved results for some of the benchmark datasets when compared to standalone methods from the literature.

Keywords: Cooperative coevolution · Feedforward networks · Problem decomposition · Time series

1 Introduction

Cooperative Coevolution (CC) provides an architecture for evolutionary algorithms that breaks down a problem into subcomponents that are implemented as sub-populations [1]. The application of CC for training neural networks is also referred as *cooperative neuro-evolution* [2]. In cooperative neuro-evolution, problem decomposition is defined by the structural properties of the network that contains interdependencies and dependent on the architecture and the type of training problem [2].

Chaotic time series problems are highly sensitive to noise and initial conditions [3]. Neural networks have been successfully used to tackle chaotic time series problems [4,5]. Time series prediction can be improved by exploring different features of the time series data and by selecting optimal values of the associated variables that are used for pre-processing [6].

Takens theorem [7] is one of the techniques for reconstructing the original time series into a phase space that is used for training neural networks [4].

© Springer International Publishing Switzerland 2016
T. Ray et al. (Eds.): ACALCI 2016, LNAI 9592, pp. 285–297, 2016.
DOI: 10.1007/978-3-319-28270-1_24

The time lag defines the interval at which the data points are to be picked and the embedding dimension specifies the size of the sliding window. These parameters are essential for building robust prediction systems that have been the focus of recent work where a quantum-inspired hybrid method was used for financial time series [6]. A multi-objective cooperative coevolution method was also introduced using time-lag as a parameter for reconstruction of the original data into different state space vector dataset as different objectives for financial prediction [8]. A similar approach was used in [9].

Competitive island cooperative coevolution algorithm (CICC) was introduced for training recurrent neural networks for time series prediction [10]. The method used different problem decomposition methods as islands and ensured that their features are used during evolution. It was later applied for global optimization problems [11].

Previous work focused on employing competitive methods that feature problem decomposition methods in neural networks. There has not been much work done that exploited the different parameters used for reconstructed state space vectors the original time series.

This paper presents a cooperative neuro-evolution method that enforces competition and collaboration using two different reconstructed feature vectors generated from a single time series. The method is called *co-evolutionary feature selection and reconstruction* which employs feedforward neural networks for time series prediction. Taken's theorem for state-space feature reconstruction.

The remainder of this paper is organized as follows. In Sect. 2, the proposed method is introduced. In Sect. 3, experiments, results and discussion are highlighted. Section 4 concludes the paper with plans for future work.

2   Co-evolutionary Feature Selection and Reconstruction

This section provides details of co-evolutionary feature selection and reconstruction (CSFR) for training feedforward network for time series prediction.

CSFR follows the same principle as the competitive island cooperative coevolution for problem decomposition methods where the exchange of best individuals takes place between the islands after competition [10].

In the proposed method, an island is defined by different reconstructed state space vectors generated from a single time series along with sub-populations that evolve using cooperative coevolution.

The proposed method has two different islands that are created using neuron level decomposition as seen in Fig. 1. Each island is evaluated using feedfoward networks with a unique reconstructed dataset as seen in Fig. 2. The reconstructed dataset is generated using Taken's embedding theorem with the two conditions that are *time delay (T)* and *embedding dimension (D)* [7]. The embedding dimension is used to determine the number of input neurons in feedforward network. The embedding dimension is fixed while time delay is varied as shown in Fig. 3.

Details of the CSFR using feedforward network is given in Algorithm 1. Neuron level problem decomposition is used where the network is broken down into subcomponents that are based on hidden and output neurons [2].

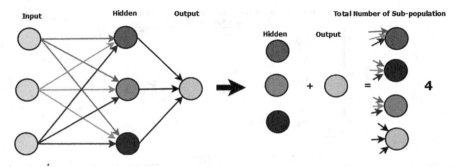

Fig. 1. Neuron level decomposition showing number of sub-components.

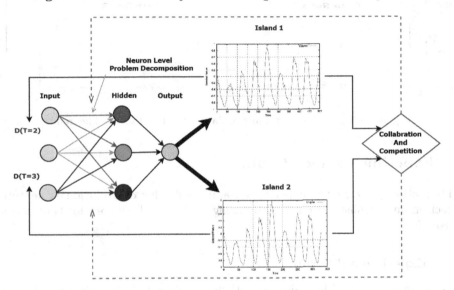

Fig. 2. The islands with different reconstructed datasets compete and collaborate with each other for Sunspot time series. Note that the same problem decomposition is used in both islands, hence the transfer of best solution is done without complications.

In Step 1, the sub-populations of both islands are initialized with random real values in a suitable range. In Step 2, the evolution of both the islands takes place where each network is evolved for a predefined time based on the number of fitness evaluations (FE) which is called *local island evolution time*. In Step 3, the competition takes place where the algorithm checks if the best solution of the particular island is better than the other island. In Step 4, the solution that is marked as best is copied to the other island which helps the other island evolve. The best solution from both the islands is used to test for generalization.

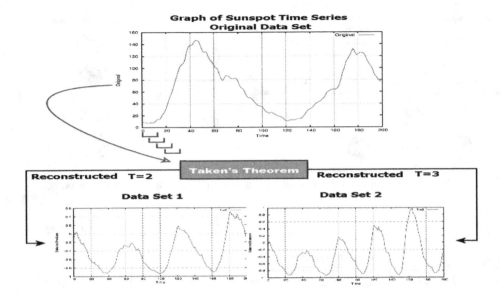

Fig. 3. Reconstruction of Sunspot data set using Taken's Theorem.

3   Experiments and Results

This section presents the experiments and results for co-evolutionary feature selection and reconstruction (CSFR) using feedforward network for time series prediction.

3.1   Experimental Setup

The proposed method is evaluated with four different chaotic time series data sets. They include the Mackey-Glass [12] and Lorenz time series [13] that are the two simulated time series. Sunspot [14] and ACI Worldwide Inc. [15] are the two real-world problems.

The data sets used is based on the same configuration as used in past work [4]. The Mackey-Glass and ACI Worldwide Inc. time series are scaled in the range of [0,1], whereas the Sunspot and Lorenz are scaled in the range of [-1,1]. Mackey-Glass and ACI Worldwide Inc., employs feedforward network with sigmoid units in the hidden and the output layer. Lorenz and Sunspot use the hyperbolic tangent unit in the output layer.

The neuron level (NL) decomposition method was used in each of the islands [2]. Standalone cooperative coevolution methods are used for comparison of the results with different time delays. The performance and results of the method were evaluated by using three different numbers of hidden neurons (3, 5 and 7), and compared with standalone methods. The maximum evolution time used is

50 000 for standalone methods. In the proposed method, both islands have 50 000 function evaluations, each similar to the approach used in [10].

The generalized generation gap algorithm with parent-centric crossover (G3-PCX) evolutionary algorithm is used to evolve the sub-populations [16]. *Depth of search* for each sub-population is 1 with pool size of 2 parents and 2 offspring [4]. We have used the population size of 300 from the literature [10]. The root mean squared error (RMSE) and normalized mean squared error (NMSE) are used to measure the performance of the network as given in Eqs. 1 and 2.

$$RMSE = \sqrt{\frac{1}{N} \sum_{i=1}^{N} (y_i - \hat{y}_i)^2} \tag{1}$$

$$NMSE = \left(\frac{\sum_{i=1}^{N}(y_i - \hat{y}_i)^2}{\sum_{i=1}^{N}(y_i - \bar{y}_i)^2} \right) \tag{2}$$

Algorithm 1. CSFR for Feedforward Networks

Step 1: Create Island-One and Island-Two with Sub-populations based on neuron level problem decomposition:
i. Cooperatively Evaluate Island-One FNN using Reconstructed Dataset-One
ii. Cooperatively Evaluate Island-Two FNN using Reconstructed Dataset-Two
Step 2: Evolution:
while *Total-FE ≤ Max-FE* **do**
   while *Local-FE ≤ Island-Evolution-Time* **do**
      foreach *Sub-population at Island-One* **do**
         foreach *Depth of n Generations* **do**
            Create new individuals using genetic operators
            Cooperative Evaluation
         end
      end
   end
   while *Local-FE ≤ Island-Evolution-Time* **do**
      foreach *Sub-population at Island-Two* **do**
         foreach *Depth of n Generations* **do**
            Create new individuals using genetic operators
            Cooperative Evaluation
         end
      end
   end
   Step 3: Competition: Compare the best solutions from both islands
   Step 4: Collaboration: Exchange the best fitness individuals from the winning island into the other island. Evaluate the other island.
end

---

where y_i, is observed data, $\hat{y}_i$ is predicted data and $\bar{y}_i$ is average of observed data and N is the length of the observed data. These two performance measures are used in order to compare the results with the literature.

3.2 Results

Tables 1, 2, 3 and 4 report the results for different number of hidden neurons using co-evolutionary feature selection and reconstruction feedforward neural network (CSFR-FNN) with time lags (T=2, T=3). The two different time lags are also used for standalone methods which are cooperative coevolutionary feedforward neural networks (CCFNN) that use different time delays (T=2 and T=3), but with same dimension (D).

The results report RMSE and 95 percent confidence interval from different numbers of hidden neurons, where each case executed 50 independent experimental runs. Note that the best results are those with the least value of RMSE for each case.

In Table 1, in the Mackey-Glass problem, it was observed that CSFR was able to beat both standalone methods (T=2, T=3), and the best result was given by 5 hidden neurons. The overall performance in terms of generalization increased as the number of hidden neurons increased.

Table 1. The prediction training and generalisation performance (RMSE) of standalone and CSFR on the Mackey-Glass time series

Prob.	H	Training	Generalisation	Best
CCFNN(T=2)	3	0.0107 ± 0.00131	0.0107 ± 0.00131	0.0050
	5	0.0089 ± 0.00097	0.0088 ± 0.00097	0.0038
	7	0.0078 ± 0.00079	0.0078 ± 0.00079	0.0040
CCFNN(T=3)	3	0.0112 ± 0.00149	0.0112 ± 0.00149	0.0039
	5	0.0081 ± 0.00063	0.0080 ± 0.00063	0.0041
	7	0.0080 ± 0.00070	0.0078 ± 0.00070	0.0047
CSFR-FNN	3	0.0090 ± 0.00109	0.00090 ± 0.001103	0.0041
(T=2,T=3)	5	0.0065 ± 0.00068	0.0065 ± 0.00069	0.0029
	7	0.0072 ± 0.00086	0.0072 ± 0.00086	0.0041

In Table 2, Lorenz problem shows that the CSFR has been able to outperform both the standalone methods. The best result was seen in the case of 3 hidden neurons for CSFR and standalone methods.

In Table 3, the Sunspot problem shows that CSFR method has not been able to outperform the one of the standalone methods (T=3). Five hidden neurons have given good results for CSFR methods.

In Table 4, the ACI Worldwide Inc. problem shows that the CSFR method gives competitive results when compared to the standalone methods (T=2,

Table 2. The prediction training and generalisation performance (RMSE) of Stand-alone and CSFR on the Lorenz time series

Prob.	H	Training	Generalisation	Best
CCFNN(T=2)	3	0.0170 ± 0.0031	0.0176 ± 0.0031	0.0043
	5	0.0249 ± 0.0062	0.0271 ± 0.0067	0.0021
	7	0.0379 ± 0.0093	0.0416 ± 0.0092	0.0024
CCFNN(T=3)	3	0.0165 ± 0.0028	0.0167 ± 0.0028	0.0030
	5	0.0278 ± 0.00830	0.0292 ± 0.00829	0.0022
	7	0.0419 ± 0.00982	0.0425 ± 0.0104	0.0031
CSFR-FNN	3	0.0159 ± 0.0037	0.0163 ± 0.0040	0.0027
(T=2,T=3)	5	0.0149 ± 0.0033	0.0162 ± 0.0039	0.0023
	7	0.0293 ± 0.0079	0.0321 ± 0.0083	0.0035

Table 3. The prediction training and generalisation performance (RMSE) of stand-alone and CSFR on the Sunspot time series

Prob.	H	Training	Generalisation	Best
CCFNN(T=2)	3	0.0207 ± 0.0035	0.0538 ± 0.0091	0.015
	5	0.0289 ± 0.0039	0.0645 ± 0.0093	0.017
	7	0.0353 ± 0.0048	0.0676 ± 0.0086	0.021
CCFNN(T=3)	3	0.0189 ± 0.0145	0.0538 ± 0.0108	0.016
	5	0.0291 ± 0.0143	0.0690 ± 0.0091	0.017
	7	0.0302 ± 0.0174	0.0849 ± 0.00859	0.015
CSFR-FNN	3	0.0211 ± 0.00034	0.0180 ± 0.00072	0.015
(T=2,T=3)	5	0.0205 ± 0.00044	0.0187 ± 0.0036	0.014
	7	0.0209 ± 0.00035	0.0181 ± 0.00077	0.015

Table 4. The prediction training and generalisation performance (RMSE) of stand-alone and CSFR on the ACI Worldwide Inc. time series

Prob.	H	Training	Generalisation	Best
CCFNN(T=2)	3	0.0246 ± 0.00348	0.0247 ± 0.00348	0.015
	5	0.0231 ± 0.00588	0.0284 ± 0.00570	0.016
	7	0.0204 ± 0.00159	0.0194 ± 0.00157	0.015
CCFNN(T=3)	3	0.0204 ± 0.0014	0.0170 ± 0.00110	0.014
	5	0.0202 ± 0.00116	0.0164 ± 0.00046	0.014
	7	0.0202 ± 0.00383	0.0199 ± 0.00383	0.014
CSFR-FNN	3	0.0206 ± 0.00054	0.0187 ± 0.00131	0.015
(T=2,T=3)	5	0.0196 ± 0.00020	0.0166 ± 0.00058	0.013
	7	0.0194 ± 0.00023	0.0183 ± 0.00274	0.014

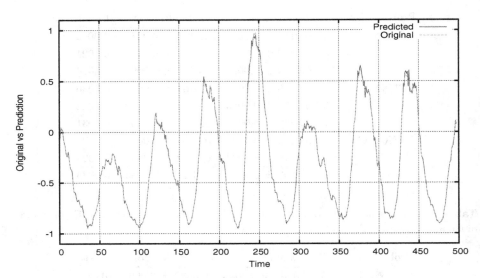

(a) Performance given by CSFR on the testing set for Sunspot.

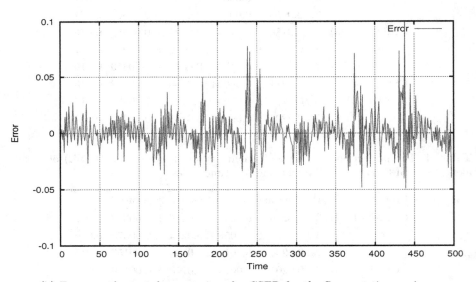

(b) Error on the test data set given by CSFR for the Sunspot time series.

Fig. 4. Typical prediction given by CSFR for Sunspot time series.

Table 5. A comparison with the results from literature for all data sets

Problem	Prediction method	RMSE	NMSE
Mackey	Radial basis network (RBF-OLS)(2006) [5]	1.02E-03	
	Locally linear neuro-fuzzy model (LLNF-LoLiMot) (2006) [5]	9.61E-04	
	Neuro-fuzzy system with time delay coordinates (2008) [17]		1.26E-03
	Neural fuzzy network (PS0) (2009) [18]	2.10E-02	
	Neural fuzzy network (CPS0) (2009) [18]	1.76E-02	
	Neural fuzzy network and DE (2009) [18]	1.62E-02	
	Neural fuzzy network and GA (2009) [18]	1.63E-02	
	Synapse Level-CCRNN (SL-CCRNN) (2012) [4]	6.33E-03	2.79E-04
	Neuron Level-CCRNN (NL-CCRNN) (2012) [4]	8.28E-03	4.77E-04
	Competitive Island Cooperative Coevolution (CICC-RNN) (2014) [10]	3.99E-03	1.11E-04
	MOCCFNN with 2-objectives (T=2)(MO-CCFNN-T=2) (2014) [8]	3.84E-03	2.80E-05
	MOCCFNN with 2-objectives (T=3)(MO-CCFNN-T=3) (2014) [8]	3.77E-03	2.70E-05
	Proposed CCFNN-CSFR	2.90E-03	1.60E-06
Lorenz	Radial basis network (RBF-OLS)(2006) [5]		1.41E-09
	Locally linear neuro-fuzzy model (LLNF-LoLiMot) (2006) [5]		9.80E-10
	Auto regressive moving average (ARMA-ANN)(2008) [19]	8.76E-02	
	Backpropagation neural network and GA (2011) [20]	2.96E-02	
	Synapse Level-CCRNN (SL-CCRNN) (2012) [4]	6.36E-03	7.72E-04
	Neuron Level-CCRNN (NL-CCRNN) (2012) [4]	8.20E-03	1.28E-03
	Competitive Island Cooperative Coevolution (CICC-RNN) (2014) [10]	3.55E-03	2.41E-04
	MOCCFNN with 2-objectives (T=2)(MO-CCFNN-T=2) (2014) [8]	2.19E-03	2.53E-05
	MOCCFNN with 2-objectives (T=3)(MO-CCFNN-T=3) (2014) [8]	2.18E-03	2.54E-05
	Proposed CCFNN-CSFR	2.32E-03	2.85E-05
Sunspot	Radial basis network (RBF-OLS)(2006) [5]		4.60E-02
	Locally linear neuro-fuzzy model (LLNF-LoLiMot) (2006) [5]		3.20E-02
	Synapse Level-CCRNN (SL-CCRNN) (2012) [4]	1.66E-02	1.47E-03
	Neuron Level-CCRNN (NL-CCRNN) (2012) [4]	2.60E-02	3.62E-03

(Continued)

Table 5. *(Continued)*

Problem	Prediction method	RMSE	NMSE
	Competitive Island Cooperative Coevolution (CICC-RNN) (2014) [10]	1.57E-02	1.31E-03
	MOCCFNN with 2-objectives (T=2)(MO-CCFNN-T=2) (2014) [8]	1.84E-02	1.02E-03
	MOCCFNN with 2-objectives (T=3)(MO-CCFNN-T=3) (2014) [8]	1.81E-02	9.98E-04
	Proposed CCFNN-CSFR	1.58E-02	7.56E-04
ACI	Competitive Island Cooperative Coevolution (CICC-RNN) (2014) [10]	1.92E-02	
	MOCCFNN with 2-objectives (T=2)(MO-CCFNN-T=2) (2014) [8]	1.94E-02	
	MOCCFNN with 2-objectives (T=3)(MO-CCFNN-T=3) (2014) [8]	1.47E-02	
	Proposed CCFNN-CSFR	1.34E-02	9.95E-04

T=3). The five hidden neurons have given best result of CSFR method. It has also been observed that the generalization performance of the CSFR and the other two methods does not deteriorate as the number of the hidden neuron increases as it does for other problems.

Figures 4 and 5 show typical prediction given by the proposed method. It shows that CSFR has been able to give a good prediction performance. CSFR has been able to cope with the noise in the Sunspot time series given in Fig. 4 and ACI time series given in Fig. 5.

The Table 5 compares the best results of CSFR given in Tables 1, 2, 3 and 4 with some of the closely related methods from the literature. The best results are used for the comparison. CSFR has given better performance when compared to the majority of the methods in the literature. However, there are specific cases that need further improvement.

In Table 5, for Mackey-Glass, the proposed method outperformed all the methods except for locally linear neuro-fuzzy model (LLNF) and radial basis network (RBF). Due to competition and collaboration, CSFR has outperformed them.

In Table 5, for problem Lorenz, it shows the best result on Lorenz time series problem that is compared with some of the related methods from the literature. CFSR outperformed all the methods for Lorenz, except for multi-objective cooperative coevolution (MO-CCFNN), radial basis network (RBF) and locally linear neuro-fuzzy model (LLNF).

In Sunspot problem, the performance of the proposed method on the Sunspot time series problem is compared to the methods in the literature. CFSR outperformed all the methods except for CICC-RNN.

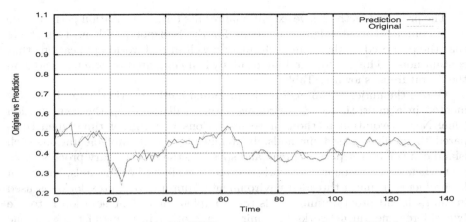

(a) Performance given by CSFR on the testing set for ACI Worldwide.

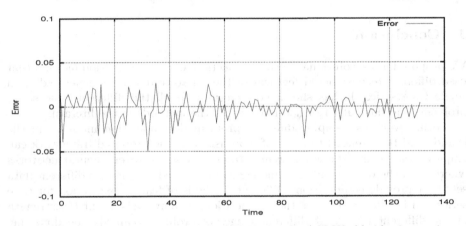

(b) Error on the test data set given by CSFR for the ACI Worldwide time series.

Fig. 5. Typical prediction given by CSFR for ACI Worldwide time series.

In ACI Worldwide Inc. problem, CFSR was able to outperform all the methods in the literature. This shows that the proposed method can handle the noise and the regions which are very chaotic in dataset as it is real world application problem.

3.3 Discussion

The main strength of the proposed method allows to explore and learn from the regions within the data set which are missed given that it is difficult to find the optimal value for the time delay parameter. CFSR was able to perform better due to information sharing during evolution via the neural network weights from two diverse features extracted datasets implemented as islands.

The proposed method gave exceptional results for generalization performance when compared to standalone methods for the Sunspot problem. This shows that the proposed method can perform very well in real world applications that contain noise. This is also the best results when compared to other methods in the literature as shown in Table 5.

One of the major advantages of the proposed method is that it can be implemented in a multi-threaded environment that will speed up the computation time. Neuro-evolution methods have limitations in terms of time when compared to gradient based methods. In a multi-threaded implementation, each island can run on a separate thread and speed up the evolutionary process. Note that when only one neural network is used to evaluate both islands, there can be problems in multi-threaded environment. Appropriate mutex locks as used in multi-thread programming needs to be implemented. One solution is to use two different neural networks that mirror each other in terms of topology one for each island.

4 Conclusion

We proposed a co-evolutionary feature selection and reconstruction method that used different reconstructed features of the separate data sets generated from single time series. It has shown good results on all the different time series problems and has outperformed majority of the methods in the literature.

Future work can employ different problem decomposition methods in the islands and be extended to three of more islands. The proposed framework can employ other neural network architectures such as recurrent neural networks where both the dimension and time lag can be varied to generate different data sets that provide competition. Different methods of feature extraction for time series can be used to enforce the competition. The analysis about the strength of the different islands at different stages of evolution can also be done, i.e. to check which island wins the competition in different time series problems. The proposed approach can also be extended for pattern classification problems where feature selection has been extensively studied.

References

1. Potter, M., De Jong, K.: A cooperative coevolutionary approach to function optimization. In: Davidor, Y., Männer, R., Schwefel, H.-P. (eds.) PPSN 1994. LNCS, vol. 866, pp. 249–257. Springer, Heidelberg (1994)
2. Chandra, R., Frean, M., Zhang, M.: On the issue of separability for problem decomposition in cooperative neuro-evolution. Neurocomputing **87**, 33–40 (2012)
3. Stephen, H.K.: In the Wake of Chaos: Unpredictable Order in Dynamical Systems. University of Chicago Press, Chicago (1993)
4. Chandra, R., Zhang, M.: Cooperative coevolution of Elman recurrent neural networks for chaotic time series prediction. Neurocomputing **186**, 116–123 (2012)

5. Gholipour, A., Araabi, B.N., Lucas, C.: Predicting chaotic time series using neural and neurofuzzy models: a comparative study. Neural Process. Lett. **24**, 217–239 (2006)
6. de A Araujo, R., de Oliveira, A., Soares, S.: A quantum-inspired hybrid methodology for financial time series prediction. In: The 2010 International Joint Conference on Neural Networks (IJCNN), Barcelona, Spain, pp. 1–8, July 2010
7. Takens, F.: Detecting strange attractors in turbulence. In: Rand, V., Young, L.-S. (eds.) Dynamical Systems and Turbulence, Warwick 1980. Lecture Notes in Mathematics, vol. 898, pp. 366–381. Springer, Berlin (1981)
8. Chand, S., Chandra, R.: Multi-objective cooperative coevolution of neural networks for time series prediction. In: International Joint Conference on Neural Networks (IJCNN), Beijing, China, pp. 190–197, July 2014
9. Smith, C., Jin, Y.: Evolutionary multi-objective generation of recurrent neural network ensembles for time series prediction. Neurocomputing **143**, 302–311 (2014)
10. Chandra, R.: Competition and collaboration in cooperative coevolution of Elman recurrent neural networks for time-series prediction. IEEE Trans. Neural Netw. Learn. Syst. (2015, in Press)
11. Chandra, R., Bali, K.: Competitive two island cooperative coevolution for real parameter global optimization. In: IEEE Congress on Evolutionary Computation, Sendai, Japan, May 2015 (in Press)
12. Mackey, M., Glass, L.: Oscillation and chaos in physiological control systems. Science **197**(4300), 287–289 (1977)
13. Lorenz, E.: The Essence of Chaos. University of Washington Press, Seattle (1993)
14. SILSO World Data Center: The International Sunspot Number (1834–2001), International Sunspot Number Monthly Bulletin and Online Catalogue. In: Royal Observatory of Belgium, Avenue Circulaire 3, 1180 Brussels, Belgium. http://www.sidc.be/silso/. Accessed 02 February 2015
15. NASDAQ Exchange Daily: 1970–2010 Open, Close, High, Low and Volume. http://www.nasdaq.com/symbol/aciw/stock-chart. Accessed 02 February 2015
16. Deb, K., Anand, A., Joshi, D.: A computationally efficient evolutionary algorithm for real-parameter optimization. Evol. Comput. **10**(4), 371–395 (2002)
17. Zhang, J., Chung, H.S.-H., Lo, W.-L.: Chaotic time series prediction using a neurofuzzy system with time-delay coordinates. IEEE Trans. Knowl. Data Eng. **20**(7), 956–964 (2008)
18. Lin, C.-J., Chen, C.-H., Lin, C.-T.: A hybrid of cooperative particle swarm optimization and cultural algorithm for neural fuzzy networks and its prediction applications. IEEE Trans. Syst. Man Cybern. Part C Appl. Rev. **39**(1), 55–68 (2009)
19. Rojas, I., Valenzuela, O., Rojas, F., Guillen, A., Herrera, L., Pomares, H., Marquez, L., Pasadas, M.: Soft-computing techniques and arma model for time series prediction. Neurocomputing **71**(4–6), 519–537 (2008)
20. Ardalani-Farsa, M., Zolfaghari, S.: Residual analysis and combination of embedding theorem and artificial intelligence in chaotic time series forecasting. Appl. Artif. Intell. **25**, 45–73 (2011)

A Subset Similarity Guided Method for Multi-objective Feature Selection

Hoai Bach Nguyen, Bing Xue[(⊠)], and Mengjie Zhang

School of Engineering and Computer Science, Victoria University of Wellington,
PO Box 600, Wellington 6140, New Zealand
Bing.Xue@ecs.vuw.ac.nz

Abstract. This paper presents a particle swarm optimisation (PSO) based multi-objective feature selection method for evolving a set of non-dominated feature subsets and achieving high classification performance. Firstly, a multi-objective PSO (named MOPSO-SRD) algorithm, is applied to solve feature selection problems. The results of this algorithm are then used to compare with the proposed multi-objective PSO algorithm, called MOPSO-SiD. MOPSO-SiD is specifically designed for feature selection problems, in which a subset similarity distance measure (distance in the solution space) is used to select a leader for each particle in the swarm. This distance measure is also used to update the archive set, which will be the final solutions returned by the MOPSO-SiD algorithm. The results show that both algorithms successfully evolve a set of non-dominated solutions, which include a small number of features while achieving similar or better performance than using all features. In addition, in most case MOPSO-SiD selects smaller feature subsets than MOPSO-SRD, and outperforms single objective PSO for feature selection and a traditional feature selection method.

Keywords: Feature selection · Classification · Multi-objective optimisation · Particle swarm optimisation

1 Introduction

Classification is one of the most important tasks in machine learning, which aims to predict the class label of an instance based on the value of instance's features. In the learning process, a set of instances, called the training set, is used to train a classification algorithm, which is tested on an unseen test set. In many problems, a large number of features is used to describe the instances well. Unfortunately, due to "the curse of dimensionality", the larger the feature set is, the longer time the training process takes. In addition, relevant features are often unknown without prior knowledge. Therefore, a large number of features often contain irrelevant or redundant features, which are not useful for classification. Those features might lower the quality of the whole feature set [4], because they usually conceal the useful information from the relevant features. Feature

© Springer International Publishing Switzerland 2016
T. Ray et al. (Eds.): ACALCI 2016, LNAI 9592, pp. 298–310, 2016.
DOI: 10.1007/978-3-319-28270-1_25

selection methods [4,9] are used to remove those redundant and irrelevant features, which will not only speed up the learning/classification process but also maintain or even increase the classification performance over using all features. However, due to the complex interaction between features and the huge search space, it is hard to develop a good feature selection approach.

In feature selection, suppose there are n features in a dataset, then the total number of possible subsets is 2^n, which is a large search space. Exhaustive search is too slow to perform in most situations. In order to reduce the searching time, some greedy algorithms such as sequential forward selection [16] and sequential backward selection [11] have been developed. However, these methods easily get stuck into local optima. Because of their global search ability, evolutionary computation (EC) techniques, such as genetic programming (GP) [12], genetic algorithm (GAs) [8] and particle swarm optimisation (PSO) [14,17,18], have been applied to solve feature selection problems. Compared with GAs and GP, PSO is more preferable because it is simple and easy to implement. In addition, PSO not only uses fewer parameters but also converges more quickly.

Feature selection can be viewed as a multi-objective problem because it needs to maximise the classification accuracy and simultaneously minimise the dimensionality of the selected subset. However, with fewer features being used for classification, the classification accuracy is likely to decrease. Those two objectives often conflict with each other and the searching process needs to consider the trade-off between them. EC techniques are particularly suitable for multi-objective optimisation since their population based mechanism can produce multiple trade-off solutions in a single run. However, directly using existing multi-objective approaches to feature selection problems may not achieve promising performance since feature selection has a very complex search space, which requires a specifically designed multi-objective algorithm to solve the problem.

Goals: The overall goal of this study is to develop a PSO based multi-objective feature selection approach, which can produce a set of non-dominated solutions that include a small number of features and achieve better classification performance than using all features. To achieve this goal, we firstly directly apply a very recently developed multi-objective PSO (MOPSO), called MOPSO-SRD [7] to solve feature selection problems. After that, we develop a new MOPSO algorithm, called MOPSO-SiD, which is specifically designed for feature selection problems. This algorithm will then be compared with MOPSO-SRD. Specifically, we will investigate

- whether the two multi-objective PSO algorithms can be applied to evolve a set of non-dominated solutions with a small number of features and better classification performance than using all features and single objective feature selection methods;
- whether MOPSO-SiD, as an MOPSO algorithm specifically designed for feature selection problems, can produce better *Pareto front* than MOPSO-SRD.

2   Background

2.1   Particle Swarm Optimisation (PSO)

Particle Swarm Optimisation (PSO) [5] is inspired by social behaviours such as bird flocking and fish schooling. In PSO, a problem is optimized by using a population (called swarm) of candidate solutions (called particles). To find the optimal solution, each particle moves around the search space by updating its position as well as velocity. Particularly, the current position of particle i is represented by a vector $x_i = (x_{i1}, x_{i2}, \ldots, x_{iD})$, where D is the dimensionality of the search space. These positions are updated by using another vector, called velocity $v_i = (v_{i1}, v_{i2}, \ldots, v_{iD})$, which is limited by a predefined maximum velocity, v_{max} and $v_{id} \in [-v_{max}, v_{max}]$. During the search process, each particle maintains a record of the position of its previous best performance, called *pbest*. The best position of its neighbours is also recorded, which is called *gbest*. The position and velocity of each particle are updated according to the following equations:

$$v_{id}^{t+1} = w * v_{id}^t + c_1 * r_{i1} * (p_{id} - x_{id}^t) + c_2 * r_{i2} * (p_{gd} - x_{id}^t) \tag{1}$$

$$x_{id}^{t+1} = x_{id}^t + v_{id}^{t+1} \tag{2}$$

where t denotes the tth iteration in the search process, d is the dth dimension in the search space, i is the index of particle, w is inertia weight, c_1 and c_2 are acceleration constants, r_{i1} and r_{i2} are random values uniformly distributed in [0,1], p_{id} and p_{gd} represent the position entry of *pbest* and *gbest* in the dth dimension, respectively.

2.2   Related Work on Feature Selection

Traditional Feature Selection Methods. Sequential search techniques are also applied to solve feature selection problems. In particular, sequential forward selection (SFS) [16] and sequential backward selection (SBS) [11] are proposed. At each step of the selection process, SFS (or SBS) adds (or removes) a feature from an empty (full) feature set. Although these local search techniques achieve better performance than the feature ranking method, they might suffer "nesting" problem, in which once a feature is added (or removed) from the feature set, it cannot be removed (or added) later.

EC Approaches to Feature Selection. EC techniques have recently been used to solve feature selection problems due to their powerful global search abilities, such as GAs [8], GP [12], and PSO [6,14,20]. Muni et al. [12] developed a wrapper feature selection model based on multi-tree GP, which simultaneously selected a good feature subset and learned a classifier using the selected features. Two new crossover operations were introduced to increase the performance of GP for feature selection. Based on the two crossover operations introduced by Muni et al. [12], Purohit et al. [13] further introduced another crossover operator, which was randomly performed for selecting a subtree from the first parent and finding its best place in the second parent. Lin et al. [8] proposed a GA-based feature selection algorithm adopting domain knowledge of financial distress prediction, where features were classified into different groups and a GA was used to search for subsets consisting of top candidate features from each group.

To avoid premature convergence in PSO, Chuang et al. [2] proposed a new *gbest* updating mechanism, which resets *gbest* elements to zero if it maintains the same value after several iterations. However, the performance of this algorithm is not compared with other PSO based algorithms. Tran et al. [14] used the *gbest* resetting mechanism in [3] to reduce the number of features and performed a local search process on *pbest* to increase the classification performance of PSO for feature selection. The proposed algorithm further reduced the number of features and improved the classification performance over [3] and standard PSO. PSO with multiple swarms to share experience has also been applied to feature selection [10], but may lead to the problem of high computational cost.

Two multi-objective PSO algorithms were used to solve feature selection problems [19]. The first algorithm applied the idea of non-dominated sorting based multi-objective genetic algorithm II (NSGAII) into PSO for feature selection. The other algorithm bases on the idea of crowding, mutation and dominance to evolve the Pareto front solutions. According to the experimental results, both algorithms can select a small number of features while achieving better classification performance than using all features. However, the above algorithms did not propose any specific design for feature selection problems. Therefore, this work will propose a new multi-objective PSO algorithm, which is specifically designed for feature selection problems.

3 Proposed Approach

PSO was originally proposed to deal with single objective problems, therefore some multi-objective PSO approaches (MOPSO) are proposed to solve multi-objective problems. In MOPSO algorithms, instead of recording *gbest* for each particle, an archive set is used to maintain a set of non-dominated solutions being discovered so far. Most of the existing MOPSO algorithms are different in terms of the way to control this archive set as well as how to select a good leader (*gbest*) for the swarm among the archive set.

Although there are many works which apply MOPSO to solve feature selection problems, most of them do not consider the properties of feature selection problems. For example, in most MOPSO approaches, if two particles have exactly same objective values, one of the particle will not be added into the archive set. However, two particles might select the same number of features and achieve the same classification accuracy, but the selected features might be different. In feature selection problems, beside the two main objectives, which features being selected is also important. Therefore, in this study we propose a new algorithm called MOPSO using the subset Similarity Distance (MOPSO-SiD), where the two main contributions are a new leader selection and a new control mechanism for the archive set.

Algorithm 1. Pseudo-code of MOPSO-SiD

1: **begin**
2: initialize the swarm and Archive A = {};
3: **while** *Maximum iterations* is not reached **do**
4:    **for** each particle i in the swarm **do**
5:        update the *pbest* of particle i;
6:        select the archive member with the shortest SiD as its *gbest*;
7:        update the velocity and the position of particle i;
8:        mutation;
9:        evaluate particles;
10:        **if** the ith particle is not dominated by any archive members **then**
11:            insert $i^{th} particle into A$;
12:        **end if**
13:    **end for**
14:    **if** A is full **then**
15:        compute SiD between all pairs of archive members;
16:        select a pair with the shortest SiD;
17:        remove the archive member (among the selected pair) with lower accuracy;
18:    **end if**
19: **end while**
20: calculate the testing classification error rate of the solutions in A (archive set);
21: return the position of particles in A;
22: return the training and test classification error rates of the solutions in A; **end**

3.1 The MOPSO-SiD Agorithm

Algorithm 1 shows the pseudo-code of MOPSO-SiD. In MOPSO-SiD, the similarity distance (SiD) and the continuous multi-objective PSO are applied to search for the non-dominated solutions. The representation of each particle is a vector of n real numbers, where n is the total number of features. Each position entry $x_i \in [0,1]$ corresponds to the ith feature in the original feature set. A threshold θ is used to decide whether or not a feature is selected. In particular, the ith feature is selected if and only if $\theta < x_i$. The two objective is to minimise the number of features and the classification performance.

3.2 Leader Selection

The main difference between PSO and MOPSO is how each particle selects its *gbest*. In PSO, each particle records its own *gbest*, which is the best position being discover by it and its neighbours. However in MOPSO, each particle will select its *gbest* from an archive set, which contains all non-dominated solutions being discovered so far. In MOPSO-SiD, for each generation, each particle freely selects its own leader by using the subset similarity distance calculation. Given two particles p_1 and p_2, the similarity distance (SiD) between two particles (i.e. two feature subsets) is calculated according to the Eq. 3.

$$SiD(p_1, p_2) = \sum_{i=1}^{n} \sqrt{(x_{1i} - x_{2i})^2} \tag{3}$$

where n is the total number of features (i.e. length of each position vector), x_{1i}, x_{2i} are the ith position entries of two particles p_1, p_2 respectively.

In each generation, for each particle in the swarm, the similarity distance (SiD) between the particle and all archive members is calculated. After that, the archive member with the shortest SiD is chosen as the leader of that particle.

This distance measure (SiD) is especially good at the early iterations comparing with SRD in MOPSO-SRD. As mentioned above, MOPSO-SRD selects the leader based on the distance of objective values. In other word, MOPSO-SRD only considers the objective space. In MOPSO-SRD a particle might select an archive member, which is the closest to it in the objective space. However, in the solution space (search space), the selected archive member might be very far way from the particle if their selected features are different. Comparing with MOPSO-SRD, MOPSO-SiD provides more exploitation ability by selecting the closest archive member in terms of the position distance rather than the objective distance.

3.3   Archive Control

Controlling the archive set is also an important part of a MOPSO algorithm. The controlling mechanism aims to decide whether or not a solution is added to the archive set or which solution should be removed from the archive set when this set is full. In general, a solution S is added to the archive set if it is not dominated by any archive members. This rule is still applied in MOPSO-SiD. However, if there is at least one archive member, which has the same objective values as the solution S, whether or not S will be added into the archive set. In MOPSO-SRD, S will not be added to the archive set since it only consider the objective values. In feature selection problems, the situation can be different. Suppose that two particles might select the same number of features and achieve the same classification, their selected features can still be different. This mean that those particles might be at the same position in the objective space but they are on different position in the solution space (search space). This is considered by MOPSO-SiD. In particular, if there is an archive member, called A, which has the same objective values as S (solution to be added), MOPSO-SiD will further check the features being selected by both A and S. If the selected features of A and S are different, S will be added into the archive set, otherwise S will be discarded. Once more, MOPSO-SiD considers not only the objective space but also the solution space.

Beside adding solutions, removing solutions from the archive set is also important in an MOPSO algorithm. In general, each MOPSO approach has a measure to rank solutions within an archive set. For example, MOPSO-SRD ranks the archive members according to the square root distance (SRD). However, most measures only consider the objective space, which might not be sufficient in feature selection problems. Two particles which are close in the objective space (similar classification accuracy and number of selected features) might select very different features. Therefore instead of using the square root distance (SRD),

Table 1. Datasets.

Dataset	#features	#classes	#instances
Vehicle	18	4	946
WBCD	30	2	569
Ionosphere	34	2	351
Lung	56	4	32
Sonar	60	2	208
Movementlibras	90	15	360
Musk1	166	2	476
Arrhythmia	279	16	452

MOPOS-SiD uses the similarity between particles (i.e. feature subsets) in the solution space to rank all archive members.

In particular, when the archive set is full, the subset similarity distance between each pair of archive members is calculated according to the Eq. 3. After that, MOPSO-SiD will select a pair of archive members with the shortest similarity distance, which means that these members are the most similar pair in terms of feature being selected. Since in feature selection problems, the classification accuracy is preferable when the number of selected features is similar, MOPSO-SiD will remove the archive member with lower classification accuracy from the above selected pair of archive members. In general, MOPSO-SiD considers not only the objective values but also which features are selected by each particle, which are both important in feature selection problems.

4   Experimental Design

Eight datasets (shown in Table 1) chosen from the UCI machine learning repository [1] are used in the experiments. These datasets have different numbers of features, classes and instances. For each dataset, all instances are randomly divided into a training set and a test set, which contains 70 % and 30 % of the instances, respectively. In the experiments, the classification/learning algorithm is K-nearest neighbour (KNN) where K = 5.

In both MOPSO-SRD and MOPOS-SiD, the parameters are set as follows [15]: $w = 0.7298, c_1 = c_2 = 1.49618, v_{max} = 0.2$, population size is 30, and the maximum number of iterations is 100. The threshold used for feature selection is set to 0.6. For each dataset, each algorithm has been run 50 independent runs. After each run, a set of non-dominated solutions are obtained. A single objective PSO algorithm (SOPSO) for feature selection is also run 50 independent times on the above datasets. SOPSO produces a single feature subset from each independent run. In order to compare MOPSO-SRD and MOPSO-SiD with SOPSO, firstly all the 50 archive sets are combined together to create an union set. In this union set, the classification error rate of feature subsets, which share the same

Table 2. Results of SFS.

Dataset	#features	Train error(%)	Test error(%)
Vehicle	5	13.0	18.3
WBCD	1	5.5	11.1
Ionosphere	2	9.4	21.0
Lung	1	13.6	10.0
Sonar	5	19.4	27.0
Movementlibras	7	3.9	7.7
Musk1	1	22.8	27
Arrhythmia	3	5.4	7.0

number of features, are averaged. A set of average solutions is obtained by using the average classification error rate and the corresponding number of features. This average set is called the *average Pareto front*. In addition, for each dataset, all the non-dominated solutions are selected from the union set to create a set of *best* solutions, called *best set*.

5 Results and Discussions

Experimental results of the three PSO algorithms on the training and test sets are shown in Figs. 1 and 2, respectively. For each dataset, the total number of original features and the classification error rate when using all features for classification are shown in the brackets on top of the chart. In each chart, the horizontal axis shows the number of selected features and the vertical axis shows the classification error rate. In Fig. 1, "SRD-Train-Ave" ("SiD-Train-Ave") stands for the average Pareto front resulted from MOPSO-SRD (MOPSO-SiD) in the 50 independent runs. "SRD-Train-Best" ("SiD-Test-Best") represents the non-dominated solutions of all solutions resulted from MOPSO-SRD (MOPSO-SiD). The results of single objective PSO for feature selection is shown as SOPSO in the figure. Figure 2 shows the same information as in Fig. 1 but the classification error rates are calculated on the test set. The results of SFS as a benchmark feature selection algorithm are shown in Table 2.

5.1 MOPSO-SiD vs All Features

According to Fig. 2, in all datasets, "SRD-Test-Ave" and "SiD-Test-Ave" contain at least one solution, which selects no more than 30 % of the available features and achieves similar or better performance than using all features. In all datasets, both "SRD-Test-Best" and "SiD-Test-Best" contains one or more solution, which select around 8 % of the available features and achieves similar or better performance than using all features.

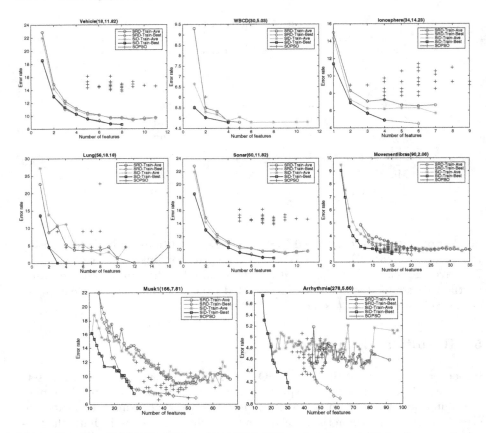

Fig. 1. Results of MOPSO-SRD and MOPSO-SiD on training set (Color figure online).

The results suggest that in all datasets, both MOPSO-SRD and MOPSO-SiD can evolve a set of features subsets with a small number of features and better classification performance than using all features.

5.2 MOPSO-SiD vs SOPSO and SFS

Comparing results from Figs. 1 and 2, and Table 2, on most datasets, both MOPSO-SRD and MOPSO-SiD can evolve at least one solution, which selects smaller number of features while achieving better classification accuracy than SFS. On Musk1 and Arrhythmia dataset, although SFS selects a smaller number of features than the multi-objective PSO approaches, its classification accuracy is even worse than the worst solution of both MOPSO algorithms. This is because MOPSO considers the interaction between features while SFS doe not.

Comparing with SOPSO for feature selection, on most of datasets, both MOPSO approaches can find better solutions than SOPSO. In particular, MOPSO approaches can evolve at least one solution that selects a smaller num-

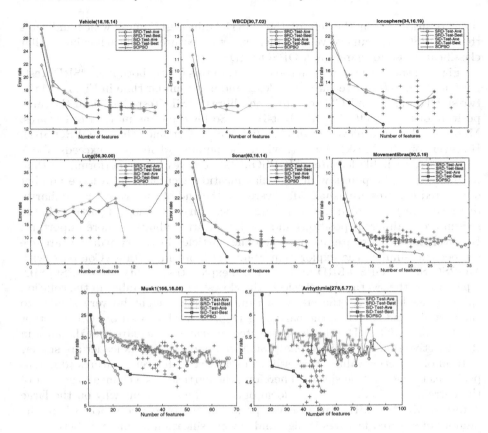

Fig. 2. Results of MOPSO-SRD and MOPSO-SiD on test set (Color figure online).

ber of features and achieves better performance than the best solution evolved by the SOPSO.

5.3 MOPSO-SiD vs MOPSO-SRD

Firstly, let consider the training results in Fig. 1, which show the searching ability of these two algorithms. As can be seen in Fig. 1, the patterns of both "SiD-Train-Ave" and "SRD-Train-Ave" are similar. However, "SiD-Train-Ave" oscillates more than "SRD-Train-Ave", which is due to the *gbest* selection mechanism. MOPSO-SRD concentrates more on the objective values to select *gbest*. Meanwhile, MOPSO-SiD selects *gbest* by mainly using the similarity in the feature search space. In addition, in all dataset, the "SiD-Train-Ave" line is mostly on the left of "SRD-Train-Ave" line, which means that MOPSO-SiD usually selects smaller numbers of features than MOPOS-SRD to achieve similar classification performance.

In terms of the best solutions, MOPSO-SiD outperforms MOPSO-SRD. As can be seen from Fig. 1, in all datasets, the "SiD-Train-Best" lines are at the same position or on the left of the "SRD-Train-Best" lines, which indicates that MOPSO-SiD can evolve a smaller subset of features while achieving similar classification performance as MOPSO-SRD.

Figure 2 shows the results on the test set. In this figure, both lines "SRD-Test-Ave" and "SiD-Test-Ave" are even closer and more similar than in Fig. 1. On the two small datasets (WBCD and Movementlibras), "SiD-Test-Best" is at the same position or on the left of "SRD-Test-Best". So for the same number of features, MOPSO-SiD can achieve better classification performance than MOPSO-SRD. However, on the Musk1 dataset, when the number of features exceeds about 13 % of the available features, MOPSO-SRD achieves better performance than MOPSO-SiD. The points with high classification accuracy and a large number of selected features are usually discovered at the end of each run. The similarity distance is very helpful at the beginning of each run, when most of particles in the swarm are at different positions and the exploitation ability is more important. However, in the later iterations, when the particles in the swarm and archive set become similar, the exploration ability is more important. Compare with MOPSO-SiD, MOPSO-SRD provides more exploration ability. In MOPSO-SiD, a particle in the swarm always selects the closest archive member in the solution space as its leader. At the end of a run, the leader might be very similar to the particle, and therefore the particle is trapped at that position. On the other hand, in MOPSO-SRD, a leader is selected by using the square root distance in the objective space. In this case, although the particle and its leader are similar in term of objective values, they still can select very different features (different positions in the solution space). Therefore, the particle has a chance to get out of the current position (probably a local optima). This explains why on the large datasets, MOPSO-SRD can discover points in the objective space, where the number of selected features is high and the classification accuracy is better.

6   Conclusion and Future Work

The goal of this study was to develop a PSO based multi-objective feature selection approach to evolving a set of non-dominated feature subsets and achieving high classification performance. To achieve this goal, a similarity distance measure to evaluate the similarity between solutions (i.e. feature subsets) is proposed to update the archive in multi-objective PSO and choose *gbest* for each particle in the swarm, based on which a multi-objective feature selection algorithm called MOPSO-SiD is proposed. The performance of MOPSO-SiD is examined and compared with a recently developed multi-objective algorithm named MOPSO-SRD, a single objective PSO, and a traditional feature selection method on eight datasets of varying difficulty. The results show that both multi-objective algorithms successfully evolved a set of non-dominated solutions, which selected a small number of features while achieving similar or better performance than using all features. They outperformed the single objective PSO and the traditional method, especially in terms of the classification performance. Furthermore, in most cases, MOPSO-SiD selects smaller number of features than MOPSO-SRD but still achieves similar classification performance.

This work starts incorporating the characteristics of feature selection problems into the multi-objective search to find a better Pareto front, which shows some success. In the future, we will further improve the exploration and exploitation abilities of multi-objective PSO for feature selection by embedding some genetic operators or a local search during the search process. We also intend to develop novel approaches to feature selection tasks with thousands or even tens of thousands of features.

References

1. Bache, K., Lichman, M.: Uci machine learning repository (2013). http://archive.ics.uci.edu/ml
2. Chuang, L.Y., Chang, H.W., Tu, C.J., Yang, C.H.: Improved binary PSO for feature selection using gene expression data. Comput. Biol. Chem. $32(1)$, 29–38 (2008)
3. Chuang, L.Y., Chang, H.W., Tu, C.J., Yang, C.H.: Improved binary PSO for feature selection using gene expression data. Comput. Biol. Chem. $32(29)$, 29–38 (2008)
4. Guyon, I., Elisseeff, A.: An introduction to variable and feature selection. J. Mach. Learn. Res. 3, 1157–1182 (2003)
5. Kennedy, J., Eberhart, R., et al.: Particle swarm optimization. In: Proceedings of IEEE International Conference on Neural Networks, vol. 4, pp. 1942–1948 (1995)
6. Lane, M.C., Xue, B., Liu, I., Zhang, M.: Gaussian based particle swarm optimisation and statistical clustering for feature selection. In: Blum, C., Ochoa, G. (eds.) EvoCOP 2014. LNCS, vol. 8600, pp. 133–144. Springer, Heidelberg (2014)
7. Leung, M.F., Ng, S.C., Cheung, C.C., Lui, A.: A new strategy for finding good local guides in mopso. In: 2014 IEEE Congress on Evolutionary Computation (CEC), pp. 1990–1997, July 2014
8. Lin, F., Liang, D., Yeh, C.C., Huang, J.C.: Novel feature selection methods to financial distress prediction. Expert Syst. Appl. $41(5)$, 2472–2483 (2014)
9. Liu, H., Motoda, H., Setiono, R., Zhao, Z.: Feature selection: an ever evolving frontier in data mining. In: JMLR Proceedings on Feature Selection for Data Mining, vol. 10, pp. 4–13 (2010). JMLR.org
10. Liu, Y., Wang, G., Chen, H., Dong, H.: An improved particle swarm optimization for feature selection. J. Bionic Eng. $8(2)$, 191–200 (2011)
11. Marill, T., Green, D.M.: On the effectiveness of receptors in recognition systems. IEEE Trans. Inf. Theory $9(1)$, 11–17 (1963)
12. Muni, D., Pal, N., Das, J.: Genetic programming for simultaneous feature selection and classifier design. IEEE Trans. Syst. Man Cybern. Part B Cybern. $36(1)$, 106–117 (2006)
13. Purohit, A., Chaudhari, N., Tiwari, A.: Construction of classifier with feature selection based on genetic programming. In: IEEE Congress on Evolutionary Computation (CEC 2010), pp. 1–5 (2010)
14. Tran, B., Xue, B., Zhang, M.: Improved PSO for feature selection on high-dimensional datasets. In: Dick, G., et al. (eds.) SEAL 2014. LNCS, vol. 8886, pp. 503–515. Springer, Heidelberg (2014)
15. Van Den Bergh, F.: An analysis of particle swarm optimizers. Ph.D. thesis, University of Pretoria (2006)
16. Whitney, A.W.: A direct method of nonparametric measurement selection. IEEE Trans. Comput. $100(9)$, 1100–1103 (1971)

17. Xue, B., Zhang, M., Browne, W.N.: Single feature ranking and binary particle swarm optimisation based feature subset ranking for feature selection. In: Australasian Computer Science Conference (ACSC 2012), vol. 122, pp. 27–36 (2012)
18. Xue, B., Cervante, L., Shang, L., Browne, W.N., Zhang, M.: Binary PSO and rough set theory for feature selection: a multi-objective filter based approach. Int. J. Comput. Intell. Appl. **13**(02), 1450009:1–1450009:34 (2014)
19. Xue, B., Cervante, L., Shang, L., Browne, W.N., Zhang, M.: A multi-objective particle swarm optimisation for filter-based feature selection in classification problems. Connect. Sci. **24**(2–3), 91–116 (2012)
20. Xue, B., Zhang, M., Browne, W.N.: A comprehensive comparison on evolutionary feature selection approaches to classification. Int. J. Comput. Intell. Appl. **14**(02), 1550008 (2015)

Applications and Games

An Evolutionary Optimization Approach to Maximize Runway Throughput Capacity for Hub and Spoke Airports

Md Shohel Ahmed$^{(\boxtimes)}$ and Sameer Alam

University of New South Wales, Canberra, Australia
md.ahmed@student.adfa.edu.au, s.alam@adfa.edu.au

Abstract. The airports have emerged as a major bottleneck in the air transportation network. Thus during the busiest time, optimal utilization of the limited airport resources such as runways and taxiways can help to avoid the congestion and delay as well as increase the airport capacity. This problem is further aggravated by use of Hub-Spoke model by airlines which sees a burst of medium size aircraft arrival followed by few heavy aircraft departure. To address this problem, strategic as well as efficient tactical approaches are essential to deal with arrivals and departures. In this paper, we propose an evolutionary optimization approach to maximize the runway throughput capacity for integrated arrival and departure in a single runway scenario. An evolutionary computation based Genetic Algorithm (GA) is developed to optimize and integrate a stream of arriving and departing aircraft sequence for a given time window. The evolved optimal arrival and departure sequencing was analyzed using the Time-Space diagrams for different aircraft configuration. The distribution shows that in Hub airports heavy and large aircrafts are sequenced consecutively where in Spoke airports similar aircraft (i.e., medium (M)-medium (M), large (L)-large (L) and so on) are positioned side by side to reduce the process time. Simulation result also shows that proposed model obtained optimal sequence that takes lower processing time as well as achieves a higher throughput comparing to First Come First Serve (FCFS) approach commonly used for arriving and departing aircraft.

Keywords: Runway capacity · Genetic algorithm · Air traffic controller (ATC) · Optimal sequencing

1 Introduction

The continued growth in air traffic presents an increasing challenge to its operating environment for example, en-route and airports [1]. The growing traffic combined with the use of "hub and spoke" operations by air carriers cause many challenges such as increased congestion at airports and en-route flight delays [2].

In hub and spoke airport system, all traffic move along the spokes (smaller airports) connected to the hub (major airport) at the center. The congestion

© Springer International Publishing Switzerland 2016
T. Ray et al. (Eds.): ACALCI 2016, LNAI 9592, pp. 313–323, 2016.
DOI: 10.1007/978-3-319-28270-1_26

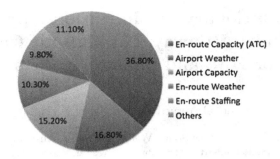

Fig. 1. Percentage of different flight delays in Europe in 2014 [3]

becomes so acute at the hub airport where air carriers schedule large numbers of flights to land and take-off within a short interval. The simultaneous arrivals and departures of several aircraft with different configurations (e.g. heavy, medium and light) can easily strain the capacity of the airport resources (runways, taxiways, gates and so on). As a result, flight delays have become routine occurrences in major hub airports. Figure 1 shows the statistics of different flight delays in Europe in 2014 [3] where airport delays have emerged as second largest cause of man-made delays. The hub-and-spoke network in intermodal transport has become one of the potential solutions to increase the intermodal market share. Such a network systems are widely used in the aviation industry due to its significant cost savings [4]. The advantages of hub-and-spoke networks are a higher frequency of transport services comparing to point-to-point networks.

To reduce the congestion and delay, it is imperative to increase the airport capacity to balance the resulting traffic load. The capacity of an airport depends on multiple factors such as the arrival-departure management, geometric layout of runway, number of runways, number of taxiways, number of gates, aprons, efficiency of the ATC and weather condition. The capacity maximization by utilizing multiple resources is a challenging task. The optimization of multiple resources make the runway capacity estimation a NP-hard problem [5].

In this paper, we propose an evolutionary optimization approach using Genetic Algorithm (GA) to integrate arrival and departure traffic sequence in a single runway configuration. The proposed model dynamically integrates (using a moving window) a set of different arriving and departing aircrafts and sequence them optimally that maximize the runway throughput capacity. The moving window size (set of arriving and departing aircraft in a given time interval) and time can be varied depending upon the communication, navigation and surveillance (CNS) system in use at a given airport. Better the CNS capability, ATC have better situation awareness of arriving and departing traffic.

In this work we also assume that for a given airport the demand for the runway is continuous (i.e. traffic is departing and arriving incessantly). For better insight into optimal arrival and departure sequencing, we further analyze the Time-Space diagrams of different aircraft configuration in hub and spoke airport.

Remainder of the paper is organized as follows: Sect. 2 describes background of the studies. Problem formulation is presented in Sect. 3. Section 4 describes the methodologies used. Experimentation is presented in Sect. 5. Section 6 presents the result analysis and discussion and finally Sect. 7 gives the conclusion of the paper.

2   Background

The airport runway capacity estimation is vital for airport operational planning and development. A number of deterministic and mathematical model have been proposed in the literature to estimate the capacity of the runway [6–9]. However such model fails to capture complex interaction of different aircraft in a mix mode (arrival and departure) operation. Further they are mode suitable for capacity estimation in a static configuration (given arrival distribution find runway capacity and likewise).

A ripple-spreading based GA (RSGA) is applied for aircraft sequencing problem (ASP) [10]. RSGA transforms the original landing-order-based ASP solutions into value-based ones. In the this scheme, arriving aircraft are projected as points into an artificial space. A very basic binary GA is then used to evolve these ripple-spreading parameters in order to find an optimal landing sequence. However, this studies only considers the optimal landing sequence of aircraft which is very simplified with respect to the complex mix operation in a single runway configurations.

Wenjing Zhao et al. [11] examine two widely used algorithms for Aircraft Landing Sequencing: First Come First Served (FCFS) and Constrained Position Shifting (CPS). They show that scenario representation affects the quality of evolutionary outputs such as variable-length chromosome representation of aircraft scheduling sequence scenarios converges fast and finds all relevant risk patterns.

The FAA-MITRE's Center for Advanced Aviation System Development (CAASD) is investigating techniques to provide computerized arrival spacing guidance. A case study on that is conducted by Diffenderfer et al. [12]. The spacing guidance communicates arrival intervals based on the order of departure traffic queued at or taxiing to the dependent runway. This approach gives the safety operations of aircrafts. However, it did not consider the optimal sequence for reducing flight-processing time.

NASA Ames has also developed the integration of trajectory-based arrival management automation controller tools and Flight-Deck Interval Management avionics to enable advanced arrival operations during periods of sustained high traffic demand [13]. However, the focus is more on human in the loop simulation and controller performance rather than dynamic capacity estimation in arrival and departure integration for a given runway operation.

The large search space (possibilities) resulting from complex interactions between aircraft type configuration (heavy, medium, light etc.), runway mode configuration (arrival or departure) and sequencing requirements (time and space between different aircraft types) with different airport configurations (hub and spoke) makes traditional search methods such as Monte Carlo Simulation unsuitable for this kind of optimization problems. Nature-Inspired techniques such as Evolutionary Computation (EC) [14] have emerged as an important tool to effectively address complex problems in the air transportation domain, in which traditional methodologies and approaches are ineffective or infeasible [15].

3   Problem Formulation

Runway is the most obvious and important resource at any airport. It directly influences to the overall capacity of an airport. The capacity of a runway system (measured hourly) depends on many factors such as strategic planning and tactical initiative for event handling (e.g. arrivals and departures). Optimized aircraft sequence and queue management are very essential for obtaining the best possible capacity.

It is observed that the inefficient utilization of the resources (i.e., runway, taxiway) and the lack of optimal sequencing tools for mix mode operation lead to the reduced overall capacity [12]. Therefore, we have been motivated to implement an approach that integrates arrival/departure traffic and optimize the sequence of arriving and departing aircraft. Figure 2 illustrates the conceptual problem formulation of our implementation. Arrival and departure aircrafts (based on distribution characteristics of hub and spoke) are integrated into a mixed queue which is optimally sequenced using a GA algorithm to maximize runway throughput capacity.

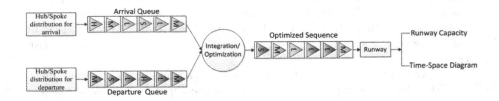

Fig. 2. Problem formulation

In this study, we focus on integrating and optimizing the sequence of arrival and departure aircraft that minimizes the processing time for each window. We assume that ATC can control up to the maximum window size (e.g. 10 arriving, 10 departing aircraft). We also assume that demand for runway occupancy is continuous. In these circumstances, proposed model optimally sequences the aircraft for each window and lock the optimized sequence for processing. Likewise, GA process another window dynamically as the demand is continuous. Consider the arrival and departure look ahead window size is W_a and W_d respectively. Hence the window size for mix operation is W_{ad}.

$$W_{ad} = W_a + W_d \tag{1}$$

Let l is the length of the final approach path and δ_{ij} is the ATC minimum longitudinal separation between two arriving aircraft. Table 1(a) shows the minimum separation of two successive arriving aircraft. Here leading indicates the operation execute first where trailing means operation execute after leading operation. For arriving aircraft, separation is indicated by nautical miles (NM). Equations (2) and (3) estimate the inter-arrival time $_{a}t_{ij}$.

$$_{aa}t_{ij} = max[\frac{l + \delta_{ij}}{v_j} - \frac{l}{v_i}, \ _{a}O_i] \ when \ v_i > v_j \tag{2}$$

$$_{aa}t_{ij} = max[\frac{\delta_{ij}}{v_j}, \ _{a}O_i] \ when \ v_i \leq v_j \tag{3}$$

where v_i , v_j and $_{a}O_i$, denote the speed on final approach path and runway occupancy time of leading and trailing aircraft respectively.

The ATC applies the separation rules between two successive departing aircraft to prevent them to simultaneously occupy the runway. The inter-departure time between aircraft i and j can be estimated as:

$$_{dd}t_{ij} = _d t_{ijmin} - (_dO_i - _d O_j) - \gamma_d(1/v_{jd} - 1/v_{id}) \tag{4}$$

where $_dt_{ijmin}$ is minimum separation time required between two departing aircraft i and j. Table 1(b) shows the minimum separation between two successive departing aircraft. Separation for two consecutive departing aircraft is measured in seconds according to the aviation practice. $_dO_i$ and $_dO_j$ is the runway occupancy time of the take-off aircraft i and j respectively.

In mix operation, when leading aircraft is departing and trailing aircraft is arriving then the inter-event time is estimated as:

$$_{da}t_{ij} = max[_dO_i, \ \frac{d\delta_{ij}}{v_j}] \tag{5}$$

where $_dO_i$ is the runway occupancy time of the departing aircraft, $_d\delta_{ij}$ is the longitudinal distance from the runway threshold and v_j is the speed of the arriving aircraft. Table 1(c) shows the values of $_d\delta_{ij}$.

When the leading aircraft is arriving and trailing is departing then the inter-event time is as follows:

$$_{ad}t_{ij} = _a O_i \tag{6}$$

where $_aO_i$ is the runway occupancy time by arriving aircraft. Likewise if a leading aircraft is departing and trailing aircraft is landing then trailing aircraft must follows the separation at least the runway occupancy time of the leading aircraft.

3.1   Objective Function

We consider a dynamic window based optimization approach. Each window consist of a stream of arriving and departing aircraft. Our objective is to minimize the processing time of each window.The formulation of this estimation problem is as follows:

$$min \ \Psi = \sum_{i,j \in C} {}_{aa}t_{ij} + \sum_{i,j \in C} {}_{dd}t_{ij} + \sum_{i,j \in C} {}_{da}t_{ij} + \sum_{i,j \in C} {}_{ad}t_{ij} \tag{7}$$

where C is the set of all arriving and departing aircraft in the window and Ψ is the summation of all aircrafts' process time in the window. The fitness function of the optimization is as:

$$Fitness = maximize(1/\Psi) \tag{8}$$

4 Methodology

Figure 3 shows the flowchart of the genetic algorithm implementation for optimization. We classify the aircraft into four categories such as heavy (H), large (L), medium (M) and small (S). Arrival and departure sequences are genetically represented as chromosome. Each chromosome is represented as a solution set of arrival and departure aircraft sequence. Initially population of possible solution sequence are generated randomly. The evolutionary process attempts to maximize the fitness function through genetic operations.

Tournament selection is used to select the candidate solution for crossover operation (described further). A fixed mutation rate of 1.5 % is used to prevent premature convergence. The elitism algorithm is used to determine the survival of parents and children in the new generation [16]. The GA is terminated at 500 generations even though the initial experiment shows that the solution converges within 200 generations.

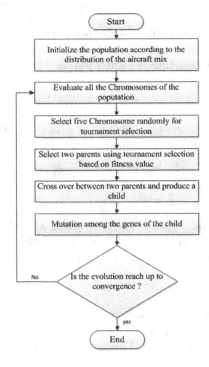

Fig. 3. Flowchart of the genetic algorithm implementation.

4.1   Genetic Operator

(1) **Crossover:** Crossover is a genetic operator used to reproduce from one generation to the next. In this crossover method a subset of gene is selected from the first parent and then add that subset to the offspring. The missing genes are then added to the offspring from the second parent ensuring that total number of genes (i.e., aircraft) remain similar to the parents. To make this explanation a little clearer consider an example in Fig. 4.

A subset of genes is taken from the parent 1 (L_a, L_d, S_a) and added to the offspring chromosome. Here subscript a indicates arrival and d indicates departure, i.e. L_a means large aircraft arrives. Next, the missing genes locations are added in order from the parent 2. Notice that first location in the parent 2 chromosome is H_d which is not exist in the offspring chromosome, thus it is added in the first available position. The next position in the parent 2 chromosome is M_d, which is not in the offspring chromosome so it is also added to offspring. The third position in parent chromosome is L_a which is already included in child chromosome so it is skipped. This process continues until the offspring has no remaining empty gene. Note that seventh position of parent 2 is again L_a which belongs to the offspring, however this time L_a is added because total number of similar gene remain same with the parents chromosome.

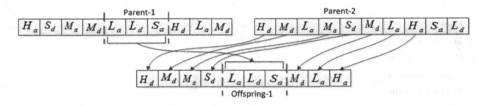

Fig. 4. An example of crossover procedure

(2) **Mutation:** Mutation is used to maintain genetic diversity from one generation of population to the next generation. In this implementation swap mutation is used. With swap mutation two genes position in the chromosome are selected at random fashion then their positions are swapped. Swap mutation is only swapping pre-existing genes, it never creates a gene which has missed or duplicates gene.

5   Experimentation

The optimization model is evaluated through simulation. The performance of the model is evaluated using the mix of arrival and departure aircraft by taking into consideration that all the ATC separation rules are satisfied. ATC rules are pairwise statements about the minimum separation requirements between

Table 1. Separation (a) Arrival-Arrival (b) Departure-Departure (c) Departure-Arrival

	Trailing			
	H_a	L_a	M_a	S_a
H_a	4	5	6	6
M_a	2.5	2.5	4	4
L_a	2.5	2.5	2.5	2.5
S_a	2.5	2.5	2.5	2.5

(a) Separation (NM) — Leading

	Trailing			
	H_d	L_d	M_d	S_d
H_d	90	120	120	120
M_d	60	60	60	60
L_d	60	60	60	60
S_d	60	60	60	60

(b) Separaton (Sec) — Leading

	Trailing			
	H_a	L_a	M_a	S_a
H_d	2.90	2.50	2.15	1.75
M_d	2.50	2.15	1.90	1.50
L_d	2.30	2.0	1.70	1.40
S_d	1.90	1.60	1.40	1.15

(c) Separaton (NM) — Leading

two aircraft. For example, if an aircraft enter the runway then another aircraft cannot enter the runway threshold area until the first aircraft clear the runway.

Table 1 shows the pair wise ATC separations for arrival-arrival, departure-departure and arrival-departure case. In practice arrival separation is measured as nautical mile (NM) and departure separation is measured in seconds(sec). In this study, we use separate distributions for arrival and departure that representing the traffic characteristics of hub and spoke airport. Table 2 shows the summary of the experimental parameters used. Each experiment is conducted 30 times to get the average value.

Table 2. Experimental setup

Parameter	Values
Mutation rate	0.015
Chromosome size	20
Population size	50
Tournament size	5
Mix distribution	Hub: H (20 %), L(35 %), M(35 %), S(10 %)
	Spoke: H (10 %), L(20%), M(35 %), S(35 %)
Generation	500
Simulation time for runway throughput	1 h

6   Result Analysis and Discussion

Figure 5 presents the convergence curve of the optimization problem. The evolutionary process where the fitness do not improve further just after 200 generations.

The simulation result presented in this section are the hourly throughput of the runway for mixed mode (i.e., arrival and departure) operation. Notice that as shown in Fig. 6(a), the average throughput of our optimized model increases up to 15 % comparing to FCFS approach.

In addition, we also measure the processing time for each window of aircraft as shown in Fig. 6(b). Our model saves average 272.83 s for each window

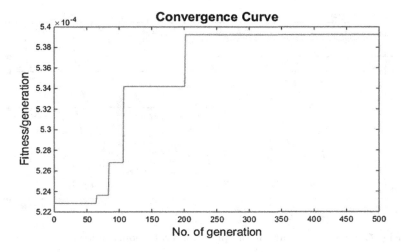

Fig. 5. Convergence curve

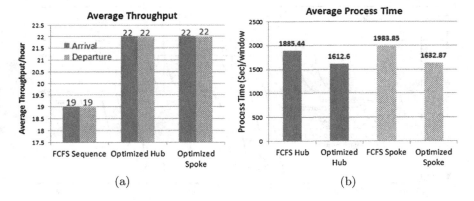

Fig. 6. Simulation result (a) Average throughput (b) Average process time/window

processing which is significant for a busy airport, where maximum process time is 2209.95 s/window and minimum process time is 1505.06 s/window. Finally, we analyze the time-space diagram of optimal sequence for hub and spoke airport. Figure 7 shows the optimal sequence for hub airport. Note that for the best possible sequence, a departing heavy (H_d) aircraft followed by a stream of medium and large arriving aircraft. An interesting result here is that heavy and large aircraft are sequenced consecutively to reduce the processing time.

Likewise, for the spoke airport configurations the time-space diagram is presented in Fig. 8. Note here that, the occurrence of medium and small aircraft are higher than heavy and large aircraft. The optimal sequence that, a large (L_a) arriving aircraft followed by a stream of departure aircraft. Another interesting outcome of the optimal sequence is that, similar aircraft (i.e., medium(M)-medium(M), large(L)-large(L) and so on) are positioned side by side.

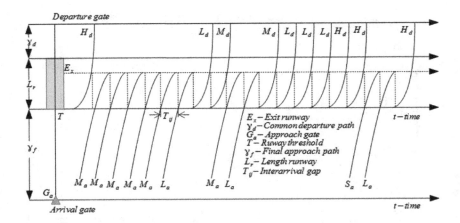

Fig. 7. Time-space diagram of optimal aircraft sequence for hub airport

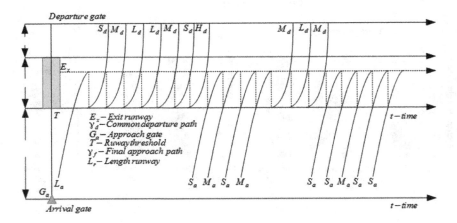

Fig. 8. Time-space diagram of optimal aircraft sequence for spoke airport

7   Conclusion

In this paper, we developed an evolutionary optimization based runway capacity maximization model that optimize the arrival-departure sequence using genetic algorithm. An optimization problem has been formulated to dynamically optimize the aircraft sequence to minimize the process time. Several simulations have been conducted considering 'hub and spoke' airport scenarios. The optimization model finds the best sequences of aircraft for the utilization of the runway. Simulation result shows that the model obtained optimal sequence that took lower process time as well as achieved a higher throughput comparing to First Come First Serve approach commonly used at aircraft sequencing. The result also demonstrates the strength of evolutionary algorithm in dealing with

NP hard problems from real world. In future, we will develop multi-objective optimization models to handle other objectives such as weather and multiple runways. We will compare our work with state of the art technology. We will also consider different CNS configurations and their effect on runway capacity however design of fitness function and solution representation can be a major challenge.

References

1. Eurocontrol: Challenges of growth 2013: European air traffic in 2035 (2013)
2. Bryan, D.L., O'Kelly, M.E.: Hub-and-spoke networks in air transportation: an analytical review. J. Reg. Sci. **39**(2), 275–295 (1999)
3. Eurocontrol: Network operations report analysis (2014)
4. McShan, S., Windle, R.: The implications of hub-and-spoke routing for airline costs. Logistics Transp. Rev. **25**(3), 209 (1989)
5. Ombuki, B., Ross, B.J., Hanshar, F.: Multi-objective genetic algorithms for vehicle routing problem with time windows. Appl. Intell. **24**(1), 17–30 (2006)
6. Jiang, Y., Yun, P.: Mathematical model and analysis of runway landing capacity. J. Southwest Jiaotong Univ. **1**, 010 (2004)
7. Harris, R.M.: Models for runway capacity analysis. Technical report, DTIC Document (1972)
8. Gilbo, E.P.: Optimizing airport capacity utilization in air traffic flow management subject to constraints at arrival and departure fixes. IEEE Trans. Control Syst. Technol. **5**(5), 490–503 (1997)
9. Gilbo, E.P.: Airport capacity: representation, estimation, optimization. IEEE Trans. Control Syst. Technol. **1**(3), 144–154 (1993)
10. Hu, X., Paolo, E., et al.: A ripple-spreading genetic algorithm for the aircraft sequencing problem. Evol. Comput. **19**(1), 77–106 (2011)
11. Zhao, W., Tang, J., Alam, S., Bender, A., Abbass, H.A.: Evolutionary-computation based risk assessment of aircraft landing sequencing algorithms. In: Hinchey, M., Kleinjohann, B., Kleinjohann, L., Lindsay, P.A., Rammig, F.J., Timmis, J., Wolf, M. (eds.) DIPES 2010. IFIP AICT, vol. 329, pp. 254–265. Springer, Heidelberg (2010)
12. Diffenderfer, P., Tao, Z., Payton, G.: Automated integration of arrival/departure schedules. In: Tenth USA/Europe Air Traffic Management Seminar (2013)
13. Callantine, T., Kupfer, M., Martin, L., Prevot, T.: Simulations of continuous descent operations with arrival-management automation and mixed flight-deck interval management equipage. In: 11th USA/Europe Air Traffic Management Research and Development Seminar, pp. 10–13 (2013)
14. Back, T., Fogel, D.B., Michalewicz, Z.: Handbook of Evolutionary Computation. IOP Publishing Ltd., Bristol (1997)
15. Delahaye, D., Puechmorel, S.: Modeling and Optimization of Air Traffic. Wiley, New York (2013)
16. Grefenstette, J.J.: Optimization of control parameters for genetic algorithms. IEEE Trans. Syst. Man Cybern. **16**(1), 122–128 (1986)

Finite Population Trust Game Replicators

Garrison Greenwood[1], Hussein Abbass[2(✉)], and Eleni Petraki[3]

[1] Electrical and Computer Engineering Department, Portland State University,
Portland, OR, USA
greenwd@pdx.edu
[2] School of Engineering and Information Technology, University of New South Wales,
Canberra, ACT 2600, Australia
h.abbass@adfa.edu.au
[3] Faculty of Arts and Design, University of Canberra, Canberra, Australia
Eleni.Petraki@canberra.edu.au

Abstract. Our previous work introduced the N player trust game and
examined the dynamics of this game using replicator dynamics for an infinite population. In finite populations, quantization becomes a necessity
that introduces discontinuity in the trajectory space, which can impact
the dynamics of the game differently. In this paper, we present an analysis
of replicator dynamics of the N player trust game in finite populations.
The analysis reveals that, quantization indeed introduces fixed points in
the interior of the 2-simplex that were not present in the infinite population analysis. However, there is no guarantee that these fixed points will
continue to exist for any arbitrary population size; thus, they are clearly
an artifact of quantization. In general, the evolutionary dynamics of the
finite population are qualitatively similar to the infinite population. This
suggests that for the proposed trust game, trusters will be extinct if the
population contains an untrustworthy player. Therefore, trusting is an
evolutionary unstable strategy.

Keywords: Trust · Evolutionary game theory · N-person trust game

1 Introduction

Human interaction is a complex process. Despite being the focus of extensive investigation for decades, a number of questions remain without adequate
answers. Social dilemmas are particularly interesting. Social dilemmas arise
whenever short-term, individual interests must be weighed against long-term,
collective interests.

Game theory is a useful vehicle for studying social dilemmas. Players compete against each other using strategies to make decisions. They receive payoffs
(rewards) for the decisions they make and their competitors make. Good strategies return high rewards. Theories can be postulated to explain how strategies

H. Abbass—Portions of this work was funded by the Australian Research Council
Discovery Grant number DP140102590.

might evolve over time and computer models can be constructed to generate empirical evidence to support or disprove these theories [3,9,15].

Consider a game with m strategies and let p_i be the frequency of strategy i in the population. At any given time the state of the population is given by $\mathbf{p} \in \mathbf{S_m}$. If p_i is a differential function of time, then the evolution of strategies in the population can be expressed using *replicator equations* [8]. (Differentiability assumes the population is infinitely large.) Each replicator equation is a 1st-order differential equation. Under replication dynamics individuals do not change strategies via mutation nor by some contrived procedure such as a Moran process [10]. Instead, strategies change frequency following Darwinian theory—i.e., reproductive success is directly proportional to fitness. Individuals with above average fitness grow in population over time while those with below average fitness die out.

Usually the N player games studied thus far only have a small number of strategies (typically $m \leq 4$). Most of these games study cooperation in populations and try to discover human characteristics that promote cooperation. These games model social dilemmas where mutual cooperation is the best outcome for the group, but individual self-interest always pays better, leading to the undesirable outcome where ultimately everyone defects. Empirical evidence from these N player games suggest that several mechanisms such as reciprocity and kin-selection promote cooperation in human populations [11].

One aspect of human interaction that has been extensively investigated in the past is trust and the role it plays in society. Schmueli *et al.* [14] maintain that the concept of trust is pervasive in social relationships and it has a great impact on social persuasion and behavioral change. Their experiment revealed that trust was significantly more effective than the closeness of ties in determining the amount of behavior change, with respect to individual fitness. High levels of trust have shown to impose social controls in political and economic institutions thereby increasing accountability, productivity and effectiveness [13].

Nevertheless, evolutionary game theoretical studies on trust are lacking and those that have been conducted were limited to 2 players. (See [12] for a notable exception.) Recently this situation changed when Abbass et al. [1] introduced a game specifically designed to investigate the role of trust in human populations. Players in this game make two choices in advance: whether to be trustworthy or not and whether to be an investor or be a trustee. Each investor contributes an amount tv. A trustworthy trustee returns an amount $R1 > 1$ to the investor (and keeps an equal amount for herself) whereas an untrustworthy trustee keeps the contribution and returns nothing. The game is designed as a social dilemma. Replicator dynamics indicate that the inevitable outcome is when the population converges to state with a mixture of trustworthy and untrustworthy players and no investors.

Replicators equations provide valuable insights into how strategies evolve in a population. Their limitation is the assumption of an infinite population. Nature does not produce infinite populations. Indeed, human populations are always finite for a variety of reasons such as geographical isolation or cultural restrictions. More importantly, it has been conclusively shown that, when comparing

Table 1. Utility matrix for a N-player trust game.

	Player in the k_1 population	Player in the k_2 population	Player in the k_3 population
Pay	tv	$R1 \cdot tv \cdot \frac{k_1}{k_2+k_3}$	0
Receive	$R1 \cdot tv \cdot \frac{k_2}{k_2+k_3}$	$2 \cdot R1 \cdot tv \cdot \frac{k_1}{k_2+k_3}$	$R2 \cdot tv \cdot \frac{k_1}{k_2+k_3}$
Net Wealth	$tv \cdot (R1 \cdot \frac{k_2}{k_2+k_3} - 1)$	$R1 \cdot tv \cdot \frac{k_1}{k_2+k_3}$	$R2 \cdot tv \cdot \frac{k_1}{k_2+k_3}$

infinite population dynamics and finite population dynamics, the latter have qualitatively different results [4–6]. This issue is important because the trust game results reported in [1] were obtained using an infinite population model.

In this paper, we extend our previous work by studying finite population models using a discrete form of replicator equations and report the findings. Our results indicate the finite population dynamics are remarkably similar to those found in the infinite population. However, the discrete replicator equations do require quantization and quantization effects introduce additional fixed points not found in the infinite population models. Surprisingly, these fixed points appear and disappear as a function of the population size. We provide an analysis of this phenomenon.

This paper is organized as follows. In Sect. 2 the trust game is formally defined and an overview of the infinite population replicator dynamics is given. Section 3 develops the replicator equations for the trust game with finite populations. Section 4 analyzes the finite population results. Finally, Sect. 5 summarizes our findings and discusses future work.

2   Background

This section gives a formal definition of the N player trust game and a brief overview of the infinite population replicator dynamics. See [1] for more detailed information.

2.1   The N Player Trust Game

Assume N players. Each player makes two decisions in advance: (1) whether or not to be trustworthy, and (2) whether to be an investor or a trustee. Let k_1 be the number of investors, k_2 the number of trustworthy trustees and k_3 the number of untrustworthy trustees. The obvious restriction is $\sum_i k_i = N$.

An investor player pays tv to the trustee, where $tv > 0$ denotes the trusted value. The dynamics of the game does not depend on the value of tv. However, we maintain tv to allow flexibility in adopting the game to different contexts. With k_1 governed players, the total money contributed is $(k_1 \cdot tv)$. Each trustworthy trustee returns to an investor a multiplier of $R1$ of what was received and keeps the same amount for herself, with $R1 > 1$. An untrustworthy trustee returns nothing but instead keeps for herself a multiplier of $R2$ of what was received, where $R1 < R2 < 2R1$. The payoff matrix for this game can then be represented as shown in Table 1 with the following constraints:

$$1 < R1 < R2 < 2R1$$

$$N = k_1 + k_2 + k_3$$

2.2   Infinite Population Replication Dynamics

The evolutionary behavior of a population playing the trust game can be studied using replicator dynamics. Let y_i be the frequency of players using strategy i in an infinitely large population with $\sum_i y_i = 1$. Then the time evolution of y_i is given by the differential equation

$$\dot{y}_i = y_i \cdot \left(f_i - \hat{f} \right) \tag{1}$$

where f_i is the expected fitness of an individual playing strategy i at time t and $\hat{f}$ is the mean population fitness. Here, fitness and net wealth are equivalent. The number of copies of a strategy increases if $f_i > \hat{f}$ and decreases if $f_i < \hat{f}$. We can calculate $\hat{f}$ as follows

$$\hat{f} = \frac{y_1 \cdot y_2 \cdot tv\,(2 \cdot R1 - 1) + y_1 \cdot y_3 \cdot tv \cdot (R2 - 1)}{(y_2 + y_3)}$$

The three replicator equations are

$$\dot{y}_1 = \frac{y_1^2 \cdot tv}{1 - y_1}\,(y_2\,(1 - 2 \cdot R1) + y_3 \cdot (1 - R2)) + \frac{y_1 \cdot tv}{1 - y_1}\,(y_2\,(R1 - 1) - y_3)$$

$$\dot{y}_2 = \frac{y_1 \cdot y_2 \cdot tv}{1 - y_1} \cdot (y_2\,(1 - 2 \cdot R1) + y_3\,(1 - R2) + R1)$$

$$\dot{y}_3 = \frac{y_1 \cdot y_3 \cdot tv}{1 - y_1} \cdot (y_2\,(1 - 2 \cdot R1) + y_3\,(1 - R2) + R2)$$

Figure 1 shows the population evolution for various initial player distributions. Figure 2 shows the effect of different $R1$ and $R2$ values (but with $R1 < R2$). The replicator equations predict a rapid growth of untrustworthiness in the population, leading to the eventual extinction of investors. However, a fraction of the population always remains trustworthy, even in the absence of investors. This predicted steady-state outcome is independent of the initial player distribution, but the ratio of trustworthy to untrustworthy players in the final population is dependent on the $R1$ and $R2$ values.

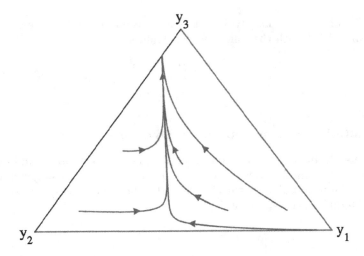

Fig. 1. A 2-simplex showing the time evolution for a game with $R1 = 6$, $R2 = 8$, $tv = 10$, and different initial distributions of y_1, y_2 and y_3. (Reproduced from [1])

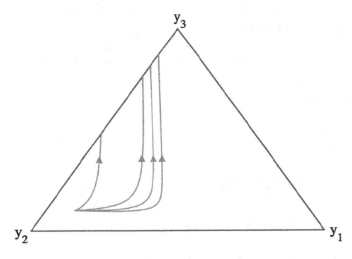

Fig. 2. A 2-simplex showing the time evolution for a game with $tv = 10$ and different $R1$ and $R2$ values ($R1 < R2$). Values increase from left to right with $R1 = 1.5, R2 = 2.9$ for the far left trajectory to $R1 = 6, R2 = 8$ for the far right trajectory. Initial distribution is $y_1(0) = 0.1$, $y_2(0) = 0.8$, and $y_3(0) = 0.1$. (Reproduced from [1])

3   Finite Population Replicator Dynamics

The population dynamics depicted in Fig. 1 and predicted by (1) apply only to infinite size populations. It has been conclusively shown that finite population dynamics can be qualitatively different from those of infinite populations [4–6]. It is therefore important to see if and, if so, how the dynamics of the trust game change for finite populations. Replicator equations can still be used to predict how a population evolves although, as will be shown shortly, the equation format is different.

Let N be the (finite) population size and k_i, $i = \{1, 2, 3\}$ be the number of players choosing strategy i. The frequency of players choosing strategy i at time t is $p_i^t = k_i/N$. With finite populations, the discrete replicator equations are now expressed as a set of first order difference equations

$$p_i^{t+1} = p_i^t F_i^t \qquad (2)$$

where $F_i^t = f_i \big/ \hat{f}^t$ with $\hat{f}^t$ the mean fitness at time t. $F_i > 1$ means the proportion of strategy i in the population grows, $F_i < 1$ means it shrinks and $F_i = 1$ it is at a fixed point. Unfortunately, the discrete form of the replicator equations introduces a couple of problems not found in the infinite population case.

The first problem is with the definition of fitness. Fitness is equated to net wealth in both the infinite population case and the finite population case. Substituting $p_i^t = k_i/N$ into the net wealth equations and simplifying yields the following finite population fitness equations

$$
\begin{aligned}
f_1^t &= tv \cdot \left(R1 \cdot \frac{p_2^t}{p_2^t + p_3^t} - 1 \right) \\
f_2^t &= tv \cdot R1 \cdot \frac{p_1^t}{p_2^t + p_3^t} \\
f_3^t &= tv \cdot R2 \cdot \frac{p_1^t}{p_2^t + p_3^t}
\end{aligned}
\qquad (3)
$$

The problem is f_1 won't be positive for all strategy frequencies. Unlike with differential equations, negative fitness values are not permitted in discrete replicator equations because this makes $p_i^{t+1} < 0$. Moreover, $\hat{f}^t$ cannot equal zero. We therefore slightly modified the fitness values as shown below.

$$
f_1 = \begin{cases}
0 < \epsilon \ll 1 & \text{if } \frac{k_2}{k_2 + k_3} \leq \frac{1}{R1} \\
tv \cdot \left(R1 \cdot \frac{k_2}{k_2 + k_3} - 1 \right) & \text{otherwise}
\end{cases}
$$

$$
f_2 = tv \cdot R1 \cdot \frac{k_1}{k_2 + k_3}
\qquad (4)
$$

$$
f_3 = tv \cdot R2 \cdot \frac{k_1}{k_2 + k_3}
$$

The second problem involves trajectories in the 2-simplex. In the finite population case each $p_i^t = k_i/N$. This means there are only a finite set of feasible points in the 2-simplex (see Fig. 3). Any trajectory must therefore consist of straight line segments between pairs of feasible points.

Clearly, the right-hand side must be an integer. This means only a finite set of points in the simplex can be visited—i.e., points where $p_i^t = k_i/N$. These points for $N = 20$ are shown in Fig. 3.

The p_i values have to be quantized to make sure only integer values for k_i^{t+1} are produced. The quantization method described in [2] is used here.

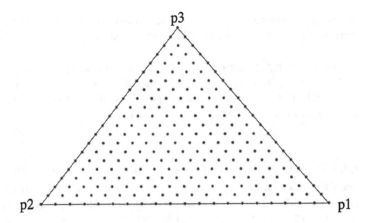

Fig. 3. A 2-simplex for a finite population with $N = 20$. Only the points shown represent an integer number of strategies in the population. Any trajectory must move between these points.

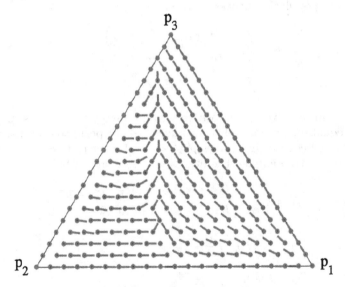

Fig. 4. A velocity plot for a finite population with $N = 20, R1 = 6, R2 = 8$ and $tv = 10$. (*c.f.* Fig. 1)

The algorithm below returns k_i' which is the new number of players choosing the i-th strategy.

1. Compute

$$k_i' = \lfloor Np_i + \tfrac{1}{2} \rfloor \quad , \quad N' = \sum_i k_i'$$

2. Let $d = N' - N$. If $d = 0$, then go to step 4. Otherwise, compute the errors $\delta_i = k'_i - Np_i$.
3. If $d > 0$, decrement the d k'_i's with the largest δ_i values. If $d < 0$, increment the $|d|$ k'_i's with the smallest δ_i values.
4. Return $[k'_1 \quad k'_2 \quad k'_3]$ and exit.

Figure 4 shows a velocity plot for a finite population with $N = 20, R1 = 6, R2 = 8$ and $tv = 10$. The vectors are shown as unit vectors because the direction is of importance here and not the magnitude. These finite population replicator dynamics are the analog of the infinite population replicator dynamics shown in Fig. 1. Notice the finite population dynamics are remarkably similar including the presence of an attractor.

4   Discussion

The finite population trust game has a Nash equilibrium at $k_3 = N$ and a Pareto optimal distribution at $k_1 = N - 1, k_2 = 1$. (See [1] for proofs.)

Many of the fixed points in the finite population are the same as those in the infinite population. For example, in the infinite population the three 2-simplex corners and every point on the $p_2 - p_3$ line is a fixed point. Similarly in the finite population model the three 2-simplex corners are fixed points but only a finite number of points on the $p_2 - p_3$ line are fixed points—i.e., the $N+1$ points where p_i is a rational number. The infinite population model also has a fixed point at

$$y_1 = \frac{R1 - 1}{2 \times R1 - 1}$$

$$y_2 = \frac{R1}{2 \times R1 - 1}$$

$$y_3 = 0$$

With R1 = 6 in our example, the fixed point is, $\mathbf{p} = [5/11 \ 6/11 \ 0/11]$. In the finite model this fixed point varies (due to quantization) but it is the rational number closest to $\mathbf{p}$.

Figure 5 shows a magnified view of a portion of the $p_1 - p_2$ line. Notice there are two fixed points that do not appear in the infinite population mode. Consider the fixed point at $[p_1 \ p_2 \ p_3] = [0.450 \ 0.550 \ 0.000]$ (equivalently, $[k_1 \ k_2 \ k_3] = [9 \ 11 \ 0]$). That population mixture yields fitness values of $f_1 = 50, f_2 = 49.09, f_3 = 0.0$ and a mean population fitness of $\hat{f} = 49.499$. The discrete replicator equations predict no change in the population mixture. It is also worth mentioning the fixed point on the $p_1 - p_2$ line at $[p_1 \ p_2 \ p_3] = [0.450 \ 0.550 \ 0.000]$ matches well to the fixed point in the infinite population at $[p_1 \ p_2 \ p_3] = [0.455 \ 0.545 \ 0.000]$.

To understand why the finite population has fixed points which are not present in infinite populations it is important to understand how quantization actually works. Quantization is a form of data compression. It maps an entire

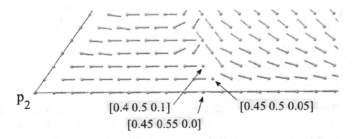

P_2

[0.4 0.5 0.1]   [0.45 0.5 0.05]

[0.45 0.55 0.0]

Fig. 5. A magnified portion of the 2-simplex for $N = 20$. The distribution of strategies is shown for the three fixed points. The fixed point with distribution [0.45 0.55 0.0] corresponds to a similar fixed in the infinite population module. The other two fixed points are a consequence of quantization (see text).

range of real numbers into a single value, which subsequently represents any real number in the range that was mapped.

For the trust game quantization must map real numbers into integers. To see why this is necessary substitute $p_i^t = k_i^t/N$ into the discrete replicator equation. After multiplying both sides of the equation by N

$$k_i^{t+1} = k_i^t F_i^t \tag{5}$$

Clearly the left-hand side must be an integer but the right-hand side typically won't be because $F_i^t = f_i^t/\hat{f}^t$ is a real number. The quantization process described previously was specifically picked because it maps a real number into an integer. However, there is no guarantee that, quantizing three frequencies that sum to 1.0 will produce three integers that sum to N—unless a repair mechanism is incorporated into the quantization process to enforce this constraint.

Each iteration of the discrete replicator equation updates the number of strategies in the population. Thus update is a mapping from $I \rightarrow I$. Unfortunately the right-hand side of (2) is rarely an integer. Quantization will produce an integer right-hand side of the replicator equation but this process introduces some fixed points not present in the infinite population model. To understand how these fixed points arise it is necessary to take a more detailed look at the quantization process.

Step 1 of the quantization process computes the new number of the i-th strategy:

$$\begin{aligned} k_i' &= \lfloor N p_i^{t+1} + \tfrac{1}{2} \rfloor \\ &= \lfloor N \tfrac{k_i}{N} F_i^t + \tfrac{1}{2} \rfloor \\ &= \lfloor k_i F_i^t + \tfrac{1}{2} \rfloor \end{aligned} \tag{6}$$

where the integer floor is necessary to make sure k_i' is an integer. It is easy to show $k_i \rightarrow k_i'$ as follows

$$k_i' = \begin{cases} < k_i & \text{if } F_i^t < 1 - 1/2k_i \\ > k_i & \text{if } F_i^t > 1 + 1/2k_i \\ = k_i & \text{otherwise} \end{cases} \tag{7}$$

The new sum $\sum_i k_i' = N'$ is calculated and then compared with N. Obviously no adjustment is required if $N' = N$. However, if $N' \neq N$ then some k_i' values must be incremented (if $N' < N$) or decremented (if $N' > N$). This adjustment is done in steps 2 through 4 of the quantization process. Which ones get incremented or decremented depends on the δ_i error values: those with the largest errors are decremented and those with the smallest errors get incremented. Thus, the only role of the δ_i values is to identify which k_i''s must be adjusted to make $N' = N$.

Now consider the upper fixed point highlighted in Fig. 5 where $N = 20$. The population mixture is $[p_1 \ p_2 \ p_3] = [0.4 \ 0.5 \ 0.1]$ at that simplex point. The corresponding fitness values are $[f_1 \ f_2 \ f_3] = [40 \ 40 \ 53.33]$ and the mean fitness is $\hat{f} = 41.33$. Consequently $F_1^t = F_2^t = 0.967$ and $F_3^t = 1.29$. Thus,

1. $k_1' = k_1$ because $0.967 \not< 1 - \frac{1}{16}$ and $0.967 \not> 1 + \frac{1}{16}$.
2. $k_2' = k_2$ because $0.967 \not< 1 - \frac{1}{20}$ and $0.967 \not> 1 + \frac{1}{20}$.
3. $k_3' > k_3$ because $1.29 > 1 + \frac{1}{4}$. (Note: $k_3 = 2$ and $\lfloor 1.29 \cdot 2 + \frac{1}{2} \rfloor = \lfloor 3.08 \rfloor$)

Readjustment is necessary because $\sum_i k_i' = 21 > N$. Step 3 of the quantization algorithm implements the repair mechanism. Specifically, in this case $d = +1$ and δ_3 is larger than δ_1 or δ_2. Thus k_3 is decremented once, which makes $k_3' = k_3$. Now $\sum_i k_i = N$ and fixed point is created since none of the k_is changed. A similar analysis can be done for the fixed point with the distribution $[0.45 \ 0.5 \ .05]$.

The fixed points in the interior of the 2-simplex caused by quantization will change as N increases and they completely disappear as $N \to \infty$. To investigate this phenomenon a simulation was run with $N = 40$. Figure 6 shows a magnified portion of the 2-simplex. The fixed point with distribution $[0.45 \ 0.55 \ 0.0]$ remains and will never disappear as N increases. Notice a new fixed point appeared at distribution $[0.45 \ 0.525 \ .025]$. More importantly, the fixed point at distribution $[0.4 \ 0.5 \ 0.1]$, which was a fixed point when $N = 20$ is no longer a fixed point when $N = 40$. An analysis conducted as done above will explain why. The same fitness values exist but now the new strategy numbers are as follows:

1. $k_1' < k_1$ because $0.967 < 1 - \frac{1}{32}$. ($k_1 = 16$; $k_1' = 15$)
2. $k_2' < k_2$ because $0.967 < 1 - \frac{1}{40}$. ($k_2 = 20$; $k_2' = 19$)
3. $k_3' > k_3$ because $1.29 > 1 + \frac{1}{8}$. ($k_3 = 4$; $k_3' = 5$)

Readjustment is necessary because $\sum_i k_i' = 39 < N$. From step 2 of the quantization algorithm $\delta_1 = -0.472, \delta_2 = -0.34, \delta_3 = -0.16$ and $d = -1$. δ_1 is the smallest so k_1' is increased from 15 to 16 making the number of strategies total to N. The simplex point with strategy distribution $[0.4 \ 0.5 \ 0.1]$ is no longer a fixed point when $N = 40$ because $k_2' \neq k_2$ and $k_3' \neq k_3$.

One area where the finite population replicator dynamics differs markedly from the infinite population dynamics is the region in the 2-simplex near the p_2 vertex (see Fig. 7). The presence of an attractor is obvious but, unlike the infinite population case, the fixed points on the $p_2 - p_3$ axis are not unique (c.f., Fig. 2). Most likely this is another effect of quantization.

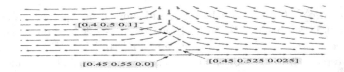

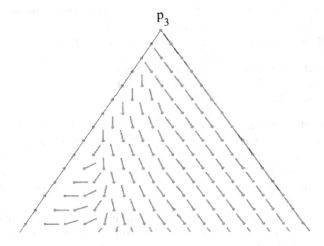

Fig. 6. A magnified portion of the 2-simplex for $N = 40$. The distribution of strategies is shown for the three fixed points. The fixed point with distribution [0.45 0.55 0.0] corresponds to a similar fixed in the infinite population module. The other fixed point is a consequence of quantization (see text).

Fig. 7. A magnified portion of the 2-simplex for $N = 40$. (*c.f.*, Fig. 1)

5   Summary

In this paper we have extended our previous work on the N player trust game by studying finite population effects. The discrete replicator equations impose certain restrictions including the necessity of quantization. Quantization introduces fixed points in the interior of the 2-simplex but these disappear (and other may take their place) as N varies. Nevertheless, the finite population evolution is qualitatively similar to the infinite population. This research extended previous research on computational measurement of trust by using game theory in both finite and infinite populations.

The replicator equations describe strategy evolution based on Darwinian principles—i.e., fitness based evolution. In particular no mutation is permitted. It will be interesting to see if trust persists when individuals are allowed to modify their strategy. Trust is the foundation of all human interactions regardless of who is involved or the duration of the encounter. This suggests emotions may play a role in whether or not individuals are seen as trustworthy and, if so, for how long. Greenwood [7], has previously shown emotions such as guilt can affect cooperation levels in social dilemmas. In our future work we intend to see how emotions may affect trust levels in social dilemmas.

References

1. Abbass, H., Greenwood, G., Petraki, E.: The n-player trust game and its replicator dynamics. IEEE Trans. Evol. Comput. (to appear). doi:10.1109/TEVC.2015. 2484840
2. Chandrasekhar, V., Reznik, Y., Takacs, G., Chen, D., Tsai, S., Grzeszczuk, R., Girod, R.: Quantization schemes for low bitrate compressed histogram of gradients descriptors. In: 2010 IEEE Computer Vision and Pattern Recognition Workshops, pp. 33–40 (2010)
3. David, O.E., van den Herik, H.J., Koppel, M., Netanyahu, N.S.: Genetic algorithms for evolving computer chess programs. IEEE Trans. Evol. Comput. 18(5), 779–789 (2014)
4. Ficici, S., Pollack, J.: Effects of finite populations on evolutionary stable strategies. In: GECCO, pp. 927–933 (2000)
5. Fogel, D., Fogel, G., Andrews, P.: On the instability of evolutionary stable strategies. BioSystems 44, 135–152 (1997)
6. Fogel, G., Andrews, P., Fogel, D.: On the instability of evolutionary stable strategies in small populations. Ecol. Model. 109, 283–294 (1998)
7. Greenwood, G.W.: Emotions and their effect on cooperation levels in n-player social dilemma games. In: Chalup, S.K., Blair, A.D., Randall, M. (eds.) ACALCI 2015. LNCS, vol. 8955, pp. 88–99. Springer, Heidelberg (2015)
8. Hofbauer, J., Sigmund, K.: Evolutionary game dynamics. Bull. Am. Math. Soc. 40(4), 479–519 (2003)
9. Li, J., Kendall, G.: The effect of memory size on the evolutionary stability of strategies in iterated prisoner's dilemma. IEEE Trans. Evol. Comput. 18(6), 819–826 (2014)
10. Moran, P.A.P.: The Statistical Processes of Evolutionary Theory. Clarendon Press, Oxford (1962)
11. Nowak, M.: Five rules for the evolution of cooperation. Science 314(5805), 1560–1563 (2006)
12. Petraki, E., Abbass, H.A.: On trust and influence: a computational red teaming game theoretic perspective. In: 2014 Seventh IEEE Symposium on Computational Intelligence for Security and Defense Applications (CISDA), pp. 1–7 (2014)
13. Putnam, R.D.: Comunidade e democracia: a experiência da Itália moderna. FGV Editora (2000)
14. Shmueli, E., Singh, V.K., Lepri, B., Pentland, A.: Sensing, understanding, and shaping social behavior. IEEE Trans. Comput. Soc. Syst. 1(1), 22–34 (2014)
15. Yeh, C., Yang, C.: Social networks and asset price dynamics. IEEE Trans. Evol. Comput. 19(3), 387–399 (2015)

Towards Evolved Time to Contact Neurocontrollers for Quadcopters

David Howard$^{(\boxtimes)}$ and Farid Kendoul

CSIRO Autonomous Systems Program, QCAT, 1 Technology Court,
Pullenvale, Brisbane, QLD 4069, Australia
david.howard@csiro.au

Abstract. Bio-inspired controllers based on visual odometry — or time to contact — have been previously shown to allow vehicles to navigate in a way that simultaneously specifies both the spatial waypoint and temporal arrival time at the waypoint, based on a single variable, tau (τ). In this study, we present an initial investigation into the evolution of neural networks as bio-inspired tau-controllers that achieve successful mappings between τ and desired control outputs. As this mapping is highly nonlinear and difficult to hand-design, an evolutionary algorithm is used to progressively optimise a population of neural networks based on quality of generated behaviour. The proposed system is implemented on Hardware-in-the-loop setup and demonstrated for the autonomous landing of a quadcopter. Preliminary results indicate that suitable controllers can be successfully evolved.

Keywords: Neurocontroller · Evolutionary algorithm · Time to contact · Tau theory · UAV

1 Introduction

Most existing Guidance, Navigation and Control (GNC) systems or autopilots for Unmanned Aerial Vehicles (UAVs) follow a conventional approach which consists of estimating the relative position and/or velocity between the UAV and a target point and then applying standard hierarchical guidance and control techniques for achieving the desired task. These methods require relatively complex planning and control algorithms and do not allow for time constraints to be specified. Furthermore, they are limited to position sensors only because computing the relative position is not always easy or even possible with bearing-only sensors such as cameras. On the other hand, flying insects and birds exhibit highly versatile and robust flight maneuvers using only the available vision and vestibular sensory information (without position sensors). It is postulated that these maneuvers are based on the processing of the time to contact (TTC) between the creature and a surface. TTC is defined as the time remaining before an anticipated contact between the approaching agent and the target object. Further research has led to the development of tau theory (e.g., [14]) — that

© Springer International Publishing Switzerland 2016
T. Ray et al. (Eds.): ACALCI 2016, LNAI 9592, pp. 336–347, 2016.
DOI: 10.1007/978-3-319-28270-1_28

TTC is embodied in a variable τ, which is directly available from neuronal circuitry and used by animals to effect precise and reliable control in dynamic environments.

Out of a desire to impart such precise and reliable control to their systems, researchers have previously studied the application of tau theory to navigation and guidance for UAVs. Rotorcraft UAVS (RUAVs) are particularly amenable to tau-based GNC as they can perform "soft" (near-zero velocity) contacts at target points. To date, RUAV tau research has focused on the replacement of the higher-level system components — guidance and navigation — with those based on tau theory [1,12], leaving the actual low-level control of these platforms to standard engineering approaches such as PID [2]. In this study we present the first demonstration of a fully tau-based GNC, by replacing traditional control approaches with a tau-controller and integrating it with existing tau strategies for navigation and guidance.

As the control mapping is anticipated to be highly nonlinear and unintuitive to hand-design, we employ an evolutionary algorithm to automatically discover useful tau-controllers. As the control mappings are highly nonlinear, feedforward neural networks [18] are our chosen representation, used as nonlinear function approximators. To assess the suitability of the neuroevolutionary system, tests are conducted on a single-axis quadcopter descent and landing manoeuver. Evolution takes place in a hardware-in-the-loop (HiL) setup, with spoofed τ generation but other parts identical to the real quadcopter setup. We envisage that this will allow for easy transfer to the real-world scenarios.

Our hypothesis is that evolutionary algorithms can provide an automatic method to discovering effective mappings between τ and the desired control outputs to allow a quadcopter UAV to follow a guidance strategy that specifies both spatial position and a desired time to reach that position. The major contributions of this work are (i) the first application of evolutionary algorithms to generate time-to-contact controllers, (ii) the first use of bio-inspired tau-based components in all three of the fundamental RUAV systems — guidance, navigation, and control, and (iii) validation of the feasibility and performance of the system in HiL simulations using real hardware and real-time implementation.

2 Background Research

2.1 Guidance, Navigation, and Control

It is important to understand how tau strategies fit into Guidance, Navigation, and Control (GNC) for autonomous UAVs, which is traditionally segregated into three parts as shown in Fig. 1. At the highest level, guidance can be viewed as a cognitive system that plans missions, generates flight paths and outputs trajectories/waypoints for the UAV to follow. Navigation is responsible for sensing, perception and state estimation — essentially how the platform is acting in it's environment. Typically, navigation outputs a multi-element state vector that comprises position information, attitude, angular rates, and optionally includes aspects such as obstacle detection, which can be passed back to guidance to update flight plans. Control takes inputs from guidance and navigation to generate control outputs which allow the platform to follow the plan specified by guidance. See [11] for an overview. Tau-GNC provides more streamlined information exchanges, and as such theoretically allows for faster processing. Tau-guidance generates a series of references τ_{ref}, based on mission parameters. Tau-navigation estimates the platforms current τ from sensing devices, i.e. a camera. By generating actuator outputs, tau-control attempts to match the actual τ to the desired τ_{ref}, thereby resulting in mission accomplishment.

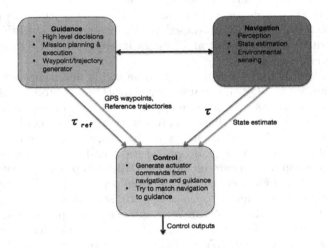

Fig. 1. GNC architecture for an autonomous UAV. Blue lines indicate traditional approaches, red lines denote tau-inspired approaches. Control attempts to follow waypoint/trajectories generated by guidance, using additional information from navigation state estimates to track the behaviour of the platform. Tau approaches potentially allow the full 4-dimensional control of a UAV based on matching the platform τ to the desired τ_{ref} (Color figure online).

2.2   Time to Contact and Tau Theory

Animals are thought to navigate in dynamic environments based on their estimated time to contact (TTC) with a given surface. It is thought to be derived from optical flow, whereby the relative motion between an observer and some scene features is used to navigate. Optical flow can be intuitively thought of as a vector field specifying the movements of such objects. Myriad TTC models have been implemented on UAVs with reasonable results. Constant optic flow is applied on a fixed-wing aircraft [3], a small quadcopter [7], and a tethered rotorcraft [17] for an autonomous landing task. Constant optic flow strategies suffer from problems including a lack of timing control and an inability to shape the dynamics of the maneuvers.

Tau Theory [14] addresses the aforementioned issues with TTC, and conceptualizes the visual strategy with which many species are believed to control and navigate. Tau theory casts the variable τ as a measure of TTC which is directly available from neuronal circuitry without the need for explicit computation (which is also called direct or Gibsonian perception [6]), and has some experimental verification [20]. It states that goal-directed movements and actions require intrinsic tau-guidance, which is generated in the brain as an intrinsic reference tau that specifies a desired TTC to the goal. Coupling this ideal intrinsic reference τ with an extrinsic τ (i.e., a measure of the agent's actual TTC) allows the agent to move to a point at a specified time [13]. A sequence of such movements allows an agent to navigate and control in 4D.

The application of tau theory to UAVs is a new research area, and very few works and papers are available. One of the most documented works [12] develops and demonstrates the application of tau theory to achieve 4D guidance and control of a quadcopter UAV during landing and docking maneuvers. A similar system [1] demonstrates autonomous landing of a quadcopter using a tau strategy and TTC from monocular camera plus inertial measurement unit. Although these works highlight the relevance and applicability of tau theory to autonomous UAVs, they all rely on traditional control methods such as PIDs to map tau information into control commands. This results in systems that are sensitive to initial conditions and don't generalise well. We aim to ameliorate this situation by evolving biologically-inspired controllers based on neural networks.

2.3   Neuroevolution for UAV Control

Neuroevolution [5] involves the use of evolutionary algorithms to optimise a population of neural networks, which are assessed on a task via a behaviour-based fitness function. Promising solutions are preserved and modified using genetics-inspired operators, which can alter e.g., synaptic connection weights, connectivity patterns, network complexity, etc. Over a number of generations, the networks are incrementally improved to be better at achieving the behaviour defined by the fitness function. Previous research includes a studies into evolving feedforward controllers for single-rotor RUAVs [4] and quadcopters [19]. Both report robust control: a higher tolerance to noise compared with standard PID controllers [2], a more graceful degradation of performance under increasing noise, and more robust handling of disturbances.

The neural model is a key determinant of the capabilities of the neuroevolutionary system. Both of the discussed works [4,19] use feedforward Multi-Layered Perceptron (MLP) neural networks [18], which are popular due to their "Universal Approximation" property — simply that an MLP of sufficient complexity can approximate any nonlinear function and hence provide highly nonlinear input-output mappings. This ability may be critical to the success of our τ-controllers. We note the promise of spiking neural models in e.g., performing waypoint-holding [8], however we use MLP networks for this study as spiking networks are only universal approximators under certain conditions (e.g., when they are made to simulate a MLP that approximates the desired function). We note that all of the above work focuses on traditional GNC. In contrast, we use τ for guidance, navigation, and control.

Justification of our approach is based on the benefits of tau-GNC (which is robust, fast, precise, and temporally sensitive), the universal approximation property and highlighted robustness of MLP RUAV controllers, and the proven suitability of evolutionary techniques to design such controllers.

3   Experimental Setup

Our chosen platform is CSIRO's in-house Eagle quadcopter. The GNC system is implemented onboard in the ESM realtime state machine framework [15], which provides guarantees on the maximum possible delays when controlling the quadcopter. This HiL setup aims to ease the transition to a real quadcopter, following e.g. [10] For our purposes, guidance takes a desired target point and arrival time as input and outputs a reference τ_{ref} for the platform to follow (computed as in [12]). The navigation system is responsible for continuously estimating the actual τ between the quadcopter and the target point using available sensors such as camera. In the current HiL experimental setup, a "virtual τ sensor" is used to emulate the computation of τ. For real flight experiments, τ will be estimated in real-time from a monocular camera. Only τ and τ_{ref} are passed to the control system (an evolved feedforward neural network), which attempts to output motor commands so that the platform accurately follows τ_{ref}.

An experiment proceeds as follows: 25 random networks are generated. Each network is trialled on the problem and assigned a fitness. Following this, 500 generations take place in which each of the networks makes 4 children, which are altered by the evolutionary algorithm, trialled, and assigned a fitness. The best network is preserved in that population slot. Each trial involves a number of steps; a step starts with the receipt of τ and τ_{ref} by the controlling network, and ends with outputting a thrust. One step is 20 ms, hence the system works in real time at 50 Hz. We conduct 10 experimental repeats, and record the current population state and associated statistics every 20 generations.

3.1   Test Problem

For our initial test we task the platform with descending from a height of 5.5 m in 7 s, the ideal result being a perfect match between τ and τ_{ref}, and subsequent arrival at the point after exactly 7 s with zero velocity. We focus only on z-axis control, x, y and yaw are controlled by PIDs which are tasked to keep their respective variable neutral. At the start of a trial, the quadcopter virtually ascends to a height of 5.5 m. When the UAV reaches this height, it switches to hover mode and waits for the flight mode manager to trigger the landing maneuver. The tau-guidance and tau-navigation systems start generating τ_{ref} and estimating the actual τ, respectively. Thrust is calculated at every step using the current controller. Note that this is a difficult task as we require highly nonlinear control in 2D with a single state variable.

Fitness is accumulated every step according to the controller's ability to follow τ_{ref}. Per step, error calculated as in (1), bounded to a maximum error e_{max} as calculated in (2). Both τ and τ_{ref} are bounded between $\tau_{min}=-100$ and $\tau_{max}=100$ — due to the nature of τ, it is possible for computational errors to occur if it approaches infinity. $\theta\tau z_{ref}=-0.01$ is a maximum value of τz_{ref}. Total trial fitness is then calculated as (3), where $t_{live} = 350$ (7 s * 50 Hz), or the final step number before the trial is aborted.

$$e = abs(\log_{10} \tau z_{ref}/\tau z) \tag{1}$$

$$e_{max} = abs(\log_{10} \tau z_{max}/\theta\tau z_{ref}) \tag{2}$$

$$f = \left(\sum_{t=0}^{t<t_{live}} (e_{max} - e)^2 \right) + v_{bonus} + z_{bonus} \tag{3}$$

A trial ends with either successful arrival at the target, or abort due to following criterea: (i) absolute velocity $> 4m/s$, (ii) absolute difference between z and setpoint $z > 8m$, $z < 0m$, e.g. platform has crashed. If a trial successfully ends, it may be eligible for fitness bonuses: v_{bonus} if final platform velocity $< 0.3m/s$, and z_{bonus}, if final platform $0 > z < 0.1m$, calculated as:

$$v_{bonus} = z_{bonus} = 70 * e_{max}^2, \tag{4}$$

where the constant is experimentally derived as a sufficient weighting. A controller can receive none, one, or both bonuses. The constant term appropriately weights the importance of arriving under those conditions. Bonuses are added to the final fitness value generated in (3) before being assigned to the controller.

To counter the effects of noise, etc., on the assignment of appropriate fitness values, a controller that receives v_{bonus} or z_{bonus} is immediately retested. If the retest also results in the award of v_{bonus} and/or z_{bonus}, the controller is flagged to indicate that it has successfully attained that bonus. If it is the first controller in an experiment to achieve that bonus, the generation is recorded. Regardless of the result of the retest, the fitness from both runs is averaged and assigned to the controller. Note that optimising based on τ allows us to create general controllers, as τ_{ref} can correspond to any setpoint/timing.

3.2   Neurocontrollers

Our neural networks allow for mapping τ to control outputs on a single axis. They are three-layer MLPs, following a standard *input, hidden, output* arrangement. The networks are feedforward with no recurrency, and are fully-connected as there are a small number of inputs and only a single output — it is likely that feature selection or connection masks (e.g., [9]) would disable connections that carry useful information and be detrimental to controller performance. The networks have four inputs, a variable-sized hidden layer under evolutionary control, and one neuron in the output layer. All neurons have a *tanh* activation function,

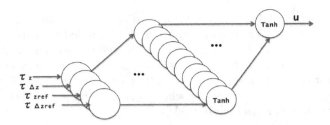

Fig. 2. Showing the architecture of our MLP networks. Networks are fully connected. Inputs are τ, τ_{ref}, and their derivatives. The single output is the quadcopter thrust.

and all connection weights w exist in the range $[-10,10]$. Each neuron has an associated bias b, also in the range $[-10,10]$. Network topology is shown in Fig. 2.

At every step during a trial, the four inputs i (τ_z, $\tau_{\Delta z}$, τ_{zref}, and $\tau_{\Delta zref}$, with range $[-100,100]$) are scaled to $[0,1]$ and passed along the appropriate connections to the hidden layer. Each hidden layer neuron sums the inputs, each input multiplied by the weight of the connection it travels down, and applies *tanh* to the sum to give the instantaneous neuron state y ($0 \geq y \leq 1$). The process is repeated for the output neuron, taking the values of the respective hidden neurons as inputs i. For an arbitrary neuron, the instantaneous state y is calculated according to (5); j is the weight layer connecting to the neuron and k indexes those connections. The output neuron's y is rescaled to $[-40,40]$ and used as the thrust u for that step.

$$y = tanh\left(\sum_{k=0}^{n}(w_{jk} * i_k) + b\right) \tag{5}$$

3.3 Evolutionary Algorithm

To search for high-fitness network configurations we use a 25+4 Evolution Strategy (ES)[16], which is chosen to give a stable search process (important given the realtime nature of the task). The networks are codified as two weight vectors (one per weight layer), a variable-length bias vector (one element per hidden neuron), and a bias for the output neuron. Connection weights, bias weights, and hidden layer size are all controlled by the ES.

Experimentally-determined mutation rates are $\mu = 0.06$ (rate of mutating a connection/bias value), and $\psi = 0.06$ (rate of performing a neuron addition/removal event). As a concession to the long evaluation times associated with the task, we include a single self-adaptive mutation parameter, ω, which controls the relative probabilities of performing node addition/removal events. As ψ is set to a low value, the mutation process is relatively incremental, however as ω can adapt itself, the ES can influence the probability of adding as opposed to removing neurons, allowing for more expedient location of suitable hidden layer sizes.

At the start of an experiment, a population of 25 uniform-randomly weighted MLPs with 10 hidden neurons are generated, together with an initial ω, uniform-randomly assigned in the range [0–1]. Each network is tested on the problem and assigned a fitness. In each subsequent generation, every network produces 4 copies of itself. Each network copies it's parents ω and modifies it as $\omega \rightarrow \omega \, exp^{N(0,1)}$ to generate a new ω for each child.

For each connection/bias, a random number [0,1] is drawn from a uniform distribution. If that number is $< \mu$, that connection/bias value is uniformly altered by $\pm 0 - 10\%$ of the total range of the value. Another number is drawn from the same distribution; if it is $< \psi$ a neuron addition/removal event takes place. This involves drawing a further number from the distribution and comparing it to ω. If $< \omega$, a fully-connected neuron is added to the hidden layer. Otherwise, a neuron is picked at random from the hidden layer and its bias and connections are removed. Each modified network is then evaluated on the test problem and assigned a fitness. Of the five candidate networks (4 children and the original parent), the best is kept and the rest discarded. Once this occurs for each of the 25 networks in the population, the generation is complete and the next generation begins.

4   Results

In terms of performance, we note a convergence of best fitness to near 7000 at ≈ 350 generations (Fig. 3(a)) — low error after this point indicates that all experimental repeats are able to find a highly fit solution that is rewarded with both v_{bonus} and z_{bonus}. Mean fitness follows a similar trend to that of best fitness, achieving a maximum value of ≈ 2600. Low fitness does not improve during the generations — this shows that at least one of the initial controllers per experiment cannot escape an initial local fitness minima through the ES, and demonstrates the difficulty of the tau-control task. A uniformly-low initial best fitness provides similar intuition — none of the controllers are good at the task by chance.

Bonuses associated with low final velocity v_{bonus} and position error z_{bonus} are attained on average after 40.1 (st.dev 11.57) and 39.9 (st.dev 11.68) generations respectively; the effects of those bonuses on population fitness can be most easily seen in the best fitness in Fig. 3(a), where best fitness rises dramatically from ≈ 3500 to ≈ 5300 between generations 20 and 60. Nine of the ten experimental repeats generated a controller that attained v_{bonus} and z_{bonus} in the same generation — one bonus was not easier to achieve than the other.

Evolved network composition (Fig. 3(b), blue line) shows a decline of mean neurons per network from 11 (10 hidden, 1 output) to ≈ 10.45 after 500 generations. Lowering the number of neurons reduces the dimensionality of the network search space as fewer connection weights need to be optimised. Simpler networks may find it easier to approximate the required function as having fewer connections reduces the effect of crosstalk and reduce the likelihood of overfitting. We note that the convergence in best fitness at ≈ 300–350 generations corresponds

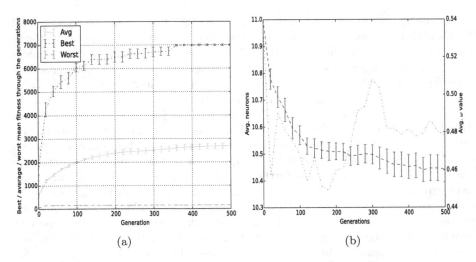

Fig. 3. (a) Best/average/worst population fitness (b) average number of neurons/ω in population through the experiment (Color figure online)

to the final significant drop in average neuron numbers from $\approx$10.5 to $\approx$10.45 over the same period.

Following an initial period of instability as many networks are replaced, the self-adaptive ω (Fig. 3(b), red line) is, apart from a small period covering generations $\approx$290-310, below the average of 0.5. This aids the evolutionary process in biasing the networks to removing neurons rather than adding them, and expedites the process of finding an adequetly-sized hidden layer. Stability is achieved after $\approx$350 generations, which corresponds to the aforementioned rise in best fitness and drop in average neuron numbers.

4.1 Evolutionary Performance

We show the progressive optimisation of control generated by the eventual best network at the end of generations 0, 20, 40, and 500. Initially, the best controller (which is functionally random), survives for 100 steps before being terminated for having velocity $> 4 m/s$ (Fig. 4(b)), at a final $z = \approx$2 m (Fig. 4(a)).

Generations 20 and 40 are very similar in terms of z, velocity and τ — the controller at generation 40 survives 15 steps longer than the controller at generation 20, (an incremental improvement) and as such is awarded higher fitness. Note that neither controller completes the full 350 steps — both are terminated for having $z < 0m$.

The best controller for generation 500 successfully arrives at the target at the desired step with $\approx$0 velocity and z$\approx$0 (Fig. 4(a)/(c)), resulting in the award of both bonuses. The z path shows that the controller descends in stages, with plateaus at steps 0-20 and 60-80 likely a way to dealing with the nondeterministic initial platform conditions. Compared to the best controllers for previous

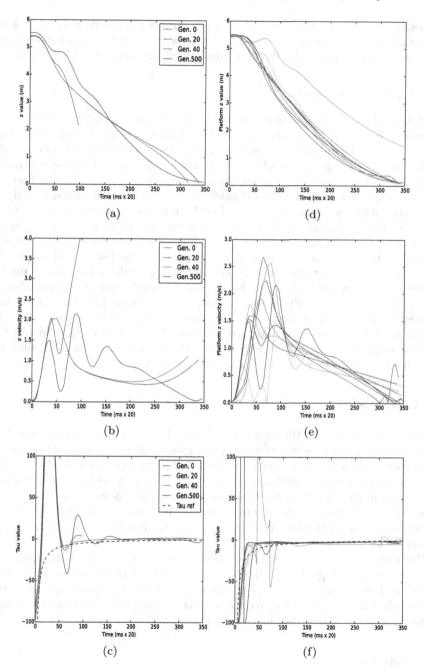

Fig. 4. Showing (a) - (c) the gradual improvement in z, z velocity, and τ following for the experiment that produced the eventual highest-fitness controller. Showing (d) - (f) z, z velocity, and τ for the best controller from each experimental repeat. (c) and (f) show the τ_{ref} as a black dashed line.

generations, the generation 500 controller generates a z profile that approaches horizontal towards the end of the trial, with a velocity that does not diverge from the target as shown by the generation 0/20/40 controller (Fig. 4(b)).

4.2   Task Performance

In-trial, z values are similar amongst 9 of the 10 repeats — Fig. 4(d). One outlier achieves a final z of 1.5 m, the rest <0.1 m. This is enough to earn these controllers z_{bonus}. In contrast, the velocities (Fig. 4(e)) generated are very variable for the first 150 steps, after which much more uniform. All of the controllers except one achieve v_{bonus}. τ values are similarly variable through the first 100 steps — controller output is based solely on τ, which is influenced heavily by the initial platform state (Fig. 4(f)). Recall that the platform must fly to its start position in simulation, hence its instantaneous initial state can include a wide range of velocities and positions, leading to a large degree of variance in both velocity and τ as the controller attempts to stabilise the platform. We also note that the variance in τ is not necessarily reflected in the z profiles attained by the controller — τ is highly variable and sensitive to disturbance, even in successful trials. By basing our fitness function on a variable with these properties, we are able to generate controllers that can robustly cope with such variations/disturbances in τ. We further note that variations in τ in the first hundred steps of a trial are less critical than those later on, as the controller has time to adapt and bring the platform under control.

5   Conclusions

In this study we present the first evolved neural τ-controller, and the first fully τ-based GNC system for bio-inspired quadcopter control. The system employs a population of neural networks that evolve to follow τ_{ref} using a self-adaptive evolution strategy, and is grounded in a hardware in-the-loop setup. Our hypothesis was proven in that MLP controllers were successfully evolved to provide precise τ control for a difficult single-axis descent task. Results indicate that the evolved controllers can generate robust and precise control, despite using only two inputs (τ and τ_{ref}).

We intend to follow up this preliminary investigation by transferring the controllers to a real quadrotor RUAV (easier thanks to the hardware in-the-loop setup), and extending the remit of the networks into the guidance and navigation parts of the GNC architecture. We envisage that this will include the use of more complex, network forms that can perform temporal processing.

References

1. Alkowatly, M.T., Becerra, V.M., Holderbaum, W.: Bioinspired autonomous visual vertical control of a quadrotor unmanned aerial vehicle. J. Guidance Control Dynam. **38**(2), 249–262 (2014)

2. Åström, K.J., Hägglund, T.: Advanced PID control. ISA-The Instrumentation, Systems, and Automation Society, Research Triangle Park, NC 27709 (2006)
3. Chahl, J., Srinivasan, M., Zhang, S.: Landing strategies in honeybees and applications to uninhabited airborne vehicles. Int. J. Robot. Res. **23**(2), 101–110 (2004)
4. De Nardi, R., Togelius, J., Holland, O., Lucas, S.: Evolution of neural networks for helicopter control: Why modularity matters. In: 2006 IEEE Congress on Evolutionary Computation, CEC 2006, pp. 1799–1806 (2006)
5. Floreano, D., Dürr, P., Mattiussi, C.: Neuroevolution: from architectures to learning. Evol. Intel. **1**(1), 47–62 (2008)
6. Gibson, J.: Visually controlled locomotion and visual orientation in animals. Br. J. Psychol. **49**(3), 182–194 (1958)
7. Herisse, B., Hamel, T., Mahony, R.E., Russotto, F.X.: Landing a VTOL unmanned aerial vehicle on a moving platform using optical flow. IEEE Trans. Robot. **28**(1), 77–89 (2012)
8. Howard, D., Elfes, A.: Evolving spiking networks for turbulence-tolerant quadrotor control. In: International Conference on Artificial Life (ALIFE14), pp. 431–438 (2014)
9. Howard, G.D., Bull, L.: On the effects of node duplication and connection-oriented constructivism in neural XCSF. In: Proceedings of the 10th Annual Conference Companion on Genetic and Evolutionary Computation, pp. 1977–1984. ACM (2008)
10. Jang, J.S., Tomlin, C.: Autopilot design for the stanford dragonfly UAV: validation through hardware-in-the-loop simulation. In: Proceedings of the AIAA Guidance, Navigation, and Control Conference (2001)
11. Kendoul, F.: Survey of advances in guidance, navigation, and control of unmanned rotorcraft systems. J. Field Robot. **29**(2), 315–378 (2012)
12. Kendoul, F.: Four-dimensional guidance and control of movement using time-to-contact: application to automated docking and landing of unmanned rotorcraft systems. Int. J. Robot. Res. **33**(2), 237–267 (2014)
13. Lee, D.N.: Guiding movement by coupling taus. Ecol. Psychol. **10**, 221–250 (1998)
14. Lee, D.N.: A theory of visual control of braking based on information about time-to-collision. Perception **5**(4), 437–459 (1976)
15. Merz, T., Rudol, P., Wzorek, M.: Control system framework for autonomous robots based on extended state machines. In: 2006 International Conference on Autonomic and Autonomous Systems, ICAS 2006, p. 14 IEEE (2006)
16. Rechenberg, I.: Evolutionsstrategie: Optimierung technischer Systeme nach Prinzipien der biologischen Evolution. Frommann-Holzboog, Stuttgart (1973)
17. Ruffier, F., Franceschini, N.: Optic flow regulation: the key to aircraft automatic guidance. Elseiver Robot. Auton. Syst. **50**, 177–194 (2005)
18. Rumelhart, D., McClelland, J.: Parallel Distributed Processing, vol. 1 & 2. MIT Press, Cambridge (1986)
19. Shepherd III, J.F., Tumer, K.: Robust neuro-control for a micro quadrotor. In: Proceedings of the 12th Annual Conference on Genetic and Evolutionary Computation, GECCO 2010, pp. 1131–1138. ACM, New York (2010)
20. Tan, H.R., Leuthold, A., Lee, D., Lynch, J., Georgopoulos, A.: Neural mechanisms of movement speed and tau as revealed by magnetoencephalography. Exp. Brain Res. **195**(4), 541–552 (2009)

The Effect of Risk Perceived Payoffs in Iterated Interdependent Security Games

Ayman Ghoneim[1] and Kamran Shafi[2]([⊠])

[1] Operations Research and Decision Support Department, Faculty of Computers and Information Cairo University, Post Box 12613, Giza, Egypt
a.ghoneim@fci-cu.edu.eg
[2] School of Engineering and Information Technology, University of New South Wales Canberra, Campbell, ACT, Australia
k.shafi@adfa.edu.au

Abstract. Interdependent security (IDS) refers to a class of problems that involve making security investment decisions under uncertainty arising from the interdependency between the actions of different decision making entities in the system. Such problems arise in many real world situations such as cyber, airline and homeland security and epidemics. IDS games provide a framework to study the behaviour of decision-makers in such environments. This paper presents a study of the IDS game dynamics in a simulation setting when the payoffs are varied based on different risk attitude functions using the concept of expected utilities. A special case of iterated IDS games is considered where the assumption of complete loss immunity, in the case where all agents cooperate in investing in their own security, is relaxed by introducing a small stochastic loss term in the payoff. The simulations are carried out using an evolutionary game-theoretic framework where strategies are evolved based on the payoffs accumulated over homogeneous iterated encounters. The results of the simulations suggest that the level of investments are reduced when agents take a risk-averse or risk-taking view of the game in comparison to risk-neutral view.

Keywords: Evolutionary game theory · Interdependent security games · Iterated evolutionary games · Risk attitude · Expected utility

1 Introduction

The role of decision makers' risk attitude in making decisions under risk has long been acknowledged and considered a vital direction in the decision analysis research [16]. While normative decision analysis approaches have been proposed to formally factor in risk attitude in decision models (e.g., prospect theory [7]), expected utility theory proposed by Cramer and Bernoulli in early 1700s [2,3], remains a dominant approach in the field due to its simplicity and elegance in representing risk attitudes using parametric utility functions. Expected utility model relaxes the risk neutrality assumption underlying the predecessor expected

© Springer International Publishing Switzerland 2016
T. Ray et al. (Eds.): ACALCI 2016, LNAI 9592, pp. 348–359, 2016.
DOI: 10.1007/978-3-319-28270-1_29

value approach, which relies only on the average outcomes for the states of nature, and provides an intuitive way to incorporate risk attitudes in making decisions.

Similar to utility theory, game theory is the long standing and dominant approach used for decision analysis in competitive environments where the individual outcomes depend on the actions of all agents involved. The concept of utility has played an important role in game theory since its inception [13]. The issue of risk attitude becomes even more important when considering decision making in competitive environments because the decision making then becomes a function of not only one's own risk preferences but also that of the opponents' risk preferences. However, game-theoretic models usually assume risk neutral agents, i.e., the relationship between utility of their preference over the choice is assumed linear for most analysis.

Notice that the risk neutrality assumption is different from the rationality principle which assumes that agents always choose the action that maximizes their expected payoffs and is also a subject of debate in game theory literature due to non-conformance of observed human behaviour in real experiments and real world scenarios. Nonetheless, while the focus of this paper is definitely not to address this debate, we do note that the evolutionary game-theoretic models, adopted in this study as well, relax the rationality assumption using the concept of fitness based evolution. Interestingly, this implies that studying game dynamics in evolutionary game-theoretic setting with utility-based agent models can potentially allow relaxing both the rationality as well as risk-neutrality assumptions. To the best of our knowledge, there is little work done in this direction in standard two-player games and specifically in interdependent securities (IDS) games.

To this end, this paper investigates the dynamics of IDS games in an evolutionary setting where agents make their decisions based on risk perceived payoffs that are moderated by a parameterized utility function. IDS games model security related investment decision problems under uncertainty which arises due to the interdependency between the actions of other agents in the system (see next section for further details). Due to the involvement of stochasticity, IDS games become a natural candidate for such a study, although we acknowledge that other stochastic games, such as stochastic prisoner's dilemma (PD) game, would also benefit from such an investigation. An extended version of the game is introduced here in order to fully map the payoffs to utility functions using a stochastic loss term in *all invest* case. IDS games have not been studied before in an evolutionary setting, except the studies reported in [14, 15], which consider a replicator dynamics-based spatial version of IDS games. In this paper, we use the same simulation set up as commonly used in iterated PD (IPD) game [1] to study the evolutionary dynamics of IDS games.

There are a few models presented in the literature that closely relate to this work. The effect of payoff magnitudes in two player games was studied in [12]. In a way the work presented in this paper also studies the effect of payoff magnitudes, however our models are evolutionary and payoffs vary using a utility function that allows us to relate the results from a risk attitude perspective. Some researchers have studied and shown the evidence of risk averse behaviour in experimental game settings [6]. Recently, Gemelli et al. [8] used a risk-aware utility model in repeated investment game. However, they have used extensive form to represent the game and focused on studying the effect of varying marginal utility on agent decisions. Further, their simulation experiments are done in a non-population and non-evolutionary setting.

The rest of the paper is organised as follows. Section 2 discusses the IDS game and presents the proposed IDS risk attitude model. In Sect. 3 we discuss our experimental framework. Experimental results and analysis are given in Sect. 4. Section 5 concludes the study and discusses future work.

2   IDS Game and Risk Attitude IDS Model

IDS Game. The IDS game was introduced in [10] to model many real-life security related problems where the lack of security in one site (e.g., house or computer node in a network) may affect other sites even if they are secured. Each player has an asset of value Y to protect against a future adversarial event. Each player has two discrete choices, either to *invest* (I) or to *not invest* (NI) in risk reducing security measures to secure its asset. The player pays a fixed cost c if it chooses to invest in security measures, which would prevent or mitigate the player's potential losses. When a bad future event occurs, a player may incur a stochastic loss of magnitude L. The probability of incurring such loss depends on the I or NI decisions made by all players. The loss is considered direct if it comes because of its own decision to not invest. Each agent faces a chance of indirect loss for every other agent in the system who decide not to invest in securing their sites. Direct and indirect losses occur with probabilities p and q respectively.

Table 1. Two-player IDS game expected payoff matrix.

		P_2	
		I	NI
P_1	I	$Y - c$	$Y - c - qL$
	NI	$Y - pL$	$Y - [pL + (1-p)qL]$

Table 2. Two-player α-IDS game expected payoff matrix.

		P_2	
		I	NI
P_1	I	$Y - c - \alpha L$	$Y - c - qL$
	NI	$Y - pL$	$Y - [pL + (1-p)qL]$

Table 1 shows the payoff matrix for a standard two-player IDS game [10]. If player 1 (P_1) invests and player 2 (P_2) does not invest, then P_1 will incur a fixed cost c for its investment, but may incur an indirect loss with probability q because P_2 does not invest. The overall payoff of P_1 will be $Y - c - qL$ where qL is its expected loss. If P_1 does not invest and P_2 invests, then P_1 may incur a direct loss with probability p. The corresponding expected loss for P_1 is pL, and its overall payoff will be $Y - pL$. If both players do not invest, then P_1 face a risk of direct and indirect losses. This results in a payoff of $Y - [pL + (1 - p)qL]$, where the factor $(1 - p)$ ensures that a (catastrophic) loss is counted only once. Conversely, if both players do invest, then P_1 incurs the investment cost with no expected loss, and its payoff is given by $Y - c$. The previous analysis holds for P_2 as we assume a homogeneous and symmetric game, i.e., players have the same set of actions and the payoffs do not change if the players' positions are reversed.

Standard IDS game (Table 1) assumes that when both players invest in security measures, no loss may occur. In other words, the security measures either prevent the bad future event from happening or completely neutralize its consequences. We propose a slightly modified version of the IDS game - denoted by α-IDS game (Table 2), where there is still a probability α for loss when both players choose to invest, i.e., If both players do invest, still there is an expected loss of αL, and the payoff will be $Y - c - \alpha L$. We assume α to be an infinitesimal probability when compared to p and q. The α-IDS game is more realistic for some security problems, where investing in security measures decreases the probability of the expected loss but does not eliminate it completely, e.g., all countries invest in their security systems but terrorist attacks still may succeed. This modified version is more suitable when studying risk attitudes, since risk is involved regardless of the players' actions, i.e., the four cells of the payoff matrix have an expected loss. Assuming that both players choose their actions simultaneously and with no communication, i.e., no precedent information about the action taken by the other players, the following three different cases can be defined for IDS game under different cost structures:

1. Both players are better off investing as investment will be a dominant strategy when $Y - c - \alpha L \geq Y - pL$ and $Y - c - qL \geq Y - [pL + (1 - p)qL]$. Thus, (I, I) is a dominant strategy equilibrium for $c \leq pL(1 - q)$.
2. Two possible Nash equilibria (I, I) and (NI, NI) for $c > pL(1 - q)$ and $c < (p - \alpha)L$ respectively. Thus for c in the interval $]pL(1-q), (p-\alpha)L[$, both (I, I) and (NI, NI) are Nash equilibria.
3. Both players are better off not investing in the security; i.e., (NI, NI) is a dominant strategy equilibrium for $c \geq (p - \alpha)L$. This case resembles the prisoner dilemma (PD) game which models the conflict between self interest and the group interest, i.e., (I, I) is a Pareto optimal solution and they would benefit by investing cooperatively.

Risk Attitude IDS Model. In game theoretic studies, players are usually assumed to be risk neutral, i.e., the player cares only about the expected payoff regardless of any taken risk. However in reality, not all decision makers have the same attitude towards the risk associated with future gains or losses. A player's risk attitude is defined by the risk premium value, which is the difference between the player's expected value (i.e., average payoff of future gamble possibilities) and the certainty equivalence (i.e., the amount the player would accept instead of the future gamble). Risk neutral represents the middle of the risk attitude continuum, which have risk averse attitude at one extreme, and risk taking attitude at the other. Risk averse player would prefer a lower but more certain expected payoff rather than a higher expected value with high uncertainty. On the contrary, a risk taking player would prefer a high uncertain expected payoff rather than a smaller more certain expected payoff. Between these two extremes, players can have different degrees of being risk averse or risk takers. Considering different players' attitude towards expected payoff in the IDS game brings the game one step closer to reality.

In the α-IDS game, other than a player's own actions of whether to invest or not invest, the opponent's actions and the effect of the bad event affect the player's payoff. Thus, from the player's perspective, there is a risk associated with the future event consequences and the opponent's moves.

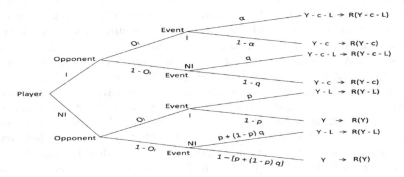

Fig. 1. The decision tree showing the α-IDS game from a player's perspective (Color figure online).

Figure 1 shows a decision tree which illustrates the α-IDS game from a player's perspective. In Fig. 1, the player take a certain action of whether to invest or not to invest in security measures. Then, the opponent may decide[1] to invest with a probability O_I or not to invest with a probability $1 - O_I$. The actions taken by the player and its opponent will define the system-wide level of security, and thus, the probability that a bad future event will cause a loss L.

Based on the choices made and the impact of the bad future event, the player's realized payoff can be either $Y - c - L$, $Y - c$, $Y - L$ or Y. Assuming the player's knowledge of the probabilities associated with its opponent actions and the bad event impact, the player will choose the action which maximizes its expected payoff. The expected payoff of the player when investing in security measures is

$$E(I) = O_I \times (\alpha \times (Y - c - L) + (1 - \alpha) \times (Y - c)) \\ + (1 - O_I) \times (q \times (Y - c - L) + (1 - q) \times (Y - c)), \tag{1}$$

while its expected payoff when not investing is

---

[1] This decision tree does not represent a sequential game where the opponent takes its decision after knowing the decision of the player. We assume a simultaneous game.

$$E(NI) = O_I \times (p \times (Y - L) + (1 - p) \times Y) + (1 - O_I)$$
$$\times ((p + (1 - p) \times q) \times (Y - L) + (1 - (p + (1 - p) \times q)) \times Y). \quad (2)$$

To capture the player's risk attitude, we use a risk function R which gives new values for the payoffs $Y - c - L$, $Y - c$, $Y - L$ and Y, where these new values (shown in Fig. 1 in red) reflects the player's attitude toward possible future gains or loses. Several risk functions were introduced in the literature, we use a bounded exponential risk function [9] defined as

$$R(X) = \begin{cases} \frac{\exp^{\frac{-(X-low)}{r}} - 1}{\exp^{\frac{-(high-low)}{r}} - 1}, & \text{if } r \neq \infty \\ \frac{X - low}{high - low}, & \text{otherwise} \end{cases}$$

The exponential risk function takes an input X and outputs a bounded value in the $[0, 1]$ interval. For scaling the input values, the function uses $high$ and low variables, which in the IDS game are the Y and $Y - c - L$, respectively. The risk function has a parameter r which defines the degree of risk aversion. Assuming values $Y = 100$, $L = 10$ and $c = 4$, Fig. 2 shows the exponential risk function with different values for the parameter r. When $r = \infty$, the risk function is a straight line corresponding to the risk neutral attitude. The values $r = 1$, $r = 3$, $r = 6$ reflect the risk averse attitude. While the values $r = -1$, $r = -3$, $r = -6$ reflect the risk taking attitude. The expected payoff of the player considering the player's risk attitude is computed according to Eqs. 1 and 2 while replacing $Y - c - L$, $Y - c$, $Y - L$ and Y by $R(Y - c - L)$, $R(Y - c)$, $R(Y - L)$ and $R(Y)$.

3   Experimental Design

Evolutionary computation approaches are frequently used to investigate how cooperation may evolve between self-interested players. Evolved complex strategies are more likely to be adopted by players in real situations than simple strategies [1,11]. Here, we use genetic algorithms (GAs) to analyse the evolutionary dynamics of single-round and iterated rounds IDS games, while investigating how different risk attitudes for players affect the investment level.

Strategy Representation. A lookup table representation for player strategies is used [1]. The lookup table is a binary representation ('0' for invest; '1' for not invest). Each table entry is split into a history portion and a strategy portion. The bit size depends on the number of players and how much historical information is recorded. For example - Fig. 3, if there were 2 players and $L = 1$ history step, then the history portion will consist of 2 bits (1 bit for the player indicating his own previous action and 1 bit indicating the other player's action). Since there are 4 possible such histories there are 4 bits needed for the strategy portion. Generally, the strategy portion size is 2^{nL} bits where n is the number of players and L is the number of historical steps.

Initialization. We consider history length of zero (Hist0) which requires a 1-bit encoding because no history is recorded and history length of one (Hist1)

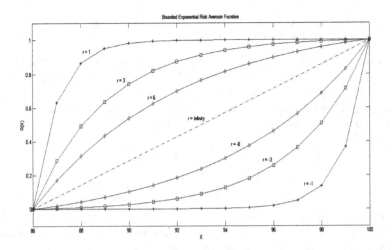

Fig. 2. The exponential risk function with different values for parameter r.

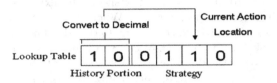

Fig. 3. The lookup table representation for $n = 2$ players with $L = 1$ bit of history recorded. Here in the previous round the players chose '10', then the player in the next round would choose to not invest '1'.

which requires a 6-bit encoding (Fig. 3). For each player (genotype), we initialize its bit(s) randomly to be '0' for invest or '1' for not to invest. We consider a population of size $PopSize = 50$.

Fitness Evaluation. Similar to [4], we evaluate each genotype (player) in a co-evolving population by making it play against every other strategy in the population. In each generation, each genotype is evaluated by playing the α-IDS game against all other strategies. The game has a single round if the players have Hist0. While the game has 200 rounds if the players have Hist1, where this number of rounds are sufficient to reach a stable payoff [5]. In each round, a player will get the expected payoff according to the α-IDS game matrix depending on his action and his opponent's action. Each genotype has a cumulative payoff from the played games against all opponents. The fitness is calculated by dividing a genotype's cumulative payoff by the number of games it participated in (i.e., the number of opponents) multiplied by the number of rounds in each game to obtain the average payoff per round for this genotype.

Selection and Reproduction Operators. Linear ranking selection is used where a new fitness is calculated for each genotype according to its position

(*Pos*) in the population, with the smallest average payoff ranked at the first position and the highest average payoff at the last position. Equation 3 is used, with $SP = 1.25$ denoting the selection pressure.

$$Fitness(Pos) = 2 - SP + 2 \cdot (SP - 1) \cdot \frac{(Pos - 1)}{(PopSize - 1)} \qquad (3)$$

We use binary crossover followed by bit mutation with probabilities of 0.6 and 0.001 respectively. All GA parameters are set according to preliminary tests.

4   Results and Discussion

In this section, we investigate the effect of different risk attitudes on the evolutionary dynamics of the α-IDS game using the risk attitude IDS game model proposed in Sect. 2 and the experimental design illustrated in Sect. 3.

We use the values $Y = 100$, $L = 10$, $p = 0.6$, $q = 0.4$, and $\alpha = 0.01$ while conducting our experiments. The values of p, q, α and L define the bounds on the cost of investment variable c and thus different cases in the α-IDS game, where $c \leq pL(1 - q) = 3.6$ corresponds to Case 1 (i.e., (I,I) is a Nash equilibrium), $c \in]pL(1 - q), (p - \alpha)L[=]3.6, 5.99[$ corresponds to Case 2 (i.e., both (I,I) and (NI, NI) are Nash equilibria), and $c \geq (p - \alpha)L = 5.99$ corresponds to Case 3 (i.e., (NI, NI) is a Nash equilibrium). We consider the values 3, 3.6, 4, 4.5, 5, 5.5, 5.99 and 6.5 for c to cover the previous three cases. In this set of experiments, we assume that a player has no information or beliefs about his opponent's actions. Thus, a player will assign a probability of 0.5 for his opponent investing in security measures (i.e., $O_I = 0.5$) and a probability of 0.5 for his opponent not investing $(1 - O_I = 0.5)$.

We use the exponential risk attitude function (Eq. 2) and experiment with different values for the parameter r to capture different risk attitudes (as shown in Fig. 2). For $r = 1$, $r = 3$, and $r = 6$, the players will be risk averse with $r = 1$ the highest risk aversion level in our experiments, while $r = 6$ is the mildest level of risk aversion. When $r = \infty$, players are risk neutral. For $r = -1$, $r = -3$, and $r = -6$, the exponential risk function expresses the risk taking attitude, where $r = -1$ is the highest level of risk taking and $r = -6$ is the mildest risk taking attitude.

When fixing the values $Y = 100$, $L = 10$, $p = 0.6$, $q = 0.4$, $\alpha = 0.01$, and $O_I = 0.5$, for a particular value c and a particular value r, the α-IDS game matrix (Table 2) will be computed according to the decision tree in Fig. 1. Thus, when fixing all other variable, each combination of c and r values will correspond to a different α-IDS game matrix. Figure 4 shows the α-IDS game matrices when $c = 3$ and different values of r.

Single-Round α-IDS Game. In order to establish a baseline for comparing the effect of different risk attitudes, we discuss first the neutral risk attitude (i.e., $r = \infty$). This is also crucial for validating our experimental implementation by showing how the evolutionary dynamics coincide with the theoretical equilibria

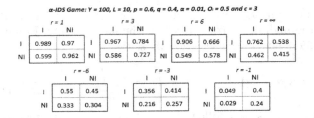

Fig. 4. The α-IDS game matrices when $c = 3$ and different values of r.

of the α-IDS game. Given a population of 50 players, each player plays pairwise games with all other players in the population (i.e., 49 games for each player), and a single round per game, we have $50 \times 49 \times 1 = 2450$ actions taken by all the players in the population in one GA generation. For each α-IDS game, we make 100 different run, each run has 150 generations. Figure 5 shows the number of investment actions taken in each run (left) and the average number of investment actions of the 100 runs (right) for $c = 4.5$. The figure shows that 150 generations was sufficient for the population to converge.

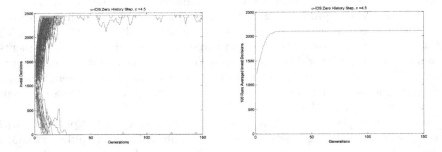

Fig. 5. The number of investment actions taken in each run (left) and the average number of investment actions of the 100 runs (right) for $c = 4.5$.

Figure 6 shows the average number of investment actions of the 100 runs (right) for all considered values of c. It shows that all the 100 runs converged to the (I, I) equilibrium for $c = 3$ and 3.6, which is the Nash equilibrium in Case 1 of the IDS game. For $c = 4.5$ (Fig. 5) or 5, some runs converge to the (I, I) equilibrium and others converge to the (NI, NI) equilibrium, which are the two possible Nash equilibria in Case 2 in the IDS game. For $c = 5.5$, 5.99 or 6.5, all runs converge to the (NI, NI) equilibrium, which is the Nash equilibrium in Case 3 of the IDS game.

Now we move to consider different risk attitudes. Figure 7 considers all risk attitudes (i.e., all considered values of r) with each c value. It plots the final convergence level of the averaged investment actions of 100 runs for each risk attitude (i.e., r value) against c values. The figure shows that the risk neutral

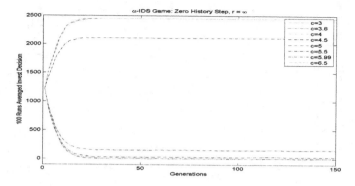

Fig. 6. The average number of investment actions of the 100 runs for different c values.

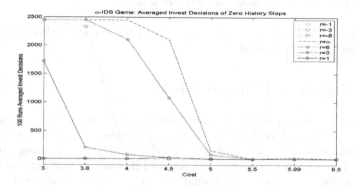

Fig. 7. Single-Round α-IDS: the final convergence level of the averaged investment actions of 100 runs for each risk attitude (i.e., r value) against c values (Color figure online).

attitude (the black dotted curve) has higher values than all other curves (i.e., other risk attitudes) for all values of c. This is followed by the mildest level of risk averse $r = 6$ (pink) and risk taking $r = -6$ (cyan). The investment level decreases dramatically for other r values. This concludes that the highest investment level in the IDS game is attained when players are risk neutral, and having any other risk attitude decreases the investment level. Further, the investment level continues to decrease as the players deviate further from being risk neutral.

Iterated α-IDS Game. In the iterated version of the α-IDS game we assume players using one history step. Again, we start with the neutral risk attitude (i.e., $r = \infty$) to establish a baseline for comparing the effect of different risk attitudes. Given a population of 50 players, each player plays pairwise games with all other players in the population (i.e., 49 games for each player), and 200 rounds per game, we have $50 \times 49 \times 200 = 490000$ actions taken by all the players in the population in one GA generation. Repeating the previous analysis, Fig. 8 shows the similar outcome that the highest investment level in the IDS game

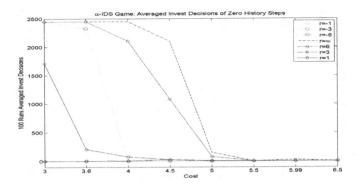

Fig. 8. Iterated α-IDS: the final convergence level of the averaged investment actions of 100 runs for each risk attitude (i.e., r value) against c values.

is attained when players are risk neutral, and having any other risk attitude decreases the investment level.

5   Conclusion and Future Work

This paper presented a study of evolutionary game dynamics when the agents perceive their payoffs based on different risk attitudes in a stochastic game settings. A parameterized utility function is used to model risk based perception and an extended version of IDS games is introduced that allows mapping between the payoff and utility functions. The simulations are run using standard evolutionary game-theoretic framework where a population of agents interact homogeneously in iterated encounters and strategies are evolved using a genetic algorithm. The simulation results suggest that agents tend to decrease security investments when they take a non-risk-neutral view of their payoffs. Future work will investigate the use of agent models with embedded risk profiles to study game dynamics in a heterogeneous setting as well as mechanisms to promote cooperation under such models.

References

1. Axelrod, R.: The evolution of strategies in the iterated prisoner's dilemma. In: Davis, L. (ed.) Genetic Algorithms and Simulated Annealing. Pitman/Morgan Kaufman, London/Los Altos, pp. 32–41 (1987)
2. Bernoulli, D.: Exposition of a new theory on the measurement of risk (translated, original 1738). Econometrica J. Econometric Soc. **22**, 23–36 (1954)
3. Cramer, G.: Letter to Nicolas Bernoulli. Reprinted in Bernoulli (1738). see ref for Bernoulli, D., 1728
4. Darwen, P., Yao, X.: Why more choices cause less cooperation in iterated prisoner's dilemma. In: Proceedings of the 2001 Congress on Evolutionary Computation, pp. 987–994. IEEE Press, Piscataway, May 2001

5. Ghoneim, A., Barlow, M., Abbass, H.A.: Rounds effect in evolutionary games. In: Randall, M., Abbass, H.A., Wiles, J. (eds.) ACAL 2007. LNCS (LNAI), vol. 4828, pp. 72–83. Springer, Heidelberg (2007)
6. Goeree, J.K., Holt, C.A., Palfrey, T.R.: Risk averse behavior in generalized matching pennies games. Games Econ. Behav. **45**(1), 97–113 (2003)
7. Kahneman, D., Tversky, A.: Prospect theory: an analysis of decision under risk. Econometrica J. Econometric Soc. **47**, 263–291 (1979)
8. Kersting, K., Toussaint, M.: Adopting a risk-aware utility model for repeated games of chance. In: Proceedings of the Sixth Starting AI Researchers Symposium, STAIRS 2012, vol. 241, p. 113. IOS Press (2012)
9. Kirkwood, C.W.: Notes on attitude toward risk taking and the exponential utility function. Technical report AZ 85287–4006, Arizona State University (1991)
10. Kunreuther, H., Heal, G.: Interdependent security. J. Risk Uncertainty **26**(2), 231–249 (2003)
11. Lindgren, K.: Evolutionary phenomena in simple dynamics. Artif. Life **II**(10), 295–312 (1991)
12. McKelvey, R.D., Palfrey, T.R., Weber, R.A.: The effects of payoff magnitude and heterogeneity on behavior in 2× 2 games with unique mixed strategy equilibria. J. Econ. Behav. Organ. **42**(4), 523–548 (2000)
13. Neumann, L.J., Morgenstern, O.: Theory of Games and Economic Behavior. Princeton University Press, Princeton (1947)
14. Shafi, K., Bender, A., Abbass, H., et al.: Evolutionary dynamics of interdependent exogenous risks. In: IEEE Congress on Evolutionary Computation (CEC), pp. 1–8. IEEE (2010)
15. Shafi, K., Bender, A., Zhong, W., Abbass, H.A.: Spatio-temporal dynamics of security investments in an interdependent risk environment. Physica A Stat. Mech. Appl. **391**(20), 5004–5017 (2012)
16. Weber, M., Camerer, C.: Recent developments in modelling preferences under risk. Oper. Res. Spektrum **9**(3), 129–151 (1987)

Genetic Algorithm Based Trading System Design

Richard Tymerski[✉], Ethan Ott, and Garrison Greenwood

Department of Electrical & Computer Engineering, Portland State University,
Portland, OR 97201, USA
tymerski@ee.pdx.edu, ethan.ott@gmail.com, greenwd@pdx.edu

Abstract. We investigate the design of trading systems using a genetic algorithm (GA). Technical indicators are used to define entry and exit rules. The choice of indicators and their associated parameters are optimized by the GA which operates on integer values only. Holding time and profit target exit rules are also evaluated. It is found that a fitness function based on winning probability coupled with a profit target and one based on the Sharpe ratio are useful in maximizing percentage of winning trades as well as overall profit. Strategies are developed which are highly competitive to buy and hold.

Keywords: Genetic algorithms · Trading systems

1 Introduction

Investors wishing to profit in the financial markets may approach it a number of different ways. Use of *fundamental analysis* may be made to evaluate the prospects of future earnings for a company and thus expect an ever rising share price. Alternatively, the underlying philosophy of *technical analysis* says that all fundamental information is reflected in the asset price and so analysis of the price itself and perhaps the associated trading volume is sufficient. A final alternative approach is a combination of the two mentioned. In this paper we utilize technical analysis alone in the development of trading systems [2].

There have been many academic investigations with the aim of developing technical trading strategies for financial markets which have used computational intelligence techniques. These include methods such as Artificial Neural Networks [8], Genetic Algorithms [6,10,13], Genetic Programming [9], a game-theoretic approach employing fuzzy logic [14] as well as other approaches [7,12]. These have been applied to a range of different financial assets such as, stocks [9], forex [11,13] and futures [10]. The techniques discussed in this paper may also be more generally applied to these assets but we will provide simulation results in the futures domain, specifically, S&P500 e-mini index futures (symbol: ES). The S&P500 index is a broad based index which serves as a proxy for the US stock market.

© Springer International Publishing Switzerland 2016
T. Ray et al. (Eds.): ACALCI 2016, LNAI 9592, pp. 360–373, 2016.
DOI: 10.1007/978-3-319-28270-1_30

In this paper a large number of widely known, as well as a couple of newer technical indicators are searched to find combinations to form entry and exit rules for trading. These indicators in essence quantify market conditions and thus when selected herald auspicious entry or exit conditions based on historical data. The selection of trading rules as well as the associated indicator parameters are evolved using a genetic algorithm. Since the rule selection and indicator parameter values (which for the main part represent lookback periods used in the indicators) are integer values, the GA reproduction and mutation operations are specifically coded with this in mind.

In this work indicator based rules are used to initiate trade entry and exits. However we first investigate the efficacy of using two alternative non-indicator based rules for exits. Furthermore, the results of using a number of different fitness functions are examined. The final results lead to strategies which are highly competitive as compared to the buy and hold strategy.

2   Trading Strategies

Mechanical trading systems are generally comprised of a set of objective rules which dictate the entry and exit conditions for trading an asset. In this paper we consider the design of long-only, end-of-day trading strategies. Consequently, entry conditions are such that there is an expectation that the asset will appreciate in value with a subsequent exit at a higher price level resulting in profitable trades. This is contrasted with trading on the short side where profits are made when the asset depreciates in value.

2.1   Technical Indicators

Objective entry and exit rules can be defined in a number of different ways. Generally for entries technical indicators are used. The indicators are simply mathematical functions which take as input the asset price and/or on occasion the asset trading volume. The price is generally aggregated to a certain time period, such as daily bars in end-of-day strategies so that a trading decision is only made at most once per day. For any time aggregation four price values can be considered. These are the opening, the high, the low and the closing prices. The output of an indicator may comprise one or more values. Generally indicators take into consideration a number of past price bars to derive the indicator value(s). The range of the historical bars considered is referred to as the lookback period.

A widely used indicator is the moving average, where generally a weighted sum of past closing prices are used to derive the indicator value. One such moving average is the exponential moving average (EMA), where more recent data points have greater weight than data further back in the lookback period. We will refer to $EMA(k, p)$ as the value of the p lookback period exponential moving average time series at time index k which is evaluated using the following formula

$$EMA(k, p) = (1 - K) \cdot EMA(k - 1, p) + K \cdot c_k \tag{1}$$

where $K = 2/(1 + p)$ and c_k is the closing price for the k-th bar.

A large number of indicators have been developed in the past and newer ones are appearing constantly. The set of indicators used in the present work are a subset of those offered in the TA-Lib library [3] which is available for use in a number of different coding languages and in particular in the language used in this paper, Matlab. The indicators used are listed in Table 1. Here we see that the value of an indicator is accessed by supplying the value of the time series index, k and also the lookback period, p. Some indicators only use the k-th bar data and so do not require a lookback specifier. An example of this is the Balance of Power (BOP) indicator which is simply determined as follows:

$$BOP(k) = \frac{c_k - o_k}{h_k - l_k} \qquad (2)$$

where c_k, o_k, h_k and l_k are the close, open, high and low prices of the k-th bar, respectively.

On the other hand a number of indicators require more than the two parameters to specify an output. One example of this is the newly developed Connors' Relative Strength Index (ConRSI) [4]. This indicator is a composite of three indicators: (1) RSI used on closing price, (2) RSI used on "streaks" of up and down closing prices, and (3) percent rank of period returns. Each component indicator has its own appropriate lookback period. For our use two of the indicator lookback values were left constant. Specifically, the RSI price period was set at 3 and the RSI streak period was set at 2. The period associated with percent rank of returns was left variable.

Another interesting indicator that was used is the Modified RSI defined as follows:

$$ModRSI(k,p) = \sqrt{p-1} \cdot [RSI(k,p) - 50] \qquad (3)$$

This formulation shifts the output indicator range of the standard RSI indicator from $[0, 100]$ to $[-50, 50]$ and also scales the output value with a value dependent on the lookback period. This was devised so as to allow RSI obtained values of different periods to be compared to each other. Apart from ConRSI and ModRSI indicators, all other indicators listed in Table 1 are standard well known indicators [5].

2.2   Indicator Based Rules

Conditions to initiate entry or exit of trades may be specified using indicators. To illustrate this, consider the widely known moving average crossover system [2]. A typical version of this system contains two moving averages with differing lookback periods, normally referred to as the short and long periods. When the short period moving average crosses above the long period moving average, this can be taken as a signal to enter a trade, i.e. to go long the asset. The condition can be stated as follows for the case of exponential moving averages:

$$EMA(k, p_{SHORT}) > EMA(k, p_{LONG}) \qquad (4)$$

Table 1. List of indicators used in defining the trading rules. All indicators are widely known and used except for the newly developed ConRSI (#5) and ModRSI (#6) indicators. k is the time-series index and p is the indicator lookback period

Ind	Indicator name and Abbreviation
1	Close(k) – bar closing price
2	EMA(k, p) – exponential moving avg
3	TEMA(k, p) – triple exponential moving avg
4	RSI(k, p) – relative strength index
5	ConRSI(k, p – Connor's RSI
6	ModRSI(k, p) – modified RSI
7	BBU(k, p) – upper Bollinger band
8	BBL(k, p) – lower Bollinger band
9	StochK(k, p) – Stochastics %K
10	StochD(k, p) – Stochastics %D
11	Range(k) – price bar range
12	ATR(k, p) – avg true range
13	NATR(k, p) – normalized avg true range
14	MFI(k) – money flow index
15	BOP(k) – balance of power
16	WILLR(k, p) – Williams' %R
17	UO(k, p) – ultimate oscillator
18	ROC(k, p) – rate of change
19	MOM(k, p) – momentum
20	OBV(k) – on balance volume
21	STDDEV(k, p) – std deviation
22	PPO(k, p) – percentage price oscillator
23	MEDPRICE(k) – median price
24	ADX(k, p) – avg directional move index
25	CMO(k, p) – Chande momentum oscillator
26	CCI(k, p) – commodity channel index
27	KAMA(k, p) – Kaufman adaptive moving avg

The result of this rule at time instant k is Boolean. The logic behind entering a long position under this rule is that it indicates a change of trend. This rule is an example of rules comprised of a comparison of the same indicator using different lookback periods.

Another category of an indicator based entry signal is the following. In the following example a long position is taken when the closing price of the current bar crosses below the lower Bollinger Band with a lookback period p—i.e.,

$Close(k) < BBL(k,p)$. Again the result of this rule at time instant k is Boolean. The logic here of entering a long position is that the price has moved sufficiently away from its moving average (which is a component of the Bollinger Bands) that a price reversion to the mean is expected. This rule exemplifies rules where a price level, or a derived price level, such as the median price $(= (h_k + l_k)/2$ where h_k and l_k are the high and low prices of the k-th bar, respectively) is compared to an indicator value.

The last category of rule is one where the indicator value is compared to a threshold level. Note that different indicators may have different ranges of possible output values. For example, the RSI indicator ranges from 0 to 100 whereas the CMO (Chande Momentum Oscillator) and Stochastics Oscillator are range bound to -100 and $+100$. This category of rule can be stated in the RSI example as $RSI(k,p) > threshold$. In this example, if $threshold \approx 80$, then this condition when satisfied signifies an over-bought market condition over the lookback period. Conversely, if the rule were $RSI(k,p) < threshold$ and if say $threshold \approx 20$ is satisfied, then this may signify an over-sold market condition and subsequent appropriate action may be taken.

To further generalize the three different categories of rules the time index k may be varied by a parameter, so that the decision is no longer dependent on the current bar but some prior bar, and the threshold level may be parameterized and scaled and/or translated so as to appropriately match the associated indicator output range. The set of rules used in this paper are listed in Table 2 where they are numbered from 2 to 65. The more generalized rules corresponding to the specific rules discussed above appear in Table 2 as rules numbers #45, #11, #9 and #8, respectively in the order presented above.

2.3 Trade Exits–Alternative Possibilities

As discussed above, a position may be exited using signals from technical indicators. However, other possibilities also exist. We will consider two of these here. The first is a time based condition: the position is exited after a certain number of days has elapsed. The second is the condition that a profit target has been reached and if this is not achieved in a certain maximum number of days the position is exited.

The results of applying indicator based signals for entry and exit as well as the alternative exit conditions just discussed are presented in Sect. 4, however in the next section we first present a discussion of the structure of a genetic algorithm and accompanying genome with which optimization may be achieved.

3   Genetic Algorithm Based Search

A genetic algorithm (GA) was used to evolve the best strategy. In this section we describe its construction and initialization.

The *genome* describes how each solution (strategy) is encoded in the GA while the *genotype* is the encoding of a particular strategy. The genome used in this research is a sequence of 12 *genes*, where each group of 3 genes encodes a rule.

Fig. 1. The genome structure consists of 12 genes. Each group of 3 genes defines a rule and a set of four rules defines an investment strategy. Light shaded groups correspond to buy rules while dark shaded groups refer to sell rules.

In the ensuing discussion we focus on the structure of the genome used for strategies where both the buy and sell rules are evolved. This is one of the three variations presented further below. For the two cases where sell rules are not dictated by indicators only half the number of genes are required. Figure 1 shows the genome structure where $r_i, \alpha_i, \beta_i \in I$. The light groups correspond to buy rules while the dark groups to sell rules. Every genotype specifies four rules where each rule checks to see if some condition exists in the asset time-series data. There are currently 64 rules, indexed from 2 to 65. Each rule r_i has two associated integer parameters α_i and β_i with a range from 2 to 65. Also associated with each rule is a *characteristic function*

$$f(r_i) = \begin{cases} 1 & \text{if condition is met in data} \\ 0 & \text{otherwise} \end{cases} \tag{5}$$

Every trading day is evaluated and a conjunction of the characteristic functions indicates what actions, if any, should be taken. An example will help illustrate how a genotype is decoded. Consider the genotype shown in Fig. 2. Rules 19 and 49 are used for buy decisions and rules 22 and 8 for sell decisions. Suppose at a given time the asset is not held. If the conjunction of $f(19)$ and $f(49)$ is "1", then the asset is purchased and the purchase price is recorded. Conversely, if the asset is held and the conjunction of $f(22)$ and $f(8)$ is "1" the asset is sold and the sell price recorded. (No action is taken if the respective conjunctions are "0".)

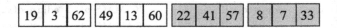

Fig. 2. An example genotype. The first six (with light background) alleles on the left represent two buy rules and their associated parameters. The second set of six (with dark background) alleles used with the indicator based sell (exit) strategy.

The GA evolves a population of 100 individuals (genotypes) over 500 generations. Reproduction is performed using uniform crossover (probability 0.7) and every gene is subject to mutation (probability 0.02). Randomly replacing an allele with another integer does mutation. Elitism is implemented by copying the best-fit individual in the current generation to the next generation. We used binary tournaments to select parents for reproduction.

Table 2. List of rules used to evolve trading strategies. k represents the time-series index. $p1$ and $p2$ are evolved parameters. The term 'adjusted($p2$)' appearing in the table refers to a threshold value parameterized by variable $p2$ and adjusted by value by scaling and/or translation to match the range of values in the corresponding indicator output.

Rule #	Rule	Rule #	Rule
2	ConRSI$(k, p1) >$ adjusted$(p2)$	34	STDDEV$(k, p1) <$ STDDEV$(k - p2, p1)$
3	ConRSI$(k, p1) <$ adjusted$(p2)$	35	STDDEV$(k, p1) >$ STDDEV$(k - p2, p1)$
4	Close$(k) >$ Close$(k - p1)$	36	OBV$(k) <$ OBV$(k - p1)$*adjusted$(p2)$
5	Close$(k) <$ Close$(k - p1)$	37	OBV$(k) >$ OBV$(k - p1)$*adjusted$(p2)$
6	Range$(k) >$ Range$(k - p1)$	38	PPO$(k, p1) >$ adjusted$(p2)$
7	Range$(k) <$ Range$(k - p1)$	39	PPO$(k, p1) <$ adjusted$(p2)$
8	RSI$(k, p1) <$ adjusted$(p2)$	40	MEDPRICE$(k) >$ TEMA$(k, p1)$
9	RSI$(k, p1) >$ adjusted$(p2)$	41	MEDPRICE$(k) <$ TEMA$(k, p1)$
10	BBL$(k, p1) <$ Close$(k - p2)$	42	MEDPRICE$(k) >$ EMA$(k, p1)$
11	BBL$(k, p1) >$ Close$(k - p2)$	43	MEDPRICE$(k) <$ EMA$(k, p1)$
12	BBU$(k, p1) <$ Close$(k - p2)$	44	EMA$(k, p1) <$ EMA$(k, p2)$
13	BBU$(k, p1) >$ Close$(k - p2)$	45	EMA$(k, p1) >$ EMA$(k, p2)$
14	StochK$(k, p1) >$ adjusted$(p2)$	46	TEMA$(k, p1) <$ TEMA$(k, p2)$
15	StochK$(k, p1) <$ adjusted$(p2)$	47	TEMA$(k, p1) >$ TEMA$(k, p2)$
16	StochD$(k, p1) >$ adjusted$(p2)$	48	ADX$(k, p1) <$ adjusted$(p2)$
17	StochD$(k, p1) <$ adjusted$(p2)$	49	ADX$(k, p1) >$ adjusted$(p2)$
18	MFI$(k) <$ adjusted$(p2)$	50	ADX$(k, p1) >$ ADX$(k, p2)$
19	MFI$(k) >$ adjusted$(p2)$	51	ADX$(k, p1) <$ ADX$(k, p2)$
20	BOP$(k) <$ adjusted$(p2)$	52	CMO$(k, p1) <$ adjusted$(p2)$
21	BOP$(k) >$ adjusted$(p2)$	53	CMO$(k, p1) >$ adjusted$(p2)$
22	WILLR$(k, p1) >$ adjusted$(p2)$	54	CCI$(k, p1) >$ adjusted$(p2)$
23	WILLR$(k, p1) <$ adjusted$(p2)$	55	CCI$(k, p1) <$ adjusted$(p2)$
24	UO$(k, p1) >$ adjusted$(p2)$	56	KAMA$(k, p1) >$ adjusted$(p2)$*Close(k)
25	UO$(k, p1) <$ adjusted$(p2)$	57	KAMA$(k, p1) <$ adjusted$(p2)$*Close(k)
26	ROC$(k, p) >$ adjusted$(p2)$	58	KAMA$(k, p1) >$ KAMA$(k - p2, p1)$
27	ROC$(k, p) <$ adjusted$(p2)$	59	KAMA$(k, p1) <$ KAMA$(k - p2, p1)$
28	MOM$(k, p) >$ adjusted$(p2)$	60	ModRSI$(k, p1) <$ adjusted$(p2)$
29	MOM$(k, p) <$ adjusted$(p2)$	61	ModRSI$(k, p1) >$ adjusted$(p2)$
30	ATR$(k, p1) >$ adjusted$(p2)$	62	ModRSI$(k, p1) >$ ModRSI$(k, p2)$
31	ATR$(k, p1) <$ adjusted$(p2)$	63	ModRSI$(k, p1) <$ ModRSI$(k, p2)$
32	NATR$(k, p1) >$ adjusted$(p2)$	64	ModRSI$(k, p1) >$ ModRSI$(k - p2, p1)$
33	NATR$(k, p1) <$ adjusted$(p2)$	65	ModRSI$(k, p1) <$ ModRSI$(k - p2, p1)$

The fitness of a genotype is based on the number of trades conducted over the time frame covered by the data set. To evolve a strategy which features a sufficient number of trades the fitness is set to 0 if less than 100 trades were conducted. Two fitness functions were used. The first type of fitness function is percentage of winning trades. The second type of fitness function is a variation of Sharpe ratio [1]. Specifically,

$$\text{fitness}(I_k) = \lambda \cdot \frac{E[I_k \text{ profit}]}{\sigma} \tag{6}$$

where the expected profit is from all trades, σ is the standard deviation of the profits and λ is a scaling factor. This second version of fitness considers risk. The numerator may result in values that are less than or equal to 0.

4   Genetic Algorithm Search Results

In this section we will present the results of a number of simulations of different trading strategies that are evolved by the GA. Each of the different strategies will use indicator based entry rules but the trade exit conditions will vary to examine the efficacy of each of these approaches. We will examine exits based on the following:

(1) A fixed holding period. That is, trade exit is initiated after a fixed number of days after entry.
(2) A fixed profit target. That is, the trade is exited when a prescribed profit target has been achieved. If the target is not reached in the prescribed time of ten days, the trade is exited after ten days.
(3) A set of indicator-based rules which are evolved to optimize the fitness function. Two different fitness functions are considered in the sequel.

The data used in the subsequent studies is the S&P500 e-mini futures contract (day session only, i.e. 8:30 am to 3:15 pm central time). The symbol for this contract is ES. The data used ranges from Sept 11, 1997 to Dec. 29, 2006, a total of 2351 daily bars. This data was segmented into three periods: (1) the period from Sept.11, 1997 to Mar. 25, 1998 (137 daily bars) is used as initial set-up data for the indicators, (2) the period from Mar 26, 1998 to Dec 31, 2002 (1205 bars) is used as the in-sample (IS) testing period, and (3) the period from Jan 2, 2003 to Dec 29, 2006 (1009 daily bars) represents the out-of-sample (OOS) period.

4.1   Fixed Holding Period Strategy

We first examine the efficacy of using a fixed holding period when trading. The market entry conditions are formed by a combination of two rules chosen from a set of technical indicators. Both entry rules must be satisfied concurrently for entry. However, the exit condition is a fixed time period from entry, here we will examine periods varying from 1 to 10 days.

Table 3. Summary of results from evolved 2-rule entry conditions and fixed holding periods after 500 generations. Performance (fitness) is measured by percentage of profitable trades.

Days	1	2	3	4	5	6	7	8	9	10
IS fit (%)	67	64	65	62	66	66	63	60	61	61
OOS fit (%)	50	62	52	59	62	63	59	62	60	59
Rule #1	13	65	63	64	6	35	35	51	51	16
	43	4	46	34	37	14	14	59	62	38
	42	52	28	38	9	12	19	58	47	10
Rule #2	15	59	35	12	36	56	20	52	12	13
	14	38	6	3	40	39	40	49	58	60
	8	42	63	44	44	31	54	10	47	11
IS profit ($)	40,425	37,225	47,088	37,288	25,815	24,338	25,950	12,074	2,451	−5,587
OOS profit ($)	8,925	10,625	6,250	3,850	21,150	20,275	17,100	24,763	27,287	22,425
# IS trades	100	110	114	114	102	106	104	104	100	106
# OOS trades	71	60	70	62	111	90	82	86	90	90

Table 4. Summary of results from evolved 2-rule entry conditions and a profit based exit strategy ($P = \{1, 2, \ldots, 10\}$ points, where 1 point = $50) after 500 generations. Performance (or fitness) is measured by percentage of profitable trade.

Profit target	+1	+2	+3	+4	+5	+6	+7	+8	+9	+10
IS fit (%)	80.37	77.19	78.26	80.58	80.39	77.88	77.45	83.17	77.31	74.51
OOS fit (%)	67.61	67.78	64.06	69.61	70.91	74.39	69.64	70.83	76.74	70.24
Rule #1	6	62	6	13	36	7	29	36	6	42
	18	34	37	7	59	32	47	56	31	3
	53	44	28	20	58	37	57	44	28	18
Rule #2	36	6	27	35	6	6	61	35	40	16
	42	18	47	14	21	19	50	15	5	18
	65	37	35	33	19	49	25	10	60	36
IS profit ($)	62,512	29,700	27,400	33,063	35,512	20,313	22,525	58,737	50,425	18,200
OOS profit ($)	11,613	10,263	11,475	13,925	21,338	14,100	6,550	17,863	28,663	15,538
# IS trades	107	115	116	104	102	105	103	101	121	102
# OOS trades	141	89	63	101	109	81	55	71	85	83

The goal of the strategy is to consistently provide positive value trades over the back-testing interval. Initially, the magnitude of the profit or loss of each trade is not considered. The assumption is that a high probability of positive value trades will result in a profitable trading strategy. Thus the performance metric used to evaluate fitness of each individual in the population is calculated as the ratio of the number of winning trades to the total number of trades.

The results of the evolved 2-rule strategies after 500 generations for the full range of holding periods from 1 day to 10 days are shown in Table 3. The mean IS performance is 63.5 % and the mean OOS performance is 58.8 %. For fixed holding periods of 5 days and more, the OOS performance is consistently close to 60 %. Additionally, each rule set achieves approximately the same total number of trades over the IS and OOS range. The maximum OOS profit of $27,287 occurs for the 9 day holding period, but the IS performance in terms of profit for both the 9 and 10 day hold periods indicate that a small number of large losing trades occur. Consequently in the next section we modify the trading strategy by adding a profit target that is taken at the earliest opportunity.

4.2   Profit Target Based Strategies

We next examine the efficacy of using profit targets and we evolve strategies using the GA under this constraint. The previous trading strategy was modified such that rather than imposing a fixed holding period, the trade may be exited when a specified profit target is achieved or, in the event that this target is not attained, a maximum holding period has elapsed. For example, if the trade was entered at price X, it will be exited when the price reaches a value of $X + P$ or if N days elapse.

Figure 3 shows the equity curve for the IS and OOS periods, for the case of a 9 point profit target, i.e. $P = 9$ (which corresponds to a profit target of \$450 per contract per trade) and a maximum holding period of 10 days, i.e. $N=10$.

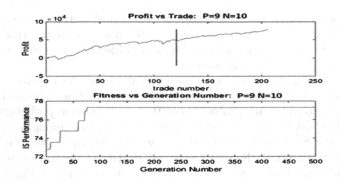

Fig. 3. Results from evolved 2-rule entry conditions with profit based exit conditions ($P = 9, N = 10$). Top graph: The equity curve achieved by the final evolved strategy with the delineation of IS and OOS range shown by the vertical line. Bottom graph: the evolution of IS performance (viz. percentage of profitable trades) over 500 generations.

Table 4 summarizes the results for profit targets of $P = 1$ to 10 points, with a maximum holding period of $N = 10$ days. Compared to the previous results, where exit was based on holding period only, we see that the average IS and OOS profitability has greatly increased from 63.5 % and 58.8 % to 78.1 % and 70.2 %, respectively. The maximum OOS profits of \$21,338 and \$28,663 occur for profit targets of 5 and 9 points, respectively. The corresponding winning probabilities were 70.91 % and 76.74 %, respectively. The limited number of holding days and high probability may make this strategy particularly useful for long option trades (since erosion of option value due to option theta decay would be minimal).

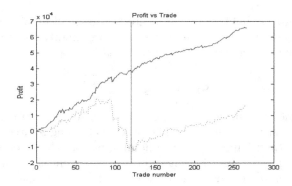

Fig. 4. Equity curves of the GA determined strategy (solid line) and buy and hold (dotted line) over the same period. The profit is given in terms of dollars (= 50 times the point value). IS (OOS) data appears to the left (right) of the vertical line.

4.3   Indicator Based Exit Strategies

In this last strategy variant GA is used to select both entry and, in particular, exit rules and their associated parameters. Similarly as in the case for trade entry, two exit rules are used which when simultaneously satisfied constitute an exit signal for the current long position.

The GA searches for a solution that maximizes the Sharpe ratio. As before, the following GA parameters were used in the simulation: population size of 100, uniform crossover with probability of 0.7, and mutation probability of 0.02. The algorithm was run for 500 generations. A number of simulations were performed and the final result discussed next was chosen where the out-of-sample performance was deemed the best based on linearity of the total equity curve.

The equity curve is shown by the solid line in the plot of Fig. 4. The buy and hold equity curve over the corresponding period is also shown in this figure by the dotted line. As before, the vertical line marks the boundary between in-sample and out-of-sample trades, with trades to the left of the line representing in-sample trades during which the GA searches for an optimal set of trading rules.

The rules discovered were encoded in the following genotype: [42, 64, 18, 65, 9, 63, 21, 59, 22, 42, 49, 22]. Decoding this genotype using Table 2 indicates the rules were:

$$\text{Entry rules}: \begin{array}{l} \text{MedPrice}(k) > \text{EMA}(k, 64) \ \ \wedge \\ \text{ModRSI}(k, 9) < \text{ModRSI}(k - 63, 9) \end{array}$$

$$\text{Exit rules}: \begin{array}{l} \text{BOP}(k) > -0.36 \ \ \wedge \\ \text{MedPrice}(k) > \text{EMA}(k, 49) \end{array}$$

(7)

In words, the entry rules state that when the current median price, i.e. the average of the high and low of the current day bar, is greater than the exponential moving average (EMA) of the past 64 closing prices and the current day nine period modified relative strength index (ModRSI) indicator value is less than its value 63 days prior to today then a position is to be entered into at the current close. Note that the newly developed ModRSI indicator has been chosen from all the available indicators providing some validation for this indicator.

Similarly, a trade exit is signaled when the balance of power (BOP) indicator for the current day is greater than -0.36 and concurrently the median price is greater than the 49 period EMA of daily closing prices. The position is exited on the next day's open. Note that the BOP indicator has values in the range $[-1, 1]$, as can be deduced from equation (2). We see in the evolved genotype that the evolved parameters in positions 3, 8 and 12 (counting left to right), specifically 18, 59 and 22 are not used in the rules but are only present to encompass the more general phenotype.

The discovered strategy shows excellent out-of-sample equity curve linearity with the performance holding up well mimicking the in-sample performance. Table 5 summarizes the performance metrics for this strategy.

Table 5. Performance metrics for the 2 rule buy and 2 rule sell, indicator-based entry and exit strategy.

Average trade length (days)	2.24
IS probability (%)	69
OOS probability (%)	74
IS profit ($)	38,212
OOS profit ($)	27,350
IS # trades	120
OOS # trades	146

5   Conclusions

In this paper a GA has been used in the design of trading strategies based on technical indicators. These indicators are used to define rules which can signal opportune trade entry and exit conditions. We have also examined a number of variations on this theme.

At first we considered a strategy where trade entry is dictated by indicator based rules but the exit signal is given after an elapsed holding period. For a given holding period, ranging from 1 to 10 days, the GA optimized the entry rules based on a fitness function which maximized the percentage of winning trades. Average IS and OOS percentages of 63.5 % and 58.8 % were achieved. However, it was found that overall profitability may not be achieved due to a few large losing trades occurring. To overcome this limitation, we next examined a modification of the first strategy where a profit target exit condition was added. So that if this target was achieved before a maximum elapsed time the trade is exited.

The GA was again used to determine optimum indicator based rules for entry for a range of profit targets. Again the fitness optimized was the percentage of winning trades. This modification to the strategy proved beneficial as the average winning percentages for IS and OOS data increased to 78.1 % and 70.2 %, respectively. At the same time a good level of profitability was attained.

The last strategy variation considered was to have exit as well as entry conditions determined by GA optimized indicator-based trading rules. The fitness function considered here was the Sharpe ratio. The Sharpe ratio is a measure of risk adjusted return and so optimizing it produced a linear equity curve since deviations from a constant return are penalized. The evolved strategy features average IS and OOS probability of winning trades of 69 % and 74 %, respectively whilst also attaining a very good level of profit. A comparison with a buy and hold strategy proved it to be highly competitive.

In this work we have also seen that the new modified RSI (ModRSI) indicator has somewhat been validated as it appears as one of the GA chosen indicators in the final strategy. Future extensions of the present work may involve setting profit targets that are adaptive to current market volatility which should improve winning percentages and profitability. Further investigations into different fitness functions are also warranted. These would include maximizing the Sortino ratio which does not penalize upside deviations in the equity curve, unlike the Sharpe ratio. It may also prove useful to consider a fitness function which minimizes the number and magnitude of losing trades.

References

1. Sharpe, W.: The Sharpe ratio. J. Portfolio Manage. **21**(1), 49–58 (1994)
2. Weissman, R.: Mechanical Trading Systems: Pairing Trader Psychology with Technical Analysis. Wiley, New York (2005)
3. TA-Lib: Technical Analysis Library. www.ta-lib.org. Accessed July 2015
4. Connors, L., Alvarez, C.: An Introduction to ConnorsRSI (Connors Research Trading Strategy Series), 2nd edn. Connors Research, Jersey City (2014)
5. Achelis, S.: Technical Analysis from A to Z, 2nd edn. McGraw-Hill Education, New York (2013)
6. Bauer, R.: Genetic Algorithms and Investment Strategies, 1st edn. Wiley, New York (1994)
7. Brabazon, A., O'Neill, M.: Biologically Inspired Algorithms for Financial Modelling. Natural Computing Series. Springer, Berlin (2006)
8. Azoff, E.: Neural Network Time Series Forecasting of Financial Markets. Wiley, New York (1994)
9. Potvin, Y.-Y., Soriano, P., Vallee, M.: Generating trading rules on the stock markets with genetic programming. Comput. Oper. Res. **31**(7), 1033–1047 (2004)
10. Wang, L.: Generating moving average trading rules on the oil futures market with genetic algorithms. Math. Probl. Eng. **2014**, 1–10 (2014)
11. Dempster, M., Payne, T., Romahi, Y., Thompson, G.: Computational learning techniques for intraday FX trading using popular technical indicators. IEEE Trans. Neural Netw. **12**(4), 744–754 (2001)

12. Ghandar, A., Michalewicz, Z., Schmidt, M., To, T., Zurbrugg, R.: Computational intelligence for evolving trading rules. IEEE Trans. Evol. Comput. **13**(1), 71–86 (2009)
13. Mendes, L., Godinho, P., Dias, J.: A forex trading system based on a genetic algorithm. J. Heuristics **18**(4), 627–656 (2012)
14. Greenwood, G., Tymerski, R.: A game-theoretical approach for designing market trading strategies. In: Proceedings of 2008 IEEE Conference on Computational Intelligence and Games, pp. 316–322 (2008)

Author Index